SYSTEMATIC APPROACHES TO A SUCCESSFUL LITERATURE REVIEW

SECOND EDITION

ANDREW BOOTH
ANTHEA SUTTON
AND DIANA PAPAIOANNOU

Los Angeles | London | New Delhi
Singapore | Washington DC | Melbourne

Los Angeles | London | New Delhi
Singapore | Washington DC | Melbourne

SAGE Publications Ltd
1 Oliver's Yard
55 City Road
London EC1Y 1SP

SAGE Publications Inc.
2455 Teller Road
Thousand Oaks, California 91320

SAGE Publications India Pvt Ltd
B 1/I 1 Mohan Cooperative Industrial Area
Mathura Road
New Delhi 110 044

SAGE Publications Asia-Pacific Pte Ltd
3 Church Street
#10-04 Samsung Hub
Singapore 049483

Editor: Mila Steele
Editorial assistant: Alysha Owen
Production editor: Tom Bedford
Copyeditor: Audrey Scriven
Marketing manager: Ben Griffin-Sherwood
Cover design: Shaun Mercier
Typeset by: C&M Digitals (P) Ltd, Chennai, India
Printed and bound by CPI Group (UK) Ltd,
Croydon, CR0 4YY

© Andrew Booth, Anthea Sutton and Diana Papaioannou 2016

First edition published 2012, reprinted 2013
This second edition first published 2016

Library of Congress Control Number: 2015955561

British Library Cataloguing in Publication data

A catalogue record for this book is available from
the British Library

ISBN 978-1-4739-1245-8
ISBN 978-1-4739-1246-5 (pbk)

CONTENTS

ABOUT THE AUTHORS

Andrew Booth BA Dip Lib MSc PhD MCLIP, Reader in Evidence-Based Information Practice, is an experienced systematic review methodologist with a background in health information. He has worked at the School of Health and Related Research (ScHARR), University of Sheffield since 1994 when he first set up a resource to support evidence-based practice. During his time at ScHARR Andrew has been involved in the creation and delivery of three different Masters modules on systematic approaches to the literature, using face-to-face, open learning and e-learning methods of delivery. He is a co-developer of three current short courses in systematic reviews, qualitative evidence synthesis and rapid reviews respectively. Andrew is a co-convenor of the Cochrane Qualitative and Implementation Methods Group and a founder member of the Cochrane Information Retrieval Methods Group. Andrew is a member of the Editorial Boards *of Systematic Reviews, Health Information & Libraries Journal* and *Implementation Science*. Andrew has been involved in over 100 individual review and synthesis products and has contributed to development of searching and qualitative synthesis methodologies. Andrew has delivered systematic review training in Belgium, the Canary Islands, Germany, Norway and Malaysia as well as participating in numerous international conferences and workshops.

Anthea Sutton BA (Hons) MA MCLIP is a Senior Information Specialist at the School of Health and Related Research (ScHARR), University of Sheffield, and has 14 years' experience of literature searching and information management for systematic review projects in health and related disciplines. Anthea co-ordinates a module for postgraduate students on systematically reviewing the research literature, and has recently led a team to design and deliver a continuing professional development course for information professionals on searching and synthesising evidence. Anthea has experience of teaching systematic review methodologies, via both face-to-face and online methods of delivery. Anthea is the Reviews Editor for *Health Information and Libraries Journal*, this role includes advising the authors of all types of reviews and offering guidance on methodology and presentation. Anthea is an author of journal articles on a range of topics, including literature searching for social science systematic reviews, and has contributed to the conducting of reviews in library and information science and workplace-based education. Anthea has a research interest in the use of tools to assist the systematic review process.

Diana Papaioannou BChD MSc is a Research Fellow at the School of Health and Related Research (ScHARR), University of Sheffield. Diana's current role is as a Proposal Developer, supporting investigators in the design and costing of the research process. Prior to this, Diana worked as Trial Co-ordinator for a multi-centre randomised controlled trial, following on from being an Information Specialist and Systematic Reviewer for five years, a role which included undertaking health technology assessments for the National Institute for Health and Clinical Excellence (NICE) and the National Institute for Health Research (NIHR) Evaluation, Trials and Studies Coordinating Centre (NETSCC). Diana's research interests and teaching experience are in the areas of clinical trial design and systematic reviews. Diana has published a wide range of systematic reviews and journal articles on topics including systematic searching, the role of the information specialist in knowledge transfer, and the validity and responsiveness of quality of life measures.

COMPANION WEBSITE

The second edition of *Systematic Approaches to a Successful Literature* is additionally supported by online resources for students that can be found at: https://study.sagepub.com/booth2e.

- **Exercises** have been provided for you to work through to help test your understanding of the text
- **Answers to Exercises** section provides solutions and explanations for all of the exercises in the book
- **A Review Protocol Template** serves as a quick guide to setting the objectives and criteria of your literature reviews
- **Weblinks** direct you to relevant resources to broaden your understanding of chapter topics and expand your knowledge

(1)

GETTING STARTED ON
YOUR LITERATURE REVIEW

 in a nutshell

Systematic approaches to a successful literature review

By the end of this book, you should be able to:

- Identify different types of reviews and their approaches, and assess their applicability to your own review topics.
- Plan the methodology, presentation and dissemination of your review.
- Define the scope of your research by applying techniques such as formulating your question and conducting a **scoping search**.
- Conduct a **systematic search** of the literature for your research question.
- Undertake **quality assessment** on a range of literature types.
- Synthesise and analyse quantitative and qualitative studies.

INTRODUCTION

This introductory chapter gives an overview of what this book will cover. It introduces the idea of applying systematic approaches to any type of literature review, and outlines the contents of each chapter. It gives a guide to the learning features you will encounter throughout the book, and also gives some ideas on how to get started with your own review, including how this book can help. The chapter concludes with some 'frequently asked questions' which will answer some common queries that you may have at this beginning stage of your review process.

SYSTEMATIC REVIEWS VERSUS SYSTEMATIC APPROACHES

All types of review should be systematic. Being systematic helps you to reduce the likelihood of **bias** and is a way of ensuring that you identify a comprehensive body of knowledge on your chosen subject. You will encounter many definitions for literature reviews, but you will find that the word 'systematic' often features as a critical element within the description of a literature review. As you will see in Chapters 2 and 3, there are numerous different types of review, but all require a level of systematicity, depending on your aims and objectives. In addition, applying systematic processes will enable you to work more efficiently.

It is not always appropriate to conduct a 'systematic review'. You should make a decision based on the nature of your research question and the purpose of your research, as well as the time and resources available to you. These issues are explored more fully in Chapters 2 and 3. However, regardless of the type of review that you conduct, you should follow a 'system' for the different processes of the review: searching the literature, quality assessment, synthesis, analysis, and reporting. This book focuses on how to conduct and then report these processes in a systematic way, utilising the approaches applied in systematic reviewing to ensure the systematicity of all review types.

CHAPTERS OVERVIEW

Below you will find an outline of each of the chapters in this book.

Chapter 2: Taking a Systematic Approach to Your Literature Review

Chapter 2 looks at the role of the literature review in research, examines some common types of review, and provides a brief history of **research synthesis**. Systematic approaches are investigated for each key element of the review process (literature searching, appraisal, synthesis, analysis and presentation).

Chapter 3: Choosing Your Review Methods

Chapter 3 examines how to choose an appropriate review method for your research topic, focusing on the factors to consider, and presenting a review choice decision tool to use in practice. It also includes some review scenarios to assist your learning.

Chapter 4: Planning and Conducting Your Literature Review

Chapter 4 outlines and then describes the main stages of the review process and their associated milestones and deliverables, allowing you to produce a draft timetable for your own review.

Chapter 5: Defining Your Scope

Chapter 5 demonstrates how to focus your research question, using a framework to define the scope. It examines the **review protocol**, presenting tips and guidance to allow you to complete a protocol for your own review. The chapter also explores the challenges and pitfalls you may encounter when defining the scope.

Chapter 6: Searching the Literature

Chapter 6 enables you to translate the research question you defined in Chapter 5 into a search strategy. It follows the stages in the literature searching process, examining the components of a systematic search, allowing you to identify appropriate sources to search for your own review. The chapter also covers conducting a scoping search, and reviewing and refining your search as necessary, as well as giving examples of research questions and their search strategies and an exercise to plan your own literature search.

Chapter 7: Assessing the Evidence Base

Chapter 7 follows the process of assessing the relevance of the studies found to your research question, presenting how to follow the **screening** process and using **reference management** software to track this procedure. The chapter then moves on to assessing your included studies along with the problems or challenges you may face, and considering the level of quality assessment required for your review type.

Chapters 8 and 9: Synthesising and Analysing Quantitative and Qualitative Studies

Chapters 8 and 9 allow you to select an appropriate strategy for synthesis to meet the particular requirements of the data found for your review. The chapters provide an overview of approaches to synthesis for both quantitative and qualitative literature. The data extraction process is covered, as are various approaches to displaying your data. The chapters then move on to analysing your findings, allowing you to produce a plan for your own review. Both chapters include key review elements for discussing limitations and recognising the likelihood of bias.

Chapter 10: Writing, Presenting and Disseminating Your Review

The final chapter describes the main elements required when writing up and presenting your review, including identifying recommendations for action and future research. It presents the key factors to consider, such as your audience, and presents a sample review structure.

WORKING YOUR WAY THROUGH THIS BOOK

The purpose of this book is to examine the **systematic review** method and how systematic approaches can be applied to your own literature review, making it more robust, transparent and ultimately a more successful review. Whilst the book does not insist that you must undertake a standardised systematic review, it will enable you to apply a more systematic approach to your own literature reviews.

It also offers a step-by-step guide to planning, conducting and writing up your literature review. If you are new to literature reviews, or systematic review methodology, you may find it useful to work through the book in sequence. If you have identified a particular skills gap or if you need to refresh your familiarity with particular processes, you can consider each chapter as a stand-alone contribution allowing you to read a single specific chapter or a selection of chapters.

Following an initial chapter on approaching the literature systematically, the subsequent chapters follow the step-by-step process of systematic review to allow you to apply a more systematic approach to your own literature reviews. Each chapter follows the same structure and has the following key features:

- *In a Nutshell* – outlining the chapter and the key points covered.
- *Toolbox* – a list of key resources you may need to assist you in your review.
- *Exercises and problem scenarios* – to test your understanding of the chapter.
- *Frequently Asked Questions* – focusing on key queries you may have at each stage of the review process.
- *Key Learning Points* – a reminder of the main elements of the chapter.
- *Further Reading* – an annotated list of references if you wish to read more about the systematic approaches covered in the chapter.

The 'In a Nutshell' feature at the beginning of each chapter offers an overview of what is to be covered in that chapter in the form of learning objectives. Once you have read the chapter, refer back to the 'In a Nutshell' section at its beginning and reflect on what you have learnt. If there are learning objectives that you feel you have not met, revisit those parts of the chapter.

For each part of the systematic review process, there are resources (such as tools, checklists, templates, etc.) to help you achieve this element of your review. The 'Toolbox' section of each chapter lists practical resources, with information on how they can aid your literature review.

You may find it helpful to complete the exercises as you work your way through the book, and subsequently to apply these exercises to your own review where appropriate. If you have queries on any of the topics, see the 'Frequently Asked Questions' feature at the end of each chapter.

Each chapter offers a recap of what has been covered in the form of 'Key Learning Points', and there is an annotated list in 'Further Reading' for each chapter topic, allowing you to follow up references around a particular systematic approach if you wish to know more.

There is also a comprehensive glossary at the end of the book. Glossary terms are highlighted in bold within each chapter, so if you wish to check the definition of a particular term then refer to the glossary as you work your way through the book.

EXAMPLES OF REVIEW CHALLENGES AND HOW THIS BOOK CAN HELP

Here are some challenges you may have encountered whilst considering your own review, with suggested solutions for each situation.

I have a general review topic in mind, but I don't know where I should focus.

Look at Chapter 5 (Defining Your Scope) to help you focus your research question. The chapter outlines various frameworks that you can use to define the scope of your question.

I have no idea how much literature exists on my review topic.

Consider conducting a scoping search on a key database for your topic to get an idea of the size of your review. The scoping search process is described in Chapter 6. Examine the number of results found and estimate how many results you are likely to find by searching a range of databases. As a rule of thumb we would recommend that you identify the single database that best covers your chosen topic, conduct a scoping search, and then multiply the number of results found in that single database by a factor of between 2.5 and 5.0 depending upon how multidisciplinary your topic is. This approach factors in duplicates that occur across multiple databases and recognises that each successive database becomes less relevant and yields fewer unique hits. You may then want to examine the title and abstracts of a proportion of the results retrieved to estimate what percentage of studies are likely to be included.

I am confident in finding and selecting studies for my review, however, I am unsure how to assess the quality of the evidence base.

Visit Chapter 7. Here you will find an overview of the quality assessment process, and all the tips and tools you need to carry this out for your own review. To practise your quality assessment skills complete the exercises within this chapter and refer to the feedback on the accompanying online resources (see https://study.sagepub.com/booth2e) to check your understanding.

I am unsure how to select an appropriate method of synthesis for my review.

Read Chapter 8 or 9 depending on whether your question will best be answered by quantitative or qualitative data or a mixture of both. Also revisit the types of review presented in Chapter 2 and the considerations when selecting a method of synthesis. You may find that the type of review you have chosen offers a more limited number of recommended synthesis approaches.

I realise that I will need to clearly report my methodology when I write up my review, so should I make notes as I go along to aid with this?

It will be easier to write up your review if you make notes as you go along. You will find the section on completing a review protocol (Chapter 5) will assist you. A good review protocol outlining your review methodology, typically written in the future tense, will facilitate your changing this to the past tense when writing up your review to produce a comprehensive account of what you have done.

GETTING STARTED

So, where to start? Firstly, think about systematic literature reviews and assess your knowledge in theory and your experience in practice. Can you identify any particular knowledge and skills gaps?

Or do you need to learn about the process from scratch? Do you have a topic in mind already? Do you know what type of review you plan to conduct?

For an overview of the systematic review process, see Chapter 2. Whatever your knowledge and experience, you will find it helpful to work your way through Chapter 4 to plan your review. If you have identified particular knowledge and skills gaps you could visit the appropriate chapters first.

frequently asked questions (FAQs)

FAQ 1.1 Is this book for me?

This book is appropriate for students and researchers undertaking any type of review. It acts as a step-by-step guide through the process but each chapter can be used as a stand-alone resource if you have specific skills and knowledge gaps or if you require a refresher in any areas.

FAQ 1.2 I don't want to do a full systematic review but I want to make my review more systematic, so how can I do this?

This book is ideal for you. It highlights particular critical steps to take to make your review more systematic. It draws on established systematic review methodology, expertise developed by the scientific and academic community in reviewing the literature in their field, and good practice for research. Start by looking at Chapter 3 which will help you decide what type of review is appropriate for your question. Each different type of review has an associated methodology so it will be useful for you to bear in mind the methodology that you will use as you work through the book.

FAQ 1.3 How do I find out the meaning of unfamiliar terms used in the book?

Throughout the book there are terms highlighted in bold, so refer to the glossary towards the end of the book for definitions of these terms.

FAQ 1.4 What if I haven't identified a review topic yet?

Think about your area of interest. You may find it helpful to find recent reviews in your general topic area – are there any research gaps you can identify? Once you have an idea of a potential review topic make sure no one else has recently undertaken a review in this same topic by searching review and protocol databases, and then work through Chapter 5 to define your scope.

FAQ 1.5 What if I don't know which type of review is most appropriate for my topic?

Chapter 3 will assist with this. Different review types and their associated methodology are presented within this chapter, along with their appropriateness for different types of topic.

FAQ 1.6 Where can I find additional resources?

Each chapter is accompanied by extensive references and further reading to allow you to immerse yourself in methodological issues or nuances that are necessarily mentioned in passing.

FAQ 1.7 I've completed one of the exercises in the book, where can I find the answers?

All answers to the exercises in this book are hosted on the accompanying website (see https://study.sagepub.com/booth2e).

suggestions for further reading

Aveyard, H. (2014) *Doing a Literature Review in Health and Social Care: A Practical Guide*, 3rd edition. Maidenhead: Open University Press.
Now in its third edition, this book provides a step-by-step guide to doing a literature review. This textbook is practical in nature, with each chapter focusing on a specific part of the process, following an introductory chapter on 'Why do a literature review?'.

Callahan, J.L. (2014) Writing literature reviews: a reprise and update. *Human Resource Development Review*, **13**, 3, 271-5.
An editorial, describing the characteristics of 'rigorous' literature reviews, and defining types of literature review, such as 'integrative', 'historic' and 'rapid structured' reviews. 'Table 1' is particularly helpful as it presents the six 'W's which should form the components of a literature review method section (Who, When, Where, hoW, What and Why).

Daigneault, P.M., Jacob, S. and Ouimet, M. (2014) Using systematic review methods within a PhD dissertation in political science: challenges and lessons learned from practice. *International Journal of Social Research Methodology*, **17**, 3, 267-83.
A reflective article reporting on the experiences of a PhD student. You may find the 'lessons learned and recommendations' section particularly helpful if you are considering doing a systematic review for your thesis or dissertation.

Gough, D., Oliver, S. and Thomas, J. (eds) (2012) *An Introduction to Systematic Reviews*. London: Sage.
Starting with the nature, logic, diversity and process of undertaking systematic reviews this book covers a wide breadth of systematic review approaches from statistical meta-analysis to meta-ethnography. It focuses exclusively on the systematic method - providing the necessary background needed to embark on the process.

Haddaway, N.R. and Pullin, A.S. (2014) The policy role of systematic reviews: past, present and future. *Springer Science Reviews*, **2**, 1-2, 179-83.
An invited expert review on how systematic reviews can inform policy and practice decisions. Includes a history of the systematic review in environmental management, and the future of systematic reviews.

Petticrew, M. (2015) Time to rethink the systematic review catechism? Moving from 'what works' to 'what happens'. *Systematic Reviews*, **4**, 1, 36.

(Continued)

(Continued)

Examines a pragmatic approach to systematic reviews, and presents examples where alternative approaches to the 'traditional' systematic review model may be more appropriate.

Petticrew, M. and Roberts, H. (2008) *Systematic Reviews in the Social Sciences: A Practical Guide*. Oxford: Wiley.
A key textbook in conducting systematic reviews in the social sciences, providing practical guidance on the main elements of reviewing – refining the question, searching the literature, appraising, synthesising and disseminating. Has a specific chapter on 'Exploring heterogeneity and publication bias' (Chapter 7) which you may find useful when analysing the results of your review. Chapter 9 challenges the 'urban myths' around systematic reviews, presenting what a review can and cannot do.

Pickering, C., Grignon, J., Steven, R., Guitart, D. and Byrne, J. (2014) Publishing not perishing: how research students transition from novice to knowledgeable using systematic quantitative literature reviews. *Studies in Higher Education*, **40**, 10, 1756-69.
Presents the pedagogical benefits of different types of literature review. Particularly interesting are the student case studies on undertaking a systematic quantitative literature review.

TAKING A SYSTEMATIC APPROACH TO YOUR LITERATURE REVIEW

 in a nutshell

Why be systematic?

- The 'literature review' has a long pedigree as an area of academic and research endeavour. However, review methods can now fulfil an even greater variety of purposes and answer a greater range of question types.
- Reviewing the literature in a systematic way helps the author to be clear, to build confidence in their work and demonstrate the rigour of their methods.
- Recent years have seen significant developments in research synthesis, starting from within healthcare and migrating across a large number of disciplines and fields.
- 'Systematic' is a requirement for any type of research, so a literature review should not be any different from this standard.
- Systematic approaches are used to reduce the potential for bias within a review.
- The main types of review can be defined by the extent to which they harness the **S**earch, **A**ppraisa**L**, **S**ynthesis and **A**nalysis (SALSA) elements.

INTRODUCTION

Fink (2005) succinctly defines a literature review as a 'systematic, explicit, and reproducible method for identifying, evaluating, and synthesising the existing body of completed and recorded work produced by researchers, scholars, and practitioners'. Particularly noticeable is the word 'systematic', key to the title and content of this book. All reviews share the requirement of original empirical research, namely to be systematic. Different types of review (see Box 2.1) should differ only in the degree to which they are systematic – according to each review's role and function – and each type should help by telling you what exactly they have and have not done.

 **box 2.1**

Some common types of review

Critical review

Integrative review

Literature review

Mapping review/systematic map

Meta-analysis

Mixed studies review/mixed methods review

Overview

Qualitative systematic review/qualitative evidence synthesis

Rapid review

Realist synthesis

Scoping review

State-of-the-art review

Systematic review

Systematic search and review

Systematised review

Umbrella review

(Note: These different types of review are defined and explained later in this chapter. For the present we acknowledge a plethora of terms for systematic approaches to a literature review.)

Hart (1998) unpicks the detail of the review process, focusing on the essential components, the documents themselves:

> the selection of available documents ... on the topic ... written from a particular standpoint to fulfil certain aims or express certain views on the nature of the topic and how it is to be investigated, and the effective evaluation of these documents in relation to the research being proposed.

To perform this *effectively* you need processes to ensure that you complete this task in an *efficient* manner and fulfil it to the right *quality*. By 'quality' we mean 'appropriate breadth and depth, rigor and consistency, clarity and brevity, and effective analysis and synthesis' (Hart, 1998).

WHY IS THE LITERATURE REVIEW SO IMPORTANT?

Bem (1995) notes that 'authors of literature reviews are at risk for producing mind-numbing lists of citations and findings that resemble a phone book – impressive case, lots of numbers, but not much plot'. When we make decisions based on evidence it makes sense to use the best that is available. By and large the best evidence for many decisions comes from a **systematic review** of *all* the evidence. Mulrow (1995) argues that reviewing in this way is a search for the whole truth, rather than just one part of it, and is thus a 'fundamentally scientific activity'. The reviewer uses a specific and reproducible method to identify, select and appraise studies of a previously agreed level of quality (either including all studies or only those that pass a minimum quality threshold) that are relevant to a particular question. The results of the studies are then analysed and summarised. Synthesising evidence helps us to find out what we know and don't know about what works and what doesn't work. A good **research synthesis** can generally give us the most trustworthy answer to a specific review question, and it can identify gaps in our knowledge that require further research. It also communicates the strength of the available evidence and the quality of included studies, thereby indicating how much confidence practitioners, service users, managers, policy makers, and the popular media should have in the results.

A research synthesis can also help us to find out how well a policy, programme, technique or intervention works in different subgroups of users and inform us about its potential to cause harm. Some research syntheses shed light on the pros and cons of different ways of organising or delivering services or policies. A research synthesis that includes considerations of cost can help shape our judgements about whether a chosen policy or course of action provides good value for money.

Yet another reason to synthesise the results of different studies of a given intervention is to learn whether findings are consistent across multiple studies. Light and Pillemer (1984) write that 'disagreements among findings are valuable ... [and that] conflicts can teach us a lot'. Thus we can identify settings in which a particular social policy might succeed, circumstances under which an educational programme might work best, or which dose of a drug is most effective.

A good research synthesis frequently highlights weaknesses in the evidence and argues for further research. What should service users, policy makers and others decide in the absence of evidence? Even when a research synthesis shows strong, unambiguous evidence to support one course of action, 'politics' may make that review's findings less influential than well-coordinated lobbying. As Chalmers and colleagues (2002) observe, 'Research synthesis sometimes yields unwelcome results that challenge strongly held opinions and other vested interests'. Yet even if the recommendations from a research synthesis are disregarded, its very existence encourages more transparency about the role of other factors in decision making. No matter how well they are done, research syntheses are not a panacea for all problems, but they do offer a valuable aid to decision making.

WHERE DOES A LITERATURE REVIEW FIT WITHIN THE CONTEXT OF RESEARCH?

Literature reviews are pervasive in academia and policy development. However, a literature review is typically showcased in three particular contexts:

1. As a major component of a dissertation, thesis or other academic deliverable.
2. As a peer-reviewed publication, typically in a journal or, depending upon the discipline, as a book chapter.
3. As a report resulting from a funded research project or other commissioned research or consultancy.

Each of these contexts shapes the final review product. For example, a literature review as part of a dissertation or thesis should be innovative. A student should be reflexive about their methods (McGhee et al., 2007) and demonstrate their personal growth through the methodology (Daigneault et al., 2014). Students are expected to demonstrate their 'knowledge about a particular field of study, including vocabulary, theories, key variables and phenomena, and its methods and history' (Randolph, 2009). Furthermore a student must demonstrate that they are sensitised to the 'influential researchers and research groups in the field'. Of course a literature review from a thesis may subsequently become a 'legitimate and publishable scholarly document' (LeCompte et al., 2003).

In producing a peer-reviewed publication the reviewer faces the challenge of squeezing a wealth of data into the tight constraints of a journal's house style and word limits, occasionally overflowing into online supplementary materials. Journals, and their parent disciplines, demonstrate very different approaches to handling reviews. Some journals will not even consider review articles. In contrast, other journals celebrate annual review-type commissioned overviews and literature surveys.

Finally if you are reviewing the literature for a funded research project or for consultancy you may face tight time constraints, a demand for answers rather than issues, and readers who want to sidestep the methodology and cut straight to the results or findings. Systematic reviews can yield:

> information about the nature and extent of a problem, and the potential benefits, harms, uncertainties, and costs of interventions and policies. Policymakers may also want to know about the impact on different groups in various settings ... [and to] answer questions about how best to disseminate information and innovations; ... whether the interventions are appropriate to local culture and context; and about the factors influencing study outcomes. (Sweet and Moynihan, 2007)

Chapter 10 acknowledges that different types of presentation suit different audiences and purposes. For the moment, we distinguish between reviews for knowledge support and those for decision support (Mays et al., 2005; Pope et al., 2007). Reviews for knowledge support summarise and synthesise research evidence (focusing on what currently exists and is known about a topic). They may highlight gaps in the evidence base as a target for future research, just as a thesis might do. Reviews for decision support go further in bringing the existing evidence to bear on a particular issue or problem. Gaps in the evidence base lead to the supplementary question '... and what shall we do about this issue or problem in the meantime?' Unsurprisingly,

Lavis and colleagues (2005) found that managers are interested in reviews that help them to decide whether to start, stop or change a programme, how to accommodate new programmes or services – tried elsewhere – within their own organisation, and how to bring about change.

The knowledge support–decision support spectrum is often caricatured within healthcare by the **Cochrane Review** at one end and the **health technology assessment** at the other. In actuality, Cochrane reviews increasingly strive to contribute to decision making while health technology assessments look beyond the immediate problem to recommend future commissioned primary research.

WHAT TYPES OF RESEARCH QUESTION ARE SUITABLE FOR LITERATURE REVIEW?

It is essential that a literature review is question-led. The question, along with the purpose of the review, the intended deliverables and the intended audience, determines how the data are identified, collected and presented. Some conclude that a literature review is only useful where a significant body of literature is already known to exist. However, even if a researcher believes that they are the first to examine a particular intervention, policy or programme they should confirm this from the previously published literature. Thus they avoid presenting 'islands without continents' (i.e. falsely claiming innovation) (Clarke and Chalmers, 1998). Cross-fertilisation of methods from a related field may similarly save a researcher from having to develop a solution from scratch.

Although you might well be the first to consider a particular issue most literature reviews assume that at least one other researcher has at least considered, if not addressed, your question. Your question is shaped and influenced by the goal and focus of the review (Hart, 1998; Randolph, 2009):

> *Effectiveness questions:* What effect does intervention X, compared with intervention Y, have on outcome Z? What are the relative cost-benefits of X versus Y?

> *Methodology questions:* What research methods have previously been used to investigate phenomenon X? What are the respective strengths and weaknesses of such methods?

> *Conceptual questions:* How has phenomenon X been identified and defined? Which theories have been used to explain phenomenon X? Which theory provides the best fit to findings from empirical studies? What are the main unresolved controversies? What are the underpinning epistemological and ontological foundations for the discipline?

WHY REVIEW THE LITERATURE?

The internet age has witnessed the so-called **information explosion** (Major and Savin-Baden, 2010). With increasing numbers of articles being published and improved open access to many of these articles, it is becoming almost impossible to navigate even the more specialised subject domains. At an individual level we face **information overload**. We are overwhelmed by the volume of information we encounter and unable to retrieve the information we need. Is there a solution to this situation? One possible approach is to become **information literate** – put simply this means acquiring the skills covered in Chapters 5 to 10 in this book that will allow us to locate, evaluate and use information effectively.

Although technologies are always changing, database interfaces and search engines are continually being upgraded, and new topics emerge with regularity, the skills of information literacy you acquire during your literature review will equip you beyond the duration of your project or dissertation and throughout your career and working life.

Many authors agree on the purposes of a literature review (see Box 2.2), irrespective of discipline (Cooper, 1989; Bruce, 1994, 1996; Hart, 1998; Galvan, 1999).

 box 2.2

Purposes for a literature review

- To place each work in the context of how it contributes to an understanding of the subject under review.
- To describe how each work relates to the others under consideration.
- To identify new ways to interpret, and shed light on gaps in, previous research.
- To identify and resolve conflicts across seemingly contradictory previous studies.
- To identify what has been covered by previous scholars to prevent you needlessly duplicating their effort.
- To signpost the way forward for further research.
- To locate your original work within the existing literature.

Which of the above points most accurately capture your reason(s) for conducting a literature review?

Your reasons may include 'taking stock' of what has gone before and identifying a niche for your own research. The literature may help you design your own research. You may identify a theory against which you will explore a specified hypothesis. You may need to select tools, instruments or scales to help you conduct your research. You may seek to identify gaps that offer opportunities as future research questions. Reasons for reviewing the literature are mirrored within the following brief history of research synthesis.

A BRIEF HISTORY OF RESEARCH SYNTHESIS

Research synthesis can have no absolute start date. Very early on in history humankind needed to record what had previously occurred, to compare experiences across cases, and to build up a knowledge base of what was now known and what remained unknown. Those who chronicle research synthesis typically identify specific landmarks (see Table 2.1) and then link these with a dotted non-continuous line.

Probably the most cited account originates from three eminent proponents, Chalmers, Hedges and Cooper (2002), in 'A brief history of research synthesis'. A more extensive treatment of the same topic is available in *The Handbook of Research Synthesis and Meta-analysis* (Cooper et al., 2009). Both works attest to the fact that research synthesis has migrated from a select number of disciplines to pervade almost every area of academic activity.

There is nothing particularly novel about research synthesis. In 1753, James Lind, the Scottish naval surgeon who was instrumental in the first **randomised controlled trial**, recognised the value of systematic methods for identifying, extracting and appraising information from individual studies as a protection against a biased interpretation of research:

> As it is no easy matter to root out prejudices ... it became requisite to exhibit a full and impartial view of what had hitherto been published on the scurvy ... by which the sources of these mistakes may be detected. Indeed, before the subject could be set in a clear and proper light, it was necessary to remove a great deal of rubbish. (James Lind, cited in Dunn, 1997)

Gathering the published research, getting rid of the rubbish, and summarising the best of what remains characterises the science of research synthesis. Subsequent developments in **information retrieval**, documentation and document delivery have made it considerably less of a challenge to identify, acquire and interpret the scattered body of published and unpublished research.

Others trace the origins of research synthesis to seventeenth-century astronomers who combined data from related studies to introduce greater precision to their individual observations (Petticrew, 2001). However, a more obvious heritage lies with statistician Karl Pearson who identified the need to bring together multiple small studies to arrive at a definitive opinion of the evidence on inoculations against fever (Pearson, 1904). Three years later, Joseph Goldberger, a scientist in the United States, reviewed 44 studies of typhoid fever and then abstracted and pooled data from 26 of the 44 studies (Chalmers et al., 2002).

Similar work was undertaken within agriculture by Ronald Fisher and colleagues in the 1930s. However, it was not until the 1970s that formal procedures for synthesising studies were labelled as **meta-analysis** by Gene Glass (1976) and other social science colleagues.

Table 2.1 Milestones in the history of research synthesis

Date	Milestones
1753	James Lind published first 'systematic review'
1904	Pearson published landmark review on effects of vaccines against typhoid
1976	Glass coined term 'meta-analysis'
1984	Light and Pillemer, *Summing Up*
1987	Mulrow, 'The medical review article: state of the science'
1989	Enkin and colleagues, *Effective Care in Pregnancy and Childbirth*
1992	Antman and colleagues illustrated value of cumulation of findings
1993	Launch of *Cochrane Collaboration*
1994	Establishment of the UK NHS Centre for Reviews and Dissemination
2000	Founding of *Campbell Collaboration*

In 1984 Light and Pillemer published *Summing Up: The Science of Reviewing Research*, arguing that new methods of research synthesis applied to many fields, including health, education and psychology:

> Without a clear picture of where things stand now, simply adding one new study to the exist-ing morass is unlikely to be very useful ... For science to be cumulative, an intermediate step between past and future research is necessary: synthesis of existing evidence. (Light and Pillemer, 1984)

Three years later, Mulrow (1987) delivered a damning verdict on 50 'review or progress articles' published in four leading medical journals. Only one of the 50 reviews 'had clearly specified methods of identifying, selecting, and validating included information'. She concluded that 'Current ... reviews do not routinely use scientific methods to identify, assess, and synthe-size information'. On the contrary, these reviews are often 'subjective, scientifically unsound, and inefficient' (Mulrow, 1987). Towards the end of the 1980s Iain Chalmers and colleagues responded to this challenge (Enkin et al., 1989), laying a platform for collaborative synthesis, from which the **Cochrane Collaboration**, and its sibling the **Campbell Collaboration**, were launched.

At about the same time Oxman and Guyatt concluded from a survey of published reviews that:

> Our data suggest that experts, on average, write reviews of inferior quality; that the greater the expertise the more likely the quality is to be poor; and that the poor quality may be related to the strength of the prior opinions and the amount of time they spend preparing a review article. (Oxman and Guyatt, 1993)

As **evidence-based policy** and **evidence-based practice** became popular in the 1990s other disciplines, such as education, started to acknowledge the importance of research syn-theses (Evans and Benefield, 2001). Not everyone welcomed such a trend (Hammersley, 2001). Nevertheless, evidence-based policy and practice gained pace in other fields such as social care and management (see, for example, Davies et al., 2000; Trinder and Reynolds, 2000). Governments also began to fund initiatives to support research syntheses, particularly system-atic reviews (Davies, 2000).

Many other organisations began producing research syntheses during the 1990s. Funding bodies began to require a systematic review of existing research before considering applications for funding a primary study. The UK Medical Research Council requires a researcher to demon-strate that a systematic review has been undertaken before it will commission a new trial (Clark and Horton, 2010). This ensures that the question has not already been answered, and that the results of previous research are used in designing the new trial.

Subsequent years have been characterised by the increasing popularity of literature review variants and derivatives, often within time-constrained policy windows and requiring a flexible toolkit of 'systematic approaches'. More than anything the proliferation of so many variants emphasises that the extent to which a review is systematic lies on a continuum running from brief **evidence summary** through to **gold standard** systematic review.

WHAT IS THE PLACE OF THEORY IN LITERATURE REVIEW?

For Webster and Watson a successful literature review:

> creates a firm foundation for advancing knowledge. *It facilitates theory development*, closes areas where a plethora of research exists, and uncovers areas where research is needed. (Webster and Watson, 2002, emphasis added)

Initially theory was considered an unwelcome distraction from the fundamentally pragmatic intent of the science of research synthesis. Pragmatic disciplines such as health services research are largely atheoretical – at least in the sense of not acknowledging a specific theoretical contribution. As you move outwards to contiguous disciplines such as public health, health promotion and nursing, theory is more plentiful. This is similarly the case for such disciplines as social care, education, management, and even information systems. A more complex panorama is emerging, particularly within the context of understanding how complex interventions might be understood to work (De Silva et al., 2014). Reviews may be broadly characterised as generating, exploring or testing theory (Gough et al., 2012). Review techniques may range from the hypothesis testing of meta-analysis through to use of interpretive techniques such as **meta-ethnography** and **critical interpretive synthesis**. Other techniques such as **realist synthesis** explore the application of mid-range **programme theory** to a mix of quantitative and qualitative data. Furthermore **concept analysis** explicitly seeks to define, expand and extend the theoretical underpinnings of a target concept, and may prove a useful starting point for a review where definitions are contested.

Literature reviews offer multiple opportunities to engage and interact with theory (see Table 2.2). Methods for searching the literature for theory in a systematic way are beginning to be proposed (Booth et al., 2013b; Booth and Carroll, 2015). An evidence synthesis may scope out theories relating to a particular issue (Campbell et al., 2014) or seek to consolidate current theory, creating a 'meta-model'. Alternatively a literature review can be used to generate new, overarching theories and interpretations (Campbell et al., 2014). Subsequently, the literature may offer a data set against which existing theories can be examined and modified. Finally, where a literature review is unable to fully explain differences that exist between apparently similar mechanisms or contexts, a reviewer may introduce theory in an attempt to analyse such differences.

THE TRADITIONAL NARRATIVE REVIEW, THE SYSTEMATIC REVIEW AND 'SYSTEMATIC APPROACHES'

All research, literature reviews included, is required to be 'systematic' in its conduct, analysis and/or presentation:

> Who would want reviews to be unsystematic, if by 'systematic' we mean no more than 'properly carried out, taking account of all the relevant evidence, and making reliable judgements about its validity and implications'? On this definition, to produce a systematic review is simply to do the job of reviewing well. (Hammersley, 2002)

Table 2.2 Examples of the interplay of literature review and theory

Type of review	Reference	Interplay of literature review and theory
Concept analysis	Teamwork: a concept analysis. (Xyrichis and Ream, 2008)	Used Walker and Avant's approach to guide analysis (2005). Searched bibliographic databases, Internet search engines and hand searches (1976–2006). Based on analysis, proposed definition for teamwork, and identified essential ingredients for it to take place.
Creation of meta-model	Fostering implementation of health services research findings into practice: a consolidated framework for advancing implementation science (Damschroder et al., 2009)	Used snowball sampling approach to identify published theories and component constructs. Combined constructs across published theories while removing redundancy or overlap. Created Consolidated Framework for Implementation Research (CFIR) as overarching typology for implementation theory development.
Meta-ethnography	Using meta-ethnography to synthesise qualitative research: a worked example (Britten et al., 2002)	Four papers about lay meanings of medicines arbitrarily chosen. Used Noblit and Hare's seven-step process for meta-ethnography (1988). Six key concepts were derived from interpretations in chosen papers and four reviewer interpretations were constructed to make sense of these. Produced middle-range theories as hypotheses to be tested by other researchers.
Meta-narrative review	Storylines of research in diffusion of innovation: a meta-narrative approach to systematic review (Greenhalgh et al., 2005)	Identified 13 key meta-narratives from literatures of rural sociology, clinical epidemiology, marketing and organisational studies. Researchers in different traditions had conceptualised, explained and investigated diffusion of innovations differently. Reconciled seemingly contradictory data, systematically exposing and exploring tensions between research paradigms.
Realist review (to complement an effectiveness review)	Realist review to understand the efficacy of school feeding programmes (Greenhalgh et al., 2007)	Complemented existing Cochrane Review by exploring detailed information on context, mechanisms, and outcomes of interventions and theories in 18 trials of school feeding programmes.
Review of theories	Healthcare professionals' intentions and behaviours: a systematic review of studies based on social cognitive theories (Godin et al., 2008)	Reviewed literature on factors influencing health professionals' behaviours based on social cognitive theories: 78 studies met inclusion criteria. Most used theory was Theory of Reasoned Action or its extension Theory of Planned Behaviour.
Review of use of theory	A systematic review of the use of theory in the design of guideline dissemination and implementation strategies and interpretation of the results of rigorous evaluations (Davies et al., 2010)	Reviewed use of theory in 235 evaluations of guideline dissemination and implementation studies (1966–1998). Classified theory according to type of use (explicitly theory based, some conceptual basis, and theoretical construct used) and stage of use (choice/design of intervention, process/mediators/moderators, and post hoc/explanation).
Scoping review	Disseminating research findings: what should researchers do? A systematic scoping review of conceptual frameworks (Wilson et al., 2010)	Searched 12 electronic databases to identify/describe conceptual/organising frameworks used in guiding dissemination activity. Narrative synthesis undertaken: 33 frameworks met inclusion criteria underpinned by three theoretical approaches (persuasive communication, diffusion of innovations theory and social marketing).
As precursor to conceptual work	The place of the literature review in grounded theory research (Dunne, 2011)	Explored the role literature review can play in grounded theory methodology.

However, reviewers have not always recognised this fact, as illustrated by our hypothetical recipe for a traditional literature review:

> Take a simmering topic, extract the juice of an argument, add the essence of one filing cabinet, sprinkle liberally with your own publications and sift out the work of noted detractors or adversaries.

Greenhalgh (2014) describes journalistic reviews of college students where, if research did not fit with their proposed theory, material is simply left out. Bias, or systematic error, may exist at the identification, selection, synthesis, analysis and interpretation stages of a review process which may demonstrate 'implicit, idiosyncratic methods' (Mulrow et al., 1997). Frequently the much maligned **narrative review** (Mulrow et al., 1997; Greenhalgh, 2014) is referred to as a 'traditional review', 'conventional review', or even more damningly, as a 'non-systematic review'. However, some non-systematic reviews openly ally themselves to different traditions of reviewing literature. Consequently a review can be poorly conducted, poorly reported, or both (Shea et al., 2002).

WHY BE SYSTEMATIC?

While many arguments are advanced for the desirability of systematic approaches to reviewing the literature, we have identified at least three principal considerations, i.e. clarity, validity and auditability.

Many systematic approaches target the *clarity* of scholarly communication. The structure of a systematic review makes it easier to navigate and interpret. Clear methodology makes it easier to judge what the reviewers have and have not done. A focused question and explicit search strategies help to clarify scope and terminology. Stated inclusion and exclusion criteria allow readers to recognise why particular articles known to them have not been included. Graphical, textual and tabular features combine to reveal rather than conceal.

A second consideration addresses internal *validity*. The review product must be defensible against potential bias (see Chapter 8). Potential biases include **selection bias** where a reviewer selects primary research studies that support his/her prior beliefs. Biases also include **publication bias** (where investigators, reviewers or editors differentially submit or accept manuscripts based on the direction or strength of the study findings) (Gilbody and Song, 2000). Systematic approaches require that items are selected for inclusion on the basis of their relevance and rigour, not on whether they report a favourable outcome or whether their results are intrinsically 'interesting'.

Finally an emphasis on transparency leads to concerns with *auditability* – how do we know that the reviewer's conclusions are grounded in the data retrieved from the review process and not an argument fabricated to support a prior conclusion?

> Systematic research syntheses are important, too, as quality control. Peer-review serves more as a check on a primary study's published report. The original data themselves seldom are subject to scrutiny. (Rousseau et al., 2008)

The science of research synthesis is thus populated by flowcharts of numbers of included studies, supplementary documents, and appendices relating to search strategies, sample data extraction forms, and increasing numbers of reporting standards (Moher et al., 2014).

 **exercise 2.1**

How systematic is this review?

Disciplines differ in the extent to which they have adopted systematic approaches to research synthesis. Identify a review article within your own subject area or discipline. (For example, search for 'review', 'overview', or 'meta-analysis' in the title or abstract.) To what extent can your chosen review be described as 'systematic'? Exercise 2.1 suggests that you construct a grid as in the following example and complete it with your own observations.

1 Features that make this review appear SYSTEMATIC	2 Features that make this review appear NON-SYSTEMATIC

Briefly reflect on what the term 'systematic' means to you. Do you consider being systematic a positive or a negative attribute? Table 2.3 suggests some words associated with being systematic or unsystematic.

Table 2.3 Words associated with being 'systematic' or unsystematic

Systematic	Either	Unsystematic
Explicit	Creative	Implicit
Transparent	Comprehensive	Opaque
Methodical	Imaginative	Whimsical
Objective	Publishable	Subjective
Standardised	Stimulating	Variable
Structured	Topical	Chaotic
Reproducible	Well-written	Idiosyncratic

The availability of time, personnel and money may further constrain the quality of the final review product (see Chapter 4). A reviewer should select a model of review that is most appropriate to the purpose required (Tricco et al., 2011; Kastner et al., 2012). The reviewer should be explicit about any limitations inherent to the chosen approach. For example, a **scoping review** that offers a snapshot of a particular topic (Arksey and O'Malley, 2005) does not usually attempt **quality assessment**. In contrast, systematic reviews (or overviews):

> use (and describe) specific, explicit and therefore reproducible methodological strategies to identify, assemble, critical appraise and synthesise all relevant issues on a specific topic. (Carney and Geddes, 2002)

Well-conducted systematic reviews should improve the reliability and accuracy of conclusions, being clearly allied to the scientific method:

> Syntheses systematically identify where research findings are clear (and where they aren't), a key first step to establishing the conclusions science supports. (Rousseau et al., 2008)

The results of systematic reviews are rarely unequivocal and require careful reading and interpretation (Hopayian, 2001). Narrative reviews often offer a 'snapshot' of **prevalent knowledge** at a particular point in time whereas many systematic reviews explicitly aim to monitor and capture **incident** (i.e. emerging) **knowledge**. Systematic reviews may be designed to be updated periodically to take into account the emergence of new evidence.

Cooper (1988a, 1988b) identifies four possible literature review approaches:

1) Exhaustive coverage, citing all relevant literature.
2) Exhaustive coverage with selective citation.
3) Representative coverage (discussion of works which typify particular groupings in the literature).
4) Coverage of pivotal works.

Cooper's choice of **exhaustivity** – often considered synonymous with the 'systematic review' – is to be preferred to the discourse of 'comprehensiveness', because the former carries the implication of finite (i.e. review-dependent) resources. Early on in the development of the systematic review process it was considered desirable to retrieve *all* studies on a clearly defined topic. Rousseau and colleagues (2008) state:

> Systematic means **comprehensive accumulation**, transparent analysis, and reflective inter-pretation of all empirical studies pertinent to a specific question. Reliance upon any sampling or subset of the literature risks misrepresenting its diversity in findings, outcomes methods, and frames of reference.

More recently there is increasing recognition that even the most exhaustive (and exhausting!) search cannot hope to identify the entire universe of studies on the most specific of topics. Interestingly Cooper's third and fourth approaches broaden our toolkit to include a wider range of sampling approaches, increasingly recognised as a more appropriate response than a 'one-size-fits-all' comprehensive approach (Suri, 2011). 'Fitness for purpose' is the appropriate aspiration, underpinned by the trade-off of rigour versus relevance (Bennett et al., 2005). Notably, however, selective citation – a danger inherent in the second of Cooper's approaches – is regarded as a potential source of bias (Song et al., 2010). Exercise 2.2 asks you to compare a systematic review with a traditional review.

 **exercise 2.2**

Compare a systematic and a traditional review

Identify a systematic review in an area of interest to you and also identify a conventional review in a similar or related topic. Place the two reviews side by side and briefly make a list of the differences between the two reviews.

Clarification of terminology

Up to now we have used the umbrella term 'research synthesis' unless specifically referring to a particular type of review. Many authors have attempted a taxonomy of literature review types (Strike and Posner, 1983; Cooper, 1988a, 1988b; Grant and Booth, 2009; Gough et al., 2012; Paré et al., 2014; Whittemore et al., 2014). Such a task is challenging because a review may be characterised across such variables as the purpose of the review (as with a **mapping review**), the types of included study (as with a systematic review of randomised controlled trials), the nature of included data (as with the qualitative systematic review), the type of question being addressed (as with the effectiveness review), the phenomenon being investigated (as in the case of **meta-theory** or **meta-method**), and the underlying intent (**meta-ethnography** for theory generation or **realist synthesis** for theory verification). Other characteristics relate to the context of the review (as for the **rapid evidence assessment**) or to the underpinning 'philosophy' regarding subsequent use of the review (as with **best evidence synthesis**). This book will attempt to define the characteristics of each type of review wherever possible. However, we would also acknowledge that:

> Only a handful of review types possess prescribed and explicit methodologies and many of the labels used fall short of being mutually exclusive ... [we recognise] that there is a lack of unique distinguishing features for the most common review types, whilst highlighting that some common features do exist. (Grant and Booth, 2009)

Researchers have a considerable incentive to invent a new label or new form of review that differs slightly from its predecessors rather than to seek standardisation. In Chapters 4 to 10 we focus on the techniques and ingredients of the review process (systematic approaches) as a counter balance to methodological 'pigeon-holing'.

Recently approaches to the synthesis of the literature have been characterised as either **aggregative** or **interpretive/configurative** (Weed, 2005; Gough et al., 2012; Sandelowski et al., 2012) (see Table 2.4). Aggregative reviews bring together studies on a similar topic such that each additional study adds 'weight' to a shared finding. Bringing studies together in this way necessitates assumptions about how similar studies are to one another (**homogeneity**). In practice all studies are different (with regard to the population studied, in how a procedure is implemented, in how an outcome is measured, etc.). The reviewer, and indeed the reader, have to judge whether studies are more alike than different.

By implication aggregative approaches can reach a point at which sufficient studies have established a finding beyond statistical doubt. Cumulative meta-analyses can demonstrate a point beyond which subsequent studies possess a certain degree of **informational redundancy** (Antman et al., 1992). Nevertheless, in theory at least, additional studies hold the potential to overturn a previous finding. Aggregative reviews therefore represent an ongoing attempt to identify studies that have previously been missed, particularly if their absence might reveal a previously neglected systematic bias.

In contrast, **interpretive/configurative** reviews seek to broaden our understanding of a particular intervention or phenomenon. Each study holds the potential to contribute additional insights and also contribute to the overall picture. Of course this potential is more limited where a broad consensus exists and authors report the same type of insights. This is analogous to **theoretical saturation** within primary research (Dixon-Woods et al., 2005). In theory, theoretical saturation should be less frequent than in primary research as, unlike interviewees, authors are not independent informants (Dixon-Woods et al., 2006). Indeed authors are incentivised to report innovative insights. To resists theoretical saturation a reviewer will make particularly strenuous attempts to sample from other fields or types of literature. Whereas aggregative reviews implicitly value the average result which adds strength to the overall result from multiple similar studies, interpretive reviews place particular value on identifying the **disconfirming case** (Booth et al., 2013a). Interpretive reviews often seek to contribute to theory (Walsh and Downe, 2005).

Occasionally the **integrative review** is used synonymously with the interpretive review. While this terminology was appropriate for as long as quantitative and qualitative reviews were separate endeavours, the **mixed methods review** now seeks to 'harness the power of stories alongside the power of numbers' (Pluye and Hong, 2014). We reserve the integrative review for cases where both types of data are brought together (Whittemore and Knafl, 2005), typically to produce a whole that is greater than the sum of its parts (Strike and Posner, 1983).

Table 2.4 Configurative/interpretive or aggregative?

Consider whether the overall intent of your intended review is interpretive or aggregative

Configurative/Interpretive	Aggregative
Will my question develop and change as new insights emerge from the literature?	Is my question fixed and focused, allowing me to decide authoritatively whether studies are relevant or not?
If new papers fail to contribute new insights will I purposively move on to different types of sources?	Will I keep searching until I have exhausted all likely sources?
Is the main value of each new study in adding a different insight to what I am investigating?	Is the main value of each new study in adding weight to, or confirming, what has previously been found?
Is my principal focus on the 'exception to the rule'?	Is my principal focus on the mean or 'average' overall result?
Will my data be presented primarily as themes or models with accompanying commentary?	Will my data be presented primarily as tables and graphs with accompanying commentary?

INTRODUCING THE SALSA FRAMEWORK

We have chosen to characterise review types against four critical steps in the review process that we embody within the mnemonic SALSA (Search, AppraisaL, Synthesis and Analysis) (Grant and Booth, 2009). The strength and quality of each step contribute to the overall 'signal' emitted by the review, whereas biases increase the distracting 'noise' (Edwards et al., 1998). Thus a **scoping review** is characterised as a broad-brush approach to finding the most notable studies in the field, minimal attempts to evaluate them for quality, a rudimentary attempt at synthesis (perhaps through listing, tabulation or mapping), and an analysis that caricatures the quantity and distribution of the literature. In contrast a gold standard **systematic review**, as endorsed by the Cochrane Collaboration, prescribes an exhaustive search of the literature, checklist-driven quality assessment, complex synthesis using textual, numerical, graphical and tabular methods and sophisticated analysis (for example, for differences between subgroups, the differential effects of study groups, and the likelihood of missing studies). Between these two extremes lie numerous variants with different levels of input at the four key stages (see Table 2.5).

Table 2.5 Types of review

Type of Review	Description	Search	Appraisal	Synthesis	Analysis
Critical review	Aims to demonstrate extensive research and critical evaluation of quality. Goes beyond mere description to include degree of analysis and conceptual innovation. Typically results in hypothesis or model.	Seeks to identify most significant items in field.	No. Evaluates by contribution.	Narrative, conceptual, chronological.	Significant component: seeks to identify conceptual contribution to embody existing or derive new theory.
Integrative review	Utilises broadest type of research review methods to include both experimental and non-experimental research in order to understand more fully a phenomenon of concern. Integrative reviews combine data from theoretical and empirical literature.	Exhaustive search to identify maximum number of eligible primary sources, using two or more strategies. Purposive sampling may be combined with exhaustive search if appropriate.	Reports coded according to quality but not necessarily excluded.	Tabular (matrices, graphs, charts, or networks) usually according to a framework.	Creativity, critical analysis of data and data displays key to comparison and identification of important patterns and themes.
Literature review	Examines recent or current literature. Can cover wide range of subjects at various levels of completeness and exhaustivity. May include research findings.	Possibly exhaustive.	Possibly.	Narrative.	Chronological, conceptual, thematic, etc.
Mapping review/ systematic map	Maps out and categorises existing literature from which to commission further reviews and/or primary research by identifying gaps in research literature.	As time allows.	No.	Graphical. Tabular.	Characterises quantity and quality of literature, perhaps by study design and other key features. May identify need for primary/secondary research.
Meta-analysis	Statistically combines results of quantitative studies to provide precise effect of results.	Exhaustive. May use Funnel plot to assess completeness.	May determine inclusion/exclusion and/or sensitivity analyses.	Graphical. Tabular. Narrative.	Numerical analysis.

Type of Review	Description	Search	Appraisal	Synthesis	Analysis
Mixed studies review/ mixed methods review	Combines methods that include review component (usually systematic). Specifically combines quantitative with qualitative research or outcome with process studies.	Sensitive search or separate quantitative and qualitative strategies.	Generic appraisal instrument or separate appraisal processes with corresponding checklists.	Narrative. Tabular. Graphical (to integrate quantitative and qualitative studies).	May look for correlations between characteristics or use gap analysis to identify aspects absent in one literature but missing in other.
Overview	Surveys literature and describe its characteristics.	Depends on how systematic methods are.	Depends on how systematic methods are.	Depends on how systematic methods are. Narrative. Tabular.	Chronological, conceptual, thematic, etc.
Qualitative systematic review/ qualitative evidence synthesis	Integrates or compares findings from qualitative studies. Looks for 'themes' or 'constructs' in or across individual studies.	Selective or purposive.	Typically to mediate messages not for inclusion/ exclusion.	Qualitative, narrative synthesis.	Thematic may include conceptual models.
Rapid review	Assesses what is already known about policy or practice issue.	As time allows, uses systematic review methods to search existing research.	As time allows, uses systematic review methods to critically appraise existing research.	Narrative. Tabular.	Quantities of literature and overall quality/direction of effect of literature.

(Continued)

(Continued)

Type of Review	Description	Search	Appraisal	Synthesis	Analysis
Realist synthesis	Synthesises large and diverse selection of literature to inform policy revision, design effective interventions and identify potentially effective and innovative interventions.	Mainly iterative and purposive.	Privileges relevance over rigour.	Narrative, causal chains and graphical.	Key output is programme theory/ies of target intervention, specifying how and why programme/ service is thought to cause intended outcomes (theory building), and then testing assumptions against further evidence, to strengthen and refine it (theory testing).
Scoping review	Identifies nature and extent of research evidence (including ongoing research).	As time allows. May include research in progress.	No.	Narrative. Tabular.	Quantity and quality of literature, perhaps by study design and other features. Attempt to specify viable review.
State-of-the-art review	Addresses current matters. May offer new perspectives on issue or point out area for further research.	Exhaustive coverage of current literature.	No.	Narrative. Tabular.	Current state of knowledge, priorities for future investigation, research limitations.
Systematic search and review	Combines strengths of critical review with exhaustive search process. Addresses broad questions to produce 'best evidence synthesis'.	Exhaustive.	Possibly.	Narrative. Tabular.	What is known, recommendations for practice.
Umbrella review	Summarises results from systematic reviews on a topic.	Exhaustive search for reviews only.	Possibly using a review specific appraisal tool (for example, AMSTAR).	Graphical and tabular.	What is known and research gaps for primary research or further reviews.

(Adapted from Grant and Booth, 2009)

The SALSA approach is anticipated by other authors: for example, Bruce (2001) specifies that a review requires 'the *analysis and synthesis* of previous work in such a manner that new understandings of that work are uncovered, and the way is opened for new scholarship or research'. More recently Major and Savin-Baden (2010) highlighted the importance of synthesis, analysis and interpretation. For us 'analysis' fuses the technical aspects of juxtaposing studies with the more imaginative and explorative aspects signified by interpretation.

SYSTEMATIC APPROACHES

By 'systematic approaches' we refer to those elements of a literature review that, either individually or collectively, contribute to the methods being both explicit and reproducible. Systematic approaches (see Box 2.3) are evidenced in both the conduct and presentation of the literature review and epitomised in the formal method of '**systematic review**'. Exercise 2.3 asks you to examine how systematic a review is. Specifically systematic approaches include:

- systematic approaches to **literature searching**, as seen in the scoping review and the mapping review (see Chapter 6);
- systematic approaches to **quality assessment** (appraisal) of the literature, as seen in an integrative review (see Chapter 7);
- systematic approaches to **synthesis** of the literature, as seen in such techniques as meta-analysis, meta-ethnography, **realist synthesis** and **thematic synthesis** (see Chapters 8 and 9);
- systematic approaches to **analysis** of the robustness and validity of review findings such as subgroup analysis, either qualitative or quantitative, or sensitivity analysis (see Chapters 8 and 9);
- systematic approaches to the **presentation** of review findings using narrative, tabular, numerical and graphical approaches (see Chapters 8, 9, and 10).

 box 2.3

What does 'systematic' look like?

- A priori specification of planned review methods/protocol.
- A clearly focused question.
- Clear, explicit criteria for inclusion and exclusion.
- Documentation of search process: sources and strategies.
- Use of tables and boxes to make methods explicit.
- Use of tables to summarise study characteristics.
- An explicit mechanism to handle quality assessment.
- Exploration of assumptions, limitations and areas of uncertainty.
- Use of tables and graphics to support interpretation of data.
- Appendices including search strategies, sample data extraction and quality assessment tools.
- Explicit Declarations of Interest.

exercise 2.3

How systematic is that review?

Look through the following fictional abstract describing 'a structured review of the literature' in light of what you have already learnt regarding the search, appraisal, synthesis, analysis (SALSA) framework. Which elements of this abstract provide evidence of a systematic approach?

performing X in Y

A structured review of the literature

Abstract

{Two brief sentences of Background}. A literature search was conducted across {list of Databases and Internet sources} of studies that evaluated X. Information on the type of activity, sample and setting, endpoints, and study design were extracted. Studies were classified based on a modified {Hypothetical Worthy} model. Four categories of activity were identified: actor, decision-support, involvement and systems. The search strategy and selection criteria yielded 21 articles. Eleven studies used an actor activity; two studies used a decision support activity, seven used an involvement activity, and one used a systems intervention. The overall quality of research was uneven: research design – nine studies were quasi-experimental in nature, endpoint measures were not consistent – three did not perform statistical analysis. Sample characteristics varied dramatically. In conclusion, the number of high-quality studies of X remains limited. Methodological limitations include measurement of an inappropriate surrogate measure when measurement of an endpoint would be more valid. Further research is needed to understand how each type of activity improves the quality of performing X in a Y setting.

SUMMARY

Like all science, research synthesis is evolving and uncertain. For example, the application of statistical methods for pooling and synthesising the quantitative results of different studies – **meta-analysis** – is steadily improving, though considerable challenges remain (Egger et al., 2002). While much early development focused on systematic reviews of evidence about healthcare interventions – drugs, therapies, technologies – the principles of research synthesis remain the same regardless of the subject matter under review. This chapter has examined the relative advantages of systematic over more traditional approaches to reviewing the literature. It has identified the main stages in the review process. Systematic approaches to the literature can improve the clarity, validity and auditability of an otherwise well-conducted conventional review. The key steps of search, appraisal, synthesis and analysis (SALSA) can help to characterise the differences between various types of review. Systematic approaches to the literature address three problems neatly encapsulated by Rousseau and colleagues (2008):

the misuse of existing research, the overuse of limited or inconclusive findings, and the under use of research evidence with substantive implications for understanding and working with organisations.

 key learning points

- Research synthesis has a long pedigree and in recent years the stimulus of evidence-based policy and practice has seen it spread across multiple fields and disciplines.
- Surveys of research syntheses consistently reveal poor reporting of review methods. All literature reviews should be systematic but reviews differ in the degree to which they are systematic and how explicitly their methods are reported.
- Systematic approaches to the literature attempt to address known deficiencies by offering greater clarity, internal validity and auditability.
- Different types of review can be characterised by the extent to which they undertake the four steps of search, appraisal, synthesis and analysis (SALSA).

frequently asked questions (FAQs)

FAQ 2.1 Will it always be possible to be systematic in conducting a literature review?

Yes. We contend that all types of literature review should contain elements of systematicity. Any type of research should access an underpinning 'system'. The flexibility of the review method allows for different degrees of being systematic. An associated challenge relates to how you describe what you have done, especially where your methods are iterative and recursive. Describing what you looked for, what you found, what you did with what you found, and what you concluded from what you found are shared characteristics of any review. Text, tables and diagrams are different ways to make your review appear more systematic – and your reader will benefit if you are able to communicate what you have done as explicitly as possible.

FAQ 2.2 If all reviews are 'systematic' should I call my review a 'systematic review'?

By all means call your review a 'systematic review' if you have followed closely a prescribed systematic review methodology, such as outlined by the Cochrane Handbook (Higgins and Green, 2011) or the Centre for Reviews and Dissemination (2009) guidelines. If a review is truly a systematic review then it will carry extra academic weight and likely be more highly cited. However, this label must be earned and not bestowed wantonly. If you call your review a systematic review and this is not the case then it will rightly receive a rough ride from editors, peer reviewers, supervisors and examiners. Choosing the most accurate label for your review will ensure that it is viewed appropriately.

(Continued)

(Continued)

FAQ 2.3 Must a minimum amount of literature exist if I am planning to conduct a literature review?

This depends upon why you are doing your literature review and what your intended audience is expecting. If your review is trying to establish whether a study exists that has previously addressed a specific question then it may be appropriate for you to demonstrate that you have conscientiously combed all likely sources and still not found any eligible study. Alternatively you may need to show that you have looked in the right places by itemising studies that are almost – but not quite – what you were looking for. If your review is required to inform a particular course of action then you may need to drop requirements for particular types of study or literature and widen this to include any source of evidence that matches your review question.

FAQ 2.4 Must the literature be of a particular quality or study type to be included in my literature review?

Again this depends on why you are doing the literature review and what your intended audience is expecting. If your review is trying to establish definitively whether or not a particular intervention works then simply adding inferior study designs or poor quality papers is not going to advance this issue. Only good quality studies will confirm or deny whether the intervention has an effect. In essence you are 'sieving out' inferior studies so that only good-enough studies remain. However, if you are seeking an overall ('all-round') picture of a phenomenon then even a poor quality study may contain a 'nugget' of valuable insight (see Chapter 7).

FAQ 2.5 Do I need to be skilled in statistics if I am planning to conduct a systematic review?

Not necessarily. Systematic reviews can analyse either quantitative literature or qualitative literature, or even combine both types of literature (**mixed methods reviews**). Generally speaking you should ensure that you have skills in reading and interpreting the type of literature that you intend to review, or plan a route by which you may obtain those skills (such as through reading or training), or identify a resource (for example, a statistician or research support service) that you can access as and when you need this. Bear in mind that not all quantitative reviews are suited to pooling in a meta-analysis. They therefore require numeracy rather than statistics. You should also recognise that your skills in qualitative research are potentially equally important even though these are a less common source of anxiety.

FAQ 2.6 Do I need to include all four steps of search, appraisal, synthesis and analysis in my literature review?

While the time you spend on each step may vary these four steps are fundamental to the review process. For example, even if you only examine a collection of full-text articles stored on your computer, or type some words into Google Scholar, you are conducting a form of 'search'. Similarly even if you decide to include any type of publication or study on your topic you are making an implicit policy about quality (appraisal) for your review. We would contend that you must describe what you have done for each step and match each step to your review purpose. Frequently analysis, although present, is comparatively neglected when squeezed out by time constraints.

suggestions for further reading

Mulrow, C.D. (1994) Rationale for systematic reviews. *BMJ*, **309**, 597-9.
An influential article that outlines why previous narrative approaches to literature review might be considered unsatisfactory.

Petticrew, M. (2001) Systematic reviews from astronomy to zoology: myths and misconceptions. *BMJ*, **322**, 13, 98-101.
An accessible introductory overview to the idea of systematic reviews and what they aim to do.

Petticrew, M.A. and Roberts, H. (2006) Why do we need systematic reviews? In M.A. Petticrew and H. Roberts (eds), *Systematic Reviews in the Social Sciences*. Oxford: Blackwell, 1-26.
The introductory chapter to a favourite textbook, notable for its clarity and excellent scholarship.

Pickering, C. and Byrne, J. (2014) The benefits of publishing systematic quantitative literature reviews for PhD candidates and other early-career researchers. *Higher Education Research & Development*, **33**, 3, 534-48.
A good starting point if you have yet to be convinced about the value of systematic reviews for your own research.

Randolph, J. (2009) A guide to writing the dissertation literature review. *Practical Assessment, Research and Evaluation*, **14**, 13.
Based within the more traditional, as opposed to systematic, review paradigm this article nevertheless provides compelling pointers to a high quality literature review.

Steward, B. (2004) Writing a literature review. *British Journal of Occupational Therapy*, **67**, 11, 495-500.
A concise and understandable guide to the steps of a systematic review

Volmink, J., Siegfried, N., Robertson, K. and Gülmezoglu, A. (2004) Research synthesis and dissemination as a bridge to knowledge management: the Cochrane Collaboration. *Bulletin of the World Health Organisation*, **82**, 10, 778-83.
Of historical interest on the development of the Cochrane Collaboration, locating reviews within the broader research-practice gap

REFERENCES

Antman, E.M., Lau, J., Kupelnick, B., Mosteller, F. and Chalmers, T.C. (1992) A comparison of results of meta-analyses of randomized control trials and recommendations of clinical experts. Treatments for myocardial infarction. *JAMA*, **268**, 2, 240-8.

Arksey, H. and O'Malley, L. (2005) Scoping studies: towards a methodological framework. *International Journal of Social Research Methodology*, **8**, 1, 19-32.

Bem, D.J. (1995) Writing a review article for Psychological Bulletin. *Psychological Bulletin*, **118**, 2, 172-7.

Bennett, J., Lubben, F., Hogarth, S. and Campbell, B. (2005) Systematic reviews of research in science education: rigour or rigidity? *International Journal of Science Education*, **27**, 4, 387-406.

Booth, A. and Carroll, C. (2015) Systematic searching for theory to inform systematic reviews: is it feasible? Is it desirable? *Health Information & Libraries Journal*, **32**, 3, 220–35.

Booth, A., Carroll, C., Ilott, I., Low, L.L. and Cooper, K. (2013a) Desperately seeking dissonance: identifying the disconfirming case in qualitative evidence synthesis. *Qualitative Health Research*, **23**, 1, 126–41.

Booth, A., Harris, J., Croot, E., Springett, J., Campbell, F. and Wilkins, E. (2013b) Towards a methodology for cluster searching to provide conceptual and contextual 'richness' for systematic reviews of complex interventions: case study (CLUSTER). *BMC Medical Research Methodology*, **13**, 1, 118.

Britten, N., Campbell, R., Pope, C., Donovan, J., Morgan, M. and Pill, R. (2002) Using meta ethnography to synthesise qualitative research: a worked example. *Journal of Health Services Research and Policy*, **7**, 4, 209–15.

Bruce, C. (2001) Interpreting the scope of their literature reviews: significant differences in research students' concerns. *New Library World*, **102**, 4/5, 158–66.

Bruce, C.S. (1994) Research students' early experiences of the dissertation literature review. *Studies in Higher Education*, **19**, 2, 217–29.

Bruce, C.S. (1996) From neophyte to expert: counting on reflection to facilitate complex conceptions of the literature review. In O. Zuber-Skerritt (ed.), *Frameworks for Postgraduate Education*. Lismore, NSW: Southern Cross University, 239–53.

Campbell, M., Egan, M., Lorenc, T., Bond, L., Popham, F., Fenton, C. and Benzeval, M. (2014) Considering methodological options for reviews of theory: illustrated by a review of theories linking income and health. *Systematic Reviews*, **3**, 114. DOI: 10.1186/2046–4053–3–114.

Carney, S.M. and Geddes, J.R. (2002) *Systematic Reviews and Meta-analyses. Evidence in Mental Health Care*. Hove: Brunner Routledge.

Centre for Reviews and Dissemination (CRD) (2009) *Systematic Reviews: CRD's Guidance for Undertaking Reviews in Health Care*. York: Centre for Reviews and Dissemination.

Chalmers, I., Hedges, L.V. and Cooper, H. (2002) A brief history of research synthesis. *Evaluation and the Health Professions*, **25**, 1, 12–37.

Clark, S. and Horton, R. (2010) Putting research into context – revisited. *The Lancet*, **376**, 9734, 10–11.

Clarke, M. and Chalmers, I. (1998) Discussion sections in reports of controlled trials published in general medical journals. Islands in search of continents? *JAMA*, **280**, 280–2.

Cooper, H.M. (1988a) The structure of knowledge synthesis: a taxonomy of literature reviews. *Knowledge in Society*, **1**, 104–26.

Cooper, H.M (1988b) Organizing knowledge syntheses: a taxonomy of literature reviews. *Knowledge, Technology and Policy*, **1**, 1, 104–26.

Cooper, H.M. (1989) *Integrating Research: A Guide for Literature Reviews*, 2nd edition. Newbury Park, CA: Sage.

Cooper, H.M., Hedges, L. and Valentine, J. (eds) (2009) *The Handbook of Research Synthesis and Meta-Analysis*, 2nd edition. New York: The Russell Sage Foundation.

Daigneault, P.M., Jacob, S. and Ouimet, M. (2014) Using systematic review methods within a PhD dissertation in political science: challenges and lessons learned from practice. *International Journal of Social Research Methodology*, **17**, 3, 267–83.

Damschroder, L.J., Aron, D.C., Keith, R.E., Kirsh, S.R., Alexander, J.A. and Lowery, J.C. (2009) Fostering implementation of health services research findings into practice: a consolidated framework for advancing implementation science. *Implementation Science*, **4**, 50.

Davies, H.T.O., Nutley, S.M. and Smith, P.C. (eds) (2000) *What Works? Evidence-Based Policy and Practice in Public Services*. Bristol: Policy.

Davies, P. (2000) The relevance of systematic reviews to educational policy and practice. *Oxford Review of Education*, **26**, 3–4, 365–78.

Davies, P., Walker, A.E. and Grimshaw, J.M. (2010) A systematic review of the use of theory in the design of guideline dissemination and implementation strategies and interpretation of the results of rigorous evaluations. *Implementation Science*, **5**, 14.

De Silva, M.J., Breuer, E., Lee, L., Asher, L., Chowdhary, N., Lund, C. and Patel, V. (2014) Theory of change: a theory-driven approach to enhance the Medical Research Council's framework for complex interventions. *Trials*, **15**, 1, 267.

Dixon-Woods, M., Agarwal, S., Jones, D., Young, B. and Sutton, A. (2005) Synthesising qualitative and quantitative evidence: a review of possible methods. *Journal of Health Services Research and Policy*, **10**, 1, 45–53.

Dixon-Woods, M., Bonas, S., Booth, A., Jones, D.R., Miller, T., Sutton, A.J., Shaw, R.L. and Young, B. (2006) How can systematic reviews incorporate qualitative research? A critical perspective. *Qualitative Research*, **6**, 1, 27–44.

Dunn, P.M. (1997) James Lind (1716–94) of Edinburgh and the treatment of scurvy. *Archives of Disease in Childhood-Fetal and Neonatal Edition*, **76**, 1, F64–F65.

Dunne, C. (2011) The place of the literature review in grounded theory research. *International Journal of Social Research Methodology*, **14**, 2, 111–24.

Edwards, A.G., Russell, I.T. and Stott, N.C. (1998) Signal versus noise in the evidence base for medicine: an alternative to hierarchies of evidence? *Family Practice*, **15**, 4, 319–22.

Egger, M., Ebrahim, S. and Smith, G.D. (2002) Where now for meta-analysis? *International Journal of Epidemiology*, **31**, 1, 1–5.

Enkin, M., Keirse, M.J., Renfrew, M. and Neilson, J. (1989) *Effective Care in Pregnancy and Childbirth*. Oxford: Oxford University Press.

Evans, J. and Benefield, P. (2001) Systematic reviews of educational research: does the medical model fit? *British Educational Research Journal*, **27**, 527–41.

Fink, A. (2005) *Conducting Research Literature Reviews: From the Internet to Paper*, 2nd edition. London: Sage.

Galvan, J.L. (1999) *Writing Literature Reviews*. Los Angeles, CA: Pyrczak.

Gilbody, S.M. and Song, F. (2000) Publication bias and the integrity of psychiatry research. *Psychological Medicine*, **30**, 253–8.

Glass, G.V. (1976) Primary, secondary and meta-analysis of research. *Educational Researcher*, **10**, 3–8.

Godin, G., Bélanger-Gravel, A., Eccles, M. and Grimshaw, J. (2008) Healthcare professionals' intentions and behaviours: a systematic review of studies based on social cognitive theories. *Implementation Science*, **3**, 36.

Gough, D., Thomas, J. and Oliver, S. (2012) Clarifying differences between review designs and methods. *Systematic Reviews*, **1**, 28.

Grant, M.J. and Booth, A. (2009) A typology of reviews: an analysis of 14 review types and associated methodologies. *Health Information and Libraries Journal*, **26**, 2, 91–108.

Greenhalgh, T. (2014) *How to Read a Paper: The Basics of Evidence-based Medicine*, 5th edition. London: BMJ Books.

Greenhalgh, T., Kristjansson, E. and Robinson, V. (2007) Realist review to understand the efficacy of school feeding programmes. *BMJ*, **335**, 7625, 858–61.

Greenhalgh, T., Robert, G., Macfarlane, F., Bate, P., Kyriakidou, O. and Peacock, R. (2005) Storylines of research in diffusion of innovation: a meta-narrative approach to systematic review. *Social Science and Medicine*, **61**, 2, 417–30.

Hammersley, M. (2001) On 'systematic' reviews of research literatures: a 'narrative' response to Evans and Benefield. *British Educational Research Journal*, **27**, 5, 543–54.

Hammersley, M. (2002) Systematic or unsystematic, is that the question? Some reflections on the science, art, and politics of reviewing research evidence. Text of a talk given to the Public Health Evidence Steering Group of the Health Development Agency, October.

Hart, C. (1998) *Doing a Literature Review: Releasing the Social Science Research Imagination.* Thousand Oaks, CA: Sage.

Higgins, J.P. and Green, S. (eds) (2011) *Cochrane Handbook for Systematic Reviews of Interventions.* Version 5.1.0 (updated March 2011). Available at: www.cochrane-handbook.org (last accessed 9 March 2016).

Hopayian, K. (2001) The need for caution in interpreting high quality systematic reviews. *BMJ,* **323**, 681–4.

Kastner, M., Tricco, A.C., Soobiah, C., Lillie, E., Perrier, L., Horsley, T. and Straus, S.E. (2012) What is the most appropriate knowledge synthesis method to conduct a review? Protocol for a scoping review. *BMC Medical Research Methodology,* **12**, 1, 114.

Lavis, J.N., Davies, H.T.O., Oxman, A.D., Denis, J-L., Golden-Biddle, K. and Ferlie, E. (2005) Towards systematic reviews that inform health care management and policy-making. *Journal of Health Services Research and Policy,* **10**, Suppl. 1, S35–48.

LeCompte, M.D., Klinger, J.K., Campbell, S.A. and Menke, D.W. (2003) Editor's introduction. *Review of Educational Research,* **73**, 2, 123–4.

Light, R. and Pillemer, D. (1984) *Summing Up: The Science of Reviewing Research.* Cambridge, MA: Harvard University Press.

Major, C. and Savin-Baden, M. (2010) *An Introduction to Qualitative Research Synthesis: Managing the Information Explosion in Social Science Research.* London: Routledge.

Mays, N., Pope, C. and Popay, J. (2005) Systematically reviewing qualitative and quantitative evidence to inform management and policy-making in the health field. *Journal of Health Services Research and Policy,* **10**, Suppl. 1, 6–20.

McGhee, G., Marland, G.R. and Atkinson, J. (2007) Grounded theory research: literature reviewing and reflexivity. *Journal of Advanced Nursing,* **60**, 3, 334–42.

Moher, D., Altman, D., Schulz, K., Simera, I. and Wager, E. (eds) (2014) *Guidelines for Reporting Health Research: A User's Manual.* London: BMJ Books.

Mulrow, C. (1987) The medical review article: state of the science. *Annals of Internal Medicine,* **106**, 485–8.

Mulrow, C.D. (1995) Rationale for systematic reviews. In I. Chalmers and D. Altman (eds), *Systematic Reviews.* London: BMJ Publishing Group, 1–8.

Mulrow, C.D., Cook, D.J. and Davidoff, F. (1997) Systematic reviews: critical links in the great chain of evidence. *Annals of Internal Medicine,* **126**, 5, 389–91.

Noblit, G.W. and Hare, R.D. (1988) *Meta-ethnography: Synthesizing Qualitative Studies.* Newbury Park, CA: Sage.

Oxman, A.D. and Guyatt, G.H. (1993) The science of reviewing research. *Annals of the New York Academy of Science,* **703**, 125–33.

Paré, G., Trudel, M.C., Jaana, M. and Kitsiou, S. (2014) Synthesizing information systems knowledge: a typology of literature reviews. *Information & Management,* **52**, 183–99.

Pearson, K. (1904) Report on certain enteric fever inoculation statistics. *BMJ,* **iii**, 1243–6.

Petticrew, M. (2001) Systematic reviews from astronomy to zoology: myths and misconceptions. *BMJ,* **322**, 98–101.

Pluye, P. and Hong, Q.N. (2014) Combining the power of stories and the power of numbers: mixed methods research and mixed studies reviews. *Annual Review of Public Health,* **35**, 29–45.

Pope, C., Mays, N. and Popay, J. (2007) *Synthesizing Qualitative and Quantitative Health Evidence: A Guide to Methods.* Maidenhead: Open University Press, 13–15.

Randolph, J. (2009) A guide to writing the dissertation literature review. *Practical Assessment, Research and Evaluation,* **14**, 13.

Rousseau, D.M., Manning, J. and Denyer, D. (2008) Evidence in management and organizational science: assembling the field's full weight of scientific knowledge through syntheses. *Academy of Management Annals,* **2**, 475–515.

Sandelowski, M., Voils, C.I., Leeman, J. and Crandell, J.L. (2012) Mapping the mixed methods–mixed research synthesis terrain. *Journal of Mixed Methods Research*, **6**, 4, 317–31.

Shea, B., Moher, D., Graham, I., Pham, B. and Tugwell, P. (2002) A comparison of the quality of Cochrane Reviews and systematic reviews published in paper-based journals. *Evaluation and the Health Professions*, **25**, 116–29.

Song, F., Parekh, S., Hooper, L., Loke, Y.K., Ryder, J., Sutton, A.J., Hing, C., Kwok, C.S., Pang, C. and Harvey, I. (2010) Dissemination and publication of research findings: an updated review of related biases. *Health Technology Assessment*, **14**, 8, 1–193.

Strike, K. and Posner, G. (1983) Types of synthesis and their criteria. In S. Ward and L. Reed (eds), *Knowledge Structure and Use*. Philadelphia: Temple University Press, 345–62.

Suri, H. (2011) Purposeful sampling in qualitative research synthesis. *Qualitative Research Journal*, **11**, 2, 63–75.

Sweet, M. and Moynihan, R. (2007) *Improving Population Health: The Uses of Systematic Reviews*. New York: Milbank Memorial Fund.

Tricco, A.C., Tetzlaff, J. and Moher, D. (2011) The art and science of knowledge synthesis. *Journal of Clinical Epidemiology*, **64**, 1, 11–20.

Trinder, L. and Reynolds, S. (eds) (2000) *Evidence-based Practice: A Critical Appraisal*. Oxford: Blackwell Science.

Walker, L.O. and Avant, K.C. (2005) *Strategies for Theory Construction in Nursing*, 4th edition. Upper Saddle River, NJ: Pearson Prentice Hall.

Walsh, D. and Downe, S. (2005) Meta-synthesis method for qualitative research: a literature review. *Journal of Advanced Nursing*, **50**, 2, 204–11.

Webster, J. and Watson, R.T. (2002) Analyzing the past to prepare for the future: writing a literature review. *MIS Quarterly*, **26**, 2, 13–23.

Weed, M. (2005) Meta interpretation: a method for the interpretive synthesis of qualitative research. *Forum Qualitative Sozialforschung/Forum: Qualitative Social Research*, **6**, 1, Art. 37.

Whittemore, R. and Knafl, K. (2005) The integrative review: updated methodology. *Journal of Advanced Nursing*, **52**, 5, 546–53.

Whittemore, R., Chao, A., Jang, M., Minges, K.E. and Park, C. (2014) Methods for knowledge synthesis: an overview. *Heart & Lung: The Journal of Acute and Critical Care*, **43**, 5, 453–61.

Wilson, P.M., Petticrew, M., Calnan, M.W. and Nazareth, I. (2010) Disseminating research findings: what should researchers do? A systematic scoping review of conceptual frameworks. *Implementation Science*, **5**, 91.

Xyrichis, A. and Ream, E. (2008) Teamwork: a concept analysis. *Journal of Advanced Nursing*, **61**, 2, 232–41.

CHOOSING YOUR
REVIEW METHODS

 in a nutshell

How to choose your review methods

Your choice of review methods is determined by five main considerations captured by the acronym, TREAD:

- Available **T**ime for conducting your review.
- Any **R**esource constraints within which you must deliver your review.
- Any requirements for specialist **E**xpertise in order to complete the review.
- The requirements of the **A**udience for your review and its intended purpose.
- The richness, thickness and availability of **D**ata within included studies.

Throughout this chapter we encourage you to TREAD carefully!

INTRODUCTION

If you had been conducting your review in the early days of evidence synthesis you would have viewed the process very much as a logical sequential series of steps. Each stage in the review process was completed in turn, and each stage in turn determined the subsequent steps of the process (Thomas et al., 2004). The review process resembled a production assembly line in a factory where each operative performs a specific function with very little autonomy in order to deliver a product according to a pre-specified protocol (PLoS Medicine Editors, 2007). Viewing the review process as a production line risks 'dumbing down' the reviewers' expertise and contribution. Nowadays, in contrast, the concept of 'systematic approaches' evokes the toolbox of the skilled craftsman where you, as reviewer, respond to certain cues that will shape your review methods. These cues and choices derive from the nature of the literature and the needs and wants of the customer or consumer. They also reflect decisions made within the external environment. As a reviewer you will select judiciously from a toolbox of methodologies, methods and review types in order that you can deliver according to the review's intended purpose. As a consequence you may consider the review process to be more iterative and flexible both in what is done and indeed the order in which certain procedures are carried out (Victor, 2008).

The 'system' of our title conveys the idea of an overall conception of a scheme or method by which you plan to deliver your review output rather than a minute specification of individual interlocking procedures. This presents both an opportunity and a threat – with a wide knowledge of the choice of available methods you have greater freedom to select an appropriate route. This increases your likelihood of success in delivering a meaningful product. Yet, at the same time, you must hold fast to principles that attempt to minimise the likelihood of bias (Kitchenham, 2004). Steering between the Scylla of rigour and the Charybdis of relevance is the modern-day challenge that you face when you review the published literature (Laupacis and Straus, 2007).

ACKNOWLEDGING YOUR REVIEW CONSTRAINTS

Factors to consider when choosing your review methods are captured in our mnemonic TREAD (with our injunction being to TREAD carefully!). In our experience the five elements embodied in TREAD represent those factors most likely to impact on the scale and complexity of any review.

Time/Timeframe – This refers both to the time you have available to spend on review activity and the timeframe within which you intend to concentrate your activity. For example, the equivalent of three months' work may be performed by one researcher spending 25% of their time over one year or by six reviewers over a two-week period. When considering what type of review you are going to carry out you will need to think of the available time. You may want to identify whether you are going to make the review more manageable by reducing its scope or by fast-tracking some of the review processes.

Resources – When time and other resources are restricted then you might undertake a **rapid review** where you choose to limit some aspect of the review; for example, breadth of review question, sources searched, data coded, quality and relevance assurance measures, and depth of analysis (Government Social Research Unit, 2008; Abrami et al., 2010). As Gough and colleagues (2012) observe, however, you must be aware that if you make too many concessions and compromises you will undermine the rigour of the resulting review. Indeed it may be preferable, under resource-constrained circumstances, to drop any pretence that you can still describe such a review process as 'systematic' and decide to describe it overtly as 'non systematic':

> If rigor of execution and reporting are reduced too far then it may be more appropriate to characterize the work as non systematic scoping rather than as a systematic review. (Gough et al., 2012)

 **box 3.1**

What do we mean by scoping?

Scoping is an exploratory process of assessing the literature for its likely quantity and quality. It has four principal functions: methodologically it helps in determining appropriate review methods (Chapter 3) and logistically it assists in estimating how much time, money and reviewer effort will need to be expended for a specific review (Chapter 4); conceptually it facilitates decisions about what type of topics are to be included/excluded from a subsequent review (Chapter 5); and practically it helps in the identification of terms and synonyms to be used in the literature searching phase (Chapter 6). Scoping may be carried out at several stages in the review process, e.g. when preparing the funding application or in finalising the review protocol and commencing the full systematic review process. A particular type of review, the **scoping review**, embodies the scoping process as the main deliverable.

As we shall demonstrate, even if resources are limited you can still demonstrate that your scoping review is systematic. Indeed the extra time and effort that a systematic (as opposed to non systematic) scoping search and scoping review may require can yield dividends. Not only might you communicate its coverage to others more clearly, but also the certainty of its findings will be stronger and it will offer the potential of a stable launch pad for a subsequent systematic review if required.

Expertise – Most stages of a systematic review may be carried out by a researcher with basic research skills. However, certain other processes may require specialist input. Areas requiring specialist input that immediately come to mind include information specialist expertise for the literature searching, statistics for meta-analysis, and skills in data analysis for a qualitative review. Once you identify these needs you face several choices – to add a specialist to the team, to access the expertise on a selective 'need to know' basis, to acquire the skills yourself, or to attempt to circumvent or substitute problematic parts of the process. All these strategies carry implications for resources or for the quality of the review. For example selective access to specialists presumes that a reviewer knows exactly when and why to draw on this additional experience. Accessing a specialist too early may mean that you are unable to articulate the information that they require to provide advice. On the other hand accessing expertise too late may result in a missed window of opportunity or the repeating of tasks. Circumventing problematic parts of the process may simply be deferring criticism and storing up subsequent problems for either external review or for the peer review stage of the publication process.

Audience and Purpose – Increasingly we have identified a need to start from what the intended audience for the literature review wants and then to 'reverse engineer' the subsequent shape of the review. You can then manage time and resource constraints by planning your available resources backwards from this starting point. At first sight what the Audience requires may appear simply to restate the Purpose of the review. However, these are two fundamentally different considerations.

To illustrate, if you are selecting a particular review topic for your PhD your choice may be determined by personal interest, supervisor support or available funding – preferably a combination of all three factors. However, your supervisor is not the primary audience for your review. Your examiners are! Of course your supervisor should serve as a surrogate, representative or advocate for what your examiners are looking for. So what do your examiners expect from your review, and indeed more generally from your thesis as a whole? A thesis should showcase work of publishable quality. Your review needs to adhere to any appropriate standards of reporting, such as PRISMA (Moher et al., 2009), MOOSE (Stroup et al., 2000), or ENTREQ (Tong et al., 2012) (see Chapter 10). A thesis is also required to contribute new insights or understandings to the chosen area of investigation. While these new insights will not necessarily originate exclusively from the literature component of the thesis, as any primary research or data analysis will also contribute, your literature review should identify what is already known about the topic and which questions have yet to be answered. Your examiners will want to see an auditable link between the work of others and your own contribution. They will not simply expect a descriptive map of what has gone before but will require that you perform some level of analysis with the potential to reveal new insights. After all you may be the first person who has ever brought this particular set of studies together side by side in juxtaposition! What patterns can you identify from the literature you have so carefully assembled?

Similarly when we conduct a review for an external commissioner we find ourselves going beyond the actual review question to try to understand what the decision problem is that the review is expected to resolve. For example, if a funder is trying to decide whether to introduce a new policy or programme frequently they are not in actuality interested in all possible solutions to the problem being addressed. More typically they are interested in how their proposed policy or programme performs in comparison to other alternatives. Evidence that compares their candidate policy to other options is of primary value to their decision problem. Evidence comparing two different alternatives, or evaluating an alternative policy in isolation, is of less interest to them. We can therefore plan our review resources and effort accordingly. Of course if the commissioners genuinely do not have a preferred policy or programme then instead we might conduct a broad scoping search on which alternatives have been tried and then work with the commissioners to agree some criteria (e.g. local feasibility or acceptability) by which we can narrow these wider alternatives to a shortlist of interventions for detailed review.

Data: Quality, Quantity, Thickness, Richness (Popay et al., 1998) (characteristics of the literature) – Systematic approaches to reviewing the evidence are collectively flexible enough to accommodate all types of data. However, the actual choice of method is very much determined by the characteristics of the literature to be included. This can be illustrated with reference to both quantitative and qualitative data. Quantitative reviews require retrieved literature that presents a finite number of important outcomes, measured using common measurements or scales, present across a sufficient number of studies that have investigated the same research question using a similar enough research design (Tseng et al., 2008).

Where there is variation from this ideal you will often need to expend effort in exploring this variation, rather than simply presenting the results of the studies themselves. So, for example, if identified studies have all measured educational attainment using a common scale then statistical pooling using **meta-analysis** becomes possible. If the studies have measured educational attainment using different scales, that are sufficiently similar and reveal a common overall pattern of effect, then a degree of mapping across studies is possible. If, however, the scales used are substantively different in terms of their underpinning rationale or the results of such measurements are so disparate as to provide conflicting conclusions then the review is necessarily more descriptive (e.g. a **narrative synthesis**). Such a review may well focus on possible methodological explanations for such differences.

Sometimes no clear evidence exists simply because the primary studies did not include the outcomes of interest (Petticrew, 2003). In public health, in particular, the problem often seems to be an absence of evidence rather than evidence of absence of effect. This is partly because few studies have evaluated the outcomes of social interventions, including policies, and even fewer measure health outcomes. For example, a major uncertainty in public health concerns the health effects of changes in taxation or benefits. One systematic review found seven trials involving income supplementation, all US based, which examined the impact of a rise in people's income; unfortunately, none of the studies had reported reliable data on health outcomes (Connor et al., 1999).

Qualitative reviews require that the data contained within retrieved literature are *contextually* thick, i.e. in terms of enhancing our understanding of what is happening. Furthermore the data will optimally need to be *conceptually* rich to facilitate our explanation of why a particular phenomenon is occurring (Booth et al., 2013). If the literature is characterised by thin levels of detail we may be able to describe the frequency of particular phenomena or themes and do so via narrative synthesis (e.g. text and tables) but have a limited facility to provide an explanation. If the literature lacks detailed theorising then we may either have to access separate, wider bodies of literature in order to provide an explanation, or simply describe what we have observed and leave a detailed explanation to those who will actually use the review's findings.

From the foregoing we can see that narrative synthesis, which essentially describes or portrays the characteristics of the literature, is a versatile tool. Narrative synthesis provides an 'entry' level approach for most types of synthesis. Very often you will be able to identify patterns from the data or generate hypotheses by using simple forms of synthesis, such as tabulation in quantitative reviews or thematic synthesis in qualitative reviews. However, if you are to go beyond this, in seeking conclusive results or explanations, you will need your data to be more plentiful and of higher quality.

toolbox

A review choice decision tool

Although the choice of actual approaches is extensive it can be helpful to follow a few brief decision rules when deciding which approach to use. We have produced a brief review choice decision tool, based on existing work (Noyes and Lewin, 2011), to help you identify an appropriate path for your review (see Table 3.1).

exercise 3.1

Thinking about your audience

Use the following review choice decision tool worksheet (see Table 3.1) to plan where your review is located. Discuss your choice with your team or supervisor.

Table 3.1 Strategies for conducting an evidence synthesis

	Which type of data have I got?						
	Quantitative	**Qualitative**			**Quantitative and qualitative**		
	Are outcomes reported in a comparable format?	Is the review objective validation or generation of a theory?			Is the review objective validation or generation of a theory?		
		Generation	Validation	No/not sure	Generation	Validation	No/not sure
No	Use narrative synthesis and tabular presentation	Consider meta-ethnography or grounded theory approaches	Consider framework synthesis	Consider narrative synthesis or thematic synthesis	Consider critical interpretive synthesis, meta-narrative or use of logic models	Consider realist synthesis or Bayesian meta-synthesis	Consider narrative synthesis or thematic synthesis
Yes	Consider using meta-analysis						

Are the studies heterogeneous?

No	**Yes**	**Not sure**
Use fixed effects method	Use random effects method	Use random effects method

(Continued)

(Continued)

	Which type of data have I got?							
	Quantitative		**Qualitative**			**Quantitative and qualitative**		
	Are outcomes reported in a comparable format?		Is the review objective validation or generation of a theory?			Is the review objective validation or generation of a theory?		
	No	**Yes**	**Generation**	**Validation**	**No/not sure**	**Generation**	**Validation**	**No/not sure**
	Use narrative synthesis and tabular presentation	Consider using meta-analysis	Consider meta-ethnography or grounded theory approaches	Consider framework synthesis	Consider narrative synthesis or thematic synthesis	Consider critical interpretive synthesis, meta-narrative/ logic models	Consider realist synthesis/ Bayesian meta-synthesis	Consider narrative synthesis/ thematic synthesis
My Review (Mark with X)								
Comments								

SOME REVIEW CHOICE SCENARIOS

Below we present some realistic scenarios, based on real-life reviews but fictionalised, for instructional purposes to enable you to practise choosing appropriate review methodologies. In each case read the section *What are you aiming to do?* and see if you can isolate clues to potential review types. Then review the factors that we have isolated as informing your choice (*What factors will influence your choice?*). Finally consider our suggested choice(s) (*What choice(s) might you make?*) particularly with a view to understanding why we have rejected alternative labels or choices for this particular scenario. We have provided references on which each scenario is based should you wish to follow up the detail of a particular example.

Scenario A: Coding and categorising a cross-sectional sample from the literature

What are you aiming to do?

You and your colleagues wish to gain a better understanding of how qualitative research has been used to enhance the usefulness of **randomised controlled trials**. You are not trying to evaluate how well this has been done, merely to describe the different types of contribution. For example to which stages of the trial process have they contributed? Your readers will want you to demonstrate that you have gathered together a representative sample of how qualitative research has been used. However, you do not need to perform a comprehensive and exhaustive search of every instance of the use of qualitative research. Optimally you want to produce a framework that depicts all the possible contributions of qualitative research to trials. The main output from your review requires you to categorise the types of contribution together with a count of how often each type of contribution has been made. This framework may help future researchers plan how they will incorporate qualitative research alongside randomised controlled trials. This is an extensive piece of research with a time-span dependent on the extent of your chosen sample.

What factors will influence your choice?

The review is primarily descriptive. The team is more interested in what has been done and how it has been done, rather than in what the outcomes are. They need to create an interpretive framework but not to sample the literature comprehensively – essentially it is a cross-sectional snapshot of activity. The literature will be coded and classified, allowing for further analysis at a subsequent stage if desired. The team does not require an in-depth synthesis of the contents of each included article. Indeed if the sample of literature is to be adequately representative then the team are unlikely to have time to examine all sampled studies in depth.

Suggested Answer: Scenario A – mapping review

What choice(s) might you make?

Clearly you do not require a sophisticated interpretive method in order to undertake this review. Analysis will likely be superficial, except for problematic examples where the review team might need to reach a consensus on how they are labelled and whether they require a new category. Once a category exists, however, it is a fairly rapid process to slot articles into existing categories. You are not examining the actual topics investigated by the trials so this is not a **rapid evidence assessment**. Neither are you reviewing the literature with a view to defining the scope of a planned future review so this is not a **scoping review**. Essentially you are mapping out the field within a predefined scope and sample. Mapping includes characterising the sample (hence the use of categories) and then depicting the frequency or percentages of the categories in either tabular or graphical form, e.g. via a pie chart. This approach does not rule out the chance of a more in-depth review of either the entire dataset or a subset of particular interest but, unlike a scoping review, this is not a primary focus. This is therefore a (systematic) **mapping review**.

(Scenario adapted from: O'Cathain et al., 2013.)

Scenario B: Examining whether or not a potential review topic is feasible

What are you aiming to do?

Your research team wants to decide whether it is feasible to perform a systematic review of randomised controlled trials of personal health records. What does the evidence base look like? Are there sufficient randomised controlled trials in this area? What specific aspects of personal health record systems do they address? You need to search the key database sources to estimate what is available. However, as a systematic review, if conducted later, would attempt to identify all relevant studies it is not critical to identify every study at this stage. You simply want to find out if eligible studies are relatively plentiful, e.g. are there at least 6–10 candidate studies and, if not, what would be the implications of reviewing the evidence from lesser quality comparative studies (e.g. **cohort studies** or **case-control studies**)? The outcome from this review will not necessarily be a peer-reviewed publication in its own right – it may be made available as grey literature or form the basis of a grant application.

What factors will influence your choice?

You are seeking to establish the quantity and quality of studies in a particular topic area. Initial information from this process may help you decide which settings, populations, interventions, comparators, outcomes and study designs will be included or excluded. Inclusion and exclusion may also be determined by the time and resources you have available. You may have to 'cut your cloth to suit your means (resources)'. Your investigation may or may not be subsequently written up and/or published. It will likely inform a subsequent review.

Suggested Answer: Scenario B – scoping review

What choice(s) might you make?

Although there is an element of 'mapping' about this review the main purpose is to establish feasibility rather than to characterise the literature conceptually. Essentially you are conducting

scoping searches which may or may not be transformed into a formal publishable scoping review. Increasingly, however, researchers seek to publish their scoping reviews, and indeed subsequently publish the operational details of the intended review within a **review protocol**. This is therefore a scoping review.

(Scenario adapted from: Archer et al., 2011.)

Scenario C: Arriving at a bottom line of 'effect'

What are you aiming to do?

You are a member of an educational research team that seeks to establish whether providing breakfast to schoolchildren has an impact on their attendance at school and their subsequent academic performance. A preliminary look at the literature review has identified some randomised controlled trials and observational studies that have examined these outcomes. The few studies that have been found to date seem to share a limited number of outcome measures, e.g. attendance rates and improvement in academic performance. You want to be able to integrate the results of such studies and arrive at an overall bottom-line of whether providing breakfast 'works'.

What factors will influence your choice?

This review offers the possibility of quantitative outcome measures which appear broadly comparable. At least some randomised controlled trials are known to exist. Although the included studies may examine different populations and different contexts the outcomes and measures used appear to be broadly comparable. Essentially this is an effectiveness question with a requirement to conclude with an overall summation or bottom-line of effectiveness.

Suggested Answer: Scenario C – systematic review with meta-analysis

What choice(s) might you make?

Clearly if you are to provide an unbiased estimate of effect you will want to take systematic steps to ensure that you identify all relevant studies, that you take into account any differences in study quality and communicate explicitly to your potential audience what you have and have not done and which studies are included or not included. Clearly too, an incomplete or imperfect answer might lead to flawed decision making and unwarranted expenditure. All of these factors impress the need for a conventional **systematic review**. However, this particular dataset seems to offer additional potential. The apparent **homogeneity** of the outcome measures and their presence as quantitative measures that might be standardised and pooled offer the potential for meta-analysis. At this early stage of the project we can entertain a plan for a systematic review with meta-analysis. If, subsequently, the study outcome measures are found to be sufficiently different to make combining them problematic or not meaningful then we can backtrack and produce a systematic review with a narrative summary and tabulation of results. This is therefore a systematic review with meta-analysis.

(Scenario adapted from: Rampersaud et al. (2005) and Murphy (2007). *Note that this is a hypothetical scenario to illustrate meta-analysis.*)

Scenario D: Bringing together qualitative data into a classification or taxonomy

What are you aiming to do?

Your research team is examining the reasons that women give for having an abortion. You plan to use a predefined, 'secure' definition of abortion to avoid issues around different perspectives on abortion and how abortion is defined. At this stage you will only include studies containing qualitative data. However, you want to keep the option open to subsequently integrate data from quantitative studies at a later date if required. You will use a qualitative approach to categorise the reasons, methodologically according to how they were generated (e.g. by survey, focus group, personal interview, etc.). You will therefore summarise data about the research aims, samples and methods of each included study. You then wish to summarise the included data according to 'families' of shared associations (e.g. a family of factors relating to the individual, a family of factors relating to the environment and so on). Where factors use different wording to convey the same meaning or similar wording for different concepts, the taxonomy or classification will be refined with a view to making the categories and sub-categories exhaustive. Any debate over classification of studies and creation of concepts will be resolved through discussion among the research team. The completed review will be used to develop instruments for collection of routine data and the generation of a standard data collection template.

What factors will influence your choice?

The planned review is clearly a type of qualitative synthesis. It will use data from qualitative research studies and possibly surveys. The concept being explored is relatively 'secure' (i.e. not subject to continual re-interpretation and change) and indeed the team has taken steps to ensure that this is the case – for example, by employing a standard definition of 'abortion'. The team is planning to construct an exhaustive framework. However, their primary interest is not on nuances of interpretation but on a drive towards homogeneous categories that are well-defined and mutually exclusive. The review procedures will privilege consensus over dissonance. In a sense then this review will be using an approach typically used to bring together quantitative studies but in the context of qualitative studies. This will then allow them to bring together quantitative and qualitative studies together at a later date although this is not a primary objective of the review.

Suggested Answer: Scenario D – an aggregative qualitative evidence synthesis

What choice(s) might you make?

At first sight this review looks similar to the mapping review described in Scenario A above. However, closer inspection reveals that we have moved beyond examining the study as the unit of analysis to focusing on the study contents – in this case the themes. We are using an **aggregative** approach by bringing themes from different studies and attempting to organise those themes alongside each other. Aggregative approaches are characterised by (i) a focus on summarising data, and (ii) an assumption that the concepts (or variables in a quantitative context) 'under which those data are to be summarised are largely secure and well specified' (Dixon-Woods et al., 2006a). In contrast to an **interpretative** or **configurative** approach, 'the primary focus of an aggregative synthesis is not on the development of concepts, or their specification' (Dixon-Woods et al., 2006b). Of course this does not mean that this type of review is entirely devoid of theoretical or interpretive functions, but the sophistication of the interpretation is likely to be fairly limited and to focus on more easily discernible types of relationship such as cause and effect. For example, we might use an aggregative qualitative synthesis to identify that religious reasons for having an abortion are more likely to occur in certain geographical regions of the world or in a typically older population. Such a top-level summary may be considered a **meta-summary**. It may be useful for hypothesis testing using the data you have extracted. The earlier stage of the review that looks at the effect of different types of research method on the data the authors have presented is known as **meta-method**. The umbrella science of **meta-study** therefore includes meta-method, **meta-synthesis** and meta-summary. Generically meta-study is an aggregative qualitative synthesis, specifically including meta-method.

(Scenario adapted from: Kirkman et al., 2009.)

Scenario E: Using qualitative data to understand and theorise about a phenomenon (e.g. an intervention or living under particular circumstances)

What are you aiming to do?

You are part of a multidisciplinary research team seeking to capitalise upon growing interest in e-government. You wish to examine and characterise existing models of e-government with a view to identifying the different stages in the development of e-government programmes. In essence you are seeking to create an innovative conception of e-government by synthesising elements from existing models with a view to creating a framework that is superior to the sum of its parts. The resulting framework will be useful to those seeking to introduce e-government and to those who are evaluating particular e-government approaches.

What factors will influence your choice?

Clearly this project description focuses on conceptual and theoretical innovation. It may therefore be broadly characterised as an interpretive, alternatively configurative review. What type of data is it likely to include? Models are typically described qualitatively, particularly in terms of the concepts or themes that they use. The output from this review process is essentially a meta-model. This cannot be simply constructed by bringing together different models and frameworks and then 'welding' them together into a new superframework – as in the aggregative method. Careful attention has to be paid to the interrelationships between the different components and any nuances that are carried by one framework, particularly if a particular dimension is not already part of any of the other existing models. Clearly a large degree of sophisticated analysis will be required once studies are identified and their findings extracted.

Suggested Answer: Scenario E – an interpretive qualitative synthesis

What choice(s) might you make?

At first it seems you have a good choice of qualitative interpretive approaches to tackle this particular task. However, approaches that seek to characterise *a body of literature* (i.e. a collective evidence base) in terms of its historical development, underpinning theory or other shared attributes are quite different from qualitative approaches that focus on the message contained within *the synthesised findings from individual studies*. Approaches such as **critical interpretive synthesis** and **meta-narrative** examine the body of the literature. A review team would use such approaches to theorise about the research studies and their characteristics, and not so much to explore the phenomenon of interest. They are not therefore suitable for this task.

The simplest interpretive approach is thematic synthesis. You could use such an approach for elementary synthesis but this particular project implies that a more advanced method is required. If an existing framework that characterises models of e-government already exists then **framework synthesis** may be used. However, it is less likely that a framework exists for this topic because the authors state that they are trying to construct such a framework as a key deliverable from this project. If they already knew such a framework existed then they would not be seeking to duplicate this work. Of course, once the authors create this framework then either they, or other authors, may well draw on this to perform framework synthesis in future updates or further extended investigations. **Meta-ethnography** can build upon initial stages of theme identification that may, indeed, resemble thematic synthesis, and extend them to conduct more sophisticated theorising. Essentially meta-ethnography moves beyond description to a more interpretive examination of their relationships and indeed any inherent contradictions.

(Scenario adapted from: Siau and Long , 2005.)

Scenario F: Bringing together quantitative and qualitative evidence

What are you aiming to do?

As part of a wide-ranging review of regional library services you and your team are examining how useful it is to provide different types of professional with information skills training. To what extent is such training effective and what factors have a bearing on whether it is acceptable to the professionals themselves? Your review therefore requires comparative effectiveness studies and studies examining the attitudes, views and opinions of the professionals, and indeed the skills trainers themselves. You intend to produce well-rounded recommendations that determine the circumstances under which local libraries might deliver training in information skills.

What factors will influence your choice?

Comparative effectiveness studies are typically quantitative in nature and use designs such as randomised controlled trials, cohort studies and case-control studies. In contrast studies on people's views, especially their attitudes and opinions, require qualitative data. Where a decision problem is particularly complex you will want to bring together both types of data to inform your decision. We are therefore looking for a review method that is suitable for accomplishing the bringing together of both quantitative and qualitative data into a single review product.

Suggested Answer: Scenario F – a mixed method quantitative/qualitative review

What choice(s) might you make?

Bringing together both quantitative and qualitative evidence within a review requires both robust methods for carrying out each type of review rigorously and separately and then innovative methods for integrating the findings from both evidence streams. The EPPI-Centre review method conceptualises its outcomes-focused randomised controlled trials and qualitative process evaluations as two distinct streams of evidence (Oliver et al., 2005) to be kept apart until findings and results are placed side by side at the very end of the review process. However, such an approach may miss opportunities for iteration and sense-checking as the reviews continue to proceed separately. The **matrix method** (Candy et al., 2011) uses tables to explore factors found to be important in a qualitative synthesis as components within quantitative trials. More formally, **Bayesian synthesis** offers the prospect of exploring the values people place upon the different features of an intervention by attaching numerical values to previously qualitative priors. Ten years on this particular review would probably be conducted as a mixed method quantitative and qualitative review, probably using the matrix method.

(Scenario adapted from: Brettle, 2003.)

SUMMARY

This chapter has demonstrated that the purpose and intended use of the review deliverable will have a major impact on the feasibility and desirability of review options, either in planning the original review or in responding to problem scenarios. Other considerations relate to available time, expertise and the expectations of the intended audience. Clearly a review team must deliver what they have previously agreed with those commissioning the review. However, what they undertake to deliver must be informed by a sufficiently circumspect scoping process – a topic to which we return in Chapter 5.

key learning points

- Numerous methods exist for synthesis of published research, particularly for reviewing qualitative research.
- A key consideration relates to whether the intention of the review is aggregative or configurative (interpretive).
- Additional considerations include the available skills and expertise, the aims and objectives of the review, its intended purpose and audience.
- With practice you will be able to identify key indicators that relate to the choice of review method.

frequently asked questions (FAQs)

FAQ 3.1 What if scoping identifies too many studies?

You will find detailed advice in the section on the scoping search in Chapter 6. However, simply speaking, you should revisit the individual elements of the **PICOS** formulation – i.e. the Population, Intervention, Comparison, Outcomes and Study Type. Narrowing your inclusion criteria within any of these elements will likely reduce the number of includable studies. Narrowing the inclusion criteria within more than one element will reduce the number of included studies even more dramatically.

Example: A review examining techniques of teaching mathematics to children may retrieve too many experimental studies. Restricting the population to secondary school children, e.g. the age group of 11 to 16 years, may reduce the number of studies to more manageable quantities. It may also improve the overall coherence of the studies as included populations share a common age group.

FAQ 3.2 What if scoping identifies too few studies?

Expanding an individual element within the PICOS formulation will likely increase the number of includable studies. Expanding more than one element at a time will likely increase the number of includable studies even more dramatically. In some cases you may find it helpful to expand the theoretical resources of the review through analogy, e.g. people's attitudes to health messages being placed on alcohol products may share characteristics with their attitudes to health messages on cigarettes. Again more detailed advice is contained in Chapter 6.

Example: An interpretative review of the effects of performance league tables in hospitals may be informed by a classification of factors involved for performance league tables in schools. If you expand your review to include other uses of performance league tables that operate at an institutional level, you may be better able to explain findings from a relatively limited number of primary qualitative studies.

FAQ 3.3 What if scoping reveals studies are poor in quality?

Where studies are poor in quality you face three options. First you can exclude all studies that fail to meet an agreed number of quality criteria. This may dramatically reduce the number of studies for inclusion in your review. This approach is frequently used in reviews that privilege rigour over the need to provide a pragmatic answer for day-to-day policy or working practice. A compromise between rigour and pragmatism comes in a second option where a review team specifies in advance minimum quality criteria (often related to so-called methodological 'fatal flaws') for a study to be included. This prevents a policy or practice recommendation being based on flawed studies. A third option is to include studies of any quality, as long as they meet the review question and the list of required study designs. You should then conduct a **sensitivity analysis** (Jüni et al., 2001) which essentially looks at the results of included studies all together and then with poor quality studies taken out.

FAQ 3.4 What if eligible studies lack detail?

Reviews that seek to understand the context or specific components of an intervention or programme, or how it works, may be hampered by lacking required detail. Deficiencies may lie in an absence of *contextual detail* (where a reader cannot understand which external factors are impacting on the success of the intervention) or in the incompletely described, or even completely absent, detail of underpinning theory with a lack of *conceptual detail*. Primary papers may not detail the components of an intervention resulting in a so-called **black box effect** (Pope and Mays, 1996). Facing these scenarios a reviewer has four main options:

1. *To seek supplementary data, published alongside the included intervention studies*, so-called **sibling studies** such as study protocols, pilot studies, feasibility studies, process evaluations, accompanying qualitative studies or surveys and audits, etc. to add detail to the investigation (Booth et al., 2013).
2. *To identify related, but not directly linked, papers* exploring how and under what circumstances an intervention or programme might work. Editorials or theoretical contributions, not in themselves eligible for inclusion in the review, may be referenced and drawn upon in the 'Discussion' and 'Conclusions' of your review.
3. *To supplement available published data by engaging with stakeholders, such as those using or those delivering the service*. Additional qualitative data obtained may help to explain how an intervention might work or which components stakeholders feel are most critical to a successful intervention. Of course, such consultation may have a significant effect on the time required to deliver the review.
4. To stop short of trying to explain how and why a programme or intervention works and simply *to concentrate on whether it works*. By limiting the ambition of the review, a reviewer may conclude further analysis requires a newly-commissioned primary study.

FAQ 3.5 What if I am short of time?

If you find yourself short of time you should recognise that a telescoped review is infinitely preferable to a truncated one. You should examine the complete available time period and then plan the duration of, and milestones for, the review accordingly. Throughout the book our SALSA framework breaks a review into four important stages – namely **S**earch, **A**ppraisa**L**, **S**ynthesis and **A**nalysis (Grant and Booth, 2009). Time savings can be achieved at each stage of the process (see Chapter 4). Frequently the 'Analysis' suffers most from time shortages. Major time savings will often impact on the rigour of the overall review. Where you depart from accepted systematic review methods you will need to communicate what exactly you have and have not been able to achieve within the timeframe of the review.

━━━━━ **suggestions for further reading** ━━━━━

Grimshaw, J. (2010) *A Guide to Knowledge Synthesis – CIHR.* Available at www.cihr-irsc. gc.ca/e/41382.html.
An excellent online overview covering the broadest possible range of systematic review types.

Hannes, K. and Lockwood, C. (2011) *Synthesizing Qualitative Research: Choosing the Right Approach.* Abingdon: Wiley.
Examines six different types of synthesis, with worked examples. Assists choice within qualitative synthesis.

Noyes, J. and Lewin, S. (2011) Supplemental guidance on selecting a method of qualitative evidence synthesis, and integrating qualitative evidence with Cochrane intervention reviews. *Supplementary guidance for inclusion of qualitative research in Cochrane systematic reviews of interventions, version, 1* (updated August 2011). Cochrane Collaboration Qualitative Methods Group. Available at http://methods.cochrane.org/qi/sites/methods. cochrane.org.qi/files/uploads/Data%20synthesis%20supplemental%20guidance_2010% 2012%2023B.doc.
Online chapter that outlines different choices for qualitative and mixed methods synthesis.

Petticrew, M., Rehfuess, E., Noyes, J., Higgins, J.P., Mayhew, A., Pantoja, T. Shemilt, I. and Sowden, A. (2013) Synthesizing evidence on complex interventions: how meta-analytical, qualitative, and mixed-method approaches can contribute. *Journal of Clinical Epidemiology*, **66**, 11, 1230-43.
Recent example reviewing a variety of methods within the specific context of complex interventions.

Snilstveit, B., Oliver, S. and Vojtkova, M. (2012) Narrative approaches to systematic review and synthesis of evidence for international development policy and practice. *Journal of Development Effectiveness*, **4**, 3, 409-29.
Overview of non-statistical methods of systematic review and synthesis, particularly in the context of international development.

REFERENCES

Abrami, P.C., Borokhovski, E., Bernard, R.M., Wade, C.A., Tamim, R., Persson, T. and Surkes, M.A. (2010) Issues in conducting and disseminating brief reviews of evidence. *Evidence & Policy: A Journal of Research, Debate and Practice*, **6**, 371–89.

Archer, N., Fevrier-Thomas, U., Lokker, C., McKibbon, K.A. and Straus, S.E. (2011) Personal health records: a scoping review. *Journal of the American Medical Informatics Association*, Jul–Aug, **18**, 4, 515–22.

Booth, A., Harris, J., Croot, E., Springett, J., Campbell, F. and Wilkins, E. (2013) Towards a methodology for cluster searching to provide conceptual and contextual. *BMC Medical Research Methodology*, **13**, 1, 118.

Brettle, A. (2003) Information skills training: a systematic review of the literature. *Health Information & Libraries Journal*, **20**, S1, 3–9.

Candy, B., King, M., Jones, L. and Oliver, S. (2011) Using qualitative synthesis to explore heterogeneity of complex interventions. *BMC Medical Research Methodology*, **11**, 1, 124.

Connor, J., Rogers, A. and Priest, P. (1999) Randomised studies of income supplementation: a lost opportunity to assess health outcomes. *Journal Epidemiology & Community Health*, **53**, 725–30.

Dixon-Woods, M., Bonas, S., Booth, A., Jones, D.R., Miller, T., Sutton, A. J., Shaw, R.L., Smith, J.A. and Young, B. (2006a) How can systematic reviews incorporate qualitative research? A critical perspective. *Qualitative Research*, **6**, 1, 27–44.

Dixon-Woods, M., Cavers, D., Agarwal, S., Annandale, E., Arthur, A., Harvey, J., Hsu, R., Katbanma, S., Olsen, R., Smith, L., Riley, R. and Sutton, A.J. (2006b) Conducting a critical interpretive synthesis of the literature on access to healthcare by vulnerable groups. *BMC Medical Research Methodology*, **6**, 1, 35.

Gough, D., Thomas, J. and Oliver, S. (2012) Clarifying differences between review designs and methods. *Systematic Reviews*, **1**, 1, 28.

Government Social Research Unit (2008) *Rapid Evidence Assessment Toolkit*. Available at www.civilservice.gov.uk/networks/gsr/resources-and-guidance/rapid-evidence-assessment.

Grant, M.J. and Booth, A. (2009) A typology of reviews: an analysis of 14 review types and associated methodologies. *Health Information & Libraries Journal*, **26**, 2, 91–108.

Jüni, P., Altman, D.G. and Egger, M. (2001) Assessing the quality of controlled clinical trials. *BMJ*, **323**, 7303, 42–6.

Kirkman, M., Rowe, H., Hardiman, A., Mallett, S. and Rosenthal, D. (2009) Reasons women give for abortion: a review of the literature. *Archives of Women's Mental Health*, **12**, 6, 365–378.

Kitchenham, B. (2004) 'Procedures for performing systematic reviews', Keele University Technical Report TR/SE-0401, July, ISSN:1353-7776, **33**.

Laupacis, A. and Straus, S. (2007) Systematic reviews: time to address clinical and policy relevance as well as methodological rigor. *Annals of Internal Medicine*, **147**, 4, 273–4.

Moher, D., Liberati, A., Tetzlaff, J. and Altman, D.G. (2009) Preferred reporting items for systematic reviews and meta-analyses: the PRISMA statement. *Annals of Internal Medicine*, **151**, 4, 264–9.

Murphy, J.M. (2007) Breakfast and learning: an updated review. *Current Nutrition & Food Science*, **3**, 1, 3–36.

Noyes, J. and Lewin, S. (2011) Supplemental guidance on selecting a method of qualitative evidence synthesis, and integrating qualitative evidence with Cochrane intervention reviews. *Supplementary guidance for inclusion of qualitative research in Cochrane systematic reviews of interventions, version, 1* (updated August 2011). Cochrane Collaboration Qualitative Methods Group. Available at http://methods.cochrane.org/qi/sites/methods.cochrane.org.qi/files/uploads/Data%20synthesis%20supplemental%20guidance_2010%2012%2023B.doc.

O'Cathain, A., Thomas, K.J., Drabble, S.J., Rudolph, A. and Hewison, J. (2013) What can qualitative research do for randomised controlled trials? A systematic mapping review. *BMJ Open*, **3**, 6.

Oliver, S., Harden, A., Rees, R., Shepherd, J., Brunton, G., Garcia, J. and Oakley, A. (2005) An emerging framework for including different types of evidence in systematic reviews for public policy. *Evaluation*, **11**, 4, 428–46.

Petticrew, M. (2003) Why certain systematic reviews reach uncertain conclusions. *BMJ*, **326**, 7392, 756–8.

PLoS Medicine Editors (2007) Many reviews are systematic but some are more transparent and completely reported than others. *PLoS Medicine*, **4**, 3, e147.

Popay, J., Rogers, A. and Williams, G. (1998) Rationale and standards for the systematic review of qualitative literature in health services research. *Qualitative Health Research*, **8**, 3, 341–51.

Pope, C. and Mays, N. (1996) Opening the black box: an encounter in the corridors of health service research. In N. Mays and C. Pope (eds), *Qualitative Research in Health Care*. London: British Medical Association.

Rampersaud, G.C., Pereira, M.A., Girard, B.L., Adams, J. and Metzl, J.D. (2005) Breakfast habits, nutritional status, body weight, and academic performance in children and adolescents. *Journal of the American Dietetic Association*, **105**, 5, 743–60.

Siau, K. and Long, Y. (2005) Synthesizing e-government stage models – a meta-synthesis based on meta-ethnography approach. *Industrial Management & Data Systems*, **105**, 4, 443–58.

Stroup, D.F., Berlin, J.A., Morton, S.C., Olkin, I., Williamson, G.D., Rennie, D., Moher, D., Becker, B.J., Sipe, T.A. and Thacker, S.B. (2000) Meta-analysis of observational studies in epidemiology: a proposal for reporting. *JAMA*, **283**, 15, 2008–12.

Thomas, B.H., Ciliska, D., Dobbins, M. and Micucci, S. (2004) A process for systematically reviewing the literature: providing the research evidence for public health nursing interventions. *Worldviews on Evidence-Based Nursing*, **1**, 3, 176–84.

Tong, A., Flemming, K., McInnes, E., Oliver, S. and Craig, J. (2012) Enhancing transparency in reporting the synthesis of qualitative research: ENTREQ. *BMC Medical Research Methodology*, **12**, 1, 181.

Tseng, T.Y., Dahm, P., Poolman, R.W., Preminger, G.M., Canales, B.J. and Montori, V.M. (2008) How to use a systematic literature review and meta-analysis. *Journal of Urology*, **180**, 4, 1249–56.

Victor, L. (2008) Systematic reviewing. *Social Research Update*, **54**, 1.

PLANNING AND CONDUCTING YOUR LITERATURE REVIEW

 in a nutshell

Planning and conducting your literature review

- Planning and conducting your literature review requires that you identify the main stages of the review process and their associated milestones and deliverables.
- You can use software to manage technical processes and facilitate project management and communication.
- To conduct a literature review you will require technical and project management skills.
- Updating or converting a systematic review requires particular consideration.

INTRODUCTION

A literature review should be planned and managed just like any other research project (Lyratzopoulos and Allen, 2004). Because formal methods exist for conducting literature reviews project planning should in fact be noticeably easier. However, you will still need considerable skill to tailor a generic plan to the specific needs of a particular review. As for any project, the reviewer or review team should consider the elements of time, quality and money (see Box 4.1). Balancing these three within an agreed timescale for delivery, whether one year for a dissertation or thesis or a longer (or indeed shorter) period of time for a commissioned project, is key to the success of a literature review.

 **box 4.1**

Three key questions for planning a review

- How much time must I allocate to the critical path of activities that must be done (and cannot be abbreviated)?
- What quality is required for processes that are key to the review but where there is some scope for flexibility or possible negotiation?
- Where can I save time (and by implication money) by efficiencies, either by one reviewer multitasking or by members of a review team dividing up the workload?

With regard to *time*, every literature review embodies a **critical path** that represents a minimum time for completion. For example, all materials for the review have to be identified, acquired and read before the review can be completed, unless agreed otherwise with the commissioner or supervisor. In addition to this minimum time there are processes where the more time you spend is rewarded by increased reader confidence in your review method. How comprehensive will the search be? Will there be formal processes for data extraction and quality assessment? How thorough will the processes of synthesis and analysis be? Typically, all reviewers, and students in particular, struggle with two areas. These are:

- knowing when to stop reading for the literature review (Bruce, 1993);
- allowing enough time at the end for editing.

For these reasons you will find it helpful to set clear deadlines. Allow a certain period of time for reading and documenting the literature review. If you have time, you can revisit this later. In addition, you should try to allow time for your work to 'rest' in order that you can come back to it with fresh eyes. To avoid a feeling of 'wasted time' you could use this downtime to ask a critical friend to check your English for spelling, grammar and style. Alternatively, this could be the time when you share your review with your supervisor, a mentor or external advisors – in the meantime you could be getting on with some other task such as tabulating data or checking the format, consistency and completeness of all of your references.

Decisions on how much time you will spend on specific processes will have a bearing on the *quality* of the final review. If you pre-specify your methods, for example in a review plan or protocol (see Chapter 5), you will have relatively little room for subsequent negotiation. Clearly, however, if you are permitted a degree of flexibility then a decision, for example, to switch from a formal checklist-based process of quality assessment to a holistic judgement of quality based upon general prompts offers you an opportunity to considerably reduce the time taken by your review. The literature on **rapid reviews** offers suggestions on how you might accelerate or abbreviate your planned review (see for example National Collaborating Centre for Methods and Tools, n.d.).

While *money* may appear relevant only if your review is externally commissioned, this concern is equally present, although implicitly, in all types of review. For example, the concept of the 'opportunity cost' ('If I wasn't doing this what else might I be doing?') underlies both the *absolute* time and resource that you allocate to the review as a whole and the *relative* time you spend on each component of the review process. In the context of a PhD if you spend too much time on the literature review this may delay subsequent primary research (Randolph, 2009). Similarly if you decide to postpone reading of a body of literature until you have exhausted all avenues for finding relevant studies you may end up with a review with an underdeveloped, stunted or truncated analysis phase. This third consideration, relating to resourcing of the review, determines such decisions as 'Can I be doing certain processes together or in parallel?', 'Is there something that I can be doing during "downtime" for another process?', and 'Can this process be divided up and apportioned clearly to different members of a review team?'

PROJECT MANAGEMENT

Managing a literature review is similar to managing any research project. You need to identify necessary skills and resources. You also need to consider the major milestones and deliverables throughout the process. This chapter revisits the stages of the typical review process and the specific project management requirements for each stage. Working around an exemplar review it illustrates the different considerations and how they impact upon the final review product. It also examines key problems within the review process and how these might be overcome. A final section examines the various tools available for managing the complex process of the literature review as an exemplar of research project management.

Project management and literature reviews

Baker and colleagues (2010) suggest that producing a review follows four phases of project management:

1. Concept.
2. Planning and definition.
3. Implementation.
4. Finalisation.

These four stages apply generically to any review project: the concept phase includes assembling the team (see this chapter); the planning and definition phase of the review includes protocol development (Chapter 5) which will include specific allocation of roles and responsibilities and identification of any training and resource requirements; the implementation phase covers all the operational aspects covered in Chapters 6 to 9 of this book; the finalisation stage involves the write-up and publication of the review and making plans for future updates (Chapter 10).

   A study by the Australasian Cochrane Centre found that the most critical barriers to completion of a **Cochrane Review** were a lack of time (80%), a lack of financial support (36%), methodological problems (23%), and problems with group dynamics (10%) (Piehl et al., 2002). More recently, another study identified time and author communication as the major barriers hindering the completion of Cochrane Reviews (Gillies et al., 2009). Considerations of time and financial support are particularly marked for Cochrane Reviews, which are very vulnerable given that many are subsidised by individuals or organisations and are given neither protected time nor funding. Nevertheless, all of these reported barriers are important for all reviews whether systematic or not. Later in this chapter, we consider some barriers and how they might be tackled. However, as with most research projects 'an ounce of prevention is worth a pound of cure'. Anticipating likely areas of difficulty and developing strategies to avoid them is by far the preferred course. Project management 'is a discipline of planning, organizing, and managing resources to bring about the successful completion of specific goals' (Cleland and Gareis, 2006).

No review can expect an entirely trouble-free progress from initiation to completion. However, most types of difficulty encountered within the relatively controlled environment of a literature-based project can be anticipated. Project management seeks to foresee or predict risks, and to plan, organise and manage activities so that projects are successfully completed in spite of those risks (Baker et al., 2010). Review methodology provides a ready-made phased structure for planning and conducting a review. It also supplies a repository of approaches with which to counter the more common types of problem. For this reason, some teams find it helpful to conduct their review using established project management methodologies. While we would stop short of recommending specific project management methods, we would emphasise that structures for quality assurance and stakeholder engagement translate well between generic project management and the specific requirements of a review project.

When thinking about your own review you should consider what risks pose threats to your completing a successful literature review. Ask yourself, 'What is the worst thing that could possibly happen? How likely is this?' Create a mental picture of the main risks to your project and how likely these are to occur. How would you tackle them? Two specific project management challenges merit brief consideration. These are:

1. updates to existing reviews;
2. conversion of reviews to a different format.

In theory, both tasks sound relatively easy when compared with undertaking a full-blown systematic review. This may explain why reviewers and commissioners of reviews commonly underestimate the time and resources required to deliver review updates and conversions.

UPDATES TO EXISTING REVIEWS

Early in our systematic review careers we were invited to update an existing systematic review previously conducted by a Spanish organisation. As only a handful of years had elapsed between completion of that review and our planned review update, the commissioners and the review team agreed a cost that represented about one-sixth of our standard price for systematic reviews. After all, it appeared that the team was only required to identify and synthesise more recent eligible studies. Although the original review was of good quality, we found that we had to check, validate and essentially repeat all the stages of the review process. Search strategies had to be updated and inclusion criteria had to be reconceived to facilitate consistency between original and newly added studies. This cautionary tale concluded with an update that cost at least three times more than its budget, equivalent to half the cost of a standard review, and probably significantly more. These extra costs were invisible to the funder as they were absorbed in extra time spent on the project and lost opportunities of working on other projects. This represented a valuable, but costly lesson. We suggest that a team contemplating an update to a review should start from the standard price of a review and works downward, discounting only the real and not imagined savings from the pre-existing review. For example, if the team can access studies originally included in the review, this represents a real saving, otherwise the budget should cost the acquisition of both original and newly added studies. Moher and Tsertsvadze (2006) confirm that

> updating a systematic review can be as costly and time-consuming as conducting the original review or developing the original guideline. Therefore, it is of paramount importance to know whether or not a systematic review needs to be updated.

Within an academic context a supervisor/mentor will want to discuss whether a proposed update is 'worthwhile'. Being 'worthwhile' depends upon the extent to which your objectives are to gain new skills, generate new knowledge, or a combination of both. Clearly little is gained from exactly replicating an existing high-quality review. However, if your objectives are to acquire skills in systematic review and **meta-analysis**, then identifying a few additional studies, extracting data, critically appraising them and possibly incorporating these in a **Forest plot** will prove valuable. On the other hand, given that the methods of systematic review favour adherence to standards over innovation, completing standard review tasks may contribute little if the objective is to create new knowledge. In such a case you will probably be looking for something more – perhaps supplementary analysis, possibly disambiguation or even reversal of a previous pattern of effect (Barrowman et al., 2003).

To decide whether or not to update a review requires that you or your mentor possess a detailed knowledge of the characteristics of a field and its associated literature. Moher and Tsertsvadze (2006) propose that, when updating a systematic review, the proper timeframe depends 'on the rate of development of a particular ... field'. Frequent updating of systematic reviews in slowly developing areas may waste resources, whereas systematic reviews in rapidly developing areas may quickly become outdated. Arbitrarily choosing fixed updating frequencies (e.g. every two to three years) of systematic reviews or clinical guidelines, as suggested by some authors, may be overly simplistic. Box 4.2 suggests possible justifications for updating a literature review on academic grounds. However, we should emphasise that these are indicators and not rules. Furthermore, they are informed by evidence on review update characteristics (Moher et al., 2008).

 **box 4.2**

Academic justifications for updating an existing review

1. Publication of a single large study (i.e. more participants than all previously included studies combined or larger than the previously largest included study).
2. Publication of multiple small studies (i.e. total number of participants greater than all previously included studies).
3. Interventions likely to have seen measurable improvements in delivery (e.g. progression up learning curve, a volume-outcome relationship, etc.).

(Continued)

(Continued)

4. Appearance and use of validated outcome measures (where a previous review relies on subjective or unvalidated measures).
5. Stimulation of both uptake and research by policy initiatives (i.e. more activity and more evaluation).
6. A four-year gap (or, by exception, two years or even less for volatile topic areas) since completion of the previous review.
7. Appearance of new conceptual thinking/theory to supply an alternative framework for analysis.
8. Similar reviews with common included studies that provide conflicting interpretations or results.

If you are considering updating an existing review, you should clarify expectations for the update with your academic supervisor/mentor. Considerations could include those covered in Box 4.3.

 **box 4.3**

Agreeing expectations for an updated review

1. Will the reviewer extract, appraise and reanalyse both new and existing studies or simply compare an interim cumulative result from the previous review with a cumulative result from all new studies?
2. Will the reviewer repeat searches for the period covered by the previous review or only search for studies published since that review (allowing for up to two years' overlap in recognition of publication delays)?
3. Will the reviewer extend the search process to cover additional sources and identify additional types of materials or additional study designs?
4. Will the reviewer enhance the interpretation of the review by including complementary qualitative/quantitative data (e.g. relating to effectiveness or acceptability)?
5. Will the reviewer conduct supplementary analyses looking at specific subgroups, sensitivity to certain study characteristics, or examining the likelihood of publication bias?
6. Will the reviewer unpick and isolate factors relating to the implementation of interventions, their fidelity and their external validity?
7. Will the reviewer enhance the scope and extent of qualitative discussions of review limitations, implications for practice and implications for further research?
8. Will the reviewer re-examine the applicability of the review findings in light of a different context, culture or political environment?

CONVERSION OF REVIEWS TO A DIFFERENT FORMAT

Another task not to be underestimated involves converting reviews to a different format. The most typical, and most studied, context for this is 'importing' or 'exporting' reviews for the

Cochrane Collaboration. Existing reviews may be converted for adoption by the Cochrane Collaboration (importing) or Cochrane Reviews may be suggested as the starting point for more extensive reviews commissioned by other funding agencies (exporting). Recent years have seen increased questioning regarding whether reviews or technology assessments are transferable across agencies and countries.

A survey by the Australasian Cochrane Centre sought to explore why review authors had chosen not to undertake a Cochrane Review. Most frequently cited reasons were a lack of time (78%), the need to undergo specific Cochrane training (46%), unwillingness to update reviews (36%), difficulties with the Cochrane process (26%) and the review topic already registered with the Cochrane Collaboration (21%) (Piehl et al., 2003). These findings illustrate how difficult it can be to comply with an external organisation's procedures and documentation when converting a review. To become familiar with such procedures you will definitely need orientation and probably training. You will need to read and comprehend documentation to gain an overall view of how the process works. You may then need to revisit operational details as you approach each stage of the review.

Nearly half of survey respondents stated that they would consider converting their review to the Cochrane format (Piehl et al., 2003). Such conversions require dedicated time – time that typically lies outside the original project, and which may compete with new and existing priorities. Not to be underestimated is the need for assistance in navigating the synthesis organisation's peer review system and procedures and to identify potential assistance with updating and financial support. While some organisations may offer 'conversion grants' these typically require you to produce a research proposal. Any further delays in processing the application could result in a window of opportunity becoming shut. Even though 86% of those surveyed were willing to have their review converted to the Cochrane format by another author, the previous cautions regarding review updates may apply, namely the need to validate the entire process and re-analyse new and existing data side by side.

A related idea of 'killing two birds with one stone' is to plan to undertake, for example, a systematic review for a Master's dissertation or a PhD, and at the same time to offer the resultant review to synthesis organisations such as the Cochrane Collaboration. Apparent economies of scale are very beguiling, particularly given the challenges faced in keeping up with the demand for coverage by new reviews (Sambunjak and Puljak, 2010). Nevertheless, we consistently recommend that students do not pursue such a course. In practice, students undertaking such dual purpose reviews face a tension similar to that for joint supervision, except greatly magnified. The two deliverables typically have different timescales, peer review processes and quality checks. While the starting point may be shared, what will the student do, for example, if their supervisor approves their review protocol, they start work and then, several weeks later, external review comments from the synthesis organisation recommend modifications and amendments? The dual purpose model works best where the educational process is flexible enough to permit the requirements of the synthesis organisation to take precedence. It is to be hoped that dual purpose reviews increase in the future, perhaps requiring that supervisors or mentors occupy dual roles (as academics and representatives of the synthesis organisation) and that the standards of the synthesis organisation are accredited and thus adopted 'off the shelf' by academic organisations. Synthesis organisations will also want to make provision for subsequent updating of the review with the supervisor, not the reviewer, offering continuity and a mechanism for 'succession planning'.

SKILLS AND RESOURCES

A successful review does not simply require technical skills. If you have never managed a review before, or you are being advised by someone with limited experience of project management, you will need to put in place a rigorous structure. You should document your methodology, review an explicit timetable with frequent deliverables and internal and external deadlines, and regularly access input on methodology.

Most reviews are multidisciplinary, requiring both methodology and subject experts. Consequently, most are conducted by collaborative review teams. Ideally, review teams should engage with representatives of stakeholders using appropriate project management structures. Many reviews have a *steering group* that meets at least monthly. There should also be a secretary, or *secretariat/administration* in larger projects, to support the project on a day-to-day basis – arranging meetings, handling correspondence and perhaps supporting document delivery, database administration or tabulation of data. The steering group may choose to create small, *ad hoc groups to address specific issues* as they arise, for example in bringing in meta-analysis expertise when required. A wider *advisory group*, comprising methodology or subject experts and, most importantly, practitioners from the field, may meet quarterly or every six months to provide advice to the steering group or secretariat on clinical, technical or other issues impacting on the review.

Study skills and techniques

As a novice reviewer, or a scratch review team, you must not assume that you already have the skills you need to plan and conduct a literature review. Most researchers consider themselves familiar with 'reviewing the literature'. They may fall into the trap of thinking that methods for conducting reviews appear obvious and straightforward. To illustrate, many experienced librarians consider that they already have excellent information retrieval skills. However, typically, their strength is in identifying specific key references for a research paper or proposal. This is a considerably different scale of endeavour from conducting sensitive searches designed to minimise the chances of missing something relevant. Similarly, if you are previously familiar with critiquing research papers (the so-called 'science of trashing papers'; see Greenhalgh, 2014) you will have a useful starting point for quality assessment. However, again critical appraisal of an individual study is nothing like as demanding and intense as the level of skills required for systematic approaches to reviewing. Notwithstanding the increased availability of systematic review courses, a skills deficit remains in fields where systematic approaches to literature review are in their infancy. Review expertise is distributed differentially across disciplines. Most trained reviewers work in health with pockets of expertise in management, education and social care amongst others. Suggestions for building capacity in reviewing include funding research training, supporting on-the-job training with experienced researchers, and collaboration with other funders (Educational Research Funders' Forum, 2005).

Generic study skills applied to review

To be able to plan and conduct a literature review you will need to follow a methodical approach and be well-disciplined in documenting your methods and progress. Individual review tasks, such as planning and executing a search strategy, will extend over multiple occasions and many days. You must document how far you have got, what remains to be done, and any false starts or blind alleys to avoid repeating these in the future. You may need to re-execute an identical search strategy towards the end of an extended review to identify more recent materials. You may even need to re-examine search strategies to try to establish why an included study, subsequently identified, was not retrieved from your original searches.

You will find that keeping a bench book or project diary for the duration of the review will yield dividends at later stages of the writing-up process. It will also be helpful to create a dedicated project folder with sub-folders clearly labelled as follows: Searches, Data extraction forms, Included studies, Review drafts, Reference management database, etc. Preferably this will be networked via an Intranet, or increasingly via the Cloud, and shared amongst the review team. If this is not possible, then you should take regular 'snapshots' of the folder contents and save these to external storage media such as hard drives or USB data sticks.

If your review is a more interpretive type of work, then a project diary will not simply be a procedural manual but will document reflectively major insights or decisions made along the way. This will assist you in documenting your review process and subsequently in justifying your decisions to a peer reviewer or examiner.

Conducting a review is both a disciplined scientific process and a creative artistic one. Although review methods may appear prescriptive, they offer a frame or structure within which you can be imaginative. You will need to structure and order your data to help you recognise patterns and carry out subsequent analysis. Picture the meticulous care with which an artist assembles materials, organises their palette and selects their vantage point before giving full rein to their creative energies. The required blend of skills and attributes further attests to the considerable advantages to be gained by undertaking such a process as a review team (Nicholson, 2007). We can conclude that such skills extend beyond a single, impossibly multi-faceted, individual.

Acquiring skills in systematic searching

Even if you are able to identify and retrieve a few key studies in your subject area this does not mean that you are able to conduct sensitive searches that won't miss relevant studies (Dickersin et al., 1994). We recommend that you involve a librarian or information specialist in any literature review (McGowan and Sampson, 2005). As a minimum a librarian might advise on search terms or database selection. They may offer tutorials on key databases. However, many review projects benefit from including a librarian or information specialist as a fully integrated member of the review team (Beverley et al., 2003; Harris, 2005; Swinkels et al., 2006; Wade, 2006; Wilkinson et al., 2009; Hausner et al., 2012).

Many academic or organisational libraries either run regular training or support sessions for literature searching or offer one-to-one support on an *ad hoc* basis. We recommend that you seize such opportunities, perhaps bringing along your own attempts at searching to date. You can then trial your own review topic or ask specific questions about your search strategy. In addition many libraries, or indeed database providers, offer online tutorials or support documentation for key databases with materials increasingly accessible via the internet. Particularly helpful are videos or screencasts that walk you through the functions of a specific database source. Similarly, you will need to acquire, or at the very least need to access, expertise in reference management. Again you should enquire about what your local library is able to offer.

Developing skills in systematic appraisal

To be successful in conducting your literature review you will need to identify the characteristics of the main types of included study. If you are planning a review of **randomised controlled trials** you will need to recognise the key features of such a study, their likely limitations, and consequent threats to validity. This is equally true for other study designs such as case studies or those associated with qualitative research. You can start with a checklist designed specifically for studies of a particular type: review each question to make sure that you understand the terminology, what is being assessed and where to find the design features in one of your included studies. You can also pilot the checklist for your review, sharing your results with colleagues or with a mentor or supervisor. Where you identify gaps in your knowledge address these through targeted reading or by attending courses.

In preparing to assess the quality of your included studies you will find it helpful to access books and articles that describe research methods or **critical appraisal** (Greenhalgh, 2014). You will also find it invaluable to read through published critiques of research studies performed by others. Above all you will find it productive to read through published research studies, focusing on their 'Methods' sections and making notes of any limitations as you go. Check the authors' own sub-section or paragraphs on the limitations of their study (typically included in a well-written 'Discussion' section) and compare their list with your own.

Refining skills in systematic synthesis

To a large extent skills in systematic synthesis are the most difficult to anticipate. After all, only when you start engaging with individual studies will you be able to assess what will or will not be possible in the way of synthesis. Nevertheless, as a bare minimum you will need to tabulate data and craft an accompanying narrative commentary for your review. Familiarise yourself with word processing packages, such as OpenOffice or Microsoft Word, and particularly with features associated with referencing (including **cite-while-you-write**) and with how to produce tables of contents and to format tables.

With such a variety of methods of synthesis, both quantitative and qualitative, to select from, you will find it helpful to read comparative overviews of multiple techniques (Dixon-Woods et al., 2004; Pope et al., 2007; Barnett-Page and Thomas, 2009). You can assess the strengths and weaknesses of each technique and their suitability for your particular purpose. Try to find published reviews that address a similar review question to your own (whether it relates to effectiveness, barriers and facilitators, attitudes, etc.). Look at the methods the authors have chosen and any observations that the authors make upon their experience of using such a technique.

As soon as you have a clear indication that you might require advanced synthesis techniques, such as **meta-analysis** or **meta-ethnography**, you should investigate opportunities to attend formal courses in these methods. If formal courses are not available you should identify local expertise, such as a resident statistician or qualitative researcher. Many published worked examples exist to help you follow the steps of a specific technique. You can access discussion lists to ask more experienced researchers to clarify detailed points arising from your reading. Attend presentations by reviewers who have used particular methods. Take the opportunity to ask why they chose their particular method and any observations and advice that they might now have on use of their chosen method.

Honing skills in systematic analysis

You will find that it is difficult to acquire skills associated with analysis through formal training. Novice reviewers often make the mistake of thinking that by assembling and 'cataloguing' their included studies they have concluded their review. Frequently when their data have been assembled in a clear and explicit way, a more experienced supervisor or mentor will identify previously neglected insights. In conducting your analysis you must maximise opportunities to identify patterns from the data. We will cover this in more detail in subsequent chapters, so for the moment we will simply flag up the three main types of 'pattern' to be explored, regardless of whether data are quantitative or qualitative. You must be able to identify *similarities* across studies, recognise the *differences* between studies, and *isolate subgroups* of studies where characteristics or effects are reduced, heightened or completely absent. These patterns may relate to subgroups of the population, subclasses of the intervention, or to subsets of outcomes and how they are measured. You may spot variations by setting or in how closely the study kept to its protocol (fidelity). Equally your included studies may differ according to their study design or study quality. You will need to be continually alert to identifying, exploring and explaining any patterns in the data you are synthesising.

You can gauge how likely it will be that you are expected to use particular techniques by seeing how frequently these appear within published examples of reviews on the same topic. For example, once you decide that your data are suited to meta-analysis you will note, from other published meta-analyses, that meta-analysis is frequently accompanied by such analytical techniques as the *Funnel plot* (to detect possible publication bias) or sensitivity analysis (to establish whether results would be changed by including or excluding particular studies). Bear in mind that many techniques will help you formatively as you conduct interim investigations and analyses. A handful of these techniques will be sufficiently informative to survive through to the summative phase of presentation and reporting.

POLISHING SKILLS IN WRITING AND PRESENTATION

Writing and presentation is common to all areas of academic activity. You will have acquired many such skills in the course of your academic career. Again, the requirements for reviewing the literature differ not so much in their nature but more in their intensity and degree. Writing-up makes demands on textual, tabular, graphic and numeric modes of presentation. Opportunities to polish these skills may present themselves through formal research training programmes, lunchtime sessions and technical or software-specific training courses.

In particular you will need to expand your writing style from itemisation (e.g. 'Study A was conducted in a population of X') to narrative summary (e.g. 'Five of the eight studies were conducted in secondary schools with the remainder in training colleges. Six were from the United States with one from Canada and one from New Zealand'). Such synthetic principles assist you in identifying similarities, differences and subgroups as mentioned previously.

━━━━━━ **personal skills audit** ━━━━━━

Having briefly reviewed the skills needed to conduct a successful literature review, reflect on: Which skills do I already possess? Which do I need to acquire? How will I acquire such skills?

Time

'How long does a literature review take?' is the synthesis equivalent to 'how long is a piece of string?' The standard 'it depends' reply is predicated on the type of review and on the phasing of the review process. This chapter presents a range of timescales of between 6 and 12 months for systematic approaches to the literature. **Rapid evidence assessments**, which abbreviate time spent on quality assessment and synthesis, may be turned around in as little as 8 to 12 weeks. The primary challenge is how to agree and communicate expectations, focusing on constraints and limitations and not the more technical issue of how to complete a systematic review in a telescoped timescale. Gall et al. (1996) estimated that completion of an acceptable dissertation literature review takes between three and six months of effort. However, this estimate predates the era of systematic approaches to the literature which have 'upped the ante' in recent years.

In our workshops on preparing a successful literature review proposal, we emphasise a distinction between processes that lie within the reviewer's own control (and that are consequently more flexible) and those that depend on external agencies (conceived as 'fixed'). The latter typically include obtaining interlibrary loans or photocopies from other libraries (see Chapter 3) and subsequent dependencies such as follow-up of citations, quality assessment and extraction of data. Depending on how review tasks are allocated, external constraints may also include the searching of bibliographic databases through an information specialist or librarian and access to a specialist in meta-analysis. Once you have all the included articles to hand, you can work through the remainder of the process at your own pace, 'burning the midnight oil' if necessary. However, a rushed, last-minute approach will typically impact negatively on the quality of the review, particularly the analysis. Our own calculations are informed by early research on a series of meta-analyses which found that the average time taken for a meta-analysis was 1,139 hours, but with a range from 216 to 2,518 hours (Allen and Olkin, 1999). When attempting to calculate the time required for a meta-analysis, you should realise that additional studies (i.e. more of the same) may not contribute too greatly to an increased workload because much of the preparatory work has already been completed. However, if the additional studies require additional subgroup analysis or include additional groups of outcomes, they can add significantly to the overall time taken.

Students often ask 'what are the minimum/maximum numbers of articles required for a review?' Again, our response is 'it depends.' Numbers vary according to the type of review, the type of analysis and any educational or personal development objectives. To establish reviewer competencies for a Master's programme we set a mini-review assignment which requires that students assess, synthesise and interpret an arbitrary five or six studies. Other institutions set a 'systematic search and review' assignment that requires students to focus on formulation of the review question and identifying relevant studies, but to conduct less rigorous synthesis and summary of results. Our take-home message is that systematic approaches to the literature are flexible and varied enough to meet most educational requirements. Indeed if a specific competency is required (for example meta-analysis) students may be able to use a dataset from an existing review rather than having to complete the entire process.

Qualitative evidence synthesis in particular is witnessing ongoing debate regarding the optimal number of studies to be included. Here the determinants relate to the overall approach and the accompanying type of analysis. A qualitative synthesis published in *The Lancet* included 32 studies (Smith et al., 2005). However, where an interpretive approach is required, much smaller numbers of studies have been proposed.

If this guidance seems particularly evasive we could add (off the record, of course) that an ideal review, in an educational context and from our personal perspective, would include somewhere between 8 and 12 studies. This is large enough to provide rich data (either quantitative or qualitative) and significant variation between studies. It also offers the possibility of multiple meta-analysis displays if relevant and yet proves small enough to be feasible within a typical academic timescale. However, we certainly would not advocate reverse engineering, by which the review question is shaped by the intended number of studies. Indeed, many students have tried to arrive at a 'magic number' of included studies, either underestimating the number of hits (and having thousands of references to sift through) or misjudging the effect of inclusion criteria (and pruning down to too few included studies). The integrity of the review question, to a large extent independent of the volume of the literature, remains the best single marker of systematic approaches to a successful literature review.

Costing

Two critical factors impact on the time and cost of a review. The first is the **conversion ratio**, namely the number of bibliographical references and abstracts that the review team has to sift through in order to identify one relevant potentially includable study. Different types of review are likely to have different conversion rates, so for example public health, management and education topics have lower conversion ratios than drug interventions or surgical procedures. Qualitative review topics have lower conversion ratios than those addressing quantitative questions. Factors affecting the conversion ratio include the sensitivity or specificity of the search strategy, the 'tightness' of review terminology, the diffuseness of the literature and the experience and expertise of the review team. The second critical factor relates to the absolute number of included studies. Each included study carries workload implications in terms of quality assessment, data extraction and synthesis. In addition to these variable factors, a fixed component relates to the overall planning, conduct and management of the review. While calculating resources required for a review is far from an exact science, a knowledge of these components helps a review team to arrive at a ball park figure.

Communication

Communication is key to the success of a review. Effective communication strategies should be planned from the outset of the project. Whether communication is formalised as a documented communications plan will depend upon the scale of the review. For large-scale international reviews, such a plan will help to meet the challenges that having review authors in different time zones, distant locations and even speaking different languages, brings. Personal communication between collaborators, typically via email, can speed a review process beyond a regular cycle of face-to-face or virtual meetings. Nevertheless, where issues require rapid resolution it may be more effective to discuss issues synchronously. Resources that harness voice-over internet protocols and video services, such as Skype video, offer an attractively cheap alternative for communication (Baker et al., 2010).

STAGES OF THE LITERATURE REVIEW

The Educational Research Funders' Forum (2005) defines literature reviews as follows:

> Systematic reviews take varying amounts of time according to the topic but usually take between nine months to a year to complete. The duration is gradually reducing as expertise and systems develop.

Typical timescales are provided for six-month, nine-month and one-year versions of a literature review (see Tables 4.1 to 4.3).

Table 4.1 Sample project timetable for six-month literature review project

Note: A six-month timescale is most appropriate for a literature review that does not require significant appraisal, synthesis and analysis (e.g. for a scoping review, a mapping review of a well-defined and focused area, or for a rapid evidence assessment). Mapping/scoping reviews are primarily descriptive (What does the literature look like? Where are the gaps?) rather than analytical (What does the literature tell us?). A rapid evidence assessment makes little claim to in-depth quality assessment. Similarly a tightly-defined conceptual analysis, perhaps to inform a subsequent framework analysis, may be achieved within six months.

Task	Timescale
First project team meeting	Months 0-1
Search	
Finalise scope	Months 0-1
Preliminary literature searches	Months 0-1
Identify and contact key organisations	Months 0-1
Second project team meeting/discussion	Months 1-2
Full literature searches and reference management	Months 1-2
Selection of articles	Month 2
Obtain articles	Month 2-3
Follow-up cited references	Month 3
Third project team meeting/discussion	Month 3
AppraisaL	
Quality assessment and selective data extraction	Months 3-4
Fourth project team meeting/discussion	Month 4

Task	Timescale
Synthesis	
Data synthesis	Month 5
Analysis	
Data analysis	Month 5
Fifth project team meeting/discussion	Month 5
Report writing	Month 6
Draft report	Month 6
Sixth project team meeting/discussion	Month 6
Final report	Month 6

Table 4.2 Sample project timetable for nine-month literature review project

Note: A nine-month timescale is most appropriate as a component of a large-scale (e.g. two or more years) project where findings from the literature review feed into subsequent primary research. Similarly nine months may be suitable if you are planning to use the literature review component of a thesis to inform the design of primary data collection and as a deliverable in an upgrade report. This timescale assumes that you are conducting other tasks, e.g. applying for ethical approval, during the concluding phases of the literature review.

Task	Timescale
First project team/supervisor meeting	Months 0–1
Search	
Finalise scope	Months 0–1
Preliminary literature searches	Months 1–2
Identify and contact key organisations	Months 1–2
Second project team/supervisor meeting/discussion	Months 1–2
Full literature searches and reference management	Months 2–3
Selection of articles	Months 2–3
Obtain articles	Months 3–4
Follow-up cited references	Months 4
Third project team/supervisor meeting/discussion	Month 4
Appraisal	
Quality assessment	Month 5
Synthesis	
Data extraction	Month 5–6
Fourth project team/supervisor meeting/discussion	Month 6
Data synthesis	Month 7

(Continued)

(Continued)

Task	Timescale
Analysis	
Data analysis	Month 7-8
Fifth project team/supervisor meeting/discussion	Month 8
Report writing	Months 8-9
Draft report	Months 9
Sixth project team/supervisor meeting/discussion	Month 9
Final report	Month 9

Table 4.3 Sample project timetable for 12-month literature review project

Note: 12 months is a typical timescale for a stand-alone literature review such as a systematic review with meta-analysis or a qualitative evidence synthesis (whether aggregative with many included studies or interpretive with in-depth analysis of 10 to 12 studies). In the latter case the aim is to complete search, appraisal and data extraction as early as possible to maximise the time spent on synthesis and analysis.

Task	Timescale
First project team meeting	Months 0-1
Search	
Finalise scope	Month 1
Preliminary literature searches	Months 1-2
Identify and contact key organisations	Month 2
Second project team meeting/discussion	Months 2-3
Full literature searches and reference management	Months 2-3
Selection of articles	Months 3-4
Obtain articles	Months 4-5
Follow-up cited references	Month 6
Third project team meeting/discussion	Months 6-7
AppraisaL	
Quality assessment	Months 6-7
Data extraction	Months 7-8
Fourth project team meeting/discussion	Month 8
Synthesis	
Data synthesis	Months 8-9
Analysis	
Data analysis	Months 9-10
Fifth project team meeting/discussion	Month 10
Report writing	Months 11-12
Draft report	Month 11
Sixth project team meeting/discussion	Month 12
Final report	Month 12

For comparative purposes you may find it helpful to consider the published one-year timeline for a typical Cochrane (systematic) Review (Green and Higgins, 2008). Obviously within these generic templates there is considerable scope for variability according to:

1) the quantity of the literature that you have to review;
2) the scope of your literature review;
3) the number of team members, and proportions of their time, available to your review;
4) the format and quality of the review deliverables.

Nevertheless these templates are a useful starting point. You may also use these as a starting point for negotiations with a review commissioner or a supervisor. Pai and colleagues (2004) provide a useful step-by-step guide to the review process.

 toolbox

A SMART plan

Nicholson (2007) suggests that you should produce a SMART plan to identify the specific, measurable, agreed, realistic and timed objectives of the review project. He advises that the person managing the review plans each phase carefully, identifies each strand of work, and sets realistic completion dates. Such a SMART plan would have the format provided in Table 4.4.

Table 4.4 Extract from a SMART plan for a review

What?	By whom?	By when?	Cost?	Status?
Conduct scoping searches	Information specialist	01/09/2016	£240 (per day)	Not started/ in progress/ completed
Completion of pilot searches				
Completion of full searches				
Quality Assessment				
Draft Report				
Final Report				

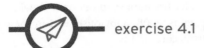

exercise 4.1

Producing a draft timetable for your review

Produce a draft timetable for your own review. Include the phases of scoping and planning; searching and obtaining references; data extraction and quality assessment; synthesis and analysis; and writing up and disseminating.

Now identify milestones (i.e. time deadlines) or deliverables (specific outputs from each phase of the review process) and where these lie in your review timetable. These may include, but not necessarily be restricted to, a review protocol or review plan (scoping and planning); a search strategy for a principal database with sample search results (searching and obtaining references); a draft data extraction form with completed quality assessment for an included article (data extraction and quality assessment); tables of included study characteristics (synthesis and analysis); and a draft report or article (writing up and disseminating). If you are undertaking a dissertation or thesis, use the timescale that you produce for these deliverables to identify useful points at which to meet with your supervisor. If you are conducting a commissioned review or working with a review team, use review milestones as critical points for either internal or external team meetings. You may find it helpful to use the format for a SMART plan (see Table 4.4).

Once you have given attention to the 'TQM (Time-Quality-Money) of Review Management' you are ready to consider the more detailed logistics of your review project. Aspects frequently overlooked include the following.

Access to databases

You may be conducting your review within an academic institution that carries a wider range of database resources than typically required for your discipline (e.g. health, management, education, social science). However, you cannot assume that you have access to all the databases required for your topic. You may need to negotiate ad hoc access to particular sources, identified from the 'Methods' sections of related reviews. Such access may be afforded direct to you and your team, in which case you need to think not only about payment of any fees or subscriptions but also about orientation or training. Alternatively access to databases may only be available via an intermediary from the hosting organisation and thus require payment, for information specialist time for the actual searching and, not to be overlooked, information specialist time for preparing and planning the search strategy.

Reference management software

The scale of managing references makes use of **reference management** software virtually essential for any substantive literature review project (Sayers, 2007). Again you may already have access to reference management software, either via your institution or via free software on the internet. However, you should be aware that institutional agreements often relate to 'cut down' versions of software geared to general student use and comparatively ill-equipped for the heavier demands of a major literature review.

Furthermore the software may restrict the number of simultaneous users of a reference management database, the number of copies of a database that may be made, whether you are permitted to have versions running both at the office and at home, and whether external collaborators may also access the system. For free versions on the internet you should explore the functions available, whether it is worth paying an additional premium for added functionality, and issues such as backup and security of data. Ultimately the bottom line involves your asking, 'What is the worst case scenario if the system malfunctions?' and 'What would be the implications for my review?' Faced with such questions you will frequently find that it is better to spend money on more robust and secure systems in terms of improved risk management and resulting peace of mind.

Obtaining literature

Most institutional libraries hold a collection of key journal and book resources to support core subject areas. However, where you move beyond these core subjects, you will typically need to access other journal articles through inter-library loan and document delivery services. Few information units, aside from those specifically created to support systematic reviews, are geared up for processing possibly hundreds of journal article requests. You therefore need to seek out those who manage local libraries to alert them to your likely needs and negotiate preferential arrangements to handle bulk quantities of requests. For large-scale projects you may be required to pre-check the holdings of other libraries in advance of your request. You may even need to employ a temporary member of staff specifically for this purpose. You should also consider whether it might be more advantageous to arrange trips to specialist libraries, e.g. national libraries or specialist collections, for you to access materials in person. You will need to prepare by researching opening hours, access arrangements and eligibility, photocopying facilities and transport times and costs.

Analysis software

While you may not be able to predict the exact form that your final analysis of data will take, you will usually be able to identify whether quantitative (i.e. meta-analysis) or qualitative (e.g. **thematic synthesis**) analysis will be possible. For a meta-analysis you should budget for meta-analysis software and possibly statistical support. For a qualitative synthesis you may wish to consider qualitative data analysis software. Again your decision on whether to use commercial proprietary or free software will depend on such factors as how central the analysis is to your final deliverable, the available resources and how much demand there is for such software from elsewhere in your organisation.

You will find it extremely helpful to project the likely size and scale of the literature. You can do this in several ways. Bibliographic databases with data mining or analytical facilities (Scopus, Scirus, PubMed PubReMiner, Web of Knowledge) supply statistics regarding the frequency of certain terms or phrases. For example PubMed PubReMiner helps you identify key authors, key journals and countries of publication, as well as terms used most frequently by authors and/or indexers.

Such decisions serve two main purposes. First, they help you create your initial review plan or protocol together with associated milestones and deliverables. Second, they offer you a toolkit of 'rescue' techniques that you can use to bring your review back on track (see Table 4.5). This is particularly critical if time, quality or money aspects of a literature review are deflecting you from your original plan.

Table 4.5 Some areas of review efficiency

- Could I use a methodological filter to reduce the numbers of studies that I have to sift?
- Can I identify a likely law of diminishing returns so that I can prioritise certain databases according to likely yield?
- Could someone eliminate duplicate citations retrieved from different bibliographic databases instead of the team having to repeat decisions on inclusion/exclusion for the same research study?
- Could I select studies (i.e. sifting from abstracts) from core databases in parallel to ongoing searching of additional databases?
- Could I request and obtain potentially relevant articles while undertaking study selection?
- Could I read and/or check initial articles received for relevant citations as soon as they are received rather than wait for the full set of retrieved studies?
- Could I start data extraction and quality assessment in advance of obtaining all studies?
- Could I conduct data extraction and quality assessment as a combined single operation?
- Will I extract data via data extraction forms or direct into summary tables?
- Do I need to use more than one reviewer for sifting or selecting all included studies (or could I use a second reviewer for a random sample of records or until we reach an adequate level of agreement)?

PROBLEM SOLVING AND TROUBLESHOOTING

The following section presents realistic scenarios relating to problems that you may encounter when undertaking a literature review. Choose one or more scenarios of interest. Try to diagnose where the problems lie and how they might be overcome. Once you have identified potential responses examine our suggested solutions (see https://study.sagepub.com/booth2e).

 **exercise 4.2**

Problem-solving scenarios

Scenario A: Adebola

Adebola is starting a literature review as part of a funded pilot project on the social determinants of ill-health in Sub-Saharan Africa. She is interested in the causes of mortality for mothers and infants, She feels she must definitely look at some leading causes of disability among adults. Then there is the increasing high profile of illness in the ageing population. In her country, there is a particular concern around HIV and AIDS. As she starts to build a list of all possible population–illness combinations she realises that her topic has started to get out of hand.

What are the root causes of this particular problem?

What strategies might you suggest to help Adebola overcome this problem?

Scenario B: Brenda

Brenda is a member of a small team working on a funded review in a management topic. After spending considerable time devising comprehensive search strategies for the specific review question, using the **PICOS** formulation, she has completed an initial sift of retrieved titles and abstracts. She applies the rigorous inclusion criteria devised by the team. Not a single article would make it through to the full article stage. She is concerned that the team has made their review topic too exclusive and may have only an 'empty review' to offer to the research funders.

What are the root causes of this particular problem?

What strategies might you suggest to help Brenda overcome this problem?

Scenario C: Sanjay

Sanjay is a part-time student conducting a literature review for his academic thesis. He has devised a comprehensive search plan for his literature review and meets with his supervisor to discuss his next steps. His supervisor suggests that, in addition to the topics he has already identified, he needs to access key concepts from the psychological literature. Discussing his review question with a work colleague, who has recently completed an MBA, she suggests that the management literature may also have something to contribute. Revisiting his search plan, he now finds that these suggested revisions have tripled the size of the literature to be screened and sifted.

What are the root causes of this particular problem?

What strategies might you suggest to help Sanjay overcome this problem?

Scenario D: Eloise

It is month 10 of a 12-month funded project and Eloise is worried. She has completed data extraction and quality assessment of about half of the 80 articles to be included in her literature review. She has no idea what are the main findings that are going to emerge from her review, let alone how the literature review is going to be written on time.

What are the root causes of this particular problem?

What strategies might you suggest to help Eloise overcome this problem?

Scenario E: Sandra

Sandra has just received the monthly budget report for her first ever 18-month literature review. It is month 7 and she has spent well over half the budget allocation for the project. The project is proceeding on schedule but she is concerned that she is going to have to report a likely end of project overspend to her line manager at her next three-monthly review meeting. She is concerned that she has underestimated the project budget for the literature review.

(Continued)

(Continued)

What are the root causes of this particular problem?

What strategies might you suggest to help Sandra overcome this problem?

Scenario F: Tomasz

Tomasz is undertaking a systematic review on attitudes to citizenship of first-generation East European migrants. He is at a crucial stage of his literature project. He has identified all studies for likely inclusion in his review. However, he is unsure which method of synthesis to use to summarise these qualitative research reports. His supervisor has extensive experience of supervising systematic review projects, but these have all involved meta-analyses and he has never supervised a qualitative evidence synthesis.

What are the root causes of this particular problem?

What strategies might you suggest to help Tomasz overcome this problem?

Scenario G: James

James is feeling frustrated. For some time he has been sending e-mails to topic experts on the review team asking for their input. Although they are located only 40 miles (64 km) away, in the nearest adjacent city, they seem to have 'disappeared into a black hole in the ether'. James is concerned that, without their cooperation and input, the literature review will fall behind its time schedule and lack credibility with practitioners.

What are the root causes of this particular problem?

What strategies might you suggest to help James overcome this problem?

Such decisions constitute a toolkit of 'rescue' techniques to help you to bring your review back on track if time, quality, money or even methodological aspects of a literature review appear to be deviating from the original plan.

 toolbox

To support the review process

Very few articles identify tools to support the review process. Articles that do identify review support tools typically focus on literature searching, reference management and analysing quantitative or qualitative data. Tools can also facilitate communication and project management (see Table 4.6). Many resources are covered in more detail throughout this book. You can use this section as a checklist when planning requirements to support your own review.

Table 4.6 Tools to support the review process

Stage of review process	Types of tool	Examples
Communication (Baker et al., 2010)	Meeting planning tools Voice and video communication File sharing Remote sharing of PC Desktop	Google Calendar Skype Dropbox Adobe Connect
Project Management	Project management software	Microsoft Project
Review Management	Integrated review management software	RevMan EppiReviewer
Review Development	Concept development Data mining	Freemind EppiReviewer
Literature Searching	Reference management Reference sharing	Reference Manager, Endnote, Refworks Citeulike, Mendeley
Data Extraction	Extraction forms	Google Forms, Access, Excel
Data Analysis	Quantitative data analysis Qualitative data analysis	SPSS, Stata NVivo
Word Processing	WP software	Word, OpenOffice Write
Dissemination	Presentation software	Powerpoint, OpenOffice Impress
Distribution	Report conversion/distribution software	Acrobat, Winzip

 toolbox

Avoiding common pitfalls

According to Gall et al. (1996) seven common mistakes are made when reviewing the literature. These mistakes may be mapped against the SALSA framework (see Table 4.7).

You will find it helpful to review these common pitfalls at various stages throughout the planning and conduct of your own review.

Table 4.7 Common reviewer errors

Stage	Reviewer error
Search	Does not take sufficient time to define the best search terms and identify the best sources to use in review literature related to the topic.
	Does not report the search procedures used in the literature review.
Appraisal	Relies on secondary sources rather than on primary sources in reviewing the literature.
	Uncritically accepts another researcher's findings and interpretations as valid, rather than examining critically all aspects of the research design and analysis.

(Continued)

(Continued)

Stage	Reviewer error
Synthesis	Reports isolated statistical results rather than synthesising them using meta-analytic methods/*reports isolated themes or categories rather than examining the relationships between them.*
	Does not consider contrary findings and alternative interpretations in synthesising quantitative or *qualitative* literature.
Analysis	Does not clearly relate the findings of the literature review to the researcher's own study or the original review question.

Items in italics are added in making this checklist applicable to a range of review types beyond the original context of meta-analysis.

SUMMARY

Project management for any review conducted according to systematic principles is complex and time-consuming. As a reviewer you must pay close attention to initial planning. Established project management principles provide a good basis for both planning and managing the production of the review (Baker et al., 2010). You must consider planning, management, effective communication and stakeholder engagement. All these elements, if handled appropriately, will improve your potential to deliver a successful review on time and within budget, as well as enhancing the experience of the review team and the capacity of the hosting organisation. Of course the converse is also true; a lack of planning and management, poor mechanisms for communication and inappropriate engagement of stakeholders are likely to hamstring your review project. Project management is therefore a key element of systematic approaches to a successful literature review.

This chapter has focused on the planning of a review, a topic frequently omitted from published guidelines for the review process. It offers useful frameworks for planning and tackling your own review. Far from shackling your creativity, paying attention to logistics early on in the review process offers you the freedom to engage effectively with your data. Having removed anxieties and uncertainties about your direction of travel you will find yourself able to liberate your imagination for synthesis and analysis.

 key learning points

- Planning a systematic review requires good project management skills.
- A project timetable should be constructed around milestones and deliverables.
- Review updates require just as much planning as full systematic reviews and may prove equally demanding on resources.
- Software is available to help you with most stages of the review process.

frequently asked questions (FAQs)

FAQ 4.1 Should I update an existing review?

Updating a systematic review can be both inefficient and introduce bias (Tsertsvadze et al., 2011; Takwoingi et al., 2013; Mayhew et al., 2015). On the other hand delaying an update may delay the introduction of an effective intervention or disinvestment from a policy or programme suspected of being ineffective. Recent years have seen several research teams try to identify circumstances under which a review update is more likely to prove useful. Such circumstances include situations where a new includable study involves more participants than have previously been analysed, or where this new study is larger than the largest previously included study. Less obviously a review update may prove useful where the confidence intervals are wide (indicating uncertainty) or where they cross the line of no effect, thus indicating genuine **equipoise** (i.e. an objective reader genuinely entertains the idea that the intervention and its alternative are equally likely to be effective and so neither represents a compelling choice).

FAQ 4.2 Will updating a review be cheaper than the original review?

Updating a review is not significantly less resource-intensive than a full systematic review. Although a review update is apparently focused on newly emergent studies, to determine whether the new body of evidence challenges conclusions from the previous review, it is usually heavily dependent upon the previously included studies. A systematic review team may consider it necessary to re-execute the previous analysis. Where the quality of the previous review is uncertain a review team may re-execute the entire review process, effectively conducting a new, more extensive systematic review for the previous review period *and* the intervening years since its completion. The criticality of the topic, the volatility of the discipline and uncertainties surrounding the previous verdict will influence this decision. Repeating a review to cover both former and current review periods, although expensive, does increase the confidence that the evidence is being handled consistently. Update searches should cover the time period from the date of last search, not from the date of publication of the review, preferably with an additional allowance for database or indexing irregularities. You should review your search strategies for changes or additions to search terminology. You can use included studies from the older review to validate the new search strategies. A new search strategy should retrieve all the original included studies in addition to more recently published articles.

FAQ 4.3 What are the main things that could go wrong when conducting a review?

Frequently subject experts under-estimate the quantity of literature available and seek to expand the scope of the original review question. Finalising the review question and conducting the literature search often take longer than anticipated. Often a team may work to external deadlines and miss the opportunities offered by setting internal deadlines. Production and formatting of the final report and assembling and checking of references are often time-consuming. Production of templates can be helpful where reviews are being undertaken as part of a regular publication series.

▬▬▬▬▬ suggestions for further reading ▬▬▬▬▬

Baker, P.R., Francis, D.P., Hall, B.J., Doyle, J. and Armstrong, R. (2010) Managing the production of a Cochrane systematic review. *Journal of Public Health*, **32**, 3, 448-50.
One of the few items to focus on project management aspects of the review process.

Boote, D.N. and Beile, P. (2005) Scholars before researchers: on the centrality of the dissertation literature review in research preparation. *Educational Researcher*, **34**, 6, 3-15.
Interesting perspective on the academic literature review and its role within a dissertation.

Levy, Y. and Ellis, T.J. (2006) A systems approach to conduct an effective literature review in support of information systems research. *Informing Science Journal*, **9**, 181-212.
Highly cited paper that highlights a framework for doctoral students, with an information systems focus.

Randolph, J. (2009) A guide to writing the dissertation literature review. *Practical Assessment, Research and Evaluation*, **14**, 13.
Useful tutorial paper on writing an academic literature review outlining pitfalls to avoid and offering a framework for self-evaluation.

Sayers, A. (2007) Tips and tricks in performing a systematic review. *British Journal of General Practice*, **57**, 545, 999.
An accessible 'How to' guide that includes some valuable know-how.

Staples, M. and Niazi, M. (2007) Experiences using systematic review guidelines. *Journal of Systems Software*, **80**, 9, 1425-37.
Walks through a recent systematic review project and compares and contrasts their experience against published guidelines.

REFERENCES

Allen, I.E. and Olkin, I. (1999) Estimating time to conduct a meta-analysis from number of citations retrieved. *JAMA*, **282**, 7, 634–5.

Baker, P.R., Francis, D.P., Hall, B.J., Doyle, J. and Armstrong, R. (2010) Managing the production of a Cochrane systematic review. *Journal of Public Health*, **32**, 3, 448–50.

Barnett-Page, E. and Thomas, J. (2009) Methods for the synthesis of qualitative research: a critical review. *BMC Medical Research Methodology*, **9**, 59.

Barrowman, N.J., Fang, M., Sampson, M. and Moher, D. (2003) Identifying null meta-analyses that are ripe for updating. *BMC Medical Research Methodology*, **3**, 13.

Beverley, C.A., Booth, A. and Bath, P.A. (2003) The role of the information specialist in the systematic review process: a health information case study. *Health Information and Libraries Journal*, **20**, 2, 65–74.

Bruce, C. (1993) When enough is enough: or how should research students delimit the scope of their literature review? In *Challenging the Conventional Wisdom in Higher Education: Selected Contributions Presented at the Nineteenth Annual National Conference and Twenty-First Birthday Celebration of the Higher Education Research and Development Society of Australasia Inc.*, HERDSA, University of New South Wales, Sydney, Australia, 435–9.

Cleland, D. and Gareis, R. (2006) *Global Project Management Handbook: Planning, Organising and Controlling International Projects*. New York: McGraw-Hill.

Dickersin, K., Scherer, R. and Lefebvre, C. (1994) Identifying relevant studies for systematic reviews. *BMJ*, **309**, 6964, 1286–91.

Dixon-Woods, M., Agarwal, S., Young, B., Jones, D. and Sutton, A. (2004) *Integrative Approaches to Qualitative and Quantitative Evidence*. London: NHS Health Development Agency.

Educational Research Funders Forum (2005) Systematic literature reviews in education: advice and information for funders. NERF Working Paper 2.1 (January).

Gall, M.D., Borg, W.R. and Gall, J.P. (1996) *Education Research: An Introduction*, 6th edition. White Plains, NY: Longman.

Gillies, D., Maxwell, H., New, K., Pennick, V., Fedorowicz, Z., van Der Wouden, J., Oliver, J., Scholten, R., Ciapponi, A. and Verbeek, J. (2009) *A Collaboration-wide Survey of Cochrane Authors*. Oxford: The Cochrane Collaboration.

Green, S. and Higgins, J.P.T. (eds) (2008) Preparing a Cochrane Review. In J.P.T. Higgins and S. Green (eds), *Cochrane Handbook for Systematic Reviews of Interventions*, Version 5.0.1 (updated September 2008), The Cochrane Collaboration. Available at: www.cochrane-handbook.org (last accessed 9 March 2016).

Greenhalgh, T. (2014) *How to Read a Paper*, 5th edition. London: BMJ Books.

Harris, M.R. (2005) The librarian's roles in the systematic review process: a case study. *Journal of the Medical Library Association*, **93**, 1, 81–7.

Hausner, E., Waffenschmidt, S., Kaiser, T. and Simon, M. (2012) Routine development of objectively derived search strategies. *Systematic Reviews*, **1**, 1, 1–10.

Lyratzopoulos, G. and Allen, D. (2004) How to manage your research and audit work. *BMJ Career Focus*, **328**, 196–7.

Mayhew, A.D., Kabir, M. and Ansari, M.T. (2015) Considerations from the risk of bias perspective for updating Cochrane reviews. *Systematic Reviews*, **4**, 1, 136.

McGowan, J. and Sampson, M. (2005) Systematic reviews need systematic searchers. *Journal of the Medical Library Association*, **93**, 1, 74–80.

Moher, D. and Tsertsvadze, A. (2006) Systematic reviews: when is an update an update? *Lancet*, **367**, 9514, 881–3.

Moher, D., Tsertsvadze, A., Tricco, A., Eccles, M., Grimshaw, J., Sampson, M. and Barrowman, N. (2008) When and how to update systematic reviews. Cochrane Database of Systematic Reviews, Issue 1. Art. No.: MR000023. DOI: 10.1002/14651858.MR000023.pub3.

National Collaborating Centre for Methods and Tools (n.d.) Methods: Synthesis 1. Rapid reviews: Methods and implications [fact sheet]. Hamilton, ON: National Collaborating Centre for Methods and Tools. Available at www.nccmt.ca/pubs/Methods_ Synthesis1.pdf.

Nicholson, P.J. (2007) How to undertake a systematic review in an occupational setting. *Occupational and Environ Medicine*, **64**, 5, 353–8, 303.

Pai, M., McCulloch, M., Gorman, J.D., Pai, N., Enaroria, W., Kennedy, G., Tharyan, P. and Colford, J.M., Jr (2004) Systematic reviews and meta-analyses: an illustrated, step-by-step guide. *The National Medical Journal of India*, **17**, 2, 86–95.

Piehl, J.H., Green, S. and McDonald, S. (2003) Converting systematic reviews to Cochrane format: a cross-sectional survey of Australian authors of systematic reviews. *BMC Health Services Research*, **3**, 1, 2.

Piehl, J.H., Green, S. and Silagy, C. (2002) Training practitioners in preparing systematic reviews: a cross-sectional survey of participants in the Australasian Cochrane Centre training program. *BMC Health Services Research*, **2**, 1, 11.

Pope, C., Mays, N. and Popay, J. (2007) *Synthesizing Qualitative and Quantitative Health Evidence: A Guide to Methods*. Maidenhead: Open University Press.

Randolph, J. (2009) A guide to writing the dissertation literature review. *Practical Assessment, Research and Evaluation*, **14**, 13.

Sambunjak, S. and Puljak, L. (2010) Cochrane systematic review as a PhD thesis: an alternative with numerous advantages. *Biochemia Medica*, **20**, 3, 319–26.

Sayers, A. (2007) Tips and tricks in performing a systematic review. *British Journal of General Practice*, **57**, 545, 999.

Smith, L.K., Pope, C. and Botha, J.L. (2005) Patients' help-seeking experiences and delay in cancer presentation: a qualitative synthesis. *Lancet*, **366**, 9488, 825–31.

Soll, R.F. (2008) Updating reviews: the experience of the Cochrane Neonatal Review Group. *Paediatric and Perinatal Epidemiology*, **22**, Suppl. 1, 29–32.

Swinkels, A., Briddon, J. and Hall, J. (2006) Two physiotherapists, one librarian and a systematic literature review: collaboration in action. *Health Information and Libraries Journal*, **23**, 4, 248–56.

Takwoingi, Y., Hopewell, S., Tovey, D. and Sutton, A. (2013) A multicomponent decision tool for prioritising the updating of systematic reviews. *BMJ*, **347**, f7191.

Tsertsvadze, A., Maglione, M., Chou, R., Garritty, C., Colman, C., Lux, L., Bass, E., Balshem, H. and Moher, D. (2011) Updating comparative effectiveness reviews: current efforts in AHRQ's Effective Health Care Program, *Journal of Clinical Epidemiology*, **64**, 11: 1208–15.

Wade, C.A. (2006) Information retrieval and the role of the information specialist in producing high-quality systematic reviews in the social behavioural and education sciences. *Evidence and Policy*, **2**, 1, 89–108.

Wilkinson, A., Papaioannou, D., Keen, C. and Booth, A. (2009) The role of the information specialist in supporting knowledge transfer: a public health information case study. *Health Information and Libraries Journal*, **26**, 118–25.

DEFINING YOUR SCOPE

 in a nutshell

How to define your review scope

- Try to focus your research topic into an answerable research question that is clearly structured to show the 'who, what and how' of your review.
- Setting out the aims of your research at this early stage informs the remainder of your project. A good research question helps your decision making for literature searching and study selection.
- To focus your question, you may find it helpful to use one of the given frameworks to define the key concepts of your research.
- Mapping processes such as descriptive mapping, data mining, concept mapping and logic models can help you refine your review scope and choose an appropriate review type.
- You will find it helpful to complete a review protocol at this stage to help you carefully plan the process of your review and adhere to it.
- When defining your scope you must be aware of common challenges and pitfalls.

INTRODUCTION

So you have an idea for a topic area that you would like to review and you're probably wondering where to start. It is important to have a plan from the outset – you know the destination but you need to think about how you will actually get there. The first step is to identify the parameters of your review, i.e. the scope. Identifying the scope is a useful way of defining from the outset what your review will cover and what it won't. This chapter takes you through the process, from formulating an answerable **research question**, undertaking an initial **scoping search** to evaluate the size and nature of the evidence base, some approaches for mapping the literature, various challenges and pitfalls to avoid and how to resolve them, and writing a review protocol (the plan).

WHY IS DEFINING THE SCOPE IMPORTANT?

A good **systematic review** is based on a well-formulated, answerable question (Counsell, 1997). It is important to start with a clearly defined scope for any type of review, but particularly one that claims to be systematic. John Ruskin wrote in 1886: 'To be able to ask a question clearly is two-thirds of the way to getting it answered' (Booth, 2006). This still resonates. Most problems with the conduct of a literature review can be attributed to initial problems with the scoping process – 'Fuzzy questions tend to lead to fuzzy answers' (Oxman and Guyatt, 1988). If you ask too broad a question you may have little chance of answering it. Similarly you may, in fact, be asking a series of questions which need to be disentangled and separately articulated.

Defining the scope involves focusing your research question so that it contains explicit, specific information about your topic. Typically, you may have an idea for a broad area of research. Defining the scope allows you to focus your research question, which informs the subsequent literature review process. Essentially, defining the scope involves deciding on the 'who', the 'what' and the 'how' (Ibrahim, 2008) (see Box 5.1).

 **box 5.1**

The three elements of defining the scope

WHO = who is the research question about?
WHAT = what must the researcher find out to answer the research question?
HOW = how will the study impact on the 'who'? (what is the outcome?)
(Adapted from Ibrahim, 2008.)

In short, defining the scope can take you from

'I'd quite like to do some research on under-age drinking … '

to

'I'm going to do some research on the economic and social implications *[HOW]* of school age *[WHO]* drinking *[WHAT]*.'

Clearly setting out the aims of your research from the start helps you to determine all the subsequent aspects of your review. For example, a good research question can inform your literature search, making it easier for you to identify the key concepts of the question and therefore your key search terms. (This idea is explored more fully in Chapter 6.) It will also inform your **inclusion criteria** (in helping you to select studies) as you will know exactly the type of study you are looking for (Stern et al., 2014). (This is explored more fully in Chapter 7.) For now we present a brief example (see Box 5.2).

 box 5.2

Example of a research question informing inclusion criteria

Research question: What are the economic and social implications of school age drinking?
Inclusion criteria
Study must include:

1. Subjects of school age (5-16 years) [WHO].
2. Drinking of any alcohol in any quantity [WHAT].
3. Economic and/or social implications [HOW].

You will also find that clearly defining your scope from the outset proves invaluable in helping you to determine the resources you will need for your research. Knowing exactly what your research does and does not include allows you to allocate the required time and money throughout the project (see Chapter 4). This, in turn, helps you in writing a project plan or protocol – for your own use and for sharing with a wider project team. You will also need to define your scope prior to applying for, and securing, any research funding.

DEFINING YOUR SCOPE WITH AN AUDIENCE IN MIND

You need to consider your review audience when defining the scope for your review. Does your review question match the question that your review audience most wants answering? To check, you could consult with key people likely to be interested in, or affected by, your review to confirm that your review question is appropriate. If your review findings are likely to inform professional practice or enable decision makers to change policy, contact experts for their input.

Petticrew and Roberts (2006) suggest that where there is a commercial or professional interest in your review findings, it might be wise to involve key opinion leaders or stakeholders from the outset and jointly devise the review question. Boote and colleagues (2011; 2012) offer case studies of user involvement in systematic reviews. This does not mean that individuals dictate your review findings, but does allow you to define a review question that is useful for your review audience.

FRAMEWORKS FOR DEFINING THE SCOPE

Splitting your research question into the 'Who?', 'What?' and 'How?' can help to identify the fundamental elements of your question. However, you may find it useful to use a formal structure to focus your question to allow you to 'unpack' that question further into its component concepts. Various frameworks are available to help you do this, depending on your field of research (Davies, 2011), but for this chapter we will concentrate on **PICOC** (Petticrew and Roberts, 2006) (see Table 5.1).

Table 5.1   The elements of PICOC

Population	Who or what is the problem or situation you are dealing with? In a human population, for example, which age, sex, socioeconomic or ethnic groups are involved? What are the technical terms, synonyms and related terms?
Intervention OR *Exposure*	In what ways are you considering intervening in the situation? What sort of options do you have for tackling the problem? For example, this could be an educational intervention such as online tutorials on plagiarism (population = undergraduate students).
	NB: For non-intervention studies you may find it helpful to replace Intervention (a planned procedure) with Exposure (an unintentional occurrence or happening). For example, exposure to radio waves from mobile phone transmitters.
Comparison	What is the alternative? This is optional. For when you wish to consider, for example, the effect of two or more interventions, comparing their outcomes possibly in terms of what they deliver and/or cost. So you may want information on the relative merits of: <ul><li>buses versus trams for urban congestion;</li><li>natural versus chemical methods of agricultural pest control;</li><li>surgery versus drugs for an illness.</li></ul>
Outcome(s)	How is it measured? This may be more difficult to identify: you have a technical terminology for your problem and a range of management options, but what do you want to achieve? This stage does, however, focus your mind on what your desired outcome(s) might be and how you will assess the impact – what you are going to measure and how.
Context	What is the particular context of your question? Are you looking at specific countries/areas/settings?

Continuing with our previous example on school age drinking, Box 5.3 shows how a focused question might look using the PICOC model.

 box 5.3

Worked example of PICOC

Population = children and adolescents/teenagers/young adults of school age – that is 5–16 years (Years 1–11 and international equivalents). Male and female. All school ages (when legally required to attend) – primary, infant, junior, secondary, high, grammar, comprehensive, state and public/private, home schooling.

Intervention/exposure = underage drinking of alcohol.

Comparison = none (not drinking alcohol).

Outcomes = economic and/or social impact. Impacts include, but are not limited to, future economic prospects (earning levels and growth), emotional development, educational and occupational achievement, antisocial and/or violent behaviour, sexual harassment, sexually transmitted diseases, teenage pregnancy, increased healthcare costs (including increased emergency admissions).

Context = primary focus is on the UK, but international studies will be considered if the results can be applied to the local setting.

This example illustrates that time spent formalising the scope of your question is time well spent, as it also provides an opportunity to identify potential search terms and consider the types of studies you are going to include in your review.

Other frameworks exist for defining the scope. Many frameworks have been developed to answer a specific type of question. PICOC itself is derived from the PICO (Population, Intervention, Comparison, Outcome(s)) formulation which was developed in the field of medicine to answer clinical queries (Richardson et al., 1995). SPIDER (Sample, Phenomenon of Interest, Design, Evaluation, Research type) (Cooke et al., 2012), ProPheT (Problem, Phenomenon of Interest, Time) or SPICE (Setting, Perspective, Intervention/Interest, Comparison, Evaluation) may be particularly useful for qualitative questions (Booth, 2004). Denyer and Tranfield (2009) have devised a management version of PICO, known as Context-Intervention-Mechanisms-Outcomes (CIMO) (see Box 5.4). However, note that when such frameworks are translated into search strategies their **sensitivity** and **specificity** may be suboptimal. There is evidence to suggest that not all frameworks are suitable for fully comprehensive reviews (Methley et al., 2014).

 box 5.4

Context-Intervention-Mechanisms-Outcomes (CIMO) framework

Context - Which individuals, relationships, institutional settings or wider systems are being studied?

Intervention - The effects of what event, action or activity are being studied?

Mechanisms - What are the mechanisms that explain the relationship between interventions and outcomes? Under what circumstances are these mechanisms activated or not activated?

Outcomes - What are the effects of the intervention? How will the outcomes be measured?

(Continued)

(Continued)

Example of a focused question using CIMO: 'Under what conditions (C) does leadership style (I) influence the performance of project teams (O), and what mechanisms (M) operate in the influence of leadership style (I) on project team performance (O)?' (Denyer and Tranfield, 2009)

Now practise using a framework to focus your research question by completing Exercise 5.1.

 **exercise 5.1**

Using a framework to focus your question

Choose a framework that best fits your research areas and formulate your own research question. So if you're using the PICOC model, consider:

Population

Intervention OR Exposure

Comparison

Outcome(s)

Context

COMPLEX INTERVENTIONS

The examples we've used thus far are fairly straightforward, involving simple 'does this work?'-type questions. Review questions become harder to define when they involve more **complex interventions**. Interventions can be considered complex if they incorporate one or more of the following characteristics:

1) They have a number of interacting components (which may or may not work together).
2) They are attempting to modify one or more behaviours of those delivering or receiving the intervention.
3) They are targeted at more than one group or different organisational levels.
4) They are attempting to affect more than one outcome.
5) They allow flexibility so that they are personalised (Craig et al., 2008).

There is much written on complex interventions, both on how to design and how to evaluate them. This chapter does not go into great detail and we suggest you refer to the further reading suggested later in this chapter. (Note, however, that although this reading focuses on health care interventions, it is highly transferable to other subject areas.)

Consider the example intervention below (see Box 5.5). We have listed *some* ways in which this intervention could be considered complex.

 **box 5.5**

Example of a complex intervention

Education programmes to teach Type 1 diabetic patients how to self-manage their condition effectively:

- Number of interacting components: lecture-type sessions, small group role play, diary keeping, discussion of problems/successes amongst group.
- Delivery of the intervention: intense week-long course, weekly sessions, online packages.
- Change of behaviour in participants: enabling increased control of their own condition and integrating effective self-management into their daily lives.
- Change in behaviour in health professionals: less 'do as I say' and more about patient empowerment.
- Programme can be tailored to an individual: one-to-one sessions available to discuss specific goals and targets.
- Therapist effect: delivered by diabetic nurses or dietitians or peer volunteers trained in delivery of the education programme, personality types.
- Outcomes: control of their diabetes, long-term health outcomes (such as heart disease), patient-rated quality of life, time off work, admissions to hospital, health care resource use.

This example illustrates how much supporting detail is available to help to unpack this type of intervention and, consequently, the variety of review questions that could be asked. So how do you begin to define the scope of your review question for this type of complex intervention? Squires and colleagues (2013) discuss how three specific complexity issues might guide how you define your review question.

1. *Type of question*

As for simpler interventions, the question your review seeks to answer should be guided by what you or your review audience need to know. This decision is made more complicated with so much choice as to which question to ask! Therefore, discuss your question widely with peers or stakeholders to make sure it addresses their needs (Squires et al., 2013).

You may still consider it appropriate to focus on a narrow review question such as determining the effectiveness of an intervention. As Petticrew and colleagues (2013) note, just because an intervention is complex doesn't mean your review question must adopt a complex perspective. If you do approach your review from a simpler perspective, you'll need to consider the outcomes on which you specifically want to focus. It is also important, even for simpler reviews, to provide descriptive information on the key characteristics of complex interventions so as not to ignore their complexity (Petticrew et al., 2013).

However, often you will need to know more than whether an intervention is effective or not. Perhaps you want to explore why an intervention works (mechanisms of action), explore factors that modify effects of the intervention, whether the intervention is implementable in 'real life', or something else such as what is the theory underpinning the intervention (Petticrew et al., 2013; Squires et al., 2013).

Let us consider our example complex intervention again and identify some review questions that we might ask (see Box 5.6).

 box 5.6

Questions which could be asked in a complex intervention review

Does it work? What is the average effect?

For whom does it work? (Effect on multiple levels?)

- For the individual with Type 1 diabetes.
- Particular subgroups within the Type 1 diabetic population.
- For family members.
- For wider society.

How does the intervention work?

- Theory behind the education interventions – what's it based on?
- Barriers and facilitators of education programmes.
- Mechanism of action and interactions.

2. *Scope of the review: Lumping or splitting*

As apparent from our complex intervention example, you may not find it feasible to ask all the pertinent questions in a single review. So also at this stage, you need to consider what is manageable within the time and resources available. It is likely that much of the evidence will be **heterogeneous** particularly in terms of multiple different study types. To determine how broad the scope of your review should be, you will need to decide whether to lump or split (Squires et al., 2013) your review evidence.

Consider our example again (see Box 5.7).

 box 5.7

Lumping or splitting in our example complex intervention review

Could a study looking at an intense five-consecutive-day education programme be lumped together with a programme which delivered five weekly day sessions?

Could a study delivered by diabetes nurses and dietitian personnel be compared with a programme delivered by peer supporters?

Could a study looking at the effects of education programmes on patient quality of life be compared with those investigating family quality of life?

'Splitters' combine studies that are very similar to each other in terms of design and such PICO attributes as intervention and population. In contrast, 'lumpers' think that, unless there is reason to believe that results from two interventions are opposing, they should be combined (Squires et al., 2013). There is clearly a resource issue here, and those considering either lumping or splitting should consider the implications for the available resources as well as which approach best matches the original decision problem (Weir et al., 2012). To find out more about lumping and splitting, look at the further reading suggested at the end of the chapter.

3. *Specification of the intervention*

When defining your review question you should be as precise as possible in describing the intervention so that you can identify which studies to include in your review. You will find it helpful to carry out a certain amount of background work such as specific scoping searches to investigate how the intervention is described in the literature. Unfortunately, complex interventions are often poorly described, making such definition problematic. One way to overcome inadequate reporting of detail in an index study is to focus your scoping searches on secondary study types such as **process evaluations**, which may provide more detail on the intervention, or to contact authors directly (Squires et al., 2013). You may find it easier to describe interventions pragmatically rather than by theoretical descriptions. Consider, at this stage, whether components of an intervention are essential and core to the description of the intervention, or alternatively whether they may be present yet not essential to the intervention (Squires et al., 2013).

 **box 5.8**

Example review of complex interventions

Crime, fear of crime, environment, and mental health and wellbeing: Mapping review of theories and causal pathways (Lorenc et al., 2012).

Scope of review: The primary aim of the study was to develop a holistic framework on the theoretical links between crime, fear of crime, the environment, and health and wellbeing. The review finding allows an outline of the broader context in which interventions take place and therefore has identified factors which may affect intervention success rate. This information can be used in subsequent reviews of complex interventions in this area.

As complex intervention reviews can involve more background or investigative work at the 'defining the scope' stage, we suggest you consider using tools to assist with this process, the first being logic models which may be particularly useful.

Logic models

A logic model (also known as an impact model) is a type of concept map, originating from programme evaluation. Logic models can be used as summary diagrams of complex interventions and are designed to identify key components and relationships (Anderson et al., 2011; Baxter et al., 2014). Used widely in the field of health promotion, these are considered particularly useful in public health, for exploring complex relationships between practice (inputs and outputs) and outcomes (Baxter et al., 2010). An example of a logic model can be found in Figure 5.1.

Logic models can be useful to clarify and prioritise the review question when defining the scope. Logic models can be used at this stage to understand the complexity of the intervention and make sure that all contributing elements will be explored (Squires et al., 2013).

FURTHER DEFINING YOUR SCOPE

Once you've broken down your research question into concepts, you will need to consider what type of review you will undertake. This will be informed by the quantity of literature on your topic area, and also the type of review that is most useful to answer your question. Chapter 3 discusses how to choose your review methods including the type of literature review appropriate to different scenarios. Typically, focusing your question is an iterative approach that develops during the initial or scoping literature searches (Khan et al., 2001). You may have a relatively clear idea of the area you want to research. By carrying out initial searches of **bibliographic databases** you can identify where the research gaps are and where a review is needed. (Chapter 6 provides details on how to conduct a scoping search.)

At this stage, when you have some results from a scoping search, you can use mapping techniques to define the scope of your research question further. We have already discussed logic models, which although time-consuming and resource intensive are nevertheless useful, particularly for complex reviews. Other mapping processes such as **descriptive mapping**, **data mining** or **text mining** and **concept mapping**, may help you gain a sense of the quantity and characteristics of the literature. In this section we outline these tools with examples and links to resources, where available, that may be used to scope or map the literature.

Descriptive mapping

Descriptive mapping is a way of defining the body of literature on a given topic, by allocating defined keywords to the studies found. It is a form of classification and can help determine what research has been previously carried out as well as identify research gaps (EPPI-Centre, 2010). Organisations such as the EPPI-Centre have devised purpose-specific sets of keywords (EPPI-Centre, 2003). Alternatively you could devise your own keywords tailored to the purposes of your own review.

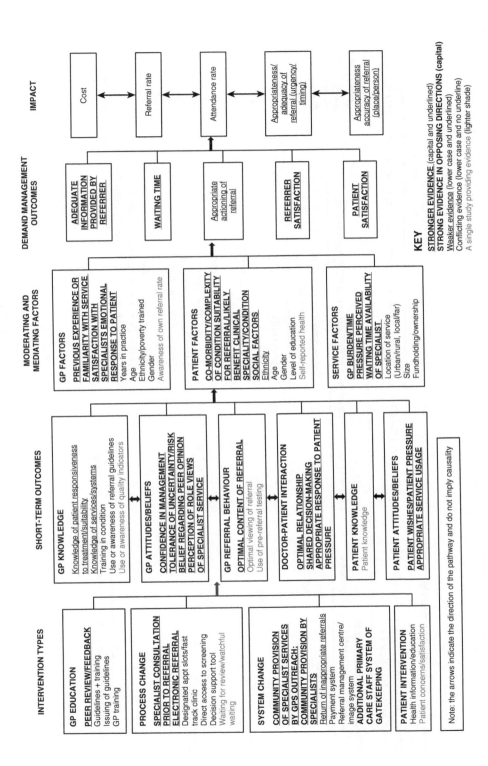

Figure 5.1 Example of a logic model (Baxter et al., 2014)

Table 5.2 Example of a descriptive map

EPPI-Centre team (2003) A systematic map and synthesis review of the effectiveness of personal development planning for improving student learning (EPPI-Centre, Appendix 3.1).

First author and date	Educational setting(s)	Discipline	Course/ qualification	Country	Main features of PDP intervention	Context of learner using PDP
Abbas (1997)	HEI	*Education: teacher training*	*Physical science course*	*USA*	Learning logs/journals/diaries Reflective practice Cooperative learning between students Cooperative learning between student(s)/teacher(s)	Course
Alderman (1993)	HEI	*Psychology*	*BA/BSc*	*USA*	Goal setting Learning logs/journals/diaries Learner training Self-assessment/evaluation	Course
Alvarez (2000)	HEI	*Cosmology*	*Summer school course in astronomy*	*USA*	Independent/autonomous learner Learning logs/journals/diaries Problem-based learning Reflective practice Self-assessment/evaluation Cooperative learning between students Cooperative learning between student(s)/teacher(s)	Course

Source: This table is an extract from Gough et al. (2003). See this publication for the cited references.

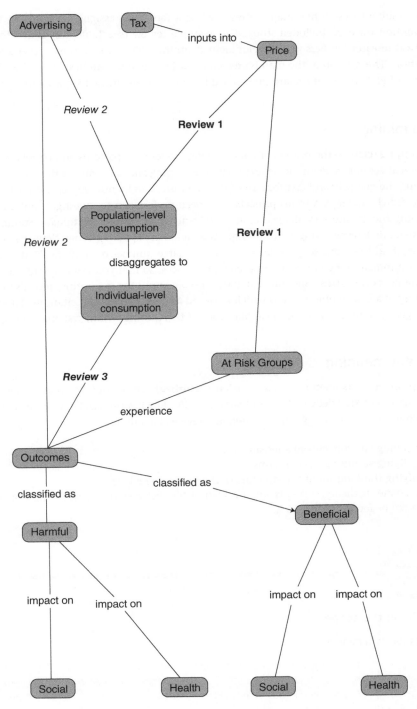

Figure 5.2 Example of a concept map (Booth et al., 2008)

The resultant descriptive map is presented as a table and assigns keywords to the main intervention for each included study. The example review (see Table 5.2) aimed to identify empirical research on Personal Development Planning (PDP) processes in higher and related education. This section of the map is created from 157 included studies. (Note that the 'Main features of PDP intervention' are categorised by a set of standardised keywords.)

Data mining

Data mining refers to the process of analysing data to identify patterns and correlations. It can be useful at various stages of the review, including scoping and determining the review question, mapping the quantity and distribution of the literature, and identifying terminology (useful to inform search strategy). Various projects have been undertaken to investigate automatic ways of mining the literature (Malheiros et al., 2007) including ASSERT (Automatic Summarisation for Systematic Reviews using Text Mining) (Ananiadou et al., 2009). When defining your scope you may find that your scoping searches return a large number of citations. Text mining can help to automate some of the citation screening process so that you can map out the literature (O'Mara-Eves et al., 2015). Shemilt et al. (2014) used text mining to prioritise records for manual screening in a large scoping review which retrieved around 1.85 million citations. Thomas et al. (2011) give a good summary of the applications of text mining within systematic reviews.

Concept mapping

Concept mapping (sometimes know as **idea webbing**) can be useful in making sense of the 'messy nature of knowledge' (Alias and Suradi, 2008). Rowley and Slack (2004) list benefits for using concept maps when planning a literature review, including:

- identifying key concepts in a research area;
- identifying additional search terms;
- clarifying thinking about the structure of the literature review;
- understanding theory, concepts and the relationships between them. An example of a concept map can be found in Figure 5.2.

 toolbox

Defining the scope

Tools for data mining

Scopus is a multidisciplinary database (see Chapter 6 for more details) allowing you to refine search results by source (journal title), author, year, affiliation or subject area. This helps you quickly identify the characteristics of the evidence base for a particular topic area. Categories for refining results are ranked in order, allowing you to see the top journals and authors in your field. You can also add further categories, such as language, document type, keyword and source type.

Web of Knowledge provides access to multidisciplinary databases including Web of Science (see Chapter 6 for more details). Search results can be refined by several categories including subject area, document type, source (journal title), and several others. An advanced option allows you to 'analyse results' where the results can be ranked by various fields (for example source title), helping you to rapidly identify the most common journals in your topic area. This function is available for other fields, such as author, document type, etc.

PubMed PubReMiner searches PubMed on your research topic and ranks your results so that you can see which journals, authors and terms appear most frequently.

Note that other data mining tools specifically for PubMed include:

MScanner – provides rapid statistical classification on the MEDLINE database of biomedical literature.

GoPubMed – uses MeSH terms to increase search possibilities. Results are clustered with results grouped according to MeSH subject headings. An advanced statistics module provides summary statistics for top authors etc.

To find other tools, *Systematic Review (SR) Toolbox* provides a searchable online catalogue of tools to assist you during the systematic review process, including data mining.

Tools for concept mapping

A **mind map** is a diagram used to represent words, ideas, tasks or other concepts linked to, and arranged around, a central key word or idea. You can use free mind-mapping software to construct a **concept map**, including:

- FreeMind;
- Freeplane;
- Docear (note this software is compatible with reference management software, such as Mendeley);
- XMind.

DEFINING THE SCOPE: CHALLENGES AND PITFALLS

As with any stage of a literature review, certain challenges and pitfalls may occur when defining the scope. These range from minor 'nuisance' complications, such as identifying duplicate and/or multiple citations, to more substantive challenges such as deciding which types of studies to include or exclude and how to assess their quality (Kennedy, 2007). In this section, we identify common problems to look out for when defining the scope for your own projects.

Comprehensiveness versus selectivity

A common challenge when defining the scope relates to knowing 'when to stop'. Debate centres on whether you should aim for comprehensiveness (in quantitative terms), **theoretical**

saturation (in qualitative terms), or whether you should aim for a 'representative' approach. Alternatively you might aim to cover key 'pivotal' works in your chosen field (as for a **meta-narrative** review or a **concept analysis**). Whichever approach you choose, and this may be influenced by the time and resources available (a completely comprehensive review may not be feasible), you should be explicit in your methods so that the reader is fully aware of the scope of your review, and the criteria for selection and relevance (Bruce, 2001).

The type of review you choose to write will help you define your scope, as reviews differ in the degree to which they use and report systematic methods. Table 5.3 outlines three review types (scoping, mapping, systematic) and their respective purposes. For each review type it provides an illustrative example together with details of the scope covered.

Table 5.3 Types of review: scope

Type of review	Purpose	Example
Scoping review	To find out how much literature exists. To find out the characteristics of the literature.	O'Malley and Croucher (2005): the scope of this review focuses on UK studies of housing and accommodation related to dementia published since the early 1980s, with the aim of identifying gaps in existing knowledge.
Mapping review	Aims to identify gaps in the literature in order to commission further research.	Groves et al., 2006: the scope of this review focuses on Australian research (although some international research has been included for context). The timeframe is from 1990 onwards, although the authors state that research prior to this has been included if appropriate.
Systematic review	Aims to be comprehensive. Scope should be well-defined and clearly stated. Systematic reviews tend to focus on the highest quality evidence available.	Edwards et al., 2002: the scope of this review was to find all RCTs of strategies to influence the response to a postal questionnaire. Note that although the authors are based in health research, the review is not restricted to medical surveys, it covers any questionnaire topic in any population. Studies in all languages were included.

Scope creep

A major problem in the literature review process is **scope creep**, i.e. your review question getting wider and wider until it is unmanageable. Scope creep is defined as:

> uncontrolled changes over time to a project's aims, direction, scale and/or timescale and, more specifically, the gradual unchecked expansion of the project's objectives. (Saunders, 2009)

Scope creep can occur at any point during the review process, particularly when you are searching the literature. You should constantly refer back to your original scope to ensure your project does not go off track. There is a tension between what is interesting and what is useful – references may catch your attention, but may not be directly relevant to answer your research question. Of course, you may face a situation where you need to make an amendment to the original scope. You can manage this using a **changes clause** (Matchar et al., 2006), which is particularly important when working on official contracts and/or as part of a wider research team.

THE REVIEW PROTOCOL

Once you have defined your review scope, you can start to write your review protocol. As with any project, your literature review should be carefully planned (see Chapter 4). It is good practice to write a review protocol in advance as this is where you outline what you are planning to do. As with a research proposal for a primary research project, the protocol describes each step of the review process: 'The protocol sets out the methods of the review' (Centre for Reviews and Dissemination, 2009).

The review protocol has three main functions:

1. Protection against **bias** – by clearly describing your methods you are ensuring rigour and minimising potential bias.
2. As a practical tool for conducting the methods of the review – by following your protocol closely you protect your review from deviating from the agreed methods. This is particularly useful when working within a wider project team as it ensures that all members follow the same procedures. A protocol can also be very useful when you are writing up your project – in writing a protocol you are effectively writing your 'Methods' section in the future tense, so if you follow it closely you will only need to change the wording to the past tense for your final report.
3. Staking your claim to the topic – this is vital if your protocol is to be published, for example if you are conducting a **Cochrane Review**.

The main components of a protocol are shown in Box 5.9.

 box 5.9

Components of a protocol

- Background.
- Review question.
- Search strategy (including search terms and resources to be searched).
- Study selection criteria and procedures.
- Study quality assessment checklists and procedures.
- Data extraction strategy.
- Synthesis of the extracted evidence.
- Project timetable.

Examples of review protocols

Look at protocols from your own research area to see how a protocol looks in practice (see Table 5.4 for suggested examples).

Table 5.4   Review protocol examples

Area of research	Topic
Computer science	Protocol for systematic review of within- and cross-company estimation models (Kitchenham et al., 2006)
Education	The impact of collaborative CPD on classroom teaching and learning (Cordingley et al., 2004)
Healthcare	PROSPERO: International prospective register for systematic reviews
Information science	Impact of school library services on achievement and learning (Williams et al., 2001: 77)
Management	Exploration into the relationship between managers' sensemaking and CSR outcomes (Jackson, 2009: 11)
Social care	Protocol guidelines for systematic reviews of home modification information to inform best practice (Bridge and Phibbs, 2013)

To familiarise yourself with reviews in your own subject area and to identify what you can learn from them for your own review, complete Exercise 5.2.

 **exercise 5.2**

Examining a review protocol

Either examine one of the review protocols from Table 5.4 or one that you have identified yourself, and consider the following:

- What are the key databases and sources within my discipline?
- What methodological documentation does the author cite that may be of value for my own review?
- What does the way that the review protocol is organised and presented tell you about the quantity and quality of the literature available in your field?

Now consider your own review, and begin to fill in the review protocol template in Exercise 5.3.

 **exercise 5.3**

The review protocol template

Start to fill in the blank version of the review protocol template (see https://study.sagepub.com/booth2e) for your own review. Table 5.5 provides further information on which sort of information you should include within each section in the review protocol template. You may find that you are only able to complete the first few sections at this stage. As you work your way through the remaining chapters of this book, you can add to each section of the template, ultimately to create a complete protocol. You will find it helpful to follow the reporting standards for review protocols (PRISMA-P) (Moher et al., 2015)

Table 5.5 Instructions for completing the review protocol template

Background

The background should set the context for your review, introducing the reader to your topic, without needing specialist knowledge to understand the area of research. This may include relevant current statistics and previous research, highlighting the importance for your review.

Objectives

Here you should outline the aims of your review and the research question(s) you are attempting to answer.

Criteria for inclusion and exclusion of studies

In this section, you should record how you will decide which studies to include and which to exclude. It is helpful to define this by key concepts such as study design, population, intervention, etc., as outlined in the following sections.

Types of studies

Which type of study design(s) are you going to include/exclude? For example, randomised controlled studies/cohort studies/qualitative studies/surveys?

Types of populations

Revisit your focused question and record the type(s) of population you are going to include/exclude.

Types of interventions or exposure

Revisit your focused question and record the type(s) of intervention(s)/exposure(s) you are going to include/exclude.

Types of outcome measures

Revisit your focused question and record the type(s) of outcome you are going to include/exclude. If you have a broad outcome such as whether an intervention is 'effective' you may want to define this further here. For example, in the question 'Is e-learning effective in teaching undergraduate students information literacy skills?' you may define effectiveness in terms of assignment marks and you would exclude any studies that did not measure this outcome. Note that it is possible to look at more than one outcome here.

Setting/context (where applicable)

If your research question applies to a particular setting or context, record which you will include/exclude here. For example, if you are only interested in studies taking place in a particular country, you can exclude studies from other countries. However, please be aware that this may limit your review too much, so you may have to look at any comparable settings also – for example, Europe rather than the UK.

Search strategy for identification of studies (see Chapter 6 for more details)

Here you should record your methodology for finding studies under the following headings:

Electronic databases to be used – which sources will you search?

Other search methods – such as hand searching, reference checking, citation searching, etc.

Keywords and sample search strategy – here you should include initial ideas for search terms. You may also find it useful to provide an example search strategy from any scoping searches you have done.

Study selection (see Chapter 7)

- Remember to include who will select studies and how they will do so. For example, if you are working within a project team you should state which project team members will be selecting the studies and how any disagreements would be resolved. If you are conducting all aspects of the review single-handedly, record that it is you who will be selecting the studies. It may be useful to record the process you will follow here – such as title sift, abstract sift, full-text sift, etc.

(Continued)

(Continued)

Assessment of methodological quality (see Chapter 7)

- Here you will record how you plan to assess the methodological quality of your included studies. Remember to include details of any specific checklists that you will use.

Data extraction (see Chapters 8 and 9)

- What data will you extract (variables, themes, etc.)? If you plan to use/adapt an existing data extraction form you should record the details here. If you plan to design your own, state this intention here.

Data synthesis (see Chapters 8 and 9)

- What will your data look like – qualitative or quantitative or a combination?
- How you will synthesise those data – will you use narrative synthesis, thematic synthesis or some other method? Tables, figures or as text?

Timeframe (see Chapter 4)

List the stages of the review and outline how long each stage of the review will take you. This will help you set milestones by which you can assess your progress.

Task	Timescale
Literature search	
Study selection	
Data extraction	
Data synthesis	
Writing up review	

You may find it helpful to construct a Gantt chart or similar if several stages will take place at the same time. Computer-based project management programs allow you to do this, such as Microsoft Project. It is possible to use Excel for this purpose. Free open source software is also available such as GanttProject.

SUMMARY

Defining the scope provides a solid foundation for your subsequent review. You may find it useful to use a published framework for formulating your research question. Conducting a scoping search is useful at this stage to assess if your review is feasible, both in terms of establishing its uniqueness (are there any existing reviews in your topic area?) and in terms of the size and characteristics of the evidence base. Consider mapping the literature identified in your scoping search. Various tools and approaches can assist you with this, including logic models, data mining and concept mapping. Challenges you may face during your scoping, in deciding on the aspiration of your review (is your aim to be comprehensive or selective?), will be informed by the literature and the type of review that you choose to undertake. Beware of scope creep, where items of interest distract you from the original aim of your review. You can avoid scope creep by drawing up a review protocol at the outset and following the protocol during your decision making, particularly in implementing inclusion and exclusion criteria. If you need to change the scope of your review you can handle this by including a **changes clause** in your protocol.

key learning points

- Formulate your research question using a published framework (such as PICO) to assist you where possible.
- Consider the requirements of your audience when defining the scope of your review.
- Conduct a scoping search on key databases to identify the literature available.
- Consider mapping the literature using a tool such as a logic model or similar.
- Beware of challenges and pitfalls, such as scope creep.
- Complete a review protocol before embarking on your review.

frequently asked questions (FAQs)

FAQ 5.1 None of the frameworks fit my question. How can I formulate my research idea?

The frameworks are only prompts so don't feel that you have to use every element of a framework. For example, it might not be relevant to define a Comparison when using the SPICE framework, so simply leave it out. Secondly, take a step back and approach your research from using the simplest 'framework' – ask the 'Who, what and how?' questions to break down your idea (see Box 5.1).

FAQ 5.2 With so much literature in my review topic, how can I review this systematically?

If there is a wealth of literature, you need to consider, a) what is the most important aspect that you need to glean from the literature, and b) how much is manageable. You might need to start with a scoping or mapping review to systematically map out the literature before deciding on elements of the literature to be explored in more depth. Tools such as data/text mining may help make screening the literature more manageable.

FAQ 5.3 My research question is actually four or five questions, is this a problem?

Given the variety of possible questions that you might like to ask when defining your review scope you will need to limit your questions to what is manageable and answerable. Otherwise you'll discover the hard way that it is not possible to answer all the questions. Consider using a logic model to prioritise your research question. Time spent planning at the beginning of your review is time well spent to avoid tackling an unanswerable question.

FAQ 5.4 I had identified a defined question but my scoping search identified nothing in this area, what shall I do?

Don't be disheartened! This is common and defining your research question is an iterative process. You may need to modify, expand or even eventually reject your question. However, it

(Continued)

(Continued)

is better to discover this at the scoping stage than to get too far into the review process and then realise that your question is not answerable.

FAQ 5.5 Is it really necessary to formally complete the review protocol as I have notes on how I will conduct the review?

Yes, your review will benefit greatly from having a formal review protocol. It serves as a document to which you can constantly refer in order to keep your review on track. The review protocol is particularly useful when working as part of a wider review team as it ensures that you are all following the same review recipe. In addition, a well-written review protocol assists when writing the methodology section of your review – you should be able to change the future tense into the past tense!

FAQ 5.6 When is is appropriate to make changes to the review scope?

There are various reasons why you might need to change the scope during your review. Hopefully, a well-planned review will avoid this, but sometimes you have to change scope due to resourcing, funding or scheduling issues. By conducting a scoping search you should be aware of the characteristics of the literature. This helps ensure that you do not need to broaden or narrow the scope later down the line. It is also important to ensure there is not a recent existing review on your topic. Also check the PROSPERO systematic reviews register for existing reviews being undertaken, to ensure that a similar review is not just about to be published!

--- **suggestions for further reading** ---

Durham University (2009) *Template for a Systematic Literature Review Protocol.*
A useful list of section headings and the various elements to include in a protocol for a systematic literature review.

Craig, P., Dieppe, P.A., Macintyre, S., Michie, S., Nazareth, I. and Petticrew, M. (2008) Developing and evaluating complex interventions: the new Medical Research Council guidance. *BMJ*, **337**, 979, e83.
Guidance from the Medical Research Council on developing and evaluating complex interventions. Provides a good overview to increase your understanding, including what makes an intervention complex.

Petticrew, M., Anderson, L., Elder, R., Grimshaw, J., Hopkins, D., Hahn, R., Krause, L., Kristjansson, E., Mercer, S., Sipe, T., Tugwell, P., Ueffing, E., Waters, E. and Welch, V. (2013) Complex interventions and their implications for systematic reviews: a pragmatic approach. *Journal of Clinical Epidemiology*, **66**, 11, 1209–14.
A practical approach to undertaking systematic reviews of complex interventions, including clarifying the review question, implications for inclusion criteria and approaches to synthesis of a multiplicity of outcomes.

Rowley, J. and Slack, F. (2004) Conducting a literature review. *Management Research News*, **27**, 4, 31–9.

See the section on developing conceptual frameworks and mind mapping.

Software Engineering Group, School of Computer Science and Mathematics, Keele University and Department of Computer Science, University of Durham (2007) *Guidelines for Performing Systematic Literature Reviews in Software Engineering.*
See Section 5 on Planning which covers formulating your research question and developing a review protocol.

Squires, J.E., Valentine, J.C. and Grimshaw, J.M. (2013) Systematic reviews of complex interventions: framing the review question. *Journal of Clinical Epidemiology*, **66**, 11, 1215–22.
A helpful guide to formulate a review question for a systematic review of complex interventions.

REFERENCES

Alias, M. and Suradi, Z. (2008) Concept mapping: a tool for creating a literature review. In A.J. Canas, P. Reiska, M. Åhlberg and J.D. Novak (eds), *Concept Mapping: Connecting Educators*. Tallinn and Helsinki: The Second International Conference on Concept Mapping.

Ananiadou, S., Okazaki, N., Procter, R., Rea, B., Sasaki, Y. and Thomas, J. (2009) Supporting systematic reviews using text mining. *Social Science Computer Review*, **27**, 4, 509–23.

Anderson, L.M., Petticrew, M., Rehfuess, E., Armstrong, R., Ueffing, E., Baker, P. and Tugwell, P. (2011) Using logic models to capture complexity in systematic reviews. *Research Synthesis Methods*, **2**, 1, 33–42.

Baxter, S., Killoran, A., Kelly, M.P. and Goyder, E. (2010) Synthesizing diverse evidence: the use of primary qualitative data analysis methods and logic models in public health reviews. *Public Health*, **124**, 2, 99–106.

Baxter, S.K., Blank, L., Woods, H.B., Payne, N., Melanie, R. and Goyder, E. (2014) Using logic model methods in systematic review synthesis: describing complex pathways in referral management interventions. *BMC Medical Research Methodology*, **14**, 1, 62.

Boote, J., Baird, W. and Sutton, A. (2011) Public involvement in the systematic review process in health and social care: a narrative review of case examples. *Health Policy*, **102**, 2–3, 105–16.

Boote, J., Baird, W. and Sutton, A. (2012) Involving the public in systematic reviews: a narrative review of organizational approaches and eight case examples. *Journal of Comparative Effectiveness Research*, **1**, 5, 409–20.

Booth, A. (2004) Formulating answerable questions. In A. Booth and A. Brice (eds), *Evidence Based Practice for Information Professionals: A Handbook*. London: Facet, 59–66.

Booth, A. (2006) Clear and present questions: formulating questions for evidence based practice. *Library Hi tech*, **24**, 3, 355–68.

Booth, A., Meier, P., Stockwell, T., Sutton, A., Wilkinson, A., Wong, R., Brennan, A., O'Reilly, D., Purshouse, R. and Taylor, K. (2008) *Independent Review of the Effects of Alcohol Pricing and Promotion. Part A: Systematic Reviews*. Sheffield: University of Sheffield.

Bridge, C. and Phibbs, P. (2013) *Protocol Guidelines for Systematic Reviews of Home Modification: Information to Inform Best Practice*. Faculties of Health Science and Architecture, University of Sydney: Home Modification and Maintenance Information Clearinghouse Project.

Bruce, C. (2001) Interpreting the scope of their literature reviews: significant differences in research students' concerns. *New Library World*, **102**, 158–65.

Centre for Reviews and Dissemination (2009) *CRD's Guidance for Undertaking Reviews in Health Care*. CRD, University of York.

Cooke, A., Smith D. and Booth, A. (2012) Beyond PICO: the SPIDER tool for qualitative evidence synthesis. *Qualitative Health Research*, **22**, 10, 1435–43.

Cordingley, P., Bell, M. and Thomason, S. (2004) *The Impact of Collaborative CPD on Classroom Teaching and Learning. Protocol: How do Collaborative and Sustained CPD and Sustained but not Collaborative CPD Affect Teaching and Learning?* London: EPPI-Centre.

Counsell, C. (1997) Formulating questions and locating primary studies for inclusion in systematic reviews. *Annals of Internal Medicine*, **127**, 5, 380.

Craig, P., Dieppe, P.A., Macintyre, S., Michie, S., Nazareth, I. and Petticrew, M. (2008) Developing and evaluating complex interventions: the new Medical Research Council guidance. *BMJ*, **337**, 979, e83.

Davies, K.S. (2011) Formulating the evidence based practice question: a review of the frameworks. *Evidence Based Library and Information Practice*, **6**, 2, 75–80.

Denyer, D. and Tranfield, D. (2009) Producing a systematic review. In D.A. Buchanan and A. Bryman (eds), *The Sage Handbook of Organizational Research Methods*. London: Sage, 671–89.

Edwards, P., Roberts, I., Clarke, M., DiGuiseppi, C., Pratap, S., Wentz, R. and Kwan, I. (2002) Increasing response rates to postal questionnaires: systematic review. *British Medical Journal*, **324**: 1183–92.

EPPI-Centre (2003) *EPPI-Centre Educational Keywording Sheet*. London: Social Science Research Unit, UCL Institute of Education.

EPPI-Centre (2010) *Methods for Conducting Systematic Reviews*. London: Social Science Research Unit, UCL Institute of Education.

Gough, D.A., Kiwan, D., Sutcliffe, K., Simpson, D. and Houghton, N. (2003) *A Systematic Map and Synthesis Review of the Effectiveness of Personal Development Planning for Improving Student Learning*. London: EPPI-Centre, Social Science Research Unit.

Groves, S., Mousely, J. and Forgasz, H. (2006) *Primary Numeracy: A Mapping, Review and Analysis of Australian Research in Numeracy Learning at the Primary School Level*. Waurn Ponds, Australia: Centre for Studies in Mathematics, Science and Environmental Education, Deakin University.

Ibrahim, R. (2008) Setting up a research question for determining the research methodology. *ALAM CIPTA, International Journal on Sustainable Tropical Design Research and Practice*, **3**, 1, 99–102.

Jackson, S. (2009) *Exploration into the Relationship between Managers' Sensemaking and CSR Outcomes*. MSc by Research in Leading, Learning and Change Thesis, Cranfield University.

Kennedy, M.M. (2007) Defining a literature. *Educational Researcher*, **36**, 3, 139.

Khan, K.S., ter Rief, G., Glanville, J., Sowden, A.J. and Kleijnen, J. (2001) *Undertaking Systematic Reviews of Research on Effectiveness: CRD's Guidance for Those Carrying Out or Commissioning Reviews*. York: NHS Centre for Reviews and Dissemination, University of York.

Kitchenham, B., Mendes, E. and Travassos, G. (2006) *Protocol for Systematic Review of Within- and Cross-Company Estimation Models*. Evidence-Based Software Engineering. Available at https://community.dur.ac.uk/ebse/study.php?type=protocol&id=5.

Lorenc, T., Clayton, S., Neary, D., Whitehead, M., Petticrew, M., Thomson, H. and Renton, A. (2012) Crime, fear of crime, environment, and mental health and wellbeing: mapping review of theories and causal pathways. *Health & Place*, **18**, 4, 757–65.

Malheiros, V., Hohn, E., Pinho, R., Mendonça, M. and Maldonado, J.C. (2007) A visual text mining approach for systematic reviews. In *ESEM '07: Proceedings of the First International Symposium on Empirical Software Engineering and Measurement*. IEEE Computer Society, Washington, DC, 245–54.

Matchar, D.B., Patwardhan, M., Sarria-Santamera, A. and Westermann-Clark, E.V. (2006) *Developing a Methodology for Establishing a Statement of Work for a Policy-Relevant Technical Analysis. Technical Review 11*. (Prepared by the Duke Evidence-based Practice Center under

Contract No. 290–02–0025.) Agency for Healthcare Research and Quality, Rockville, MD, AHRQ Publication No. 06–0026.

Methley, A.M., Campbell, S., Chew-Graham, C., McNally, R. and Cheraghi-Sohi, S. (2014) PICO, PICOS and SPIDER: a comparison study of specificity and sensitivity in three search tools for qualitative systematic reviews. *BMC Health Services Research*, **14**, 579. Available at http://bmchealthservres.biomedcentral.com/articles/10.1186/s12913-014-0579-0

Moher, D., Shamseer, L., Clarke, M., Ghersi, D., Liberati, A., Petticrew, M., Shekelle, P. and Stewart, L.A. (2015) Preferred reporting items for systematic review and meta-analysis protocols (PRISMA-P) 2015 statement. *Systematic Reviews*, **4**, 1, 1.

O'Malley, L. and Croucher, K. (2005) Housing and dementia care – a scoping review of the literature. *Health and Social Care in the Community*, **13**, 6, 570–7.

O'Mara-Eves, A., Thomas, J., McNaught, J., Miwa, M. and Ananiadou, S. (2015) Using text mining for study identification in systematic reviews: a systematic review of current approaches. *Systematic Reviews*, **4**, 1, 5.

Oxman, A.D. and Guyatt, G.H. (1988) Guidelines for reading literature reviews. *Canadian Medical Association Journal*, **138**, 8, 697.

Petticrew, M., Anderson, L., Elder, R., Grimshaw, J., Hopkins, D., Hahn, R., Krause, L., Kristjansson, E., Mercer, S., Sipe, T., Tugwell, P., Ueffing, E., Waters, E. and Welch, V. (2013) Complex interventions and their implications for systematic reviews: a pragmatic approach. *Journal of Clinical Epidemiology*, **66**, 11, 1209–14.

Petticrew, M. and Roberts, H. (2006) *Systematic Reviews in the Social Sciences: A Practical Guide*. Malden, MA: Blackwell.

Richardson, W.S., Wilson, M.C., Nishikawa, J. and Hayward, R.S. (1995) The well-built clinical question: a key to evidence-based decisions. *ACP Journal Club*, **123**, 3, A12.

Rowley, J. and Slack, F. (2004) Conducting a literature review. *Management Research News*, **27**, 6, 31–9.

Saunders, L. (2009) *The Policy and Organisational Context for Commissioned Research*. London: British Educational Research Association, TLRP 29 November.

Shemilt, I., Simon, A., Hollands, G.J., Marteau, T. M., Ogilvie, D., O'Mara-Eves, A. and Thomas, J. (2014) Pinpointing needles in giant haystacks: use of text mining to reduce impractical screening workload in extremely large scoping reviews. *Research Synthesis Methods*, **5**, 1, 31–49.

Squires, J.E., Valentine, J.C. and Grimshaw, J.M. (2013) Systematic reviews of complex interventions: framing the review question. *Journal of Clinical Epidemiology*, **66**, 11, 1215–22.

Stern, C., Jordan, Z. and McArthur, A. (2014) Developing the review question and inclusion criteria. *American Journal of Nursing*, **114**, 4, 53–6.

Thomas, J., McNaught, J. and Ananiadou, S. (2011) Applications of text mining within systematic reviews. *Research Synthesis Methods*, **2**, 1, 1–14.

Weir, M.C., Grimshaw, J.M., Mayhew, A. and Fergusson, D. (2012) Decisions about lumping vs. splitting of the scope of systematic reviews of complex interventions are not well justified: a case study in systematic reviews of health care professional reminders. *Journal of Clinical Epidemiology*, **65**, 7, 756–63.

Williams, D., Wavell, C. and Coles, L. (2001) *Impact of School Library Services on Achievement and Learning*. Aberdeen: The Robert Gordon University.

6

SEARCHING THE LITERATURE

 — in a nutshell

How to conduct a literature search

- Identification of evidence is a key component within any literature review.
- Having developed a structured research question, this chapter helps you translate your question into its relevant search concepts.
- A systematic literature search is an essential component of any systematic review.
- Tools and exercises can assist you to devise a search strategy and identify appropriate sources of information to be searched.
- Several techniques exist to make your literature search more systematic, and to identify how to review and refine your search as necessary.

INTRODUCTION

The purpose of the literature search is to identify information for your research topic. A successful literature search allows you to identify 'research gaps' enabling you to investigate a unique aspect of a topic. Literature searching also helps you design the methodology for your own research by identifying the techniques or methodologies most appropriate for your topic (Hart, 2002).

Searching the literature systematically entails more than seeking a quick answer from one or two selected articles. For whatever type of literature review you undertake, you can enhance the credibility of your review findings and conclusions by demonstrating that you have thoroughly searched for evidence.

Systematic literature search techniques optimise **sensitivity,** i.e. they maximise the chance of retrieving relevant items for your review. Of course, the downside to this approach is that whilst you reduce the risk of missing a relevant item, the number of irrelevant records you have to look through may increase (**number needed to read (NNR)**). In contrast, whenever you are looking for a specific known item, you utilise techniques that optimise **specificity**, i.e. where you do not spend much time looking at irrelevant articles but face a higher likelihood that you have missed some additional relevant ones.

This chapter covers the processes and methods that make a literature search more systematic. Throughout the chapter we reference various tools, of different degrees of usefulness, depending on your topic and the extent to which you require your review to be systematic. The chapter draws upon methods used in **systematic review**. As discussed in Chapter 2, a systematic review is commonly defined as a type of literature review that aims to identify *all* the available evidence so as to reduce the effect of **bias** on the review findings. Methods for literature searching to identify evidence for systematic reviews of healthcare interventions were the first to be developed (Centre for Reviews and Dissemination, 2009; Higgins and Green, 2011), however, extensive guidance has been developed for identification of evidence for systematic reviews of non-health topics such as the social sciences (Petticrew and Roberts, 2006). Similarly, whilst the guidance on systematic searching for health topics tends to focus on the retrieval of quantitative evidence, methods for identifying evidence for qualitative systematic reviews are increasingly documented (Booth, 2011).

This chapter cannot teach you how to undertake a literature search for a systematic review. Rather by examining the ways in which systematic reviews identify evidence, we show you how you can utilise the same techniques to make the way in which you search the literature for your review more systematic, whatever the topic area. Depending on the purpose of your review, some techniques are more appropriate than others. Nevertheless, carrying out a literature search in a more systematic manner will result in more comprehensive retrieval of literature and therefore more meaningful and credible review findings that are less prone to bias.

As with the previous chapter on 'Defining Your Scope', this chapter explores literature searching in general, with a focus on relatively simple research questions – for example is X effective for Y? However, the techniques presented transfer to all types of research question. You may find that the approach you would take for a **complex intervention** question, such as the one presented in Chapter 5 (*Education programmes to teach Type 1 diabetic patients how to self-manage their condition effectively*) may require alternative approaches in both the planning and conducting of your literature search. This is explored briefly in this chapter, but we recommend that you visit further reading on the topic before embarking on a literature search for complex interventions.

The chapter starts by describing the five different stages in the search process and the various methods or techniques to systematically identify the evidence for a literature review. The next section considers the search methods for different types of literature reviews such as **scoping**, mapping and systematic reviews (including qualitative reviews). A practical section then demonstrates how to translate the clearly formulated research questions from Chapter 5 into a **search strategy**. Throughout the chapter, we refer to examples from different disciplines; however, you will find it useful to consider each section in the light of your own literature review topic.

STAGES IN THE LITERATURE SEARCHING PROCESS

A systematic search necessitates multiple approaches or techniques which may comprise some (but not always all) of the following major search strategies: (a) searches in **subject indexes**, (b) consultation with experts in the topic area, (c) browsing, (d) **citation searching**, and (e) **footnote chasing** (Wilson, 1992). This is not an exhaustive list and the approaches are not mutually exclusive; however, we will examine how they are used in the five distinct phases of the search process (see Table 6.1).

Table 6.1 The stages of the search process

Stage	Description	Steps
Stage 1	Initial search of the literature: scoping search	• Search for existing reviews and familiarise yourself with the topic and volume of literature by a scoping search on select databases (one or two key databases) • Determine which databases are to be included in the full search • Identify key search terms • Develop and document a search strategy
Stage 2	Conduct search	• Search all databases using the identified search terms and the key search principles where appropriate: free-text terms and tools, thesaurus terms, operators and limits • Conduct a search for unpublished or **grey literature** • Consider the appropriateness of a methodological search filter • Ensure if the search is modified, this is documented
Stage 3	Bibliography search	• Search the reference lists and bibliographies of all included studies for any additional relevant studies • Identify any key citations and conduct citation searches • Consider hand searching key journals
Stage 4	Verification	• Check indexing of any relevant papers that have apparently been missed by search strategies • Revise search strategies if necessary • Consider contact with experts to determine if all relevant papers have been retrieved
Stage 5	Documentation	Record details such as the sources searched, search strategies used, and number of references found for each source/method of searching (NB: although listed as Stage 5 here, it is helpful to document your searches and any additional techniques as you perform them)

 box 6.1

An important reminder

Remember, this chapter is not suggesting that to carry out a systematic search you have to use every single one of these techniques! It is true that by using all the techniques described in this chapter, there is less risk of missing a relevant study for your review. However, you have to weigh up these techniques in relation to the purpose of your review, and the time and resources available. The approaches used in different types of literature review are presented in Table 6.6.

STAGE 1: SCOPING SEARCH

To begin you will find it helpful to undertake a **scoping search**. This is a preliminary search usually focusing on identifying existing reviews, and giving an indication of the existing quantity and quality of **primary studies** relevant to the objectives of your review. This scoping search is ideally performed on a selection of core **electronic databases** and **grey literature** sources (see sources for Tables 6.2 and 6.3) relevant to your topic area.

sources

Table 6.2 lists common electronic databases (by subject area) together with sources of grey literature. Most electronic databases provide a free guide to searching on the database, offering hints, tips and search tutorials as well as explaining the individual features of the database.

Table 6.2   Electronic databases: subject specific

Database	Coverage
Health	
Allied and Complementary Medicine Database (AMED)	Professions allied to medicine
	Alternative and complementary medicine
	Palliative care
BIOSIS	Biology and biomedical sciences (including botany, zoology, microbiology, biomedical science, ecology, biotechnology, biophysics, biochemistry and agriculture)
British Nursing Index	Nursing and midwifery
CINAHL	Nursing and allied health
The Cochrane Library includes:	
Cochrane Database of Systematic Reviews (CDSR)	Cochrane systematic reviews and protocols
Cochrane Central Register of Controlled Trials (CENTRAL)	Controlled trials included in Cochrane systematic reviews
Centre for Reviews and Dissemination Databases includes:	
Database of Abstracts of Reviews of Effects (DARE)*	Abstracts of systematic reviews including quality assessment of reviews
Health Technology Assessment database (HTA)	Health technology assessments from around the world
NHS Economic Evaluation Database (NHS EED)*	Health economic papers including economic evaluations
*Please note that DARE and NHS EED ceased to be updated on 31 March 2015	

(Continued)

(Continued)

Database	Coverage
Embase	Biomedical and pharmacological sciences, as well as general medicine
MEDLINE/PubMed (includes the MEDLINE database plus additional citations such as 'in process' and 'ahead of print')	General medical and biomedical sciences. Includes medicine, dentistry, nursing, allied health
PsycINFO	Psychology and related fields
ScHARRHUD	Studies reporting health state utility values
Social sciences	
ASSIA	Social sciences, includes sociology, psychology and some anthropology, economics, medicine, law and politics
Campbell Library	Systematic reviews of the effects of social interventions produced by the Campbell Collaboration: includes social welfare, crime and justice, education
International Bibliography of Social Sciences	Social sciences including economics, sociology, politics and anthropology
Sociological abstracts	Sociology and related disciplines
Social Science Citation Index	Social sciences
Social care	
Social Care Online (replaced Caredata)	Social work and community care
Social Services Abstracts	Social work, human services and related areas
Social Work Abstracts	Social work and human services
Education	
Australian Education index	Education (Australia)
British Education Index	Education (Europe)
Education Resources Information Centre (ERIC)	Education (US emphasis)
Information studies	
Library, Information Science Abstracts (LISA)	Library and information sciences
Library, Information Science and Technology Abstracts (LISTA)	
Computer sciences	
Computer and information systems abstracts	Broad coverage of computer sciences
IEEE/IET Electronic Library (IEL)	Electrical engineering, computer science and related technologies
Business and management	
Business Source Premier	Business research including marketing, management, accounting, finance and economics

Database	Coverage
Multidisciplinary	
Web of Science	Comprises: • Arts and humanities citation index • Science citation index expanded • Social sciences citation index • Conference proceedings citation index – science • Conference proceedings citation index – social sciences and humanities (NB these indexes can either be searched individually or simultaneously)
Scopus	• Chemistry, physics, mathematics, engineering • Life and health sciences • Social sciences, psychology and economics • Biological, agricultural and environmental sciences
Emerald Insight	Books and journals relating to a range of subjects including accounting and finance, management, marketing, education, information studies and engineering.
Google Scholar	Search tool dedicated to academic content

Table 6.3 Grey literature

General sources:

• GreySource, which contains a selection of online grey literature in a variety of subject areas
• Touro College Libraries: Gray Literature, contains a number of online grey literature sources including sources for Humanities, Business, Jewish Studies, Education and Psychology, Mathematics and Science, Health Sciences and the Social Sciences

Ongoing research: Research registers

• UKCRN
• ISRCTN Register

Databases

• OpenGrey
• Social care online
  o ProQuest Dissertations & Theses (UK and International)
  o EThOS e-theses online (via The British Library)

Conference abstracts

• Web of Science indexes international conference proceedings and has two conference proceedings databases: (i) Science (ii) Social sciences and humanities
• British Education Index includes conference proceedings index
• Topic specific conferences: check websites. For example in cancer: ASCO, ESMO; or in library and information science: UMBRELLA/CILIP Conference

Websites – examples

• Social research: Joseph Rowntree Foundation
• Social sciences: Economic and Social Research Council
• Mental health research: Centre for Mental Health
• Education research: Higher Education Academy
• Economics Research: National Bureau of Economics Research Working Papers
• Criminology, University of Toronto, CrimDoc (Criminology Library Grey Literature)

If your topic is multidisciplinary, you will want your scoping search to purposively sample from a range of subject disciplines. To conduct the scoping search, revisit your research question and list the various synonyms for each concept of your query (defined using the PICOC framework or similar).

Example

Revisiting the research question presented in Chapter 5: what are the economic and social implications of school age drinking? Here is what a first attempt at generating synonyms to be used for a scoping search might look like:

P = children, adolescents, teenagers, young adults, young people, girls, boys, school age ...

I = drinking, alcohol.

C = NB as the comparator is 'nothing' - not drinking, it is not necessary to include this in the search.

O = NB for the scoping search, try the search without outcomes and see whether you retrieve a manageable number of results. If you need to narrow the search further, add outcome terms as identified in Chapter 5. Note that the search will be most effective if you search for 'outcomes' in general and also specifically named outcomes such as 'emotional development' etc.

C = *UK, United Kingdom, Great Britain, England, Scotland, Wales, Northern Ireland. For information on Search Filters to identify studies from specific geographic locations, please see the section on search filters below.*

Complex intervention scoping search

To conduct a scoping search for a complex intervention question you will probably start with the key concepts – from the example *Education programmes to teach Type 1 diabetic patients how to self-manage their condition effectively* you may search for 'self-management', 'diabetes' and 'education' as a starting point. From this initial search, you could examine the titles and identify relevant papers, visiting the reference lists of these papers to identify further relevant studies. By taking this approach, you will gain an overall picture of the types of literature that may contribute to answering the question. For complex interventions, you will need to take an iterative approach to your searching, conducting focused searches on electronic databases supplemented with additional search techniques, such as citation searching (Levay et al., 2016), reference list checking, snowballing and hand searching, so it makes sense to use a similar approach to your scoping search (Greenhalgh and Peacock, 2005; Booth et al., 2013).

Results from the scoping search can help you focus or refocus your literature review, depending on what you find. For example, if you identify an unmanageable amount of literature you may need to narrow the focus of your question. Conversely, if you retrieve too little literature, making comparisons difficult, you may need to broaden your question. Whilst viewing the titles, abstracts, subject headings and keyword descriptors of relevant citations, you can refine your search strategy to make it as exhaustive (that is sensitive) as possible. The scoping process, therefore, enables you to begin developing the search strategy to be used in conducting the search itself (Stage 2). After completing the scoping search, you will have identified key search terms for each database and drawn up a list of databases to search. It is important at this stage to document your search strategy, as this will help you in writing up the methodology. (See the 'Stage 5: documenting your search' section of this chapter for information on the search details to document.)

During the 'scoping the literature stage', **pearl-growing** is an alternative way to start developing your search strategy. Pearl-growing refers to identifying a known, highly relevant article (the 'pearl') to identify terms (both **free-text** and **thesaurus** – these different ways of searching are examined later in Stage 2 of the search process) on which a search can subsequently be based. If you haven't already identified a key article for your topic area, you can conduct a very specific search, such as looking for key concepts in an article title to identify a key reference. This pearl-growing process may be repeated several times until no further relevant terms are identified. The pearl-growing technique assumes that articles on the same topic are indexed on a database in similar ways. However, this may not always be the case, particularly in multidisciplinary topics (Papaioannou et al., 2010). Figure 6.1 describes the use of pearl-growing to identify relevant articles for the research question, 'What is the psychological wellbeing of individuals with high debt?' A relevant article by Shen et al. (2014) yields the free-text search terms 'debt' and 'stress'. In addition, the article/pearl is indexed in the PsycINFO database under the term 'financial strain'. These terms can then be used to search for further articles that are likely to be relevant and match our research question.

STAGE 2: CONDUCT THE SEARCH

By this stage, you should have a fairly well-defined list of search terms. You will need to organise these into a search strategy (Aromataris and Riitano, 2014). During Stage 2, you will probably

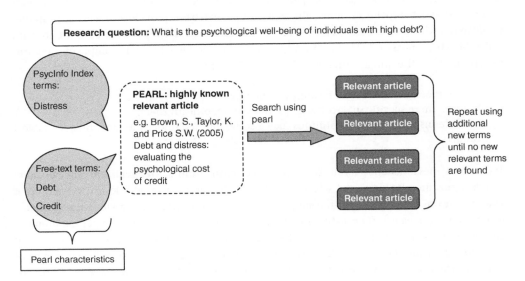

Figure 6.1 Pearl-growing

need to modify your defined search strategy on each database that you have chosen to search as each database works in a slightly different way. In addition, you will need to consider other potential sources of studies for your review such as reference list checking and contact with experts (see Stages 3 and 4). Some methods of searching to assist with Stage 2 are described in the following paragraphs.

Free text searching

Electronic databases typically allow free-text searching. You can use this approach to search for **textwords** in fields such as the title and abstract. The drawbacks of this approach are well-documented, such as problems associated with different spellings (such as organisation or organization) and different terminology (such as young person, adolescent, teenager, youth, child, children, etc.). Fortunately, many databases offer features such as **truncation** ('*' or '$') and **wildcard** ('?') symbols. Searching on teenage*, for example, would retrieve records containing the words teenage, teenager, teenagers. Searching for "wom?n" would retrieve records containing the words woman, women, etc. Check the help pages on each database you are searching to find out if these techniques are available and the relevant symbols you should use.

Thesaurus searching

A thesaurus (or **controlled vocabulary**) is a list of terms produced by database indexers and used to categorise references on an electronic subject database. The terms are called subject headings or descriptors. Indexers use these to apply consistent subject headings to articles which describe the same concept, but in a variety of ways. For example, the term 'reiki' translates to the MeSH term 'therapeutic touch' on the MEDLINE database. In ASSIA, the thesaurus term 'prisons' is used for 'jail', 'gaols' or 'penitentiaries'. Subject headings also take into account plurals and variable spellings. Some, although not all, databases provide a thesaurus. Examples of databases with thesauri are MEDLINE and the **Cochrane Library** (which both use thesauri called **MeSH**), Embase (EMTREE), ASSIA and ERIC. (See Figure 6.2 for an example of thesaurus searching.) Most thesauri are arranged hierarchically, with:

- broader, more general subject headings at the top;
- narrower, more specific subject headings indexed underneath them;
- related terms with similar definitions may also be indexed under the same broader subject heading.

Typically, a thesaurus allows you to select subject terms from a **hierarchical vocabulary**; related terms are also suggested which may be worth searching in addition. For example, if you look at the **scope note** for the subject term *'Pets'* on MEDLINE, you will see a suggested related term is *'Bonding, Human-Pet'*. In addition, free-text terms such as 'companion animals' are suggested. A thesaurus may contain the actual term for which you intend to search, and if not you search the thesaurus to find its closest match (see Figure 6.2). Your chosen thesaurus term can then be used as a search term to retrieve all records to which the selected thesaurus term is assigned.

Population interested in = Teenagers
ASSIA Thesaurus term = Adolescents
[+} indicates there are narrower terms below the term.

Adolescents [+] (Use For Teenagers)
Broader Terms = Children [+]
Narrower Terms =

- Autistic adolescents
- Behaviour disordered adolescents
- Blind adolescents
- Conduct-disordered adolescents
- Deaf adolescents
- Developmentally-disabled adolescents
- Disadvantaged adolescents
- Emotionally-disturbed adolescents
- Gifted adolescents [+]
- Hearing-impaired adolescents
- Hyperactive adolescents
- Learning-disabled adolescents
- Low-intelligence quotient adolescents
- Reading-disabled adolescents [+]
- Runaway adolescents [+]
- Sexually-abused adolescents
- Sick adolescents
- Special-needs adolescents
- Violent adolescents
- Visually impaired adolescents

Figure 6.2 Example of thesaurus searching

Thesaurus searching is an effective way of searching a database, but some concepts may be absent from thesauri. For example, relatively new concepts (such as 'credit crunch') and those specific to a particular country's administration (for example county councils in UK local government) may not appear in a globally used thesaurus. In such instances, you should carry out a free text search as an alternative. An optimally exhaustive search strategy will combine both free text and thesaurus terms. Remember thesauri terms vary between databases which means you will need to translate your search strategy for each database. Have a go at identifying appropriate thesaurus terms in Exercise 6.1.

 exercise 6.1

Thesaurus searching

To explore thesaurus searching, use an appropriate database for your discipline (see Table 6.2 for subject coverage) and find appropriate thesaurus terms for the concepts below. Note that you may want to use more than one term if relevant.

(Continued)

(Continued)

Database	Concept	Thesaurus Term(s)
ASSIA	Neighbourhood watch	
	Lifelong learning	
	Foster care	
ERIC	Online learning	
	English as a foreign language	
	Peer harassment	
LISA	Outreach librarian	
	Information retrieval	
	Dewey	
MEDLINE	Prozac	
	Shingles	
	Cost effectiveness	

(HINT – if you are not sure, view the scope notes/description of thesaurus terms to make a judgement on their relevance to the concept.)

Boolean, adjacency and proximity operators

Once you have devised a focused question and identified multiple terms for each concept within your search strategy, you can use **Boolean logic** to combine terms appropriately. Whilst this may sound complicated, Boolean logic denotes the simple concept of combining search terms using the words AND, OR, NOT (Boolean Operators) to devise a search strategy. Hart (2002) explains Boolean logic as a way of *'adding to, subtracting from and multiplying your search terms in order to expand (add), narrow (subtract), or include terms (multiply or combine) to your search'*. In practical terms, this means using the Boolean operators AND, OR and NOT to define how you want the databases to combine your individual search terms together. When constructing a search, remember the following rules:

1. OR is used to combine terms within the same concept together (for example child* OR adolescent* OR teenage*), thus expanding the search.
2. AND is used to combine different concepts together (for example child* AND inequalit*), thus narrowing the search by combining terms.
3. NOT is used to exclude irrelevant terms (for example NOT letter*), thus narrowing the search by removing terms.

(Note the use of truncation in the above examples.)

To get a clearer idea of how AND, OR and NOT are used within search strategies, examine the search strategies in the 'Translating your search question' section of this chapter.

Many databases allow you to specify how closely two or more words are positioned relative to each other by using operators to specify that terms must be near each other (**proximity**) or directly next to each other (**adjacency**) (see Figure 6.3 for examples). Check the help pages of databases to clarify which operators are used by a particular database.

ADJ# (where #= number of words), two or more words within the same field in any order (MEDLINE, Embase, PsycInfo via OVID)

NEXT finds adjacent terms (The Cochrane Library)

NEAR/# (where #= number of words), two or more words within the same field in any order (The Cochrane Library)

SAME finds two or more words in the same sentence (Web of Science)

exact phrase: use inverted commas to search for an exact phrase (ASSIA)

Figure 6.3 Examples of proximity and adjacency operators

Limits

Most databases provide a **limit function**, with the most common limits relating to publication year and/or language. Ideally, you should not limit your search to English language only to protect your review against potential language bias; however, resources for translation are frequently limited and you will often be unable to pursue an all language option for a thesis or dissertation.

An effective way of restricting a search is to limit it to specific publication and/or study types. MEDLINE, for example, allows you to limit searches by publication type (PT), while the Citation Indexes (Web of Science) offer the option of limiting to various document types, including *'article'* and *'review'*. ERIC allows limitation to document types such as *'dissertations'* and *'opinion papers'* and *'journal articles'*. If you do decide to limit by publication type, be sure that you know how each publication or document type is defined (check the help pages of each database to assist with this).

Search filters

Search filters or **methodological filters** are standardised search strategies designed to retrieve studies of a particular methodology type such as **randomised controlled trials**, systematic reviews, economic evaluations. By using search filters, you can also restrict your search to particular outcomes of interest. For example, you may want to limit your search to studies reporting the costs of an intervention. Search filters limit to types of question (for example, in healthcare studies diagnosis, aetiology, prognosis or therapy) or types of article, (for example, reviews, economic evaluations, guidelines or qualitative research). Filters are also available for geographic settings and specific populations (age groups). Good sources of search filters are the Scottish Intercollegiate Guidelines Network, the McMaster Hedges Project, and the InterTASC Information Specialists' Sub-Group (ISSG).

Searching the grey literature

As well as searching the published literature, you will find it useful to find and include relevant unpublished studies within your systematic review. **Grey literature** is defined as 'Information produced on all levels of government, academics, business and industry in electronic and print formats not controlled by commercial publishing, i.e. where publishing is not the primary activity of the producing body' (GreyNet, 2008). This literature is referred to as 'grey' (sometimes 'gray') or 'fugitive' literature because it is typically difficult to identify and obtain.

The rationale for searching the grey literature is to minimise **publication bias**. McAuley and colleagues (2000) examined a random sample of systematic reviews in a range of disease areas. Only 33% of included systematic reviews contained both grey and published studies. Generally, published studies showed larger effects of the intervention when compared with grey literature, thus demonstrating that excluding grey literature from systematic reviews can lead to exaggerated estimates of effectiveness (McAuley et al., 2000). Within the social sciences, the need for searching the grey literature is even more apparent since a vast quantity of evidence exists in practitioner journals, books and reports from public, private and voluntary sector bodies as well as official publications (Young et al., 2002; Grayson and Gomersall, 2003).

Sources of grey literature are listed in Table 6.4.

Table 6.4   Sources of grey literature

Type of grey literature	Potential sources
All types	Grey literature databases such as:
	• OpenGrey: System for Information on Grey Literature in Europe
Ongoing research	Research registers such as:
	• UK Clinical Research (UKCRN) Study Portfolio
	• ISRCTN Register
Governmental or quasi-governmental reports and guidance	Organisational websites such as:
	• Department of Health
	• National Institute for Health and Care Excellence (NICE)
Reports from key organisations	Specialist library catalogues and databases such as:
	• Health Management Information Consortium (HMIC)
	• Social Care Online
Conference abstracts for ongoing or unpublished literature	Conference Proceeding Indices such as:
	• Conference Proceedings Citation Index - Science via Web of Science
	• Conference Proceedings Citation Index - Social Science & Humanities via Web of Science
	• COS Conference Papers Index via ProQuest
	(Note that some databases such as Embase include conference abstracts)
	• Conference websites in your chosen field
Dissertations and theses	Databases such as:
	• ProQuest Dissertations & Theses (UK and International)
	• EThOS e-theses online (via The British Library)
Information from key websites in the field of interest	• For example for social research - The Joseph Rowntree Foundation

Many academic institutions maintain open-access repositories which can be searched for many types of research outputs, including reports, monographs, journal articles, electronic theses and dissertations. OpenDOAR provides a searchable Directory of Open Access Repositories.

The majority of the examples given above represent UK sources, but most have international equivalents. Look for published lists in your topic area, for example in evidence-based medicine the Canadian Agency for Drugs and Technologies in Health (CADTH) produces 'Grey Matters' which lists relevant sources to search, categorised by type and geographic location (CADTH, 2014).

STAGE 3: BIBLIOGRAPHIC SEARCHING

Checking bibliographies and reference lists

Since electronic searching may still miss important published studies, particularly when concepts are difficult to define or where the level of indexing is limited (due to errors, inaccuracy, or concepts lacking appropriate subject headings) (Garg et al., 2009), you must take further steps to ensure identification of studies. One simple approach involves examining bibliographies or reference lists of relevant retrieved studies to check that nothing has been missed. You may also find it useful to check the reference lists of existing reviews. Several studies have demonstrated the importance of reference list checking for identifying further studies for inclusion in reviews (Brettle and Long, 2001; McNally and Alborz, 2004; Stevinson and Lawlor, 2004; Greenhalgh and Peacock, 2005; Papaioannou et al., 2010).

Citation searching

Citation searching focuses on following a chain of references that cite one or more earlier studies. The citation search begins with identifying a key article on a given topic. Next, you use a database with the facility for citation searching (such as Social Science Citation Index via Web of Science) to locate all articles referred to by this key article. There is some discussion on the advantages and disadvantages of the various sources that provide a citation searching function. Google Scholar can be used, as each reference has a 'Times Cited' link. However, it is known to provide an inflated citation rate, due to indexing a number of non-refereed document types, including websites, and duplicates citations if they appear in different forms (for example pre-print and published journal articles). There are also technical issues when dealing with large sets of references as it is only possible to export one citation at a time (Yang and Meho, 2006). As with any type of searching you should weigh up the benefits of searching multiple sources, based on the time available and the potential yield of unique references.

Once additional materials have been located, you can repeat this process (**snowballing**) using newly retrieved materials as the starting point for additional citation searches, until no further relevant studies are found. As such citation searching is extremely useful for tracing the development of a body of literature. In contrast to many other search strategies, recall and precision tend to be high for well-constructed citation searches. Again, citation searching has been shown to identify studies missed from the main bibliographic search (Brettle and Long, 2001; McNally and Alborz, 2004; Papaioannou et al., 2010; Hinde and Spackman, 2015).

Author searching

Where a particular author is influential or prolific in your area of interest, **author searching** may be useful to identify further relevant studies by that specifically named author. However, author searching carries the risk of retrieving a biased sample of references, perhaps reflecting only one line of argument, so you should only use author searching in conjunction with other search methods as outlined above.

Hand searching

Some topics may be concentrated in a few key journals or inconsistently indexed or not indexed at all by the databases being searched. You must also allow for a time lag of references being added to databases. MEDLINE is updated daily; however, some databases have a longer time lag for indexing articles and therefore you are more likely to find recently published articles via journal websites, particularly as many maintain an 'early view' or 'pre-print' section. For these reasons, **hand searching** of key journals in the topic area is often conducted as a supplementary search method, examining the contents pages of individual journals (electronically or in print). To identify key journals in your research area, consider using a tool such as PubMed PubReMiner, where literature is mapped by several categories, including journal, so you can quickly identify those journals that publish most articles on your topic.

A Cochrane Review of studies compared hand searching with searching one or more electronic databases (Hopewell et al., 2009). Hand searching found between 92% to 100% of the total number of reports of randomised controlled trials and was particularly useful in finding trials reported as abstracts, letters and those published in languages other than English as well as articles in journals not indexed in electronic databases. In areas where the research question is less well-defined, hand searching has also been shown to be useful (Armstrong et al., 2005). However, it is very time consuming and should be used sparingly. Greenhalgh and Peacock (2005) found that in searching for a systematic review of complex evidence, 24 papers identified from hand searching made the final report. It took a month to complete the hand search, and thus one paper was included on average for every nine hours of hand searching. The authors also found that other supplementary methods such as reference list checking and citation searching proved much more fruitful and less time intensive for their diffuse topic (Greenhalgh and Peacock, 2005). Therefore, as with other methods, it is important to examine time versus yield. For some topics, hand searching the most recent journal issues (for example for the previous twelve months) may be a pragmatic approach. However, for diffuse topics where subject indexing is known to be problematic, it may be beneficial to search over a longer time period.

STAGE 4: VERIFICATION

Consultation with experts

Consultation involves locating references by corresponding with others. It tends to be a low-recall strategy, since it is limited by the knowledge, memory and biases of correspondents. In addition, response rates are often low if the experts are unknown to the researcher. Conversely, consultation is generally high in precision because the references provided have been pre-screened for relevance. A major advantage of consultation is the ability to locate unpublished materials. Internet technology and social media (e-mail, discussion groups, Twitter, blogs) have greatly increased the utility of consultation as a search technique. Consulting experts in your topic area (perhaps your supervisor or tutor) provides validation that relevant studies have been found and instils confidence that the efforts to identify such studies have been wide-ranging and encompassing (Ogilvie et al., 2005; Petticrew and Roberts, 2006). For example, contact with experts yielded two additional unique studies for inclusion in a review of the student experience of e-learning that we might otherwise have missed (Papaioannou et al., 2010).

Indexing and revision

If you subsequently discover that you have missed one or more relevant articles for your review in Stage 2, you should consider revising your search strategy. First, you need to establish whether articles you missed are actually indexed within your selected databases. If they are indexed, examining the **descriptors** and free-text terms assigned to the missed articles will help to identify terms that you can incorporate within your revised search strategy. If the articles that were missed are not indexed, you may need to use additional search techniques such as browsing contents pages, citation searching or checking of reference lists. No single method can identify all the literature on a topic, so you should employ multiple search methods to minimise the risk of missing a relevant item.

Your local librarian/information specialist

Carrying out a systematic literature search may appear daunting. You face many choices regarding how broad to make a search, what databases to search, and what search techniques to use. So don't forget to ask a specialist. If you have access to an academic or workplace library, make use of the librarian or information specialist (Campbell and Dorgan, 2015). They will be able to advise you on how best to search the literature according to your topic area and the purpose of your review.

STAGE 5: DOCUMENTING YOUR SEARCH

Whilst you may not use all the search techniques discussed in this chapter so far, you should always provide an accurate account of the process that you followed to identify evidence for the review. By describing exactly which sources were searched and with which search terms, as well as recording other techniques used to locate evidence (such as checking of reference lists), you will fulfil two criteria of a systematic search: transparency and reproducibility. Readers will know exactly what you did to find the evidence for your review and also, in theory, should be able to repeat the process for themselves, a key aspect of systematic reviews.

You should document your search process as you go along so that you find it easier to write up the literature search methodology for your review (Booth, 2006). Details to record include:

- the sources searched (database and database provider, and timespan of databases);
- search strategies used (for each database);
- number of references found for each source/method of searching;
- the date searches were conducted.

Many databases allow you to save your search strategy online (advisable to allow you to quickly re-run your search at a later date) and generate an electronic copy of the strategy (typically as a text file to be copied and pasted into a Word document). The **PRISMA** (Preferred Reporting Items for Systematic reviews and Meta-Analyses) statement (Moher et al., 2009) aims to help authors improve the reporting of systematic reviews and meta-analyses. The 27-item checklist included in the PRISMA statement contains two items relating to the documentation of the literature search in a systematic review or meta-analysis (see Box 6.2). Chapter 10 discusses additional items included in the PRISMA statement.

 box 6.2

Items from the PRISMA statement relating to searching

The PRISMA statement is a published reporting standard for systematic reviews and meta-analyses. These two items from the PRISMA statement specifically deal with reporting the literature searching methods.

Item 7: Information sources

Describe all information sources (databases with dates of coverage, contact with study authors to identify additional studies etc.) in the search and the date last searched.

Item 8: Search

Present full electronic search strategy for at least one database, including any limits used, such that it could be repeated.

(Note that search strategies often appear in the appendices as additional material to the main review.)

(Source: the PRISMA statement, Moher et al., 2009)

Other standards have been proposed for the reporting of literature searches, including the STARLITE mnemonic (sampling strategy, type of study, approaches, range of years, limits, inclusion and exclusions, terms used, electronic sources) (Booth, 2006). Use these examples to help you, and it may be useful to consult existing reviews to see how other authors have reported the search write-up (Rader et al., 2014). The important issue is to be consistent with the method you use across all the searches for your review, reporting the same elements each time.

Reference management

Reference management was mentioned earlier in the context of managing your review (see Chapter 4). It refers to any systematic means of organising your references. Manual reference management involves recording reference details on index cards and storing articles in a filing system. Electronic reference management involves the use of specialist software, such as Endnote. Other online reference management systems host reference libraries on the web, meaning if multiple users wish to share a reference database they do not require access to a shared computer network drive. Examples include RefWorks, a subscription-only service, whereas Mendeley, CiteULike and Zotero are free to use. A list of software for reference management can be found in the Systematic Review Toolbox (SRToolbox), an online resource of tools to assist with the systematic review processes.

Management of references greatly assists the process of a systematic literature review. All references retrieved in the search can be accounted for during the systematic literature review ensuring a transparent process.

Electronic reference management software allows references to be directly imported from individual databases. From this bank of references, you can keyword, sort and search references, as well as create in-text citations and the reference list for your final report.

Having explored the stages of the systematic literature search process, we will move on to look at a case study of the search process. Complete Exercise 6.2 which examines the search methods used in a published systematic review.

 exercise 6.2

Case study of the search process

Table 6.5 details methods of identifying literature for a systematic review looking at 'Social inequality and infant health in the UK' (Weightman et al., 2012): 5,173 references were retrieved. Consider Table 6.5 and attempt the following questions.

Questions

1 How would you rate this search in terms of the number and types of sources searched? Is this adequate?
2 What disadvantages are there in the author's search approach?
3 What aspects of the search process in the case study might be applied to your own review?

TYPES OF LITERATURE REVIEWS

Remember that systematic approaches to reviewing the literature do not necessarily require that you conduct a fully exhaustive systematic review-style search. The search techniques you choose, and the breadth of your approach, depend on the type of literature review you undertake, guided in turn by the review's aim. For example, a **systematic review** aims to be exhaustive in identifying literature and thus adopts a similarly exhaustive search process. In Table 6.6, Webb and colleagues (2009) searched seven electronic databases, checked reference lists of included studies, and contacted experts in order to identify studies for a systematic review of workplace interventions for alcohol-related problems. In comparison, a **scoping review** may seek to provide a preliminary assessment of the potential scope and size of the available literature in a topic area and thus adopt a less exhaustive approach (Peters et al., 2015). In our example of a scoping review (see Table 6.6), the review authors limited their approach by searching only key databases within the field (although in this instance this was still ten databases!) and searched for ongoing

Table 6.5 Anatomy of the search process

Focused review question	Description of review	Details of the search process used in this review
Population: infants (0-12 months)	The objective of this review is to determine the association between area and individual measures of social disadvantage and infant health in the UK.	*Stage 1*: initial search of the literature (scoping search)
Exposure: social determinants		Search terms were developed and tested by qualified librarians in one database (MEDLINE), to a high recall of relevant studies (sensitive) without too many irrelevant studies (specific).
Comparison: none		
Outcomes: preterm birth, birth weight, mortality, diagnosed illness, attendance at primary or secondary care in relation to ill-health, infection, injury or disability, growth and development	36 prospective and retrospective observational studies with socioeconomic data and health outcomes for infants in the UK, published from 1994 to May 2011.	
		Stage 2: conduct search
Context: UK	This review quantifies the influence of social disadvantage on infant outcomes in the UK. The magnitude of effect is similar across a range of area and individual deprivation measures and birth and mortality outcomes.	• Searches were carried out in 26 databases and websites. • Conducted a search for grey literature on various sources including OpenGrey and organisational websites. • Exhaustive search strategy including terms for the setting, population, exposures and study design.
		Stage 3: bibliography search
		• Reference lists of identified studies, including relevant systematic reviews, were scanned. • Contents pages of three key journals were hand-searched. • Citation tracking of relevant studies.
		Stage 4: verification
		• Contact with subject experts and organisations.

Table 6.6 Types of review

Type of review	Search Methods			Example
	Definitely Use ✓	Consider Using ?	Not Essential X	
Scoping review: – Aims to identify key research in the topic area. – May restrict the number of sources searched to key ones in topic discipline(s). – Often involves an assessment of ongoing research.	– Database searching	– Grey literature – Ongoing research	– Reference list checking – Citation searching – Hand searching – Contact with experts	**Kavanagh, J., Trouton, A., Oakley, A. and Harden, A. (2005) A scoping review of the evidence for incentive schemes to encourage positive health and other social behaviours in young people. London: EPPI-Centre, Social Science Research Unit, Institute of Education, University of London.** This review undertook comprehensive searching of ten databases covering the disciplines relating to the topic area. In addition, there was a thorough attempt to identify ongoing research/projects. This search is well-documented and the process for identifying evidence is transparent.
Mapping review: – Several examples exist of exhaustive, comprehensive searching in mapping reviews. – It would be reasonable to use any/all of the techniques (be guided by your topic area and/or aim of review).	– Database searching – Grey literature – Reference list checking – Citation searching	– Grey literature – Hand searching – Contact with experts – Ongoing research		**Graham-Matheson, L., Connolly, T., Robson, S. and Stow, W. (2006) A systematic map into approaches to making initial teacher training flexible and responsive to the needs of trainee teachers. Technical report. In Research Evidence in Education Library. London: EPPI-Centre, Social Science Research Unit, Institute of Education, University of London.** This review undertook a number of different approaches to identify evidence including comprehensive database searching, hand searching of journals, contact with experts, citation searching and reference list checking. This search is well-documented and the process for identifying evidence is transparent.

(Continued)

(Continued)

Type of review	Search Methods			Example
	Definitely Use ✓	Consider Using ?	Not Essential X	
Systematic review: – Exhaustive, comprehensive searching – use all search techniques available.	– Database searching – Grey literature – Reference list checking – Citation searching – Hand searching – Contact with experts – Ongoing research			**Webb,G. et al. (2009) A systematic review of work-place interventions for alcohol-related problems. Addiction, 104, 3, 365-77.** This review demonstrates a systematic literature search both in practice and in the reporting. A variety of sources were searched and search terms were adapted for each database. The search strategies used for each database are presented. Additional search methods were also used; networking with colleagues and checking the reference lists of the studies found in the electronic searches. Searches were limited to papers published between 1995 and 2007. This paper presents the search method in a flowchart diagram as well as describing the search within the text. This is commonly seen in systematic reviews.
Qualitative systematic review: – May employ selective or purposive sampling. – Database searching may be limited to key databases. – More emphasis may be placed on using other search techniques (such as citation searching and contact with experts).	– Database searching – Grey literature – Reference list checking – Citation searching – Contact with experts	– Hand searching – Ongoing research		**Duggan,F. and Banwell, L. (2004) Constructing a model of effective information dissemination in a crisis. Information Research, 9 (3).** This review demonstrates an extensive search of a variety of sources, including electronic databases, web resources and other sources of grey literature. In addition hand searching of a key journal was carried out and checking of the reference lists of relevant papers. A full search strategy is not included in the paper.

research. Note that although the authors did not use additional methods such as reference list checking and contact with experts, the search approach used was well-documented, transparent, and thus entirely reproducible.

Table 6.6 explores appropriate literature searching methods for different types of review. Each review type is defined with suggested guidance on the types of literature search methods to be used. Methods are categorised as 'definitely use' (essential for this type of review), 'consider using' (this may or may not be appropriate, depending on your review question and scope), and 'not essential' (not usually a necessary method for this type of review). Note that it is challenging to stipulate which methods should be used within a type of review as this is largely determined by the topic area and aim of your review. Think about what each technique might bring to your literature search, both in terms of positive aspects and negative aspects – this will help you weigh up which techniques to use.

TRANSLATING YOUR SEARCH QUESTION

As previously discussed, each database you search has unique functions and specific thesaurus/index terms particular to that database. Once you have developed your search strategy, you will need to translate it for each additional database you search. Using a variety of topics and databases, Exercise 6.3 presents worked examples on how to derive a search strategy from a focused research question.

 exercise 6.3

Examining search strategies

Look at each search strategy in turn, and consider the following:

- How would you rate the search strategy? Have the concepts of the research question (population, intervention/exposure, outcome(s), etc.) been successfully translated into search terms? Are there any other search terms that you might have included?
- What types of searching (thesaurus searching, free-text searching) have been used and are these appropriate?
- Which search tools have been used (Boolean operators, truncation, etc.)? Have these been used successfully?

(Note that the searches were conducted in May 2015, so re-running the search at a later date may produce a different number of results.)

Research Question A

Is the location of schools near to electromagnetic fields from electricity pylons liable to have adverse health effects on schoolchildren?

(Continued)

(Continued)

Suggested Search Strategy for MEDLINE via OvidSP

1. exp Schools/ (84101)
2. school*.ti,ab. (202965)
3. 1 or 2 (252115)
4. location*.ti,ab. (280578)
5. near.ti,ab. (248671)
6. next to.ti,ab. (135447)
7. adjacen*.ti,ab. (140275)
8. proximity.ti,ab. (37018)
9. 4 or 5 or 6 or 7 or 8 (804037)
10. 3 and 9 (8342)
11. exp Electromagnetic Fields/ (14956)
12. electromagnetic* field*.ti,ab. (7175)
13. 11 or 12 (18367)
14. 10 and 13 (18)

Research Question B

Do ICT interventions improve primary schoolchildren's performance in solving maths problems?

Suggested Search Strategy for ERIC via EBSCO

S1 DE "Elementary Schools"
S2 primary school*
S3 DE "Children"
S4 child* or infant* or junior*
S5 S1 OR S2 OR S3 OR S4
S6 (DE "Problem Solving")
S7 DE "Information Technology"
S8 ICT or IT or information technolog* or ("information and communication* technolog*")
S9 S7 OR S8
S10 DE "Mathematics Achievement" OR DE "Mathematics Skills"
S11 maths or mathematics
S12 S10 or S11
S13 S5 AND S6 AND S9 AND S12

Research Question C

Is the provision of solar-powered cars likely to result in benefits to society in an industrialised nation?

(Note that this search has focused on environmental and financial benefits.)

Suggested Search Strategy for Science and Social Sciences Citation Indexes via Web of Science

#1 Topic = (solar power*) AND (car* OR vehicle* OR automobile*)
#2 Topic = (environment* OR pollut* OR emission*)
#3 Topic = (financ* OR econom* OR cost effective* OR cost benefit*)
#4 Topic = #2 OR #3
#5 Topic = #1 AND #4

Research Question D

Is early discharge of stroke patients from hospital into the community more effective than standard hospital care?

Suggested Search Strategy for EMBASE via Ovid

1. exp stroke patient/ or exp stroke/ (109752)
2. stroke$.ti,ab. (238972)
3. cerebrovascular accident$.ti,ab. (7569)
4. 1 or 2 or 3 (274896)
5. exp hospital discharge/ (70481)
6. early discharge$.ti,ab. (2844)
7. 5 or 6 (72179)
8. 4 and 7 (4588)
9. Meta Analysis/ (92310)
10. ((meta adj analy$) or metaanalys$).tw. (97880)
11. (systematic adj (review$1 or overview$1)).tw. (79847)
12. or/9-11 (179356)
13. cancerlit.ab. (661)
14. cochrane.ab. (43593)
15. embase.ab. (42596)
16. (psychlit or psyclit).ab. (955)
17. (psychinfo or psycinfo).ab. (10333)
18. (cinal or cinahl).ab. (12994)
19. science citation index.ab. (2375)
20. bids.ab. (476)
21. or/13-20 (68987)
22. reference lists.ab. (10967)
23. bibliograph$.ab. (15905)
24. hand-search$.ab. (5107)
25. manual search$.ab. (3063)
26. relevant journals.ab. (907)
27. or/22-26 (32392)
28. data extraction.ab. (13180)
29. selection criteria.ab. (21579)
30. 28 or 29 (33477)
31. review.pt. (2049037)
32. 30 and 31 (16910)
33. letter.pt. (884438)
34. editorial.pt. (475548)
35. animal/ (1652198)
36. human/ (15705953)
37. 35 not (35 and 36) (1245364)
38. or/33-34,37 (2590629)
39. 12 or 21 or 27 or 32 (217204)
40. 39 not 38 (210173)
41. 8 and 40 (88)

(Continued)

(Continued)

Note how this search demonstrates the use of a search filter (Steps 9–40) (Scottish Intercollegiate Guidelines Network, 2014), in this case to limit the search to retrieve systematic reviews only.

Now you have examined existing search strategies, it is time to turn your attention to your own review. Complete Exercises 6.4, 6.5, and 6.6 to plan your literature search.

exercise 6.4

Searching for your own review

Having read through the information on literature searching, it is time to start thinking about the searching for your own review. Work through the following exercises for your own research topic.

Start to plan your literature search

Practise by working through the following questions.

Think ...

- about the purpose of your review – how systematic does your search need to be to fulfil the purpose of your review?
- about your focused question – what types of databases may index articles on your topic area? Which terms might describe each concept in your focused question?
- do you know of any key citations or authors in your topic area? (Hint: ideally these papers should have been published between five and ten years ago in order to have accrued sufficient impact.)

Decide on the following ...

- database sources to search, including sources of unpublished or grey literature (for assistance with identifying sources, see Tables 6.2 and 6.3);
- additional searching techniques: reference list checking, contact with experts, citation searching;
- brainstorm search terms for each concept within your focused question – think of all the synonyms;
- identify thesaurus terms for your search terms;
- include free-text terms where appropriate;
- combine your search terms using an appropriate operator.

exercise 6.5

Pearl growing and author searching

In the grid provided list three or four key citations you might consider useful 'pearls' in your topic area. List authors or institutions who might have conducted research studies in your topic area.

Candidate pearls:

Candidate authors or institutions for author searching:

1	1
2	2
3	3
4	4

 exercise 6.6

Sources to search

Using the search planning worksheet in the Toolbox section of this chapter, list the different sources that would be useful to search for your chosen review topic area. Check your list with a local librarian/information specialist if possible.

At the end of Chapter 5 ('Defining the Scope'), you defined your research question as concepts and brainstormed synonyms for each concept. The next stage is to identify thesaurus and free-text terms for each synonym within a concept. Once you have derived a set of terms for each concept, you should assemble your search strategy using the steps outlined in Box 6.3.

 box 6.3

Assembling your search strategy

1. Combine terms within the same concept (all population search terms) using OR; and terms for different concepts (population AND intervention terms) with AND.
2. First combine population AND intervention/exposure terms to refine your strategy.
3. If your search result set is unmanageable, combine population AND intervention/exposure AND outcome terms.
4. If your search result set is still unmanageable, combine population AND intervention/ exposure AND outcome terms AND comparison terms. Remember that the first step of the screening process is to read the titles to ascertain whether the reference will be potentially relevant to answer your research question. This is relatively quick to do, so bear this in mind when considering the number of search results you can manage.

(Note that if your search does not fit a PICOC question (see Chapter 5), carry out the same process with the headings for the method you used to define your question (for example SPICE), brainstorming terms and combining together in a similar way.)

(**Tip, if you are struggling to assemble a search, take a look at the examples in the 'Translating your search question' section for guidance.)

 **toolbox**

Searching the literature

Tool	Where to find it	Useful for
PubMed PubReminer	http://hgserver2.amc.nl/ cgi-bin/miner/miner2.cgi	• Scoping searches. • Identifying key journals and authors. • Identifying MeSH headings for search strategies.
ISSG Search Filters Resource	https://sites.google.com/a/ york.ac.uk/issg-search-filters-resource/home	• Identifying search filters to apply to search strategies. Filters are categorised by type and database.
Grey Matters: a practical search tool for evidence-based medicine (CADTH 2014)	www.cadth.ca/resources/ finding-evidence/grey-matters-practical-search-tool-evidence-based-medicine	• Identifying grey literature sources. • Documenting the grey literature search process. • Ensuring grey literature searching is done in a standardised and comprehensive way.
SR Toolbox	http://systematic reviewtools.com/	• A searchable, online catalogue of tools to support systematic reviews. • Covers the healthcare, social science and software engineering disciplines. • Includes generic or multidisciplinary tools. • Browse the 'Search' and 'Reference Management' approaches for tools to support the searching the literature process.

Search planning worksheet

We have devised a template for you to record what sources you will search to find the literature to answer your research question. Adjust the number of sources you will search accordingly to meet the requirements of your topic and the time and resources available.

Databases	Grey Literature	Journals (hand searching)	Experts to Contact

SUMMARY

Systematically searching the literature ensures that you identify relevant studies for your research question. The breadth and type of approach you take will depend on the type and topic area of the review. This chapter has outlined five key stages in the literature search and techniques to be used to make your literature search more systematic. Identifying the evidence for your review may include: scoping searches; conducting the full search; further search techniques such as reference list checking; citation searching and hand searching; search verification and search documentation. Database tools such as thesaurus searching, free-text searching, Boolean operators and application of limits will help in the development of a search strategy for electronic databases. Sources to search are determined by your subject area, and may include electronic databases, national registries of ongoing research, websites and conference proceedings. Central to systematically reviewing the literature is that your research question and your search approach must be fit for purpose (according to review type) and designed to identify the studies to answer your research question. It is good practice for all types of literature review to report how they have identified evidence in a transparent manner so that someone else might reproduce the process from the methods described, and doing so will strengthen your review.

 key learning points

- Pre-plan your search and carry out a scoping search.
- Select the most appropriate sources to search.
- Take into account limitations of the literature, such as inconsistent terminology and problematic indexing, and brainstorm alternative search terms.
- Select the most appropriate search techniques for the sources that you have chosen (is it appropriate to use search filters?).
- Employ more than one search approach (for example citation searching as well as traditional database searching).
- Evaluate your search results, modify your search strategies accordingly and be sure to document the search process.

frequently asked questions (FAQs)

FAQ 6.1 How do I identify synonyms for my research topic concepts?

You can identify synonyms during the scoping search, and the more you read within your area, the more familiar you will become with the terminology used. Consulting experts at the planning stage will help verify whether you have overlooked any search terms. If you discover later in the process that you have missed a key term, you can always conduct a supplementary search (see the section on Verification).

(Continued)

(Continued)

FAQ 6.2 How do I know when to stop searching?

There is some debate on the stopping rules to apply to searching for reviews. Again this depends on the purpose of your review, for example for a qualitative review you may reach data saturation whereby no new themes are identified. This topic is explored in Booth (2010).

FAQ 6.3 Is it sensible to use NOT in a search strategy?

Use NOT with caution as it may exclude studies that are potentially relevant. In a review on art therapy (Uttley et al., 2015) many references about anti-retroviral therapy (ART) for HIV were retrieved from the searches. If 'NOT HIV' had been included in the search strategy, an included study on art therapy for relief of symptoms associated with HIV/AIDS would have been missed (Rao et al., 2008). Think carefully before using the operator NOT and test to see the types of studies are excluded. NOT tends to be most useful as part of a search filter, excluding document types such as letters and editorials, or to eliminate records found in a previous version of the search, as outlined below.

FAQ 6.4 I have completed my searching, but have now discovered an additional search term that might be useful, what should I do?

Add the term to your existing search strategy and re-run the search to see if any additional studies are identified. To view only the additional studies and avoid duplication with your original search, use the Boolean operator NOT – for example:

#20 [original search results]

#21 [search results plus additional term]

#22 [#21 NOT #20]

FAQ 6.5 Shall I use abbreviations in my search terms?

Abbreviations can be useful in search strategies. However, if you find your search results increase dramatically with a large number of irrelevant references, check that the abbreviation is not meaningful in multiple different contexts. For example a search for evidence on attendance at GP appointments, focusing on factors that predict 'did not attend' rates, using the abbreviation 'DNA' would retrieve a large number of irrelevant studies relating to 'deoxyribonucleic acid'.

FAQ 6.6 I've contacted some experts in the field but had no response, what should I do?

It is frustrating to receive no response but the important factor in terms of your review methodology is that you have attempted to identify all the studies by using multiple retrieval methods, including contact with experts (albeit unsuccessfully). Document this in your 'Methods' section, including the number of experts contacted, noting that there were no responses. It may be worth sending a follow-up email as a reminder, or asking peers or colleagues if they have contact with experts in your field.

FAQ 6.7 There is substantial duplication between the databases I've searched, how do I handle this?

This is where reference management software proves useful. It is possible to import all references from each bibliographic database you search into a single reference management library and then perform an automated duplicate check. Note that it is also worth performing an additional manual duplicate check as automated checks only identify duplicates that are an exact match in format. When writing up, note the total number of references found before de-duplication, and the total number of unique references (after de-duplication).

FAQ 6.8 Do I need to use a search filter?

This depends on your topic, the number of search results found, and the purpose of your review. For example, if you are conducting a systematic review of RCTs only, it may be worth employing an RCT filter, particular where there is a wealth of literature in your area. Conduct your search strategy first, and if the number of references retrieved is manageable, you probably do not need to use a search filter. However, if you retrieve large numbers of references, this can be an appropriate way to limit your search. If you are considering a specific population, for example geographic area, a published search filter is useful in ensuring that you have identified all the appropriate search terms.

suggestions for further reading

Aveyard, H. (2014) How do I search for literature? In H. Aveyard (ed.), *Doing a Literature Review in Health and Social Care: A Practical Guide*, 3rd edition. Maidenhead: McGraw-Hill, 68–88.
This chapter provides a step-by-step guide to searching the literature. The focus is on health and social care but there are transferable skills addressed, such as identifying inclusion and exclusion criteria, identifying keywords and recording your search strategy. The chapter also briefly covers using abstracts to assess relevance, retrieving references and reference management. The tips on 'writing up your search strategy' are particularly useful, so note these before you start your literature search so that you can ensure you are keeping an accurate record of the information you require to report your search strategy efficiently.

Bettany-Saltikov, J. (2012) Conducting a comprehensive and systematic literature search. In J. Bettany-Saltikov (ed.), *How To Do A Systematic Literature Review In Nursing: A Step-By-Step Guide*. Maidenhead: McGraw-Hill, 66–83.
Focusing on doing a systematic literature review in nursing, this chapter begins with the importance and aims of undertaking a comprehensive and systematic search. Follow the steps to convert your research question into a search strategy, using the PICO framework. You may find the case study on identifying synonyms particularly useful. There is also a helpful template to assist with the documentation of searches.

Cherry, M.G. and Dickson, R. (2013) Developing my search strategy and applying inclusion criteria. In A. Boland, M.G. Cherry and R. Dickson (eds), *Doing a Systematic Review: A Student's Guide*. London: Sage, 35–60.

(Continued)

(Continued)

This chapter focuses on the planning of your review, namely the review question and review protocol. It presents the review process as a journey whereby your review question is the destination and the review protocol details the proposed route. There is a useful section on scoping your review. A handy example of an email contacting research experts is presented which you could adapt for your own purposes. There is also a number of 'frequently asked questions' answered at the end of the chapter.

Garrard, J. (2013) Paper trail: how to plan and manage a search of the literature. In J. Garrard (ed.), *Health Sciences Literature Review Made Easy*. Burlington, MA: Jones & Bartlett, 63-98.

The helpfully entitled 'paper trail' iterates the importance of keeping records during your literature searching. It covers the setting up, with five recommended parts to make notes on including keywords and sources. There are some useful searching tips, such as how to find government reports and a description of the 'snowballing' technique to identify the literature. The chapter ends with a case study ('Caroline's Quest') on managing the search, which presents a paper trail for a search on characteristics of teenage girls who smoke.

Brunton, G., Stansfield, C. and Thomas, J. (2012) Finding relevant studies. In D. Gough, S. Oliver and J. Thomas (eds), *An Introduction to Systematic Reviews*. London: Sage, 107-34.

This chapter covers the searching and screening for inclusion using eligibility criteria for a systematic review. A myth is addressed that 'every relevant study for a review can be located'. There is a substantive section on developing and implementing search strategies. Sensitivity and precision in searching are explored, and you may find the diagram on p. 124 particularly useful in familiarising yourself with these concepts. Additional search methods are discussed, such as hand searching and reference list checking. The chapter moves on to cover the screening of studies, which we will address in Chapter 7.

Oliver, P. (2012) Doing a literature search. In P. Oliver (ed.), *Succeeding With Your Literature Review: A Handbook For Students*. Maidenhead: McGraw-Hill International, 39-57.

Covers scoping (preliminary survey) and determining keywords. Helpfully explores some additional sources of literature, such as university repositories and library catalogues, and wikis, blogs and RSS for keeping up to date. Visit the three 'key questions' at the end of the chapter with regard to your own literature review.

REFERENCES

Armstrong, R., Jackson, N., Doyle, J., Waters, E. and Howes, F. (2005) It's in your hands: the value of handsearching in conducting systematic reviews of public health interventions. *Journal of Public Health*, **27**, 4, 388.

Aromataris, E. and Riitano, D. (2014) Constructing a search strategy and searching for evidence: a guide to the literature search for a systematic review. *American Journal of Nursing*, **114**, 5, 49–56.

Booth, A. (2006) 'Brimful of STARLITE': toward standards for reporting literature searches. *Journal of the Medical Library Association*, **94**, 4, 421–9.

Booth, A. (2010) How much searching is enough? Comprehensive versus optimal retrieval for technology assessments. *International Journal of Technology Assessment in Health Care*, **26**, 04, 431–35.

Booth, A. (2011) Chapter 3: Searching for studies. In J. Noyes, A. Booth, K. Hannes, A. Harden, J. Harris, S. Lewin and C. Lockwood (eds), *Supplementary Guidance for Inclusion of Qualitative Research in Cochrane Systematic Reviews of Interventions*. Version 1 (updated August 2011). Cochrane Collaboration Qualitative Methods Group. Available at http://methods.cochrane. org/qi/sites/methods.cochrane.org.qi/files/uploads/Data%20synthesis%20supplemental%20 guidance_2010%2012%2023B.doc

Booth, A., Harris, J., Croot, E., Springett, J., Campbell, F. and Wilkins, E. (2013) Towards a methodology for cluster searching to provide conceptual and contextual 'richness' for systematic reviews of complex interventions: case study (CLUSTER). *BMC Medical Research Methodology*, **13**, 1, 118.

Brettle, A.J. and Long, A.F. (2001) Comparison of bibliographic databases for information on the rehabilitation of people with severe mental illness. *Bulletin of the Medical Library Association*, **89**, 4, 353–62.

CADTH (2014) *Grey Matters: A Practical Search Tool for Evidence-based Medicine*. Ottawa: CADTH Information Sources.

Campbell, S. and Dorgan, M. (2015) What to do when everyone wants you to collaborate: managing the demand for library support in systematic review searching. *Journal of the Canadian Health Libraries Association/Journal de l'Association des bibliothèques de la santé du Canada*, **36**, 1, 11–19.

Centre for Reviews and Dissemination (2009) *CRD's Guidance for Undertaking Reviews in Healthcare*, 3rd edition. York: Centre for Reviews and Dissemination.

Garg, A.X., Iansavichus, A.V., Wilczynski, N.L., Kastner, M., Baier, L.A., Shariff, S.Z., Rehman, F., Weir, M., McKibbon, K.A. and Haynes, R.B. (2009) Filtering Medline for a clinical discipline: diagnostic test assessment framework. *British Medical Journal*, Sep 18, **339**, b3435.

Grayson, L. and Gomersall, A. (2003) A difficult business: finding the evidence for social science reviews. Working Paper 19, Economic and Social Research Council, UK Centre for Evidence Based Policy and Practice, London.

Greenhalgh, T. and Peacock, R. (2005) Effectiveness and efficiency of search methods in systematic reviews of complex evidence: audit of primary sources. *British Medical Journal*, **331**, 1064–5.

GreyNet (2008) *Grey Literature Network Service International Conference on Grey Literature* (Luxembourg, 1997 – expanded in New York, 2004). GreyNet, Grey Literature Network Service. Amsterdam: GreyNet.

Hart, C. (2002) *Doing a Literature Search: A Comprehensive Guide for the Social Sciences*. London: Sage.

Higgins, J.P.T. and Green, S. (2011) *Cochrane Handbook for Systematic Reviews of Interventions*, Version 5.1.0 (updated March 2011). The Cochrane Collaboration. Available at: www. cochrane-handbook.org (last accessed 9 March 2016).

Hinde, S. and Spackman, E. (2015) Bidirectional citation searching to completion: an exploration of literature searching methods. *Pharmacoeconomics*, **33**, 1, 5–11.

Hopewell, S., Loudon, K., Clarke, M.J., Oxman, A.D. and Dickersin, K. (2009) Publication bias in clinical trials due to statistical significance or direction of trial results. *Cochrane Database of Systematic Reviews*, **21**, 1.

Levay, P., Ainsworth, N., Kettle, R. and Morgan, A. (2016) Identifying evidence for public health guidance: a comparison of citation searching with Web of Science and Google Scholar. *Research Synthesis Methods*, **7**, 1, 34–45.

McAuley, L., Tugwell, P. and Moher, D. (2000) Does the inclusion of grey literature influence estimates of intervention effectiveness reported in meta-analyses? *Lancet*, **356**, 9237, 1228–31.

McNally, R. and Alborz, A. (2004) Developing methods for systematic reviewing in health services delivery and organization: an example from a review of access to health care for people with learning disabilities. Part 1. Identifying the literature. *Health Information and Libraries Journal*, **21**, 3, 182–92.

Moher, D., Liberati, A., Tetzlaff, J., Altman D.G. and PRISMA Group (2009) Preferred reporting items for systematic reviews and meta-analyses: the PRISMA statement. *PLoS Medicine*, **6**, 7, e1000097.

Ogilvie, D., Hamilton, V., Egan, M. and Petticrew, M. (2005) Systematic reviews of health effects of social interventions. 1. Finding the evidence: how far should you go? *Journal of Epidemiology and Community Health*, **59**, 9, 804–8.

Papaioannou, D., Sutton, A., Carroll, C., Booth, A. and Wong, R. (2010) Literature searching for social science systematic reviews: consideration of a range of search techniques. *Health Information and Libraries Journal*, **27**, 2, 114–22.

Peters, M.D., Godfrey, C.M., Khalil, H., McInerney, P., Parker, D. and Soares, C.B. (2015) Guidance for conducting systematic scoping reviews. *International Journal of Evidence-based Healthcare*, **13**, 3, 141–6.

Petticrew, M. and Roberts, H. (2006) *Systematic Reviews in the Social Sciences: A Practical Guide.* Malden, MA: Blackwell.

Rader, T., Mann, M., Stansfield, C., Cooper, C. and Sampson, M. (2014) Methods for documenting systematic review searches: a discussion of common issues. *Research Synthesis Methods*, **5**, 2, 98–115.

Rao, D., Nainis, N., Williams, L. , Langner, D., Eisin, A. and Paice, J. (2009) Art therapy for relief of symptoms associated with HIV/AIDS. *AIDS Care*, **21**, 64–9.

Scottish Intercollegiate Guidelines Network (2014) *Search Filters.* Edinburgh: SIGN.

Shen, S., Sam, A.G. and Jones, E. (2014) Credit card indebtedness and psychological well-being over time: empirical evidence from a household survey. *Journal of Consumer Affairs*, **48**, 3, 431–56.

Stevinson, C. and Lawlor, D.A. (2004) Searching multiple databases for systematic reviews: added value or diminishing returns? *Complementary Therapies in Medicine*, **12**, 4, 228–32.

Uttley, L., Scope, A., Stevenson, M., Rawdin, A., Taylor Buck, E., Sutton, A., Stevens, J., Kaltenthaler, E., Dent-Brown, K. and Wood, C. (2015) Systematic review and economic modelling of the clinical effectiveness and cost-effectiveness of art therapy among people with non-psychotic mental health disorders. *Health Technology Assessment*, **19**, 18.

Webb, G., Shakeshaft, A., Sanson-Fisher, R. and Havard, A. (2009) A systematic review of workplace interventions for alcohol-related problems. *Addiction*, **104**, 3, 365–77.

Weightman, A.L., Morgan, H.E., Shepherd, M.A., Kitcher, H., Roberts, C. and Dunstan, F.D. (2012) Social inequality and infant health in the UK: systematic review and meta-analyses. *BMJ Open*, **2**, e000964.

Wilson, P. (1992) Searching: strategies and evaluation. In H.D. White, M.J. Bates and P. Wilson (eds), *For Information Specialists: Interpretations of Reference and Bibliographic Work.* Norwood, NJ: Ablex, 153–81.

Yang, K. and Meho, L.I. (2006) Citation analysis: a comparison of Google Scholar, Scopus, and Web of Science. Paper presented at the 69th Annual Meeting of the American Society for Information Science and Technology (ASIST), Austin (USA), 3–8 November.

Young, K., Ashby, D., Boaz, A. and Grayson, L. (2002) Social science and the evidence-based policy movement. *Social Policy and Society*, **1**, 215–24.

ASSESSING THE EVIDENCE BASE

 in a nutshell

Selecting studies to include in your review and assessing their quality

- Different roles and challenges are associated with assessing the evidence base for quality and relevance.
- You must be able to undertake a relevance assessment and select studies to include in your literature review.
- The key concepts in quality assessment are validity and reliability, this chapter explores their importance within literature reviews.
- This chapter also explores the concept of applicability or generalisability.
- Advice is given on identifying appropriate quality assessment resources, undertaking quality assessment and presenting the results of quality assessments.

INTRODUCTION

Assessing the **evidence base** is the point in the review process that focuses on the particular value that individual studies hold for your research question and the practical application of research. After searching the literature (Chapter 6), you will have identified a potential evidence base for your review, which often can be large and diffuse. From this list of references, you will need to systematically select those that are *relevant* for your research question and exclude those that are not relevant. Once you have a list of included studies for your literature review, you will need to plan how to assess the evidence base. How exactly you do this depends on the type of review being undertaken. So, at one end of the scale, assessing the evidence base might involve briefly characterising the literature, for example in a mapping review. At the other end of the scale, assessment might involve a detailed examination of the methods and conduct of each study included in the review.

You may have heard of the terms **critical appraisal** or **quality assessment** (often used synonymously). Essentially, critical appraisal or quality assessment focuses on 'whether we can believe a study', and this is often referred to as **internal validity**. Systematic reviews carry out critical appraisal or quality assessment as a standard procedure, and extensive multi-disciplinary guidance exists on how this is done (Centre for Reviews and Dissemination, 2009; EPPI-Centre, 2010; Higgins and Green, 2011). Another concept to throw into the mix is assessment of **generalisability** or **applicability**, also known as **external validity**. Often this process is considered alongside quality assessment, but its focus is slightly different. Put simply, we assess the generalisability or applicability of an individual study by asking, 'Is the study relevant to the population identified by our research question?' Typically issues concerning internal validity are presented in the 'Results' section of a review, whilst external validity is considered in the 'Discussion/Recommendations/Conclusion' (see Chapter 10 for how to write up your review); however, many reviewers prefer to assess both in a single process.

This chapter discusses how to assess the evidence base, focusing on the processes of quality assessment (we will use this term for the purpose of this chapter). The chapter starts by discussing how to select relevant studies for a literature review in a systematic way. It then considers how to begin to assess the evidence base and how the depth of assessment depends on the function of, and type of, literature review. The next section introduces the need for quality assessment and outlines the different properties assessed in the studies included in your review: validity, reliability and generalisability/applicability. Next, an overview of various study designs is provided, focusing on the implications of study design features. This is followed by a section on conducting your quality and relevance assessment, including presenting results and challenges of the process. The chapter includes details of some tools for assessing the evidence base. Throughout the chapter examples from within different disciplines are referred to; however, do consider how each section applies to your own literature review topic.

ASSESSING THE RELEVANCE OF STUDIES TO YOUR RESEARCH QUESTION

At this stage, you will have completed your literature search (see Chapter 6), and as a result will have a list of potential studies for your literature review from which you will need to select those that are relevant to answering the research question you formulated in Chapter 5. In some instances, depending on the quantity of research in your topic area, this can be a very long list of studies and can seem rather daunting as you are overloaded with an abundance of information.

Applying a systematic method to selection of studies from the results of your literature search allows you to exclude studies that are not relevant to your review whilst ensuring that you do not miss studies that are relevant. This helps reduce **selection bias** within the review: the review findings should be based upon *all* relevant studies. Having a clear idea of what is relevant to your review is essential. Chapter 5 discussed formulating explicit **inclusion criteria** and **exclusion criteria**, and it is at this stage where, if you devised an appropriately focused research question, the process of selecting studies is made much easier. You look at your inclusion and exclusion criteria and assess how each study identified from the literature fulfils each of these criteria in turn. If a study does not fulfil every single inclusion criterion or meets any of the exclusion criteria, it must not be included in your review.

STEPS IN THE SELECTION PROCESS

Experience suggests that the most efficient way of screening studies for inclusion in a literature review is to first examine the *titles* of articles from your literature searches. However, where time is at a premium reviewers will often combine screening of titles with the next stage which is screening of abstracts. Often you can tell from the title of an article whether or not it is relevant. After screening the titles, you can move on to look at the *abstracts* of any studies where it was not possible to judge relevance from the title alone. Finally, you can examine the *full text* of studies obtained on the basis of the relevance of their abstracts to your inclusion criteria. When it comes to excluding studies examined at the full-text stage, it is useful to record the reasons for exclusion of each study for the sake of transparency and subsequent reporting. Some literature reviews will provide a list of studies excluded at full-text stage, together with the reasons in an appendix. This offers transparency and allows you to justify decisions made in the study

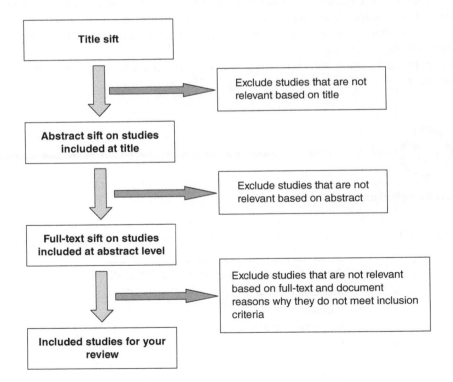

Figure 7.1 Process of selecting studies

selection phase. You are also able to anticipate queries as to why a particular study was excluded from your review. Figure 7.1 depicts the stages of the study selection process.

USING REFERENCE MANAGEMENT SOFTWARE FOR STUDY SELECTION

Chapter 6 presented the different types of reference management software available to help you manage the literature review process. One function of reference management software is the ability to tag or apply keywords to records in the reference management database. For example, you can tag all the references that have been selected for inclusion in your review at the abstract stage by using the keyword 'include abstract'. This function allows you to retrieve a list of included studies in the review, as well as providing an audit trial of decisions made in the study selection process. This means you should be able to know precisely which studies have been included or excluded and at what stage (title, abstract or full-text examination). Chapter 10 discusses the importance of providing an account of the study selection process.

Increasingly those conducting reviews, especially reviews that offer a mapping function, will import the bibliographic records into Microsoft Excel (or some similar spreadsheet package) and construct a series of pre-defined drop-down menus for each of the inclusion/exclusion criteria. The reviewer proceeds systematically through the list of studies, viewing the abstract in the top panel of the spreadsheet, and selects the relevant category from the relevant drop-down 'pick list'. The categorisation aids in completing the subsequent PRISMA flowchart (see Chapter 10), in mapping different types of studies and their frequencies, and by filtering on particular columns offers an instant result for how many studies met or failed a particular inclusion/exclusion criterion.

To apply the inclusion and exclusion criteria for your review for study selection, complete Exercise 7.1.

 exercise 7.1 ━━━━━━━━━━━━━━━━━━━━━

Study selection

Now revisit your inclusion and exclusion criteria from Chapter 5 and write them down in the grid provided. Keep this grid to hand whilst you go through your study selection process.

Tool for focusing your question - PICO, SPICE, etc.

Inclusion Criteria

Population =

Intervention/exposure =

Comparator =

Outcome(s) =

Context =

Exclusion Criteria

Population =

Intervention/exposure =

Comparator =

Outcome(s) =

Context =

ASSESSING YOUR INCLUDED STUDIES – FIRST STEPS

Once you have selected the articles for your review, the next stage is to assess the evidence base in more detail. Here you are seeking to become immersed in, and familiar with, each study so that you start to see the ways in which you might analyse and present your data. By this point, you will have produced a list of studies judged to have met all your review inclusion criteria (correct population, outcomes and study design) and so you will know that each included study will provide findings that answer your research question in some way. You need to examine each study in detail, taking all the meaningful information from each included study (**data extraction**) before you start compiling and synthesising the information. For whichever type of literature review you are undertaking, at this stage you are reading, becoming familiar with, digesting, reflecting upon, and perhaps unknowingly making judgements on each study included in your review. All these processes are involved in *assessing the evidence base*.

The depth to which you assess the evidence base depends on the type of review and its aim. For example, a **systematic review** generally involves an in-depth quality assessment of included studies. A key component of systematic reviews is to reflect upon the credibility of the review's findings; it is essential that you are aware of how the weaknesses or flaws of included studies may impact upon the review's findings. However, for a mapping review, where the aim is to map out and categorise existing literature as well as to identify gaps in the literature (Grant and Booth, 2009), you will assess the evidence base to identify its key characteristics such as study design, country of publication or general direction of study findings, offering you a rich picture of the existing literature to be described.

All literature reviews involve, and benefit from, some assessment of the evidence base, which helps to guide the subsequent stages of synthesis and writing up.

If nothing else, at this stage you will be familiarising yourself with the intricacies of each study and will start to spot where findings from studies agree with or differ from each another. More importantly, you will start to suggest possible reasons for study similarities or differences. For example, what does an individual study contribute to your review? Does it add strength to an argument, a conflicting argument, a new argument, perspective or theory, or perhaps nothing new?

To begin with, you should ask yourself what you need to find out from your included studies to help you fulfil the aim of your literature review. Table 7.1 presents four types of review (introduced in Chapter 2) and looks at their aims in relation to how you might assess the evidence base. For each review type, you can consider particular 'key questions' when assessing the evidence base. The answers to each question will help shape how you will proceed with your review. Hopefully, you will be able to identify which questions apply to each particular review type. For example, in a systematic review most, if not all, of the questions in Table 7.1 will be appropriate.

Table 7.1 Assessing the evidence base in different types of reviews

Type of review	Key questions to ask when assessing the evidence base	Practical application	Review example
Scoping review	• Are there any previous reviews? • How much evidence exists on my research question? • What type of evidence is available?	Identifies previous reviews on your topic area to avoid duplication If there is a significant volume of evidence, you might want to consider refining your scope. Too little evidence and you might want to broaden your question 'Firms up' the research question by looking at what kind of evidence is out there. For example, if your review is limited to randomised controlled trials (RCTs) but your scoping search finds no such evidence, you may need to consider other types of research design. Similarly, if you have limited your research question to only UK studies but found none in your scoping search, you may wish to widen this to include research undertaken outside UK. It will be particularly important to assess generalisability if looking at studies outside of the setting (context) of your research question	A scoping review of the association between rural medical education and rural practice location (Farmer et al., 2015).
Mapping review	• Where is evidence plentiful? • Where is evidence lacking (gaps)? • How can I describe the evidence? • Are there relationships or key themes occurring?	Focus for subsequent literature reviews Key features of evidence base might include study design, country of publication, populations or subgroups, nature of intervention or exposures analysed (are they similar or differ greatly) Explores the following: • Directional (A affects B) • Studies in agreement • Conflicting studies	Maternity care services and culture: a systematic global mapping of interventions (Coast et al., 2014).
Systematic review	• How can I describe the evidence? • Are there relationships or key themes occurring? • How credible is the evidence? • How applicable is the evidence to my situation/scenario? • Where is evidence lacking (gaps)?	Key features of evidence base might include study design, country of publication, populations or subgroups, nature of intervention or exposures analysed (are they similar or do they differ greatly?) Directional (A affects B) Studies in agreement Conflicting studies Quality of the study conduct and design: subgroup analyses Generalisability of research Areas for future research	Psychosocial interventions for school refusal with primary and secondary school students: a systematic review (Maynard et al., 2015)
Qualitative systematic review	• How can I describe the evidence? • What themes or constructs are present between or within individual studies? • What is the quality of the evidence?	Key features of evidence base – for example participants, settings (are they similar or differ greatly?) Interpretation of a phenomenon – broaden understanding Does this mediate the findings?	Treatment non-adherence in pediatric long-term medical conditions: systematic review and synthesis of qualitative studies of caregivers' views (Santer et al., 2014)

Now consider your own review, and use Exercise 7.2 to decide the level of quality assessment required.

exercise 7.2

Assessing the evidence base for your review

Consider the types of review in Table 7.1 and think about the questions you might want to ask when assessing the evidence base for your review.

Your review question:

Which key questions do you need to ask for your review?

What is the practical application of your questions?

Assessing the evidence base in detail

Some literature review types require a systematic exploration of study strengths and weaknesses to assess the impact of study quality on both the findings of that individual study and the findings of the literature review as a whole. The rest of this chapter considers quality assessment and its role in the literature review process.

The first step of quality assessment is to decide whether an article is worth reading. Complete Exercise 7.3 to practise this skill.

exercise 7.3

When is an article worth reading?

Before introducing quality assessment in more detail, when you come across a research study in a journal, consider the following:

1. How do you decide whether an article is worth reading?
2. What makes an article believable?

In addressing Exercise 7.3 you can probably divide your factors into three distinct groups:

- *Applicability* – the topic of the study, how important it is to you at the moment, the similarity of the setting to the one in which you work, the level at which it is written, the professional group or discipline for whom it is written, etc.
- *Extrinsic factors* – those external factors assumed to relate to, but not always associated with, the quality of the article: who wrote it, where they work, what their job or qualifications are,

whether you have heard of them, who paid for the study, in which journal it is published, whether the authors have written on the subject before.
- *Intrinsic factors* – factors that relate to the study itself, i.e. the appropriateness of the study design to the question being asked, the suitability of the sample, the methods used to recruit the sample, the methods used to obtain the results.

Quality assessment asks you to discard any prejudices that you have regarding the extrinsic factors. It also asks you to make an initial judgement about the general relevance of the study, and then look exclusively at the intrinsic factors using a structured checklist, before finally returning to consider issues that relate to its suitability to your own practice. In this way you will follow a process that is as objective and explicit as possible. On this basis you can judge if an article is worth reading and if it is believable.

Assessing the quality of included studies – what is it and why do we do it?

Quality assessment, sometimes referred to as critical appraisal, aims to discover if first the methods, and consequently the results of the research, are valid. It is:

> the process of assessing and interpreting evidence by systematically considering its validity, results and relevance. (Parkes et al., 2001)

Generalisability or applicability is often considered alongside quality assessment, and reflects on how research findings (if at all) impact on practice. In the context of qualitative studies you will consider whether the findings are transferable. Considering how the research is applicable, transferable or generalisable defines the difference between critical appraisal and a simple 'critical reading' of the research (Booth and Brice, 2004).

Every study included in your literature review will have weaknesses or flaws. You will need to identify each weakness or flaw to determine first its potential impact on the findings of an individual study, and second its implications for the findings of your review as a whole. You will need to become aware of both the strengths and flaws of included studies so that you can take these into account when presenting and discussing your review findings.

You will need to consider which study flaws are considered 'fatal' and which are 'non-critical'. All studies will have weaknesses, but by considering their impact upon the study findings you can determine which are critical and which are not. Remember that undertaking research is fraught with difficulties. Several things can 'go wrong' or not as originally planned in research studies (for example poor recruitment to a study). You may find yourself becoming very scathing about studies when you are assessing their quality! Sackett et al. (1997) refer to this as critical appraisal 'nihilism', i.e. no paper is ever good enough. However, the function of quality assessment is not the 'pursuit of some "holy grail" of perfection' (Petticrew and Roberts, 2006). Assessing the evidence base focuses on the practical application of research, and similar pragmatism is required when you are performing quality assessment. Therefore, if a particular flaw has minimal or limited impact on the findings of a study, is it really that important?

However, quality assessment is not simply used to identify study flaws. Using such a structured formal approach allows you to explore the detailed contents of a paper both in terms of its methodology and findings. It is therefore basically a type of 'acclimatisation' or 'sensitisation' to a study, an important journey of discovery for the reader (Booth, 2007). By critically examining published research, you will become more aware of how others have conducted research. This also means you will become better at designing and conducting your own research studies. For example, if you identify where a study has been carried out using an inappropriate study design, you might recommend that the research should be repeated using a stronger study design. If a study has been carried out but failed to recruit enough subjects, it might be useful to repeat this with a larger sample to determine the results.

Lastly, quality assessment is helpful in identifying between-study differences (the technical term here is **heterogeneity** and this is discussed further in Chapters 8 and 9). For example, smaller studies tend to overestimate findings in comparison to larger studies (Higgins and Green, 2011).

STUDY DESIGNS - IS THERE A HIERARCHY OF EVIDENCE?

Before looking at quality assessment in more detail, it is useful to understand the different types of study design used in research. Some research designs are better able to answer certain questions. Therefore, early on in the process of quality assessment, you need to consider: 'Is this the most appropriate study design to answer this research question?' If you are not familiar with study designs, take a look at the resources available on the Oxford Centre for Evidence-based Medicine website (Centre for Evidence Based Medicine, 2009).

Health research pays particular attention to the capacity of particular study designs to answer particular types of research questions; the **randomised controlled trial (RCT)** is considered the **gold standard** study design to answer questions on the effectiveness of an intervention. The idea of the 'best study design for a research question' has been used prescriptively within health research, where so-called **hierarchies of evidence** have been developed. These hierarchies rank study designs in order of robustness for answering a type of question, for example, for the effectiveness of an intervention, randomised controlled trials are normally considered at the top of the scale, in terms of robustness, with case studies at the bottom. Of course all study designs combining multiple well-conducted examples in a single systematic review will always be considered superior to the findings of an individual well-conducted study.

One of the most cited examples of a published hierarchy is the 'Levels of Evidence' produced by the Oxford Centre for Evidence Based Medicine Levels of Evidence Working Group (2011). This hierarchy allows the reader to select a particular type of research question and then identify the order of study design by robustness.

However, there are problems with classifying research designs in this way. First, hierarchies can give a false impression that a poorly conducted RCT may provide better evidence than a well-conducted observational study. Second, it is often not straightforward to determine which research design is the most appropriate since the choice may be limited by practical and ethical considerations. For example a researcher may believe that it is not ethical to randomise subjects. Third, hierarchies of evidence are limited in addressing questions on the rigour of qualitative research where different designs have different attributes (Taylor et al., 2007). Finally, most hierarchies are health research focused, and their value is contested by researchers within other disciplines (Hammersley, 2001; Taylor et al., 2007). Petticrew and Roberts (2003) offer a more flexible approach based on a taxonomy for each type of question, a so-called 'horses for courses' approach.

Whatever your discipline, you will find it invaluable to be aware of different types of study design, the flaws or biases to which they are prone, and in particular their effect on study findings. However, in a multidisciplinary setting you may find it more helpful to consider when particular studies may be reasonably used and what the strengths or weaknesses are. Thus this section takes a broad look at the three 'families' of study design: descriptive, analytic experimental and analytical observational.

Studies can be broadly classified into **descriptive** or **analytic** designs. Descriptive study designs focus on describing or giving us a picture of what is happening in a population (for example **cross-sectional surveys** and **qualitative studies**). Analytic studies try to quantify relationships between factors (Centre for Evidence Based Medicine, 2009), for example the effect of an Information and Communication Technology (ICT) intervention on maths ability. Analytic studies are further classified according to whether researchers simply measure the effects of an exposure (they do not manipulate the intervention or exposure in any way). In contrast, experimental analytic studies manipulate an intervention or exposure, for example in RCTs by allocating subjects to different intervention or exposure groups. The key characteristic of experimental studies is that they are designed to control bias. Experimental studies may be cross-sectional or **longitudinal; prospective** or **retrospective**; contain one or more groups of participants (including random or non-random allocation to groups within a study); and may be **blind** or **open label**. Each feature of an experimental study design has implications for the research, as explored in Tables 7.2 to 7.6.

Table 7.2 Cross-sectional versus longitudinal

Study design feature	Implications		Studies that often use this feature
Cross-sectional: records outcomes or examines relationships between variables at one point in time only (snapshot in time).	• Cheap and simple to set up. Ideal for pinpointing the prevalence of a particular, for example what number of higher education students visit their public library?	• Cannot determine a cause and effect relationship between two variables.	• Survey.
Longitudinal: records observations over a period of time (can be several years).	• Changes over time are recorded in a population or outcome so more plausible to determine a cause and effect relationship.	• More complicated to set up and more costly than cross-sectional studies. Causality may only be determined if confounding factors are controlled for.	• Cohort study. • Randomised controlled trial.

Table 7.3 Prospective versus retrospective

Study design feature	Implications		Studies that often use this feature
Prospective: forward-looking and observe for outcomes. Typically a group or cohort of individuals is identified and followed for a long period of time.	• Able to determine cause and effect and provide 'real' incidence rates. • Can uncover unanticipated outcomes or associations.	• Can be prone to large loss of study participants (attrition). • The outcome of interest must be common or the study will fail to recruit enough participants to make the findings meaningful.	• Cohort study. • Randomised controlled trial.
Retrospective: identify a group of individuals who have had a particular outcome and then look back in time to record details about what interventions or exposures they received.	• Able to determine cause and effect; particularly useful when an outcome is rare.	• Looking 'backwards', particularly when asking study participants to remember events or details in the past, makes retrospective studies particularly prone to recall bias.	• Case control studies. • Cohort studies (occasionally).

Table 7.4 One group versus more than one group

Study design feature	Implications		Studies that often use this feature
One group of study participants.	• Fewer participants need be recruited to the study.	• Between-group comparisons cannot be made. • Confounding factors may not be taken into account as easily.	• Survey. • Cohort study. • Case control study.
Two groups of study participants.	• Between-group comparisons to be made. • Confounding factors can be taken into account more easily. • Groups can be balanced.	• Requires extra participants to be recruited.	• Survey. • Cohort study. • Case control study. • RCT.

QUALITY ASSESSMENT: VALIDITY, RELIABILITY AND APPLICABILITY

To undertake quality assessment, you need to understand the principles underpinning the process. These can be split into three key concepts of validity, **reliability** and applicability. Each is considered in turn.

Table 7.5   Random versus not random allocation

Study design feature	Implications		Studies that often use this feature
Non-random allocation.	• Not always possible or ethical to randomise participants to different groups (for example in a study investigating smokers and non-smokers).	• Because participants may have chosen which study group they are in (or the researcher has done so for them), this significantly biases the outcomes. • For example, if there were two groups of children: Group 1 in the top set for maths, and Group 2 in the bottom set for maths, and a study investigated performance in physics, the two groups of children are not similar.	• Cohort study. • Case control study.
Random allocation.	• Allows equal balancing of confounding factors. • Limits bias in terms of participant selection of an intervention or exposure.	• Not always possible or ethical to randomise participants to different groups.	• RCT.

Table 7.6   Blind versus open-label studies

Study design feature	Implications		Studies that often use this feature
Blinding: an individual is not aware of what intervention or exposure they're given. Individuals who can be blinded in a study include the participants, the researchers and the analysts, and so a study can be single, double or triple blind.	• Anticipation of the placebo effect: a phenomenon whereby study participants experience improvement in an outcome after receiving 'something' that should in theory not produce an improvement in outcome. • Prevention of observer bias in researchers and analysts.	• It is not always possible or ethical to blind study participants or researchers.	• RCT. • Cohort study.
Open-label: an individual is aware of what intervention or exposure they are receiving. Again, this includes the participants, the researchers and the analysts.	• It is not always possible or ethical to blind study participants or research personnel, for example in a study investigating surgery versus no surgery.	• Participants may exaggerate an improvement if they think they are receiving something that is supposed to have an effect. • Researchers may exaggerate findings according to their own biases.	• RCT. • Cohort study.

Validity (Are the results of a study true?)

The way in which research is designed and undertaken has a bearing on whether the results can be considered 'true' or 'valid'. Are there any flaws in how the research has been carried out that may invalidate the findings? Simply the act of undertaking research can alter study findings from reality. Imagine if you were informed by one of your tutors that the occupational health department wanted you and your fellow course participants to take part in a study on the frequency of hand washing. Would you be likely to alter your hand-washing practices? Would the findings of the study accurately represent hand-washing practices or would they present a distorted picture?

So in assessing validity we ask, 'How much have the methods used to obtain the results thrown into question the findings themselves?'(Booth and Brice, 2004). The rigour of the research refers to the degree to which the design of the study and its conduct minimises the risk of **bias** and takes into account **confounding**; the two key flaws that can affect all studies. Bias is 'anything that erroneously influences the conclusions about groups and distorts comparisons' (Rose and Barker, 1994). Systematic errors in the conduct of a study include how subjects are selected to take part, how outcomes are measured, or how data are analysed. All of these can lead to inaccurate results (College of Emergency Medicine, 2010). Confounding is where you cannot ascertain whether an effect is caused by the variable you are interested in or by another variable. For example, a study may demonstrate a link between alcohol consumption and lung cancer. However, alcohol consumption is commonly associated with smoking, and therefore smoking is a potential confounder for your study. Studies can be designed to take account of potential confounding at the analysis stage, or to ensure that groups within the study are stratified to achieve equal distribution of participants with the confounding factor (in this example smoking). Whichever method is chosen, the researcher should demonstrate that they have identified potential confounders at the beginning of the study. Common **confounding variables** are age, sex and ethnicity.

To illustrate sources of bias and confounding, read the accompanying study scenario (Exercise 7.4) and try to answer the questions following.

 exercise 7.4

Study scenario

Can an ICT intervention improve primary schoolchildren's performance in solving maths problems?

A group of 20 primary schoolchildren are selected by their teacher to take part in this study as a reward for good behaviour. At the start of the study, each child completes a maths problems test consisting of 10 questions. Each child then completes a one-hour online workbook on the class computer, in which they complete a series of maths problems in the form of fun games and exercises. The children then complete another maths problems test of 10 questions, and the number answered correctly is recorded. The teacher asks each child to recall how many they got correct in the maths test before the study started.

(Continued)

(Continued)

1   *What sources of bias can you see?*

Hint 1 – might the children selected to take part in the study differ in any way from those who did not take part?

Hint 2 – do you think the children could accurately (and truthfully!) recall their score for the test they took at the beginning of the study?

2   *Aside from the sources of bias in this study, what other factors might limit the credibility of the study findings?*

Reliability (What are the results?)

All research results are subject to the possible effects of chance. Reliability refers to the trustworthiness of the results: 'What is the likelihood that this study reports something that is reproducible as opposed to being a "fluke" or chance result?' (Booth and Brice, 2004). Statistical tests can be undertaken to determine the likelihood that results are due to chance. Techniques exist to provide a range of plausible values for the repeated measurement of the effect. This allows you to judge whether you would make the same decision based on the very best and the very worst estimate of the effect. However, statisticians choose arbitrary thresholds for determining chance, typically 5% or 1 in 20, and if something occurs more frequently than this, it is considered unlikely to be due to the play of chance (Booth and Brice, 2004) and is labelled **statistically significant**. It is also important to determine whether results are meaningful, i.e. is the effect large enough to be **practically signifi- cant**? For example, a study might demonstrate a change in five points on a scale measuring improvement in computer skills. This change of five points might be statistically significant but it might take a change of 10 points or more before a teacher considers this to be practi- cally significant.

Applicability (Can we generalise the results?)

Once you have assessed the validity and reliability of a study, you need to determine whether the results actually are useful. Validity and reliability are concerned with estimating the strength of the evidence, whereas applicability is concerned with the strength of recommendations for practice (based on the study results).

Continuing with our study scenario, imagine you are the headteacher of a primary school and you are reading the results of a systematic literature review investigating whether an ICT intervention improves primary schoolchildren's performance in solving maths problems. The review found seven studies designed to test this research question, however the results are con- flicting between the studies. Five studies found that ICT did improve students' performance in a weekly maths test, whilst two showed no evidence of such an effect. By examining the studies in more detail, you realise that the five supportive studies were undertaken in a group of children aged eight to nine years old, whereas the two studies that did not find a positive effect were undertaken in children of a younger age group (four to five years old). Thus, it might be reasonable for you as headteacher to suggest that the ICT-based maths computer program should be taken up only by classes of older children at the school. Note this is not a flaw of the individual studies included in the review, but simply reflects a difference in age of study participants and thus relates to how applicable the findings are to your situation.

DOING QUALITY ASSESSMENT

Now that the theory has been covered, how do you tackle assessing the quality of studies? Whilst every article is different, assessment of quality can be split into four stages (LoBiondo-Wood et al., 2002) (see Box 7.1).

 box 7.1

Four stages of quality assessment

Preliminary understanding – skimming or quickly reading to gain familiarity with the content and layout of the paper.

Comprehensive understanding – increasing understanding of concepts and research terms.

Analysis understanding – breaking the study into parts and seeking to understand each part.

Synthesis understanding – pulling the above steps together to make a (new) whole, making sense of it and explaining relationships.

Even if you do not undertake full quality assessment for your review, you will always need to follow the first two steps in Box 7.1. In developing a preliminary and then comprehensive understanding of each study, you will arrive at an overall understanding of the individual contribution of that study. Most literature reviews involve some form of analysis understanding. The depth to which you break down the study into parts depends on which data are most important for your review. For example, in a systematic mapping review you may be concerned with a few items of information such as the type of studies, country and key themes. In contrast, in a systematic review, the details of study design are required in great depth, and so this will involve you 'drilling down' into the study for much of the necessary detail.

A useful place to start is by reading the abstract. The format of the abstract varies between disciplines. Increasingly within the medical literature, structured abstracts (with headings) are being adopted. These help the reader quickly assess the study design, participants and key results. Abstracts in other disciplines may be less structured but give a flavour of what the study is about. After reading the abstract, to gain a deeper understanding of the study, you would start to read the paper in full. Whilst the 'Introduction', 'Discussion' and 'Conclusion' can help in understanding the paper, it is the 'Methods' section that allows you to determine the quality of the paper. The 'Results' section may also indicate the significance of the individual study. Remember that practical relevance may not feature in the 'Results' section but may be considered in the 'Discussion' section. The National Collaborating Centre for Methods and Tools (2014) provides an 'anatomy' of a systematic review which is a useful tool to assist with critical appraisal as it presents the information that can be found in each section of a review.

EXISTING REVIEWS IN YOUR SUBJECT AREA

You can start to understand the process of quality assessment in your discipline by investigating the methods used in existing reviews in your topic area. This enables you to gain a good understanding of the general approach taken including justification for the approaches used, which checklists (or combinations of checklists) are widely used, and how the authors present the information. Finally, such a review may help you identify which key study flaws and strengths are most likely to occur in your topic area.

Some examples of systematic reviews in a variety of disciplines are presented in Table 7.7, each demonstrating a different approach to quality and relevance assessment. Similar variation is apparent for other types of literature reviews such as mapping and scoping reviews (examine the reviews we listed in Table 7.1). The other examples of different types of reviews throughout this book may also be useful. Further examples can be found at resources such as the EPPI-Centre, the Campbell Library and the Cochrane Library.

Table 7.7 Examples of systematic reviews in different disciplines

Topic area	Reference	Quality assessment strategy
Health	Portion, package or tableware size for changing selection and consumption of food, alcohol and tobacco (Hollands et al., 2015)	As per the *Cochrane Handbook* criteria of assessment of risk of bias (Higgins and Green, 2011).
Social welfare	The impact of detention on the health of asylum seekers: a systematic review (Filges et al., 2015)	Studies were assessed using an extension of the Cochrane Collaboration's risk of bias tool. The extension covers risk of bias in non-randomised studies that have a well-defined control group. The risk of bias model used is based on nine items: <ul><li>sequence generation</li><li>allocation concealment</li><li>confounders</li><li>blinding</li><li>incomplete outcome data</li><li>selective outcome reporting</li><li>other potential threats to validity</li><li>a priori protocol</li><li>a priori analysis plan.</li></ul>

Topic area	Reference	Quality assessment strategy
Psychology	Psychological and educational interventions for atopic eczema in children (Ersser et al., 2014).	Quality assessment addressed four areas: • Randomisation (method of generation and concealment of allocation) • Blinding of observers (blinding of participants was not possible because of the nature of the intervention) • Loss to follow-up (presence of dropouts and withdrawals and the analysis of these) • Other bias. Each component was categorised as low risk, unclear risk or high risk as advised by the *Cochrane Handbook for Systematic Reviews of Interventions* (Higgins and Green, 2011).
Education	Impacts of after-school programs on student outcomes (Goerlich Zief et al., 2006)	The study reviewers met and listed 39 qualities that they felt should be included in the reporting of a rigorous experimental study. These were adapted from the What Works Clearinghouse *Evidence Standards of Reviewing Studies* (2005). From these, four specific standards were selected that the reviewers believed needed to be met in order for a study to be included in this review: (a) no specific evidence of control group contamination (b) neither overall study attrition nor differential attrition would bias the impact estimates (c) appropriate statistical measures were used for the analyses, and (d) the primary impact analyses were conducted on all available sample members at follow-up (intention to treat and not 'treatment on treated'). Two reviewers independently read each full study, applied the study quality criteria, and recommended whether the study should be included in the final review.
Library and information science	The attitudes and behaviours of illegal downloaders (Williams et al., 2010).	When selecting studies for inclusion, the authors categorised the literature into four 'classes', which included an assessment of quality: • *Class A:* Studies with high validity, a robust methodology and that had been highly cited. (Note that high citations do not necessarily indicate high quality, a study could equally be cited as a bad example of research!) • *Class B:* Credible studies in which we could not place quite such a high degree of confidence. This could be a methodological issue (small-scale surveys, convenience sampling, limited case study interviews, etc.). • *Class C:* Research that was not very sound in terms of methodology, rigour and validity. • *Class D:* Minimal or no real research content (for example opinion pieces).
Computer sciences	Using text mining for study identification in systematic reviews: a systematic review of current approaches (O-Mara Eves et al., 2015)	Critical appraisal was conducted as part of the data extraction tool. Quality was assessed by two questions: a) Sampling of test cases: how generalisable is the sample of reviews selected? b) Is the method sufficiently described to be replicated?

USING CHECKLISTS

For experienced and novice reviewers alike, checklists can be particularly helpful in guiding the process of quality and relevance assessment. For the novice reviewer, checklists provide a comprehensive list of everything to consider in terms of quality assessment. Checklists may also help when considering study relevance, typically considered by the last three questions on Critical Appraisal Skills Programme checklists (Critical Appraisal Skills Programme, 2013). However, as you become experienced at quality assessment, checklists will act as a prompt to help you consider all relevant points. The tools in this chapter point to a range of multi-disciplinary sources of checklists for a range of study designs. However, be sure to investigate reviews within your discipline as they may give pointers as to how quality assessment is undertaken within your research area (Davoudi et al., 2015). For example, checklists in social work and social care have been discussed (Wells and Littell, 2009) and developed (Taylor et al., 2007). Also consider whether a generic checklist for each type of question, such as CASP, meets your needs or whether you need to adapt an existing checklist to your own topic area. If you adapt a published checklist, be sure to note this when writing up the methodology for your review.

Table 7.8 lists a few key checklist resources by study design or topic. See Box 7.2 for some tips on selecting a checklist.

 toolbox

Quality assessment checklists

Table 7.8   Key checklists resources

	Study design checklists	
Resource	**Details**	
Systematic Review Toolbox (http://systematicreviewtools.com/)	A searchable online catalogue of tools to support systematic reviews. The focus is on automated tools (software), but other tools (such as checklists) are also included. To browse the quality assessment tools, select 'quality assessment' from the feature list.	
Critical Appraisal Skills Programme (CASP)	Checklists for the following study designs: • Systematic reviews • Randomised controlled trials (RCTs) • Qualitative research • Economic evaluation studies • Cohort studies • Case control studies • Diagnostic test studies • Clinical Prediction Rules	

Study design checklists	
Resource	**Details**
STrengthening the Reporting of OBservational studies in Epidemiology (STROBE)	Checklists for the following study designs: • Cohort, case-control, and cross-sectional studies (combined) • Cohort studies • Case-control studies • Cross-sectional studies
BestBETS	Checklists for the following study designs: • Case-control checklist (including harm) • Cohort • Decision rule • Diagnosis • Economic • Educational intervention • Guideline • Prognosis • Qualitative • Randomised control trial • Review or meta-analysis • Screening • Survey (including pre-test probabilities)
AMSTAR - Assessing the methodological quality of systematic reviews	www.amstar.ca/Amstar_Checklist.php
Case studies (Atkins and Sampson, 2002)	Case studies
Qualitative research (Dixon-Woods et al., 2006)	Prompts for qualitative research
Mixed-methods studies (Pluye and Hong, 2014)	http://mixedmethodsappraisaltoolpublic.pbworks.com/w/page/24607821/FrontPage

Topic-specific checklists

Evidence-based library and Information science (http://ebltoolkit.pbworks.com/f/EBLCriticalAppraisalChecklist.pdf)

Education - ReLIANT (Readers guide to the Literature on Interventions Addressing the Need for education and Training) (Koufogiannakis et al., 2008)

Generic checklists

Standard quality assessment criteria for evaluating primary research papers from a variety of fields (Kmet et al., 2004)

Do not be put off by the first few occasions you undertake quality assessment. It takes some time – from our experience quality assessment of a complicated study can take anything up to a couple of hours. However, you will soon become more proficient and, consequently, quicker. The more quality assessment you undertake, the more adept you become at spotting the key strengths or weaknesses of a study – the same flaws in published studies often occur again and again.

 box 7.2

Tips on checklists

- Remember quality and relevance assessment vary by discipline. Take a look at reviews in your discipline and examine how authors have undertaken quality and relevance assessment, and also which checklist they have used. See Table 7.7 for examples and key features of reviews in different disciplines.
- Stick to checklists that have been validated or widely accepted in your discipline. Again, examining reviews in your discipline will help you identify the accepted checklists.
- Avoid checklists that employ scoring systems. It is dangerous to label studies with scores, and not particularly helpful in understanding how the study strengths and weaknesses contribute to the validity of the study findings. In fact, the Cochrane methods guide for systematic reviews actively discourages use of checklists that assess quality using a scoring system (Higgins and Green, 2011).
- Remember what you are trying to achieve through quality and relevance assessment – checklists are only a guide. You may spot study features that are not picked up by your checklist and these can still be reported.
- Lastly, you can get creative with checklists, and may want to select criteria from different checklists and devise your own uber-checklist. (However, do remember to justify why you have done so and reference the contributing checklists.)

Pre-existing summaries

It can be helpful to identify published examples where someone has performed a quality assessment of a published study, so investigate the journals in your discipline (particularly student versions of journals) to see if they do.

Examples include:

- Student BMJ;
- TERSE reports at the Centre for Evaluation and Monitoring: www.cem.org/terse-reports;
- Evidence Based Library and Information Practice (EBLIP) Journal.

QUALITY ASSESSMENT OF QUALITATIVE RESEARCH

There is considerable debate around the quality assessment of qualitative research as to whether it can, or indeed should, be done. There is little consensus within qualitative research, with over a hundred sets of proposals on quality in qualitative research (Dixon-Woods et al., 2004) and widely opposing views. Popay and colleagues (1998) describe two camps: those who believe that the concepts used in quantitative research apply equally to qualitative research, without further interpretation (reliability, validity), and those who believe that there are no quality criteria by which qualitative research can be assessed. There is further contention about how best to approach quality assessment given evidence that it cannot be performed reliably; Dixon-Woods and colleagues demonstrated widely different results from quality assessment using three appraisal approaches and six different reviewers (Dixon-Woods et al., 2007). In recent times, the debate has shifted away from whether or not quality assessment should be done, and towards what criteria should be used (Carroll and Booth, 2015). Hannes and Macaitis (2012) examined 82 qualitative evidence syntheses (QES) published between 1998 and 2008, and found that critical appraisal had been conducted in most cases, with only five reviews explicitly stating and justifying the absence of critical appraisal. The ENTREQ statement, a guideline to enhance transparency in the reporting of qualitative evidence synthesis, published in 2012, includes appraisal within its five domains (Tong et al., 2012), indicating that your target journals may expect you to perform quality assessment within your qualitative review.

The Cochrane Qualitative and Implementation Methods Group has published supplemental guidance to Chapter 20 of the *Cochrane Handbook* on qualitative research and **Cochrane Reviews** (Noyes et al., 2011). Chapter 4 of this guidance covers critical appraisal, affirming that quality assessment is an essential component of qualitative Cochrane Reviews (Hannes, 2011). The chapter adapts the broad principles of quality assessment in quantitative reviews, and refers to the concepts being assessed as *credibility, transferability, dependability* and *confirmability*. To find out more about quality assessment of qualitative research, read the chapter which is freely available online (Hannes, 2011). There are plans to update the guidance in 2016.

If you are undertaking quality assessment for your own qualitative research, you need to consider which checklist to use or whether to consider devising your own. Some researchers have devised their own criteria, basing them on existing quality criteria (Thomas and Harden, 2008), and others discuss quality assessment methods more generally (Barnett-Page and Thomas, 2009). Carroll et al. (2012) propose a tool that focuses explicitly on the quality of reporting, not on the appropriateness of methods used. Brief prompts for quality assessment of qualitative research have also been suggested (Popay et al., 1998; Dixon-Woods et al., 2004). Dixon-Woods and colleagues developed a brief set of prompts to investigate the quality of studies on access to healthcare by vulnerable groups (Dixon-Woods et al., 2006). The prompts they used can be seen in Box 7.3.

 box 7.3

Quality assessment prompts

- Are the aims and objectives of the research clearly stated?
- Is the research design clearly specified and appropriate for the aims and objectives of the research?
- Do the researchers provide a clear account of the process by which their findings were reproduced?
- Do the researchers display enough data to support their interpretations and conclusions?
- Is the method of analysis appropriate and adequately explicated?

(Source: Dixon-Woods et al., 2006)

Secondly, it is important to bear in mind why you are undertaking quality assessment of qualitative research. Examples exist in the literature where studies are excluded on the basis of quality (Brunton et al., 2006), however as in quantitative reviews the majority of qualitative reviews do not exclude studies on the basis of quality. Sandelowski and colleagues (1997) advise caution in using checklists to exclude studies from a review, arguing that any exclusions must be supported by an explicit account of the researcher's view of 'good' and 'bad' studies, and reason for exclusions. Carroll and Booth (2015) propose that you should routinely look at the effect on the review of both including and excluding poor quality studies (so-called 'qualitative sensitivity analysis').

Lastly, you should recognise that quality assessment of qualitative research is a developing area, and further work is being done in this field (Garside, 2014). Recent research suggests that there is little value in assessing qualitative studies for qualitative systematic reviews because the appraisal activity has little impact on the overall review findings, and the exclusion of weaker studies shows no effect (Thomas and Harden, 2008). For example, Carroll and colleagues (2012) found that in two reviews previously conducted (one on the topic of young people's views relating to school sexual health services, and one on health professionals' views of online education techniques), exclusion of 'so-called inadequately reported' studies had no meaningful effect on the synthesis. However, they also observed, in the review of online education, that excluding inadequately reported studies might leave out a disproportionate number of studies of one particular group of health professionals.

APPLYING QUALITY ASSESSMENT

Quality assessment of studies generates large quantities of information. Typically, in systematic reviews where quality assessment is standard, the 'Results' section presents a few paragraphs that attempt to synthesise information on overall study quality, focusing on its impact on individual study findings. The information can also be tabulated by drawing out the key points of the checklist. Generally the 'Discussion' focuses on the key flaws, but you should not forget to include what has been done well! As mentioned previously, you should be aware of those study flaws that are 'fatal' and those that are not – remember that it is the *impact* on the study findings that is crucial.

Reviews do not generally exclude studies on the basis of quality. However, sometimes a **subgroup analysis** is performed to examine the results of the quality assessment. This involves splitting the studies into subgroups according to a particular study design feature that might impact on study findings, for example the country in which the study was undertaken, and exploring how this might impact on the findings of the review. For example, smaller studies are known to overestimate study findings (Higgins and Green, 2011) and subgroup analysis can demonstrate this.

Finally, be cautious about labelling studies according to a level of quality (for example high, medium and low). Whilst in principle this might appear useful, you need to be explicit about the criteria by which studies are categorised, so that ultimately the classification of studies could be reliably reproduced. Given this may be a highly subjective exercise, you don't want to mislead the reader as their concept of a high-quality study may differ from your own.

ISSUES AND CHALLENGES IN QUALITY ASSESSMENT

Assessing the quality of research is time-consuming, particularly when you are new to the process. With experience, you will become quicker as you become more familiar with the study designs and their inherent and anticipated weaknesses. You may also find it difficult to choose a checklist given the number from which to choose. As discussed earlier, you could examine examples of reviews in your subject area to identify the more common and well-used checklists of your research discipline.

Quality assessment is a subjective process. For systematic reviews, methods guides suggest that quality assessment should be carried out by more than one person and the results compared (Centre for Reviews and Dissemination, 2009; Higgins and Green, 2011). However, this is not always practical or necessary. Having a second reviewer check a sample of quality assessments might be a more reasonable alternative, particularly for those elements of which you are unsure (with a supervisor or mentor perhaps). Use of checklists typically makes it easier to achieve consensus. As previously stated, fundamental issues concerning the subjectivity of quality assessment of qualitative research remain to be resolved.

Lastly, remember quality assessment examines what is reported within a study, and thus studies can only be as good as their reporting. Often studies do not report enough details of the methods of a study and thus the quality assessment measures only the quality of reporting. Whilst it is possible to track authors down to elicit missing details, a good paper should include sufficient detail to allow you to assess its quality. The quality of reporting of research has been subject to recent attention, with several standards being published regarding the quality of research reporting for specific study designs; the **PRISMA** statement in systematic reviews (Moher et al., 2009); the CONSORT statement in RCTs (Schulz et al., 2010); and the STROBE statement for observational studies in epidemiology (von Elm et al., 2014). Various extensions to the published standards also exist, for example the PRISMA-P for systematic review and meta-analyses protocols (Moher et al., 2015). The Equator Network provides a comprehensive list (www.equator-network.org/reporting-guidelines/). Over time, as more studies adopt such standards in their reporting, the task of quality assessment will become, at least in theory, much easier – assuming that standardised reporting does not make it more difficult to identify the poorer studies.

Use Exercise 7.5 to practise your quality assessment skills. We suggest you critically appraise the articles given by using the suggested checklist. When you have completed your own critical appraisal, compare with the *Student BMJ* commentary to see if you identified the same issues.

 exercise 7.5

Quality assessment

In Table 7.9, three articles from the *British Medical Journal (BMJ)* are presented for you to test out your quality assessment skills. Each of the three articles is accompanied by a commentary from the *Student BMJ*, which summarises the key issues relating to quality.

(Continued)

(Continued)

Although these examples are from the *BMJ*, the selected articles are of different study designs and are not exclusively health-focused. The skills that you acquire from undertaking this exercise are transferable when appraising studies from other disciplines.

First, read the full article (freely available online at the *BMJ* website). Then try undertaking a quality assessment using an appropriate checklist (suggested checklists are provided in Table 7.9). Then take a look at the accompanying reference provided for each of the three articles at the *Student BMJ*, which provides a critical appraisal summary of the article, drawing out the key issues. Try the quality assessment yourself (do not look at the corresponding *Student BMJ* article until you have completed it) and then take a look to see if you've identified the key points.

Table 7.9   Quality assessment of an article

Study reference	*Student BMJ* summary	Checklist
Effect of antibiotic prescribing on antibiotic resistance in individual children in primary care: prospective cohort study (Chung 2007)	Student BMJ (2007) 15, 337-82	CASP Cohort study checklist
Experiences of belittlement and harassment and their correlates among medical students in the United States: longitudinal survey (Frank et al., 2006)	*Student BMJ* (2006) 14, 353-96	BestBETS Survey worksheet
Relation between a career and family life for English hospital consultants: qualitative, semi-structured interview study (Dumelow et al., 2000)	*Student BMJ* (2000) 8, 236-40	CASP Qualitative checklist

SUMMARY

All literature reviews involve an assessment of the evidence base. The first step is to systematically select those studies identified by the literature search that are relevant to your research question. The type of review that you are undertaking and its purpose will determine the accompanying tasks related to assessing the included studies in your literature review. For some reviews, you may briefly characterise the key features of the evidence base. In other reviews, you will need to conduct a more in-depth assessment of study quality to help answer the review question. Using checklists helps you in this process, and these are particularly useful if you are a novice reviewer. Many useful resources exist to support the process. Quality assessment is, initially at least, a difficult and time-consuming process. However, be sure to persevere as it does become easier with experience and practice.

 key learning points

- Use the inclusion and exclusion criteria you devised in Chapter 5 to help you select studies for your review in a transparent manner.
- Consider the extent to which you need to assess the evidence base for your review by thinking about the aim of your review.

- Consider how the design features of studies included in your review can impact upon the research findings.
- Three core components of quality assessment to consider when reading a study are:

  o Are the results of a study true? (validity)
  o What are the results? (reliability)
  o Can I generalise the results? (generalisability)

- Quality assessment checklists are helpful in guiding the process of quality and relevance assessment.
- Look at research within your discipline, particularly existing reviews, to see how quality assessment is undertaken in your subject area.

▬▬▬ frequently asked questions (FAQs) ▬▬▬

FAQ 7.1 I am unsure whether to include a study in my review, what can I do?

You could ask for a second opinion, for example from your supervisor or mentor. Alternatively, you could hand a colleague your inclusion and exclusion criteria and ask them to apply these to the study in question to see what decision they reach.

FAQ 7.2 Do I need to record a reason for all the studies I exclude?

No, you only need to record reasons for any studies you exclude at full-text. Systematic reviews usually include in the appendices a list of these with a (brief) reason for why they did not meet the inclusion criteria (such as incorrect population).

FAQ 7.3 How do I keep track of what I have included and excluded and at what stage?

It is important that you have a system, whether manual or electronic. Reference management tools can be helpful in this regard, as you are able to tag or label references accordingly – such as include-abstract or exclude-full-text. You will then be able to retrieve lists based on the various tags/labels, for example to generate a list of excluded at full-text studies for your appendices.

FAQ 7.4 I'm unsure about the level of quality assessment required and how to go about it for my review?

Refer to Table 7.1 as a starting point. You may also find it helpful to look at existing reviews, of a similar type (so if you plan to do a scoping review look at existing scoping reviews) and from within your subject area to see if subject-specific checklists exist or if researchers tend to use and/or adapt generic ones. The Systematic Review Toolbox (http://systematicreviewtools.com/) is a good source of quality assessment checklists and guidelines as it covers multiple disciplines.

FAQ 7.5 I am critically appraising a systematic review, and I want to assess the issue of heterogeneity, whereabouts in the review should I look for this?

How the reviewers planned to deal with the issue of heterogeneity may be recorded up front in the 'Methods' section. Also, check the results section to see how this was carried out in

(Continued)

(Continued)

practice. If the review has a **meta-analysis**, you can check the **Forest plot** to see whether it was appropriate to combine the results of the individual studies. There is a useful 'Anatomy of a Systematic Review' (National Collaborating Centre for Methods and Tools, 2014) tool which will assist you in your reading of reviews for critical appraisal.

FAQ 7.6 Can I combine my data extraction with my quality assessment, to save having to read the study twice?

It is possible to record the data extraction and critical appraisal at a single sitting. Various examples of combined data extraction and critical appraisal exist, including this sample data extraction form from the Research Council for Complementary Medicine (www.rccm. org.uk/sites/default/files/files/DECA%20forms.pdf). It really is a matter of choice and what you find most effective for you as a reviewer. With any data extraction form, whether including critical appraisal or not, it is useful to pilot the form first before using it throughout your review.

━━━━━ suggestions for further reading ━━━━━

Ajetunmobi, O. (2002) *Making Sense of Critical Appraisal*. London: Arnold.
A useful book with a chapter on appraising each key study design. Read the chapter(s) that cover the study designs of your evidence base.

Aveyard, H. (2014) How do I critically appraise the literature?. In H. Aveyard (ed.), *Doing a Literature Review in Health and Social Care*, 3rd edition. Maidenhead: Open University Press, 99–135.
This chapter gives an overview of critical appraisal. Particularly helpful is the 'six questions to trigger critical thinking'. Appraisal of a variety of information types is covered – quantitative and qualitative research, theory, practice literature, policy and guidelines, and information on websites.

Greenhalgh, J. and Brown, T. (2014) Quality assessment: where do I begin?. In A. Boland, M.G. Cherry and R. Dickson (eds), *Doing a Systematic Review*. London: Sage, 61–83.
This chapter covers the process of quality assessment from beginning to end, in a six-step guide.

Greenhalgh, T. (2014) *How to Read a Paper: The Basics of Evidence-based Medicine*, 5th edition. Oxford: Wiley Blackwell.
Now in its 5th edition, this essential book gives an overview of the evidence-based medicine process. Chapter 3 on 'Getting Your Bearings' provides an introduction to quality assessment, before moving on in the following chapter to assessing methodological quality. Chapter 5, 'Statistics for the Non-statistician', is particularly useful for familiarising yourself with the key statistical aspects of studies to inform your critical appraisal.

Oliver, P. (2012) How to select literature for inclusion. In P. Oliver (ed.), *Succeeding with Your Literature Review*. Maidenhead: Open University Press, 58–74.
A good introduction to quality assessment, does not cover formal critical appraisal, but does highlight the issues to consider when selecting studies to include in your review.

Porritt, K., Gomersall, J. and Lockwood, C. (2014) JBI's systematic reviews: study selection and critical appraisal. *American Journal of Nursing*, **114**, 6, 47-52.
Part of a series presenting a step-by-step guide to systematic review, this article focuses on study selection and critical appraisal, with the aim of ensuring that your review produces valid results capable of providing a useful basis for informing policy, clinical practice and future research. The article helpfully presents appraising evidence of effectiveness (quantitative studies) and appraising evidence of experiences (qualitative studies).

REFERENCES

Atkins, C. and Sampson, J. (2002) Critical appraisal guidelines for single case study research. *ECIS 2002 Proceedings*, Paper 15.

Barnett-Page, E. and Thomas, J. (2009) Methods for the synthesis of qualitative research: a critical review. *BMC Medical Research Methodology*, **9**, 59.

Booth, A. (2007) Who will appraise the appraisers? – the paper, the instrument and the user. *Health Information and Libraries Journal*, **24**, 1, 72–6.

Booth, A. and Brice, A. (2004) Appraising the evidence. In A. Booth and A. Brice (eds), *Evidence Based Practice for Information Professionals: A Handbook*. London: Facet, 96–110.

Brunton, G., Oliver, S., Oliver, K. and Lorenc, T. (2006) *A Synthesis of Research Addressing Children's, Young People's and Parents' Views of Walking and Cycling for Transport*. London: EPPI-Centre, Social Science Research Unit, Institute of Education, University of London.

Carroll, C. and Booth, A. (2015) Quality assessment of qualitative evidence for systematic review and synthesis: is it meaningful, and if so, how should it be performed? *Research Synthesis Methods*, **6**, 149–54.

Carroll, C., Booth, A. and Lloyd-Jones, M. (2012) Should we exclude inadequately reported studies from qualitative systematic reviews? An evaluation of sensitivity analyses in two case study reviews. *Qualitative Health Research*, **22**, 10, 1425–34.

Centre for Evidence Based Medicine (2009) *Study Designs*. Oxford: CEBM.

Centre for Reviews and Dissemination (2009) *CRD's Guidance for Undertaking Reviews in Healthcare*, 3rd edition. York: Centre for Reviews and Dissemination.

Chung, A. (2007) Effect of antibiotic prescribing on antibiotic resistance in individual children in primary care: prospective cohort study. *BMJ*, **335**, 429.

Coast, E., Jones, E., Portela, A. and Lattof, S. (2014) Maternity care services and culture: a systematic global mapping of interventions. *PLOS One*, **9**, 9, e108130.

College of Emergency Medicine (2010) *Bias and Confounding*. London: RCEM.

Critical Appraisal Skills Programme (2013) *Critical Appraisal Skills Programme Tools*. Oxford: CASP UK.

Davoudi, S., Harper, G., Petts, J. and Whatmore, S. (2015) Judging research quality to support evidence-informed environmental policy. *Environmental Evidence*, **4**, 1, 1.

Dixon-Woods, M., Cavers, D., Agarwal, S., Annandale, E., Arthur, A., Harvey, J., Hsu, R., Katbamna, S., Olsen, R., Smith, L., Riley, R. and Sutton, A.J. (2006) Conducting a critical interpretive synthesis of the literature on access to healthcare by vulnerable groups. *BMC Medical Research Methodology*, **6**, 35.

Dixon-Woods, M., Shaw, R., Agarwal, S. and Smith, J. (2004) The problem of appraising qualitative research. *Quality and Safety in Health Care*, **13**, 223–5.

Dixon-Woods, M., Sutton, A., Shaw, R., Miller, T., Smith, J., Young, B., Bonas, S., Booth, A. and Jones, D. (2007) Appraising qualitative research for inclusion in systematic reviews: a quantitative and qualitative comparison of three methods. *Journal of Health Services Research and Policy*, **12**, 42–7.

Dumelow, C., Littlejohns, P. and Griffiths, S. (2000) Relation between a career and family life for English hospital consultants: qualitative, semistructured interview study. *BMJ*, **320**, 7247, 1437–40.

EPPI-Centre (2010) *Quality and Relevance Appraisal*. London: EPPI-Centre.

Ersser, S.J., Cowdell, F., Latter, S., Gardiner, E., Flohr, C., Thompson, A.R., Jackson, K., Farasat, H., Ware, F. and Drury, A. (2014) Psychological and educational interventions for atopic eczema in children. *Cochrane Database of Systematic Reviews*, Issue 1.

Farmer, J., Kenny, A., McKinstry, C. and Huysmans, R.D. (2015) A scoping review of the association between rural medical education and rural practice location. *Human Resources for Health*, **13**, 27.

Filges, T., Montgomery, E., Kastrup, M. and Klint Jørgensen, A. (2015) The impact of detention on the health of asylum seekers: a systematic review. *The Campbell Library*, **11**, 13.

Frank, E., Carrera, J.S., Stratton, T., Bickel, J. and Nora, L.M. (2006) Experiences of belittlement and harassment and their correlates among medical students in the United States: longitudinal survey. *BMJ*, **333**, 682.

Garside, R. (2014) Should we appraise the quality of qualitative research reports for systematic reviews, and if so, how? *Innovation: The European Journal of Social Science Research*, **27**, 1, 67–79.

Goerlich Zief, S., Lauver, S. and Maynard, R.A. (2006) Impacts of after-school programs on student outcomes: a systematic review. *The Campbell Library*, **2**, 3.

Grant, M.J. and Booth, A. (2009) A typology of reviews: an analysis of 14 review types and associated methodologies. *Health Information and Libraries Journal*, **26**, 2, 91–108.

Hammersley, M. (2001) On 'systematic' reviews of research literatures: a 'narrative' response to Evans and Benefield. *British Educational Research Journal*, **27**, 5, 543–54.

Hannes K. (2011) Chapter 4: Critical appraisal of qualitative research. In J. Noyes, A. Booth, K. Hannes, A. Harden, J. Harris, S. Lewin and C. Lockwood (eds), *Supplementary Guidance for Inclusion of Qualitative Research in Cochrane Systematic Reviews of Interventions*. Version 1 (updated August 2011). Oxford: Cochrane Collaboration Qualitative Methods Group. Available at http://methods.cochrane.org/qi/sites/methods.cochrane.org.qi/files/uploads/Data%20synthesis%20supplemental%20guidance_2010%2012%2023B.doc.

Hannes, K. and Macaitis, K. (2012) A move to more systematic and transparent approaches in qualitative evidence synthesis: update on a review of published papers. *Qualitative Research*, **12**, 4, 402–2.

Higgins, J.P.T. and Green, S. (2011) *Cochrane Handbook for Systematic Reviews of Interventions*, Version 5.1.0 (updated March 2011). The Cochrane Collaboration. Available at: www.cochrane-handbook.org (last accessed 9 March 2016).

Hollands, G.J., Shemilt,I., Marteau,T.M., Jebb,S.A., Lewis, H.B., Wei, Y., Higgins, J.P.T. and Ogilvie, D. (2015) Portion, package or tableware size for changing selection and consumption of food, alcohol and tobacco. *Cochrane Database of Systematic Reviews*, Issue 9.

Kmet, L.M., Lee, R.C. and Cook, L.S. (2004) *Standard Quality Assessment Criteria for Evaluating Primary Research Papers from a Variety of Fields*. Edmonton: Alberta Heritage Foundation for Medical Research (AHFMR). HTA Initiative #13.

Koufogiannakis, D., Booth, A. and Brettle, A. (2006) *ReLIANT: Reader's Guide to the Literature on Interventions Addressing the Need for Education and Training*. e-LIS: e-prints in library and information science. Available online at: http://eprints.rclis.org/8082/.

LoBiondo-Wood, G., Haber, J. and Krainovich-Miller, B. (2002) Critical reading strategies: overview of the research process. In G. LoBiondo-Wood and J. Haber (eds), *Nursing Research: Methods, Critical Appraisal, and Utilization,* 5th edition. St Louis, MI: Mosby.

Maynard, B.R., Brendel, K., Bulanda, J.J., Heyne, D., Thompson, A. and Pigott, A. (2015) Psychosocial interventions for school refusal with primary and secondary school students: a systematic review. *The Campbell Library*, **11**, 12.

Moher, D., Liberati, A., Tetzlaff, J., Altman, D.G. and PRISMA Group (2009) Preferred reporting items for systematic reviews and meta-analyses: the PRISMA statement. *PLoS Medicine*, **6**, 7, e1000097.

Moher, D., Shamseer, L., Clarke, M., Ghersi, D., Liberati, A., Petticrew, M., Shekelle, P. and Stewart, L.A. (2015) Preferred reporting items for systematic review and meta-analysis protocols (PRISMA-P) 2015 statement. *Systematic Reviews*, **4**, 1, 1.

National Collaborating Centre for Methods and Tools (2014) *Anatomy of a Systematic Review* [factsheet]. Available at www.nccmt.ca/resources/publications/70.

Noyes, J., Booth, A., Hannes, K., Harden, A., Harris, J., Lewin, S. and Lockwood, C. (eds) (2011) *Supplementary Guidance for Inclusion of Qualitative Research in Cochrane Systematic Reviews of Interventions*. Version 1 (updated August 2011). Oxford: Cochrane Collaboration Qualitative Methods Group. Available at http://methods.cochrane.org/qi/sites/methods.cochrane.org. qi/files/uploads/Data%20synthesis%20supplemental%20guidance_2010%2012%2023B.doc.

OCEBM Levels of Evidence Working Group (2011) *The Oxford Levels of Evidence 2*. Oxford Centre for Evidence-Based Medicine. Available online at: www.cebm.net/ocebm-levels-of-evidence/.

O'Mara-Eves, A., Thomas, J., McNaught, J., Makoto, M. and Ananiadou, S. (2015) Using text mining for study identification in systematic reviews: a systematic review of current approaches. *Systematic Reviews*, **4**, 5.

Parkes, J., Hyde, C., Deeks, J. and Milne, R. (2001) Teaching critical appraisal skills in health care settings. *Cochrane Database of Systematic Reviews*, Issue 3.

Petticrew, M. and Roberts, H. (2003) Evidence, hierarchies, and typologies: horses for courses. *Journal of Epidemiology and Community Health*, **57**, 7, 527–9.

Petticrew, M. and Roberts, H. (2006) *Systematic Reviews in the Social Sciences: A Practical Guide*. Malden, MA: Blackwell.

Pluye, P. and Hong, Q.N. (2014) Combining the power of stories and the power of numbers: mixed methods research and mixed studies reviews. *Annual Review of Public Health*, **35**, 29–45.

Popay, J., Rogers, A. and Williams, G. (1998) Rationale and standards for the systematic review of qualitative literature in health services research. *Qualitative Health Research*, **8**, 3, 341–51.

Rose, G. and Barker, D.J.P. (1994) *Epidemiology for the Uninitiated*, 3rd edition. London: BMJ Publishing Group.

Sackett, D.L., Richardson, S., Rosenberg, W. and Haynes, R.B. (1997) *Evidence-Based Medicine: How to Practise and Teach EBM*. London: Churchill Livingstone.

Sandelowski, M., Docherty, S. and Emden, C. (1997) Qualitative metasynthesis: issues and techniques. *Research in Nursing and Health*, **20**, 1, 365–71.

Santer, M., Ring, N., Yardley, L., Geraghty, A.W.A. and Wyke, S. (2014) Treatment non-adherence in pediatric long-term medical conditions: systematic review and synthesis of qualitative studies of caregivers' views. *BMC Pediatrics*, **14**, 63.

Schulz, K.F., Altman, D.G., Moher, D. and CONSORT Group (2010) CONSORT 2010 Statement: Updated Guideline for Reporting Parallel Group Randomised Trials. *PLoS Medicine*, **7**, 3, e1000251.

Taylor, B.J., Dempster, M. and Donnelly, M. (2007) Grading gems: appraising the quality of research for social work and social care. *British Journal of Social Work*, **37**, 335–54.

Thomas, J. and Harden, A. (2008) Methods for the thematic synthesis of qualitative research in systematic reviews. *BMC Medical Research Methodology*, **8**, 45.

Tong, A., Flemming, K., McInnes, E., Oliver, S. and Craig, J. (2012) Enhancing transparency in reporting the synthesis of qualitative research: ENTREQ. *BMC Medical Research Methodology*, **12**, 181.

Von Elm, E., Altman, D.G., Egger, M., Pocock, S.J., Gotzsche, P.C., Vandenbroucke, J.P. and STROBE Initiative (2014) The Strengthening the Reporting of Observational Studies in Epidemiology

(STROBE) Statement: guidelines for reporting observational studies. *International Journal of Surgery*, **12**, 12, 1495–99.

Wells, K. and Littell, J.H. (2009) Study quality assessment in systematic reviews of research on intervention effects. *Research on Social Work Practice*, **19**, 1, 52–62.

What Works Clearing House (2005) *Evidence Standards for Reviewing Studies.* Washington, DC: US Department of Eduction, Institute of Education Sciences.

Williams, P., Nicholas, D. and Rowlands, I. (2010) The attitudes and behaviours of illegal downloaders. *Aslib Proceedings*, 62, 3, 283–301.

SYNTHESISING
AND ANALYSING
QUANTITATIVE STUDIES

 in a nutshell

How to synthesise and analyse quantitative studies

- Quantitative data can typically be summarised and synthesised in narrative, tabular and sometimes graphical form.
- In planning whether to conduct meta-analysis first ask yourself: is it appropriate to combine my studies in meta-analysis? Justify your decision in your text.
- Your choice of meta-analysis method is primarily determined by the degree of heterogeneity in your populations, interventions, outcomes and study characteristics.
- You should always identify and discuss any heterogeneity in the meta-analysis results.

INTRODUCTION

Bringing together your review results in a synthesis is a key step in a quantitative review. Synthesis allows you to *juxtapose* the individual studies to identify patterns and direction in the findings, and to *integrate* the results to produce an overall bottom line that tells your reader whether an intervention works on average (Mays et al., 2005a). As you examine the composite **evidence base** for similarities, whether related to the **homogeneity** ('sameness') of study characteristics (i.e. how they were carried out) or relatedness of findings (i.e. what they found), you can contribute significant added value to your review process.

As Mulrow (1994) comments:

> The hundreds of hours spent conducting a scientific study ultimately contribute only a piece of an enormous puzzle. The value of any single study is derived from how it fits with and expands previous work, as well as from the study's intrinsic properties.

SYNTHESIS-ANALYSIS, ANALYSIS-SYNTHESIS?

Some authors may take issue with our SALSA framework in separating synthesis from analysis. Others may contend with our suggestion that synthesis precedes analysis. Such a distinction can be illustrated with reference to the specific technique of meta-analysis. For meta-analysis the specific steps are as follows:

1. Tabulate summary data (data extraction).
2. Graph data (synthesis).
3. Check for heterogeneity (synthesis).
4. Perform a meta-analysis if heterogeneity is not a major concern (synthesis).
5. If heterogeneity is found, identify factors that can explain it (analysis).
6. Evaluate the impact of study quality on results (analysis).
7. Explore the potential for **publication bias** (analysis).

Following data extraction, three steps associated with synthesis culminate in the production of the well-recognised **meta-analysis** display of data. However, rather than being an endpoint, this meta-analysis is actually a starting point for further investigation and inquiry. Three steps of analysis include trying to identify factors associated with variation, examining study quality as a possible explanation for variation, and investigating the likelihood that key studies have been overlooked or omitted.

OVERVIEW OF APPROACHES TO SYNTHESIS

Synthesis relies heavily on pattern recognition. Hart emphasises such techniques as *analogy* (looking for similarities between different phenomena), *metaphor* (thinking about one thing as if it were the same as another), and *homology* (looking for direct and corresponding relationships between natural and synthetic structures, e.g. between nature and human society) (Hart, 1998). Furthermore Hart and other authors emphasise how important it is to use *comparison* and *contrast* (Hart, 1998; Cresswell, 2003; Gray and Malins, 2004):

> [Some] references may be organized chronologically in parts of your review where you may be evaluating developments over time; some may be arranged thematically, demonstrating similarities and allowing you to make creative connections (cross-currents) between previously unrelated research; and some arranged to demonstrate *comparison and contrast* perhaps using a common set of criteria as an 'anchor'. (Gray and Malins, 2004)

Comparison and contrast may therefore be used within a literature review to compare study by study (usually only possible with a limited number of items for inclusion) or by findings (i.e. similarities and differences across studies). Within a larger literature review, as carried out for a dissertation or thesis, it may be desirable to combine both approaches.

Approaches to synthesis can be characterised in three main forms; quantitative (this chapter), qualitative and integrative (i.e. bringing together both quantitative and qualitative: see both of these in Chapter 9). Once you have identified which type of data you shall be using, you need to decide how best to synthesise and analyse your data. Of course your obvious choice is to use quantitative approaches for handling quantitative data and qualitative approaches for processing qualitative data. However, your synthesis toolkit includes quantitative approaches to qualitative data (i.e. where the occurrence of themes or words is quantified as in **content analysis**) or qualitative approaches to quantitative data (i.e. where different types of quantitative study are described narratively; see Mays et al., 2005b). *Quantitative* approaches are best exemplified by the technique of meta-analysis which has been in the ascendancy over the last couple of decades.

EXTRACTING QUANTITATIVE DATA FOR YOUR REVIEW

Data extraction is key to demonstrating that you have followed a systematic approach and handled different studies in a consistent manner. Pawson and colleagues (2004) characterise the centrality of data extraction to the review process and in terms of the intensive effort required:

> The next stage in systematic review is often considered its core, and a time consuming, uphill slog to boot.

This process allows the reviewer to examine which elements of data are present in each individual study report. Studies are reported differently according to the requirements of the particular journal within which they have been published. Extracting data from this disparate set of studies makes it easier for you to make comparisons in relation to what is reported and what is missing. The human brain finds it difficult to assimilate variables from more than a handful of studies at the same time, so converting these study reports into a common format (a lowest common denominator if you like) helps you interpret the body of evidence and aids the subsequent process of pattern recognition (Petticrew and Roberts, 2006). As Light and Pillemer (1984: 4) conclude:

> A reviewer unarmed with formal tools to extract and summarize findings must rely on an extraordinary ability to mentally juggle relationships among many variables. Systematic ways of exploring such relationships would make it far easier both to detect and understand them.

When designing your data extraction form you will find that extraction elements cluster around the elements of the **PICOS** structure (i.e. Population, Intervention, Comparison, Outcomes, Study design) (see Box 8.1).

 box 8.1

Possible elements for inclusion in a data extraction form

1. *Eligibility*: explicit statement of inclusion and exclusion criteria with the opportunity to indicate whether a study is to be included in the review or not.
2. *Descriptive data*: information about study characteristics including setting, population.
3. *Quality assessment data*: information about the quality of the study. A formal checklist may be incorporated within the documentation.
4. *Results*: information about the results of the study in the form of data to be used in your review. Data may be in a 'raw' format as taken directly from the paper and/or in a uniform format. Ideally it will be in both forms to indicate variation in methods but also to allow checking for accuracy.

Data extraction may be undertaken at the same time as quality assessment (see Chapter 7) or performed separately, either before or after the overall judgement of quality. Both approaches have their merits and disadvantages. It may be more efficient to examine the detail of reporting *and* the quality of the study from a single pass through the literature as both require an in-depth reading. Others contend that the two processes are dissimilar in that data extraction encourages you to focus on the minutiae of the report while quality assessment involves an overall holistic judgement of a study. For these reasons some prefer to arrive at an overall assessment of quality to temper or moderate their subsequent examination of findings. Others prefer to immerse themselves in the detail of the study report before stepping back to view the whole that emerges from the sum of its parts (Barnett-Page and Thomas, 2009).

The level of detail for data extraction, and the corresponding time spent upon the activity, will vary according to the type of review being undertaken. For a **scoping** or **mapping review** you may simply be extracting key study characteristics such as the setting, the study design, number of participants, etc. (Budgen et al., 2008; Ryan et al., 2009). As Petticrew and Roberts (2006) observe, such a study will attempt:

> to determine what sorts of studies addressing the systematic review question have been carried out, where they are published, in what databases they have been indexed, what sorts of outcomes they have assessed, and in which populations.

Rapid reviews

The time constraints associated with **rapid reviews** (see Box 8.2) may require you to extract data directly into tables rather than go through the intermediate stage of designing a data extraction form and then extracting the data from each individual study (Watt et al., 2008; Ganann et al., 2010).

box 8.2

The rapid review

What is it?

Rapid reviews are 'literature reviews that use accelerated or abbreviated (streamlined) methods as compared to traditional systematic reviews' (National Collaborating Centre for Methods and Tools, n.d.). Although the terminology draws superficial attention to the speed with which such a review is conducted, commentators observe that the reason why an accelerated process is possible, namely close interaction between those producing the review and those commissioning it, is equally key to the definition. Those conducting rapid reviews seek a clear unequivocal brief from the customer. In return they communicate the options available for an accelerated or abbreviated process and the implications of these for the uncertainty surrounding the results. There is no agreed duration for a rapid review, but as a general rule a 'rapid review typically takes 3 weeks to 6 months to complete (versus minimum 6-12 months for systematic reviews)' (National Collaborating Centre for Methods and Tools, n.d.).

What can I use it for?

Rapid reviews may be commissioned when a topic is urgent (for example Ebola) or when there is a narrow policy window. They are often a response to demands for the uptake of new technology (Harker and Kleijnen, 2012; Khangura et al., 2014) or where an area of literature is particularly volatile, requiring frequent updates. While many assume that a rapid review may be performed within limited time/resources this varies substantially between review models. For example, some reviews achieve rapidity by doubling up resource use within an intensive and truncated review period. More research is required on the implications of different shortcuts on the methodological quality of the resultant review (Polisena et al., 2015; Schünemann and Moja, 2015).

How has it been used?

In the UK there was mounting political pressure to tackle societal problems with binge drinking through pricing and taxation interventions. The Department of Heath commissioned a rapid review on the effect of these interventions on health to inform subsequent modelling work on the implications of different pricing models (Booth et al., 2008). A short time later the Home Office commissioned a follow-up rapid evidence assessment (Booth et al., 2010), within an even tighter timeframe, looking at the effect of the same interventions on crime and violence. Methodological shortcuts included collective quality assessment by study type rather than critical appraisal at the level of individual studies. Previously untried approaches to fast-track quality assessment, used in rapid reviews by the same team, include using limitations reported by different authors to compile a common assessment of data registry sources shared across multiple studies (Turner et al., 2014).

For most types of reviews data extraction can be performed easily using a questionnaire format on Google Forms. The resultant data can then be inspected within a Google spreadsheet or exported into Excel. It may be helpful to map out the data extraction form in a word processing document first (see Table 8.1) before converting it into a questionnaire format. Particular rows or columns can also be pasted into word processing documents. Time spent in extracting data is rewarded by the ease with which you are subsequently able to produce data displays, identify shared characteristics and patterns across studies, and spot particular discrepancies or inconsistencies that benefit from subsequent analysis. You can display extracted data as matrices, graphs, charts or networks (Whittemore and Knafl, 2005). Such displays can help you visualise patterns and relationships within and across the constituent studies.

Table 8.1 Sample data extraction form for a quantitative study

Title of review		
Publication details		
		Reference number
Author(s)		Year
Title of article		
Title of journal		
Volume	Issue	Pages

Study details	
Study type	
Study design	
Study aims	
Any further research questions addressed	
Country in which study was done	
User/carer stakeholder involvement in design/conduct of study	
Setting (e.g. rural/urban), context and key characteristics (e.g. of organisation)	
Target population (e.g. primary school children, secondary school children, etc.)	Number of participants
Sampling/how recruited (any info re: age, ethnicity, gender)	
Details of any theory/conceptual models used	
Characteristics of participants (e.g. practitioners, types of job roles, age, sex, gender, ethnicity, type of policy makers)	

Nature of the study	
Study date and duration	
Methods of data collection and who collected by (e.g. researcher/practitioner)	
Any research tools used	
Analysis used	
Aim of intervention	
Country	Location/setting
Target population (age, ethnicity, gender, etc.)	

Intervention	
Who provided the intervention? (e.g. teacher, volunteer, etc.)	
Description of intervention	
How was the intervention/service delivered? (e.g. groupwork, home visits, teaching module)	
Duration	Intensity
How and why was intervention developed? (e.g. reasons for development, any 'needs assessment' or involvement of target population)	
Any theoretical framework used to develop the intervention	

Results	
Outcome measures used	
Details of outcomes/findings	
Strengths/limitations of the study (including diversity of sample)	

Authors' conclusions:

Reviewer's notes or comments

Table 8.2 Matrix for examining possible correlations

Country of origin	Canada	United States	Singapore	South Africa	Australia	France	Germany	India	Poland	Japan	Netherlands	Sweden	Spain	United Kingdom	Italy	Romania
Roosevelt et al. (2009)*		X														
Cosmo et al. (2007)			X		X	X	X	X		X	X	X	X	X		
Washington et al. (2005)		X														
Bull (2004)														X		
Ceau escu et al. (2001)																X

*all references for illustrative purposes only

A data display to examine the correlations between study characteristics and study setting is given in Table 8.2 and can be produced immediately following data extraction. You can see at a glance by looking down the columns that three of the studies (by Washington et al., 2005; Cosmo et al., 2007; and Roosevelt et al., 2009) contain data from the United States. Conversely, by looking across the rows the reader can see that only one study (Cosmo et al., 2007) is a multi-country study, while all the others report data from a single country.

PLANNING YOUR SYNTHESIS STRATEGY

A key early stage in the process of synthesis is planning your **synthesis strategy** – how you will approach the literature once it has been assembled (Kitchenham, 2007). You have several choices as to how you will accomplish this task; your approach is governed by the nature of your review and its objectives (see Table 8.3). You may in fact need to switch from your initial strategy to a more appropriate alternative as patterns from the literature become clearer.

Although your *initial* synthesis strategy is open to subsequent refinement and change, you nevertheless need to have a reasonably clear picture of your direction of travel. Clearly if your final intention is to read and review an entire body of literature, albeit centred on a focused question, decisions on the order in which you will handle the papers are less critical. Each paper is given the same opportunity to contribute equally to the final map or the pooled result.

After considering techniques for handling data, we look at how such activities may be undertaken within the context of different types of data presentation, namely textual, graphical, numerical and tabular.

When seeking to identify patterns from quantitative data we should seek to answer such questions as: Are the *settings* for a particular intervention (e.g. personal counsellors in secondary education) more similar than different? Are the *interventions* themselves comparable? (For example, if something is described in multiple studies using a common terminology such as a 'policy unit' do these studies refer to the same entity?) Such questions at the synthesis stage inform subsequent analysis, e.g. whether any naturally occurring subgroups can be identified for more detailed investigation and whether the line of argument of the synthesis is overly dependent upon particular individual studies or groups of studies. In short, one can decide whether, in fact, it makes sense to treat all included studies as a group (**lumping**) or whether they make more sense as a series of separate and distinct groups (**splitting**).

Examining consistencies

It is not sufficient to simply catalogue all the variables to emerge from the individual studies and then amalgamate these into a long master list. You will want to examine possible groupings to the patterns in your data, such as **explanatory variables** or **confounding variables,** which may be recorded consistently as codes or categories.

A key step in such data analysis is data comparison. This iterative process involves examining data displays for primary source data in order to identify patterns or relationships. In quantitative studies, you are looking for shared characteristics of particular groupings of studies. For example, do particular studies share a certain type of measurement? Are some studies measured using objective measures while others use subjective measurement such as self-reporting? At

Table 8.3 Approaches to synthesis in different types of reviews

Type of review	Approaches used to synthesis	Application	Review example
Scoping review	Coding Narrative synthesis Tabular presentation	Descriptive coding was applied to include study features such as design, country of origin, type of behaviour targeted, characteristics of population and type of incentive used. Outcome studies were coded in greater depth. Paragraphs described the features of studies for each variable (e.g. types of intervention and incentive). Tables complemented narrative synthesis with frequencies and percentages of each type.	A scoping review of the evidence for incentive schemes to encourage positive health and other social behaviours in young people (Kavanagh et al., 2005).
Mapping review	Keywording Mapping studies not synthesised because they were 'disparate in their focus'	EPPI-Centre core keywording strategy used to classify studies according to a range of criteria, including bibliographic details (how the study was identified and whether it has been published), and contextual details (the language in which the study was written/published and the country where the study was conducted). Key aspects of the study also coded, such as topic focus of study, and information about the subjects of the study. Mapping stage of review describes studies found to be relevant, gives overview of the field of study, and enables reviewers to focus on particular areas of map. Brief commentary given on each study with emphasis on conclusions not methods.	A systematic map into approaches to making initial teacher training flexible and responsive to the needs of trainee teachers (Graham-Matheson et al., 2006).
Meta-analysis	Data extraction Translation into common metrics Computation of missing values	Extracted data in a standardised way: weights in pounds (lbs) transformed into kilograms (kg) and weeks transformed into months. Attempted contact with authors to obtain missing information. Assessed each study using a modified version of the Ottawa-Newcastle Scale.	A meta-analysis of weight gain in first year university students: is Freshman 15 a myth? (Vadeboncoeur et al., 2015).
Systematic review	Categorisation Data extraction Quality assessment Narrative synthesis Tabular presentation Meta-analysis not possible because of variability of studies	Articles categorised by type of publication. Data from intervention studies included study design, sample and intervention characteristics, and data collection methods and measures. Studies assessed using checklist. Narrative description and tabulation of study features and of methodological adequacy.	A systematic review of work-place interventions for alcohol-related problems (Webb, et al., 2009).

this point it is helpful to make a distinction between *descriptive* grouping that may contribute to a narrative commentary or synthesis (e.g. 'ten of the fifteen studies were conducted using the Edinburgh Depression Scale while the remainder used self reporting') and analytical grouping (where you may examine such differences to see if they might provide a possible explanation for differences in results).

Differences may typically occur across one or more specific variables. It is important at this stage not to attach too much importance to a single preferred variable when a difference may in fact be attributable to many variables working together. For example a review of change management strategies appeared to find that strategies using multiple interventions worked better than those based upon a single strategy (Grimshaw et al., 2004). However, closer examination found this relationship to be more complex. Not only are multiple intervention strategies more difficult to implement in the first place, there may also be a 'scattergun' effect (i.e. if you select multiple interventions you increase the chance of at least one working successfully). In this case it may not be that multiple interventions *work together* more effectively but rather that an individual intervention *works alone* but its specific effect is masked among accompanying interventions.

Of course, individual studies may differ from the main body of studies across a wide range of aspects (i.e. they are genuine 'outliers'). In such cases, you may wish to reconsider whether it truly makes sense to include these within an overarching analysis or whether they should be analysed separately. Such considerations of 'sameness' versus 'differentness' are fundamental to the entire process of meta-analysis.

Of course not all hypotheses generated from your data will be answerable from within the extracted data set. You may need to examine additional data sources, either within the current review or as a supplementary review step. Process evaluations may help you understand implementation difficulties or variations in implementation fidelity. Qualitative studies may help you surface assumptions about the intervention or programme held by either recipients or those delivering the intervention. You may wish to conduct a realist synthesis to move you forward from 'what works' to what works for whom under what circumstances (see Chapter 9). How has the intervention been theorised? Bear in mind the arbitrary split in many disciplines and fields between papers that generate theory and those that test theory. Papers you rejected for your intervention review might now be useful in an exploratory or explanatory capacity. Recently Booth and Carroll (2015) have outlined systematic steps by which you might retrieve papers advancing theory as a supplementary strategy to explain what has been observed from intervention studies. Greenhalgh and colleagues (2007) describe how they undertook a realist synthesis to explain why school feeding programmes did not achieve their intended effectiveness when implemented in a real world setting. The index child (receiving the intervention) did, in fact, benefit at school from the feeding programme. However, when the child returned home at night the parents redistributed that child's food to other siblings, in the knowledge that the child had already received a portion sufficient for subsistence but not growth.

APPROACHES TO SYNTHESIS

Approaches to synthesis may be characterised in many different ways. In keeping with the overview nature of this text, we characterise synthesis according to the type of data that you may be attempting to synthesise.

Narrative and textual approaches

Regardless of the type of review you are undertaking, it is likely that you will find it necessary to use some form of narrative approach. Here you have a basic choice between the traditional narrative approach and the more formalised development of narrative synthesis. Some researchers promote the benefits of a *traditional narrative approach* (Hammersley, 2001), which has evolved organically as a less formalised method for summarising large quantities of information. This traditional narrative approach largely involves compiling descriptive data and exemplars from individual studies. The output from such a process may well be conceived as a mosaic or map (Hammersley, 2001). Narrative reviews provide deep and 'rich' information (Light and Pillemer, 1984) and seek to remain faithful to the wholeness or integrity of the studies as a body while also preserving the idiosyncratic nature of individual studies (Pawson, 2001). Unlike meta-analysis, where there must be a 'fit' between the type and quality of the primary sources, a traditional narrative review can accommodate differences between the questions, research designs and the contexts of each of the individual studies. It disguises such distinctions by weaving together a common line of argument.

Rumrill and Fitzgerald (2001) argue that there are four potential objectives for this approach:

- to develop or advance theoretical models;
- to identify, explain and provide perspectives on complicated or controversial issues;
- to provide information that can assist practitioners in advancing 'best' practice;
- to present new perspectives on important and emerging issues.

Furthermore such an approach offers an opportunity for the reviewer to be reflexive and critical (Hart, 1998) (see Chapter 9). However, the traditional narrative approach falls short of the systematic approaches espoused by this book. A possible middle ground is offered by 'narrative synthesis' which focuses on how studies addressing a different aspect of the same phenomenon can be narratively summarised and built up to provide a bigger picture of that phenomenon.

Narrative synthesis is able to address a wide range of questions, not only those relating to the effectiveness of a particular intervention. It is defined by Popay and colleagues (2006) as:

> An approach to the synthesis of evidence relevant to a wide range of questions including but not restricted to effectiveness [that] relies primarily on the use of words and text to summarise and explain – to 'tell the story' – of the findings of multiple studies. Narrative synthesis can involve the manipulation of statistical data.

Despite excellent examples of its application, narrative synthesis was initially criticised within the systematic review community because of its potential bias and lack of transparency and reproducibility. However, Popay and colleagues (2006) have formalised a four-step method of narrative synthesis and have identified a range of specific tools and techniques for achieving each step.

Narrative synthesis (see Box 8.3) is therefore one means of summarising the characteristics and findings of a body of research in a succinct and coherent manner (Evans, 2007).

Essentially you are taking a series of slices through your group of included studies according to different study characteristics.

 **box 8.3**

Narrative synthesis

What is it?

A method of synthesis that primarily uses words and text to summarise the findings of multiple studies. It is therefore a process of synthesising primary studies to explore heterogeneity descriptively rather than statistically.

What can I use it for?

Narrative synthesis is appropriate for use with results from different types of empirical research, including experimental evaluative research and survey research. You can use narrative synthesis to describe the scope of existing research, summarise it into structured narratives or summary tables, and thus to account for the strength of the evidence. However, in comparison with thematic approaches it is less good at identifying commonality (Lucas et al., 2007).

How has it been used?

Rodgers and colleagues (2009) compared narrative synthesis against a meta-analysis of the same study data related to the implementation of smoke alarms. Although the conclusions of the two syntheses were broadly similar, they detected that that conclusions about the impact of moderators of effect appeared stronger in the meta-analysis. In conclusion, implications for future research appeared more extensive when derived from the narrative synthesis. They emphasised the complementarity of the two approaches and concluded that, despite the risk of over-interpretation of study data, the framework, tools and techniques itemised in their guidance had fulfilled their objective of increasing the transparency and reproducibility of the narrative synthesis process.

Rather than describing each study individually, narrative synthesis attempts to characterise studies in terms of multiple groupings. This is preferable to reviews that describe each individual study in turn. Grouping studies increase the probability that the reader, and the reviewer, can characterise the included studies as a 'body of evidence' (see Box 8.4). Most importantly it moves the reader towards identifying patterns among included studies. Narrative synthesis is often used in conjunction with tabular presentation. Both are essentially methods of **descriptive data synthesis**. This is common to use of tables of data, whether using simple counts or more sophisticated descriptions, when composing the accompanying narrative commentary.

box 8.4

The inherent advantage of narrative synthesis

You are in a lift with your supervisor or mentor. He/she asks you how your review is going. You have reviewed 20 included studies. You start with 'Study 1 is a randomised controlled trial of 150 patients conducted in Sweden … ' Before you get beyond describing your fifth included study, the lift arrives and your companion alights with thankful relief. On the way down in the same lift, later that morning, the supervisor asks a colleague, also involved in a literature review, about their progress:

> Interestingly I found that only two of my 25 included studies target children; the remaining 23 study adult populations. I had thought that the Sheffield Stress Scale was going to be the most common outcome measure but in fact there is a proliferation of researcher-designed instruments. Only five studies used validated outcome measures; three of these used the Sheffield Stress Scale. So I am already starting to plan my own primary study to be targeted at children using a validated outcome scale.

Which review will the supervisor remember (for the right reasons!) on the way home that evening?

Popay and colleagues (2006) define four processes in narrative synthesis. These helpful reference points formalise processes that should occur naturally through a review:

- *Developing a theory of change*: you can use reviews either to generate some explanatory theory or to validate or test some already existing theory.
- *Developing a preliminary synthesis*: this involves mobilising findings from the literature and stringing these together in order to tell a plausible 'story'.
- *Exploring relationships in the data*: this involves examining consistencies in the data and actively seeking the disconfirming case.
- *Assessing the robustness of the synthesis product*: this corresponds to the analysis phase of the SALSA mnemonic (see Chapter 2) and involves using a variety of tools to examine lines of inquiry suggested either a priori or as a result of the synthesis process.

Tabular presentation

In addition to narrative synthesis, included studies can be described using tabulation. Again because you are using tabulation to describe studies, not to analyse them, this is useful for all types of studies. You might use tabulation to describe characteristics of the population, intervention, comparator and outcome (measures). You may also use tabulation to describe study characteristics (e.g. study design). Some reviewers use tabulation to report how individual studies perform with regard to study quality. This makes it easier for the reader to identify higher-quality studies. In quantitative studies where meta-analysis is not an option, a table may be used to present a summary of results. Cells may indicate whether an effect is positive, negative or neutral and whether a specific effect is statistically significant or not.

Tabulation is particularly valuable within the context of cross-case comparison and for 'eyeballing' patterns across rows or down columns. However, it may be criticised, because the process of tabulation is necessarily reductive and can result in a loss of important context or detail that aids interpretation of the studies.

Numerical presentation

Where the same effect is measured by multiple similar studies, it may be possible and advantageous to statistically combine their results. Combining studies in this way, known as meta-analysis, may help to produce a conclusion about a body of research. For example it may be that there are insufficient large studies to have proved an effect conclusively. Alternatively, those studies that do exist may show different patterns of effects. In the latter case, using simple vote-counting (i.e. how many studies find in favour of an intervention and how many find against) may be misleading.

Meta-analysis

Statistical meta-analysis involves the aggregation of a weighted average of the results of individual studies in order to calculate an overall effect size for an intervention (Denyer et al., 2008). The logo of the **Cochrane Collaboration**, a stylised plot for a meta-analysis, demonstrates an actual scenario where seven small individual studies appeared to show conflicting results but which, when subject to meta-analysis, found in favour of a life-saving intervention. Although – mainly through the high profile of the Cochrane Collaboration and its associated Cochrane Library product – it is meta-analyses of **randomised controlled trials** that are best known, meta-analysis may also be used to synthesise other study types such as **observational studies**. Meta-analysis can be effective in disciplines where there are suitable and comparable quantitative data available from multiple studies (Denyer et al., 2008).

Meta-analysis as a technique meets a need to demonstrate an 'average effect'. This is at the same time its great strength and its associated weakness. As a strength, if an intervention consistently displays the same effect across a range of situational and contextual variables (e.g. country, population, ethnic group, etc.) we can conclude with increasing confidence that it will apply in our own context. This means that we do not need to replicate these studies with our own population before taking them into account locally. At the same time, it means that if an intervention works differentially in a variety of contexts, being successful in some and unsuccessful in others, we may not be able to conclude about its usefulness in our specific context. Although it may work *on average* we cannot be sure that our context is one in which it will realise such benefits. This explains why mere synthesis on its own is not enough. We also need to undertake follow-up analysis to be able to explain differences in findings across multiple studies (see Chapter 9). Where variations exist in study design, the nature of evidence and study context, meta-analysis is seen to be problematic (Hammersley, 2001):

This mixing of diverse studies can make for a strange fruit salad: mixing apples and oranges may seem reasonable enough, but when sprouts, turnips or even an old sock are added, it can cast doubt on the meaning of any aggregate estimates. (Davies and Crombie, 1998)

 **box 8.5**

Meta-analysis

What is it?

Meta-analysis is a quantitative literature review method used widely as an alternative approach to narrative literature review. It uses a set of statistical procedures to integrate, summarise or organise a set of reported statistical findings of studies that investigate the same research question using the same methods of measurement. Therefore, many reviewers endorse it as a practical and systematic way of drawing review conclusions. A meta-analysis follows the five-stage model of the integrative review suggested by Cooper (1982) corresponding to the chapters of this book: (a) problem formulation (Chapter 5), (b) data collection (Chapter 6), (c) data evaluation (Chapter 7), (d) analysis and interpretation (Chapters 8 and 9), and (e) public presentation (Chapter 10).

What can I use it for?

Meta-analysis follows prescribed procedures that seek to summarise the findings from studies in a systematic way. Provided that the reviewer makes appropriate assumptions and uses correct methods of analysis, this process reduces the chances of incorrect inter-pretation of findings and misleading review conclusions. As meta-analysis uses system-atic data collection and data analysis, it is effective when reviewing large homogeneous bodies of research. Meta-analysis is useful in highlighting gaps in an extensive literature, although the reader should bear in mind that it is dependent on outcomes that are com-parable and quantifiable. The subsequent analysis can be used to explore the influence of a large number of variables including different contextual factors. Cooper and Dorr (1995) suggest that narrative review (qualitative) and meta-analysis (quantitative) can be used to cross-validate findings from both methods. Therefore, meta-analysis can be used to quan-tify and corroborate review conclusions in preference to using only one of these methods.

How has it been used?

Chua and colleagues (1999) conducted a meta-analysis of studies to examine the relationships between computer anxiety and age, gender and computer experience. The meta-analysis found that female university undergraduates are generally more anxious than male under-graduates, but the strength of this relationship was not conclusive. The reviewers were also able to make observations about the reliability of instruments measuring computer anxiety and detected a possible inverse relationship between computer anxiety and computer experi-ence that remained to be explored in further research.

It is beyond the scope of this text to provide a full description of methods for meta-analysis (Glass et al., 1981; Rosenthal, 1991; Cooper and Hedges, 1994; or Lipsey and Wilson, 2001 are all excellent guidebooks for conducting meta-analyses). It will suffice to highlight the main considerations when using a meta-analysis. First of all, meta-analysis is only intended to be undertaken when studies address comparable populations, interventions, comparisons and outcomes using the same study design. Of course the degree of similarity between studies (**homogeneity**) requires a subjective judgement – is it meaningful to combine these studies together in pursuit of an average effect? However, such a judgement can be quantified using a test for **heterogeneity**. If studies are sufficiently similar (i.e. the test for heterogeneity has a low value) they may be combined using a **fixed effects analysis**. If, however, they are not considered sufficiently similar, they may be combined using a **random effects analysis**. In essence, this distinction means that, where studies that are dissimilar are combined using the random effects method, we produce a more conservative estimate of the intervention effect. This means that we are less likely to conclude that an intervention works where it does not. However, this is at the expense of increasing the likelihood that we conclude an intervention does not work when it is actually marginally beneficial.

Graphical approaches

Graphical approaches may make an important contribution to synthesis by assisting in the identification of patterns. They have a particular role in helping the reviewer visualise the relationship of parts to the overall whole. They also may be used for cross-linking across disparate features of a review, e.g. for depicting a link between study characteristics and findings. For example, colour coding might be used to indicate whether qualitative findings from a review are associated with negative (red), neutral (yellow) or positive (green) results from quantitative effectiveness studies. As Whittemore and Knafl (2005) observe:

> Creativity and critical analysis of data and data displays are key elements in data comparison and the identification of important and accurate patterns and themes.

Graphical methods can include techniques for exploring data (see Table 8.4) as well as those for actually presenting the data. So **mind maps**, **concept maps** and **idea webs** may be used to map out the main variables in a creative and imaginative way. **Logic models** may be used to present the inputs, processes, outputs and outcomes for a particular intervention (see Chapter 9). Graphical approaches have been developed for specific purposes (such as the Harvest plot: see Table 8.4 and Box 8.7) for 'synthesising evidence about the differential effects of population-level interventions' (Ogilvie et al., 2008). Nevertheless, outside the specific requirements of meta-analysis, graphical approaches are comparatively underdeveloped and there is much to be learnt from the use of graphics and diagrams for research in general (Wheeldon and Faubert, 2009; Umoquit et al., 2011).

One reason for the success of meta-analysis as a technique is that it supports statistical methods with a fairly intuitive method of graphical presentation known as the **Forest plot** (see Box 8.6).

Table 8.4 Graphical methods for exploring data

Method	Description	Application
Concept map	Concept maps can be a useful way of identifying key concepts in a document collection or research area. Concept maps can be used to identify additional search terms during the literature search, clarify thinking about the structure of the review in preparation for writing, and understand theory, concepts and the relationships between them (Rowley and Slack, 2004; Alias and Suradi, 2008).	Braithwaite (2010) devised a concept map of key themes in the literature on organisational social spaces, networks, boundaries and holes for his systematic review on between-group behaviour in healthcare.
Forest plot	A Forest plot is a graphical representation of a meta-analysis. The Forest plot (see Figure 8.1) depicts the relationship between the success rate of an intervention of interest and the success rate of its comparator. This relationship is pictured in relation to a 'line of no effect', i.e. the assumption that both intervention and comparator are equally effective/ineffective. Usually accompanied by a table listing references (author and date) of studies included in the meta-analysis (Sedgwick, 2012).	In a review of the Freshman 15 weight gain phenomenon a Forest plot displays the average (mean) weight change (kg) from baseline to follow-up in first year university students. The overall mean weight change across 22 studies was 1.36 kg (Vadeboncoeur et al., 2015).
Harvest plot	The Harvest plot is a method for combining research with different study designs and outcomes to give an overall visual effect. It can also demonstrate study appropriateness, quality and outcome measures. The plot groups studies based on whether they demonstrate a positive, negative or no effect, and for each study provides information on outcome measures, suitability of study design and quality of the study. The reader can judge not only where most studies lie (tally counting) but also where the most appropriate and highest quality studies lie (Ogilvie et al., 2008; Crowther et al., 2011).	In a Cochrane review of interventions for slum upgrading (Turley et al., 2013) differences between the included study interventions and outcomes precluded meta-analysis so the results were presented in a narrative summary with illustrative harvest plots. Harvest plots were used to show health, socioeconomic and quality of life findings across main and supporting studies.
Idea web	Ideas webbing is a method for conceptualising and exploring the connections among findings reported by the studies included in a review. This approach uses spider diagrams to develop a visual picture of possible relationships across study results (Clinkenbeard, 1991).	Arai and colleagues (2007) present an example of idea webbing conducted by one of their reviewers for their review of barriers to smoke alarm implementation.

Method	Description	Application
Logic model	Logic models (also known as impact models) originate from the field of programme evaluation, and are typically diagrams or flowcharts that convey relationships between contextual factors, inputs, processes and outcomes. They are considered valuable in providing a 'roadmap' to illustrate influential relationships and components from inputs to outcomes. Such models are used widely in health promotion to identify the domains underlying best practice (Baxter et al., 2010).	Dinh-Zarr and colleagues (2001) used a logic model to examine possible mechanisms involved in increased use of safety belts. For example it included the possible effect of penalties for non-use.
Mind map	A mind map is a diagram used to represent words, ideas, tasks or other concepts linked to, and organised around, a central key word or idea. A mind map is essentially a creative vehicle that operates at a conceptual level rather than representing a logical linear progression (compare logic maps). As such, they may be used at an early stage of a review, before relationships have been identified, and then the exact nature of relationships between concepts can be determined at a later stage following evidence synthesis.	In a review by Atkins and colleagues (2008) on adherence to tuberculosis treatment, each author was also asked to develop a mind map of their own model of the synthesis as a basis for subsequent discussion.
Network meta-analysis	Network meta-analysis allows readers to visualise and interpret a wide picture of the evidence for specific conditions and to understand the relative merits of multiple interventions. The geometry of the network allows one to understand how much evidence exists for each treatment, whether some types of comparisons have been avoided, and whether particular patterns exist in the choices of comparators. The addition of numerical estimates allows the reader to see how interventions that have not been directly compared with each other might perform were they to be ranged head to head.	Alfirevic and colleagues (2015) identified 280 randomised clinical trials of prostaglandin-type drugs to bring on labour compared to placebo, no treatment, alternative prostaglandin dose or administration, or a different prostaglandin. From multiple comparisons they concluded which administration was least likely to result in caesarean section or most likely to lead to vaginal delivery. Findings informed national and international guidelines for induction of labour and future research.

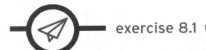

exercise 8.1

Helpful graphical display

Briefly reflect on a journal article that you have recently read, not necessarily a systematic review. Which aspects of its use of tabular or graphical display made it easier to read? Which aspects made it more difficult to understand and interpret? If so, why?

box 8.6

The Forest plot

What is it?

A Forest plot presents a series of effect sizes and their confidence intervals in a graphic manner, so that they can easily be compared. The effect sizes are represented by **point estimates** and the confidence intervals by horizontal lines.

The relationship between the intervention of interest and its comparator is pictured in relation to a 'line of no effect', i.e. against the assumption that both intervention and comparator are equally effective/ineffective. The greater the superiority of the intervention (or conversely its comparator), the further away its point estimate is plotted from the line of no effect. Multiple studies can thus be plotted on the same graph to provide a pattern of how studies relate both to each other and to the line of no effect. Each point estimate is provided with a confidence interval to illustrate the amount of variation between a best-case and worst-case scenario for that particular study. Finally, the pooled effect of combining all studies is depicted as a diamond where the centre of that diamond indicates the point estimate for all studies combined. The horizontal extremities of the diamond shape indicate the best- and worst-case scenarios for all the studies combined. The reader can therefore decide whether he/she wishes to assume a best-case result or a more conservative worst-case estimate, and indeed whether the difference between these two scenarios is important enough to affect any subsequent action (see Crombie and Davies, 2009). The Cochrane RevMan software typically displays effect size estimates as blocks proportionate to the weight assigned to a given study. A Forest plot draws the eye towards studies with larger sample sizes/larger weights, and away from smaller studies with wider confidence intervals.

What can I use it for?

General statistical packages such as SPSS, Stata, SAS and R can be used to perform meta-analyses. However, it is not their primary function and hence reviewers need to download external macros or coding. Additionally, SPSS, Stata and SAS are not available free of charge while the open source R package requires programming. Some software packages are specifically developed for meta-analyses. RevMan, a freeware program from the Cochrane Collaboration, requires the researcher to fill all steps of a systematic review. It only accepts effect sizes in traditional formats. Metawin and Comprehensive Meta-Analysis (CMA) are commercial software with user friendly interfaces. Metawin only accepts three types of primary data, while CMA has a purchase cost, but accepts more types of data. CMA can perform advanced analyses but does not allow customisation of the Forest plot produced. Finally, Meta-Analysis Made Easy (MIX), an add-on for Excel, can be used for analysis of descriptive data by selecting the input type 'continuous', but the free version does not allow analysis of original data. Neyeloff and colleagues (2012) demonstrate that it is possible to produce a statistically adequate but graphically appealing Forest plot summarising descriptive data, using only Microsoft Excel.

How has it been used?

Lewis and Ellis (1982) produced a plot for a meta-analysis showing the effect of beta blockers on mortality. They depicted the overall (combined) effect at the bottom of the plot. However, smaller less precise studies had larger confidence intervals and were more noticeable on the plots. In 1983 the statistician Stephen Evans suggested replacement of the mark with a square whose size was proportional to the precision of the estimate (Lewis and Clarke, 2001).

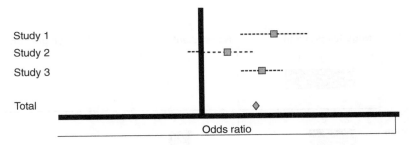

Figure 8.1 Forest plot

box 8.7

The Harvest plot

What is it?

The Harvest plot is a relatively recent innovative approach to summarising the results of a systematic review of the effectiveness of population-level interventions. In contrast to Forest plots (see Box 8.6), which are used in meta-analyses to graphically illustrate the overall results of the review, the Harvest plot can be used to display and summarise evidence from a complex and diverse group of studies. Steps for developing the Harvest plot include:

- define the hypotheses to be tested;
- allocate each study to the best supported hypothesis;
- plot the distribution of evidence;
- write a narrative synthesis to interpret the harvest plot.

(Continued)

(Continued)

What can I use it for?

The Harvest plot is a useful technique for displaying the findings of a systematic review where studies measure diverse and complex outcomes of interest. This method can be used to summarise research findings on the effectiveness of population-level interventions that are relevant to decision makers and policy makers.

How has it been used?

The method was developed by epidemiologists at the Medical Research Council Epidemiology Unit in Cambridge as a way of presenting diverse studies from a systematic review of population tobacco control interventions and their effects on social inequalities in smoking.

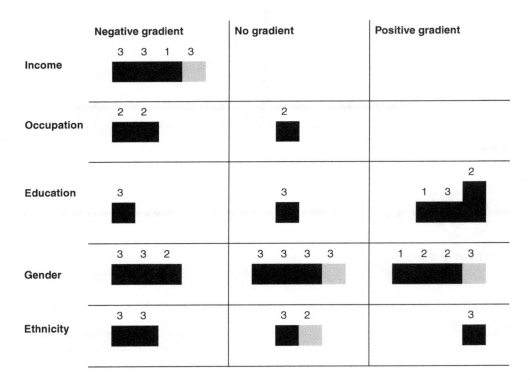

Figure 8.2 Harvest plot

Key: Each study is represented by a bar in each row for which that study had reported relevant results. Studies with hard behavioural outcome measures are indicated with full-tone (black) bars, and studies with intermediate outcome measures with half-tone (grey) bars. The highest bars represent the most suitable study designs (Education – Positive gradient) and the lowest bars represent the least suitable. Each bar is topped by how many methodological criteria (maximum six) were met by that study.

box 8.8

Logic model

What is it?

Logic models have a long pedigree within programme evaluation and public health as a graphical means by which to understand complex programmes to improve social and health outcomes. A logic model illustrates how a programme is designed to achieve its intended outcomes. It can also be used to describe connections between determinants of outcomes.

What can I use it for?

Logic models offer a potential mechanism for depicting causative relationships for such complex phenomena as low high-school graduation rates or spiralling obesity rates, thus aiding the development of interventions to target those causal factors. Logic models can aid in the conceptualisation of the review focus and illustrate hypothesised causal links, identify effect mediators or moderators, specify intermediate outcomes and potential harms, and justify a priori subgroup analyses when differential effects are anticipated. They may also be used more instrumentally to direct the actual systematic review process. They can help justify narrowing the scope of a review, identify the most relevant inclusion criteria, guide the literature search, and clarify interpretation of results when drawing policy-relevant conclusions about review findings.

How has it been used?

Zief et al. (2006) included a logic model in a systematic review of after-school programmes for low-income elementary school youth. In their logic model they specified intervention components hypothesised to change conditions necessary to improve youth outcomes. This facilitated the coding of programme characteristics thought to contribute to programme success. The logic model provided an a priori justification for subgroup analysis by illustrating the possible influence of student demographic characteristics, prior academic achievement, family background, and school and community characteristics. In this way, the logic model elucidated hypotheses for how the intervention is expected to work, and considered how disadvantage might interact with the hypothesised mechanisms of action (Tugwell et al., 2010).

box 8.9

Network meta-analysis

What is it?

Network meta-analysis (also known as a multiple treatment comparison meta-analysis or mixed treatment meta-analysis) offers a set of methods to visualise and interpret the wider picture of evidence when multiple interventions (A. B, C, D, E, etc.) have been used and compared head to head for the same disease and outcomes (Caldwell, 2014). It permits a review team to understand

(Continued)

(Continued)

the relative merits of these multiple interventions against one another. Network meta-analysis has advantages over conventional pairwise meta-analysis (i.e. A versus B or B versus C), as the technique borrows strength from indirect evidence to gain certainty about all treatment comparisons. Network analysis's particular contribution relates to being able to estimate comparative effects that have not been investigated head to head in randomised clinical trials (e.g. A versus C).

What can I use it for?

Network meta-analysis is becoming popular among clinicians, guideline developers and health technology agencies as new evidence on new interventions continues to surface and needs to be placed in the context of all available evidence for appraisals. In contrast to conventional pairwise meta-analysis, network meta-analysis can provide estimates of relative efficacy between all interventions (Neupane et al., 2014), even though some have never been compared head to head. For many comparisons, the network meta-analysis may yield more reliable and definitive results than would a pairwise meta-analysis.

How has it been used?

Over 20 years more than 20 randomised clinical trials have investigated the long-term effects of several variants of warfarin and aspirin as well as other drug treatments for the prevention of stroke in patients with atrial fibrillation. Building up the evidence on multiple treatments produces an interconnected network of interventions and comparators to allow comparison of the randomised trial evidence between all interventions (Bafeta et al., 2014).

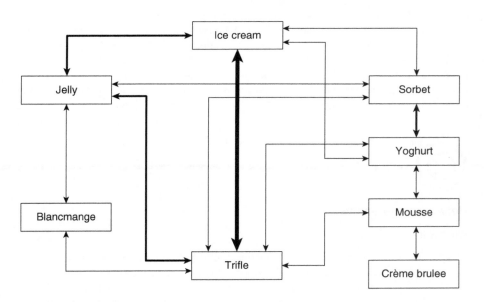

Figure 8.3 Network meta-analysis

This fictional Network Meta-analysis shows that Ice cream has been compared most frequently with Trifle. Sorbet–Yoghurt, Trifle–Jelly and Jelly–Ice cream are other more common comparisons. Crème brulee has only been compared (once) with Mousse. Jelly has never been compared with Mousse.

ANALYSIS OF QUANTITATIVE RESEARCH

Once you have performed an initial synthesis you will be ready to explore both what has been found and what is missing. The synthesis stage aims to tell you what the literature *says*. Analysis provides you with an opportunity to assess the strength of evidence for drawing conclusions about the results of synthesis and their generalisability in your intended context.

You will find it helpful to select techniques according to the robustness of the original synthesis and the underlying purpose of the analysis. For example Slavin (1986) suggests a technique known as 'best evidence synthesis'. This involves combining meta-analytic and narrative techniques so that you can gain insights on effects from the quantitative synthesis combined with contextual data from accompanying narrative descriptions.

Use of validity assessment

For quantitative studies the validity assessment is a useful method for exploring study findings. A common criticism of reviews, even those performed by the Cochrane Collaboration, is that they may conduct a validity assessment but not use it to discriminate between the findings of high-quality studies and those underpinned by lower-quality studies (de Craen et al., 2005). As previously mentioned, such an assessment can be conducted illustratively by ordering studies by quality and looking for patterns from the findings, or more typically by dividing studies into the three categories of high, moderate and low quality. This latter approach paves the way for subsequent sensitivity analysis either by removing all studies of low quality or by only including studies of the very highest quality.

Checking with authors of primary studies

Arai and colleagues (2007) report that they found checking with authors of primary studies potentially valuable. However, they point out that this process depends upon 'the accessibility and generosity' of authors. Although their prior experience of author validation is reported as overwhelmingly positive, this is more likely to be a characteristic of topic areas where researchers provide continuity over many years rather than for the more volatile areas of policy evaluation.

Subgroup analysis

During data extraction and coding you will have identified different groups or 'families' of studies, perhaps sharing population characteristics (e.g. small firms versus large firms, streamed classes versus mixed ability classes, acute hospitals versus primary care settings) or characteristics around the intensity or exact nature of a programme or intervention. Are such subgroups part of the total population, representative of the average effect, or the exception to the rule? For example, Thomas and colleagues (2004) examined interventions to promote healthy eating among children. After establishing overall effect estimates, they started to unpack the various components of the included programmes. After removing studies that contained a physical activity component, identified as qualitatively different, they further divided the studies into those that emphasised health messages and those that did not. They found that the studies that achieved the most significant gains in vegetable consumption were those with little or no emphasis on health messages. This subgroup analysis achieved two main purposes – it helped to explain significant heterogeneity between the different studies and led to the generation of a hypothesis to inform and possibly direct the development of future programmes or interventions.

Of course even a relatively homogeneous group of studies includes a significant degree of possible variation, dependent in part on how extensive the reporting of studies has been and how thorough the extraction of data. It is therefore particularly helpful, and a more robust approach methodologically, to identify possible subgroup analyses before examining any of the results. Indeed the review protocol should specify the main areas of likely variation and the principal subgroup analyses that will be used in exploring such variation. However, Thomas and colleagues (2004) state that this was not possible in their case as the key components of each programme were not identified until the qualitative component of their review had been completed. Mills and colleagues (2005) described how they explored the findings of their review on parental attitudes to childhood vaccination by analysing by variations in study methods (e.g. semi-structured interview versus focus group) and by publication date.

Sensitivity analysis

Greenhalgh (2014) neatly characterises **sensitivity analysis** as the formal 'exploration of "what ifs"'. Throughout the review process, you will have made arbitrary decisions on what to do where methods or data are missing, unclear or obviously incorrect. Depending upon the purpose of your review, and the amount of data from which to choose, you will have decided whether to interpret such limitations strictly or generously. Of course, the most extreme position is to actively exclude studies on the basis of such omissions. More typically you will include such studies, perhaps flagged with a question mark and then, once you have combined studies to look for an overall pattern, revisit such question marks to examine their implications for your review. In a meta-analysis, for example, a single effect size will typically be accompanied by a confidence interval. The simplest type of sensitivity analysis is to ask, 'Would I make the same decision based upon this review if I assume that the actual result is located at the less favourable end of the confidence interval compared with assuming that the actual result is at the most favourable end?' The most typical indications for performing sensitivity analysis are given in Box 8.10.

 box 8.10

Reasons for considering a sensitivity analysis (quantitative)

You might consider conducting a sensitivity analysis where:

- you have had significant and persistent doubts about whether a study is eligible for inclusion within a review; you could look at the effect of including and then excluding the result of that study from your review;

- you have identified significant differences in the quality of included studies; you could calculate results using all studies and then excluding poorer quality studies;
- you are uncertain about whether included studies are heterogeneous or homogeneous; you might perform calculations using the two alternative methods of meta-analysis (fixed and random effects) to assess the robustness of the results to the method used;
- you observe that one study has results very different from the rest of the studies (i.e. it is an obvious outlier); you might investigate what might happen were you to exclude this;
- you have made some assumption about a missing value (for example you have carried forward the last available measurement, or alternatively you have assumed a least favourable outcome); you may seek to explore what happens when you change the basis for your estimate;
- you consider the overall result to be particularly influenced by one particular study (e.g. the largest, the earliest, etc.); you might look at the pattern of results were this study to be excluded.

IDENTIFYING GAPS

A key concern for reviewers at the analysis stage relates to the adequacy of their literature sample – have they have identified *all* studies (comprehensive sampling)? Combs and colleagues (2010) describe the potential ambiguities for reviewers at this point in their review:

> The student might note feelings of optimism and relief, particularly as he/she begins to experience information saturation. At the same time, the student might experience anxiety related to the uncertainty of whether every possible key source has been located.

As acknowledged by the requirement of the Cochrane Collaboration to update reviews every two years, preparation of a review is an ongoing and continuous process. New studies are appearing continuously; chasing cited references may repeatedly extend the review task and reading in adjacent literatures may imperceptibly cause **scope creep** (see Chapter 4). For these reasons, it is important for the reviewer, perhaps in conjunction with a supervisor or mentor, to agree mechanisms by which closure of the study identification process might be achieved. Models of conducting systematic reviews and meta-analysis, fuelled by the 'big bang approach' to literature searching (i.e. all the literature identified a priori before the synthesis and analysis commences), might suggest that agreement on when to stop should appear at the search stage of the SALSA model. However, we have deliberately chosen to discuss this in connection with the analysis stage in recognition that some reviews are more iterative with some analytical processes suggesting further lines for inquiry.

For an **aggregative** review, such as a meta-analysis, the decision on when to stop is relatively simple and involves one of three choices: you can choose to set a time limit to a single phase of study identification after which you will not accept further studies; you can decide how many times during the life of the review project that you will repeat the full **search strategy**; you can put in place regular updating mechanisms so that new studies are identified up to the point when the final report is produced. This last approach opens up the possibility of bias in the identification of studies but may be appropriate for a literature review in a policy context (e.g. a **rapid evidence assessment**) where policy makers will not want to be 'caught out' by the appearance of an important new study.

Decisions as to whether the sample of literature is adequate allow you to demonstrate, at least to some degree, that you have followed systematic approaches. This contrasts with the typical advice given in the context of a traditional narrative review:

> Of course, it is likely that new articles will come to light after the data collection period has concluded. However, unless the new article is critically important, I suggest leaving it out. Otherwise, the reviewer may have to open the floodgates and start anew the data collection process. (Randolph, 2009)

Now we have considered the variety of techniques that comprise the analysis section of the reviewer's toolkit, we shall briefly revisit the sample reviews we have used throughout this book to see how they have utilised such techniques according to their purpose (see Table 8.5).

Table 8.5   Examining methods of analysis used in reviews

Type of review	Methods of analysis used	Application of methods	Review example
Scoping review	Identifying gaps Checking with authors of primary studies (i.e. projects in progress)	Identifies absence of systematic reviews on use of incentives in young people. Identifies existence of significant work in progress to inform future reviews. Following discussion with funders identified need for systematic review on effectiveness and implementation aspects.	A scoping review of the evidence for incentive schemes to encourage positive health and other social behaviours in young people (Kavanagh et al., 2005).
Mapping review	Identifying gaps Subgroup analysis	Failed to find research that explicitly considers how to make initial training responsive to individual needs of trainee teachers. Reports most common aspects of training. Concludes further research is needed in this area.	A systematic map into approaches to making initial teacher training flexible and responsive to the needs of trainee teachers (Graham-Matheson et al., 2005).
Systematic review	Use of validity assessment Sensitivity analysis Identifying gaps	Identified considerable methodological problems that limit internal validity and generalisability of results. Emphasises implications for future research. Suggests possible avenue of future research.	A systematic review of work-place interventions for alcohol-related problems (Webb et al., 2009).

REVISITING THE REVIEW QUESTION

While you should expect to have to return to your review protocol and question throughout the review project, for example for arbitration of scope or for planning your synthesis strategy, it is especially important that you do this at the analysis stage. Having sought to identify whether the authors of primary studies have been selective in their reporting you do not want to discover, after publication, that you have omitted important outcomes from your review. If a logic model featured in your original mapping of your review questions it will be helpful to map the literature against each node to gain a picture of which questions are well covered and which are data poor. Revisiting your review question will also suggest lines of inquiry for your analysis. For example, you may now be able to discern what you will require in the way of tables and supplementary analysis techniques such as sensitivity analysis and subgroup analysis.

DISCUSSING THE LIMITATIONS OF THE EVIDENCE

Recognising the limitations of the evidence is important in placing your review findings in context. You should clearly highlight how each article, and the review as a whole, performs with regard to its **validity**, its closeness to the truth (see Chapter 7). You can help your reader by ascribing a level of credibility to a review's conclusions. You should go beyond a mere listing of the magnitude and direction of random and systematic errors and any associated problems with validity. You should interpret what any errors mean and their likely influence on your conclusions. Your reader will be able to take away from the discussion section a clear picture of the influence of any validity problems on the published results of the review.

Recognising the likelihood of bias

In theory, systematic reviews should not only evaluate and take account of the **internal validity** (i.e. the extent to which systematic errors or bias are avoided) of each included study, but also the **applicability** and **generalisability** or **external validity** (i.e. whether the results of a study can be reasonably applied to a definable population in a particular setting in day-to-day practice) (Dekkers et al., 2009).

Key to the robustness of the results from a review is some consideration of the presence or absence of bias. The Cochrane Collaboration has developed and tested a **risk of bias tool** to appraise the internal validity of trial results included in systematic reviews (Lundh and Goetzche, 2008). Such an approach is still experimental with some evidence to suggest that those items that require more judgement achieve lower rates of consensus (Hartling et al., 2009). Comparison with established methods of quality assessment suggests little agreement indicating that the two approaches may, in fact, be capturing different study features. However, the overall assessment of the risk of bias did demonstrate potential usefulness in identifying low-quality studies that may be exaggerating likely treatment effects.

THE RISK OF BIAS TOOL

An assessment of the risk of bias using the Cochrane risk of bias tool begins by assessing bias in individual studies and then proceeds to examine systematic bias within the component studies in a review. The process begins with the quality assessment of an individual study (see Chapter 7). An example of such a structured assessment is seen in Table 8.6.

Once the tabular assessment has been completed, the data on risk of bias can be 'translated' into a quantitative form. Each threat of bias is quantified and a graphical display is produced (see Figure 8.4). This graphic display uses a red-amber-green colour (with a monochrome alternative symbols scheme to aid in the identification of patterns across the individual study).

Table 8.6 Example of a 'risk of bias' table for a single study (fictional)

Entry	Judgement	Description
Adequate sequence generation	No	Quote: 'patients were allocated according to alternate days presenting at the clinic' Comment: this opens up possibility of systematic bias
Allocation concealment	No	Quote: 'allocation was performed from a printed schedule' Comment: opportunity to break allocation via alternation
Blinding (for each outcome)	Yes	Quote: 'biochemical tests used to corroborate abstinence at three months' Comment: objective measure ascertained by laboratory
Incomplete outcome data addressed (for each outcome)	No	15 smokers missing from intervention group, only five from control group
Free of selective reporting?	No	No reporting of independently confirmed smoking cessation at one year
Free of other bias?	No	Trial supported financially by nicotine patch company

Finally, the risk of bias instrument comes into its own as a tool for synthesis. Each component study in the review (six studies in our hypothetical example) is colour-coded, again using red-amber-green notation (with monochrome alternative symbols of +, ? and -), against each of eight quality domains (see Figure 8.5). At a glance, the reviewer can identify systematic patterns of bias across studies. Such patterns can be explored in more detail and linked to an overall assessment of the robustness of the review's conclusions and the strength of its recommendations.

Just as it is important to take steps to avoid being misled by biases and the play of chance in planning, conducting, analysing and interpreting individual primary studies, similar steps must be taken in planning, conducting, analysing and interpreting evidence syntheses. When you are conducting your overall evaluation of your review and its limitations you need to ask such questions as specified in Box 8.11.

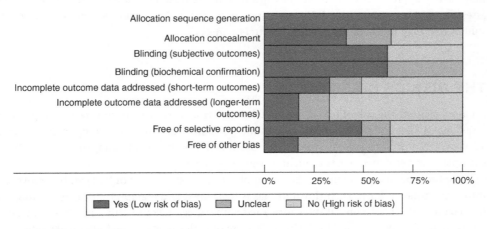

Figure 8.4 Example of a risk of bias graph

Study	Adequate sequence generation	Allocation concealment	Blinding (subjective outcomes)	Blinding (biochemical confirmation)	Incomplete outcome data (short-term outcomes)	Incomplete outcome data (long-term outcomes)	Free of selective reporting	Free of other bias
Bamboozle (1982)	+	+	+	+	−	+	−	−
Barr and Humbug (1991)	+	+	+	−	+	+	−	+
Bunkum and Hornswoggle (2001)	+	−	?	+	?	+	+	+
Hook (2002)	+	+	+	+	?	?	?	?
Line (1999)	+	+	+	+	+	+	?	+
Sinker (2011)	+	−	−	?	+	−	−	−

Figure 8.5 Example of a risk of bias summary

box 8.11

Questions to ask when assessing the likelihood of bias in your review

1. Have I clearly specified the question to be examined by my review, how included studies address this question, and the extent to which my conclusions resolve this question?
2. Have I defined explicit and objective eligibility criteria for studies to be included?
3. To what extent am I confident that I have identified all potentially eligible studies?
4. Have I ensured that the eligibility criteria have been applied in ways that limit bias (possibly resulting from inappropriate acceptance or rejection)?
5. Have I assembled as high a proportion as possible of the relevant information from the included studies (guarding against a bias in outcome selection)?
6. Have I used a variety of analyses to explore any uncertainties associated with my review findings?
7. Have I presented my findings and conclusions in a structured report with clear links between what is observed and what is concluded?

Your answers to the questions in Box 8.11 will, to a large extent, both determine what you cover in your discussion of review limitations and mediate the strength of any recommendations made on the basis of the evidence you have found. In particular questions 3 and 5 from Box 8.11 highlight two aspects that may be largely beyond your control as you are in the hands of the study authors. These points target publication bias and **selective reporting bias** respectively and are briefly expanded upon below.

toolbox

Template – Identifying Bias

The following template can be used to identify the main threats to validity (likely sources of bias) for your particular review and any steps that you might take to minimise the potential threats posed by each source of bias. This template may be used to populate your protocol and, subsequently, in discussing the limitations of your review (see Chapter 10).

Threat	How it might prove a threat to my review?	How I could counter this threat?
Change of scope		
Publication bias		
Selection bias		
Inclusion of poor quality primary studies		
Selective outcome reporting		
Misinterpretation of findings		
Researcher bias in presentation		

PUBLICATION BIAS

Criticisms of the systematic review method, and meta-analysis in particular, include that it is subject to publication bias (i.e. that *statistically significant* results tend to be published more than non-statistically significant results). Chan and Altman (2005) conclude a milestone paper by stating that 'the [medical] literature represents a selective and biased subset of study outcomes'.

Publication bias refers to an entire family of biases that include **language bias, location bias** and **database bias**, etc. These have more recently been grouped as 'Dissemination- and publication-related biases' (Song et al., 2010).

What steps can you as a reviewer take in your analysis to try to identify whether your review is a likely victim of dissemination- or publication-related biases? Some suggestions are given in Box 8.12.

box 8.12

Suggested ways of exploring dissemination or publication biases

1. Look at the list of databases and other sources that you have chosen to search. How likely is it that non-English studies/unpublished studies will be retrieved by each of these routes?
2. Look at your final list of included studies. How high a proportion of these are published in languages other than English?
3. Look at your final list of included studies. How high a proportion of these are published in the grey literature/fugitive literature?
4. If you only intend to examine English-language studies look at abstracts of non-English studies that would otherwise be included. Is the direction of effect comparable to that for your included English language studies?
5. Map sample size versus effect size on a graph as a funnel plot. Are small negative studies and small positive studies similarly represented?

Table 8.7 identifies the main types of bias that apply to quantitative studies. Some of these may also apply to other types of study but these have been less explored.

Table 8.7 Types of reporting bias with definitions

Type of bias	How does it happen?	What is its effect?
Citation bias	When chance of study being cited by others is associated with its result (Song et al., 2010).	Use of reference lists may be more likely to locate supportive studies, which could bias the findings of the review (Egger and Davey Smith, 1998).
Database bias	When there is biased indexing of published studies in literature databases (Song et al., 2010).	Journals indexed in databases are more established, in the language favoured by database producer and include larger studies. Journals from developing countries are less likely to be represented in databases produced in the developed world (Egger and Davey Smith, 1998).
Funding bias	When the design, outcome, and reporting of industry-sponsored research may result in sponsor's product showing a favourable outcome (Lexchin, 2003).	Positive studies supporting a product are more likely to be published. Negative studies may be delayed or even suppressed.
Grey literature bias	When results reported in journal articles are systematically different from those in reports, working papers, dissertations or conference abstracts (Song et al., 2010).	Studies may contain interim findings, may not have been subjected to peer review, or may include the selective reporting of outcomes.

(Continued)

(Continued)

Type of bias	How does it happen?	What is its effect?
Language bias (including English- language bias)	When reviews are more likely to include studies published in the language of that review.	Problem for English-language reviews with non-English authors more likely to publish significant results in English rather than in their own language (Egger and Davey Smith, 1998).
Multiple publication bias (duplicate publication bias)	When multiple/duplicate publications are produced from single studies.	Studies with significant results are more likely to lead to multiple publications and presentations, making them more likely to be located and included in reviews. The inclusion of duplicated data may lead to overestimation of the effect size (Egger and Davey Smith, 1998).
Outcome reporting bias	When study in which multiple outcomes were measured reports only those that are significant, rather than insignificant or unfavourable (Song et al., 2010).	Important clinical outcomes are present in some studies but not in others.
Publication bias (also known as positive results bias)	Selective submission of papers (by authors) or selective acceptance of papers (by editors).	Authors may anticipate rejection (Egger and Davey Smith, 1998) and decide not to submit their paper.
Study quality bias	Studies of (typically) lower quality are associated with positive or favourable results.	Studies of lower quality less likely to be published (Song et al., 2010).

 box 8.13

The Funnel plot

What is it?

A Funnel plot is a graphical device (scatter plot) to helping you explore the likelihood of publication bias by plotting the effect estimates from individual studies against some measure of each study's size or precision. The standard error of the effect estimate is often chosen as the measure of study size and plotted on the vertical axis such that the larger, most powerful studies are placed towards the top. The effect estimates from smaller studies should scatter more widely at the bottom, with the spread narrowing among larger studies. If publication bias is not present, and provided the studies are not demonstrably different, the scatter will be entirely due to sampling variation. In such a case the scatter plot will resemble a symmetrical inverted funnel (see Figure 8.6). A triangle centred on a fixed effect summary estimate and extending 1.96 standard errors either side will include about 95% of studies if no bias is present and the true treatment effect is the same in each study.

What can I use it for?

For a Funnel plot to be valuable requires there to be more than a mere handful of studies. (As a rule of thumb, tests for Funnel plot asymmetry should not be used when there are fewer than

10 studies because test power is usually too low to distinguish chance from real asymmetry: see Sterne et al., 2011). A Funnel plot is only an indication, not a guarantor of bias, so it is seen as a starting point for further investigation, not an end in itself (Sterne et al., 2011). Where publication bias is possibly present, there will be a missing 'chunk' of data (see Figure 8.7).

How has it been used?

Small studies of magnesium for myocardial infarction formed an asymmetrical inverted funnel, suggesting the presence of publication bias. Studies in which magnesium was beneficial were more likely to be published, and those in which magnesium was ineffective or detrimental were less likely to be reported. Hence, the overall meta-analysed effect (open diamond) suggested a beneficial effect of magnesium. However, when a large trial (ISIS-4) was subsequently completed, there was no benefit. The lack of agreement of the meta-analysis effect with a subsequent large randomised controlled trial demonstrates the importance of performing Funnel plots and related statistical tests of asymmetry and likely publication bias (Smith and Egger, 1997).

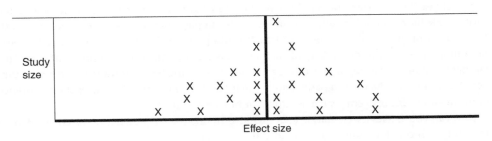

Figure 8.6   Funnel plot with no evidence of publication bias

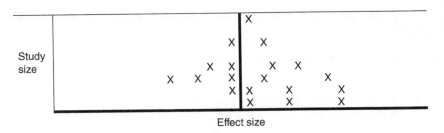

Figure 8.7   Funnel plot with possible publication bias

(Note that in Figure 8.7 a possible population of studies, i.e. those at the bottom of the left-hand side of the funnel, appears not to have been detected by the meta-analysis.)

SELECTIVE OUTCOME REPORTING BIAS

Selective outcome reporting bias is a specific instance of a generic problem, selective reporting bias, defined as the 'selection of a subset of analyses to be reported'. Whereas publication bias refers to a problem relating to missing studies, selective reporting bias is a problem of missing data within a study. Consequently it may prove more difficult to detect and requires a greater degree of familiarity with the topic area under consideration. Selective outcome reporting is the principal concern because it relates to the biased selection of outcomes and so may present a particular programme or intervention in a more favourable light and thus lead to erroneous conclusions as to whether such an intervention should be introduced into practice (Williamson and Gamble, 2005). At its most innocuous, but nevertheless still potentially harmful, a researcher may have measured the same outcome in multiple ways and then selected which measure contributes best to an understanding of the data. The researcher then only provides results using the chosen method. Obviously such an approach has particular limitations in connection with meta-analysis which is only usually possible where the same methods of outcome measurement are used by multiple studies. More serious, however, is where a study measures important and meaningful outcomes but suppresses the results because they are unfavourable to the overall verdict.

Expert knowledge of a particular topic may help you identify a more problematic variant of selective outcome reporting, namely the use of surrogate outcomes. Such outcomes are comparatively easy to measure but bear little relation to what is most important when judging the success or achievement of an 'effect'. Consider, for example, where a government agency records the number of new small businesses to which it has provided 'start-up' funds where the public is more interested in how many of such businesses return an operating profit after x years. Similarly, a drug may be reported to have an effect on lowering blood pressure by a certain number of units but the doctor and patient are more interested in whether it reduces the occurrence of health-threatening events (such as strokes or heart attacks).

How can you as a reviewer analyse your included studies for the presence of selective outcome reporting? Suggested questions are provided in Box 8.14.

 box 8.14

Questions to detect possible outcomes reporting bias

1. To what extent does the list of outcomes identified from the literature match the outcomes that stakeholders in your topic area consider important and meaningful?
2. Examine the full list of outcomes compiled across all studies. Are there any studies that seem to have neglected important outcomes from this list? Do any studies report demonstrably fewer outcomes than their counterparts?
3. Try to identify study protocols for your included studies. How does the list of proposed measurements compare with the list of actual measurements reported in the published papers?
4. Try to identify abstracts from conference proceedings for your included studies. Are any particular measurements reported in interim results but not reported in final published papers?
5. Contact authors of published papers and ask for any additional data, either on specific outcomes or on all non-reported outcomes. Can they point you towards any supplementary publications that you have not previously identified?

What steps can you as a reviewer take in your analysis to try to identify whether your own review is a likely victim of selective outcome reporting bias? Some suggestions are given in Box 8.15.

 box 8.15

Questions to detect possible reporting bias in your own review

1. In your initial reading of a paper, look at which outcome measures have been reported. Are all the outcome measures that have been reported associated with statistically significant results? If so, they are more likely to reflect selective reporting.
2. Again in your initial reading of a paper, count how many separate outcomes are reported. If there are fewer than five different outcomes there is a very high likelihood, between 5 and 10 a high likelihood, and between 11 and 20 a moderate likelihood of selective reporting bias.
3. In your initial reading, look at the outcome measure being used for calculating the sample size. Is this identifiable as the primary outcome from the 'Results and Conclusions'? Has its role as primary outcome been 'hijacked' by a less important outcome?
4. Finally, in your initial reading of the paper, look for evidence of **data dredging**, i.e. where potentially significant associations are stumbled upon during data analysis and an outcome is being attributed with greater importance than a practitioner would invest it with.
5. In following up includable papers, try to obtain relevant study protocols and compare the list of intended outcomes with the list of those actually reported in the final paper. Are they identical? Are there any missing? Have any been promoted in terms of prominence?
6. In following up includable papers via protocols, are sample size and statistical methods in published trials clearly discrepant with respect to the pre-specified protocols?
7. In synthesising your data across studies, construct a matrix of all reported outcomes (rows) against all studies (columns). Are any common outcomes missing from individual studies? Are any important outcomes comparatively under-reported?
8. In analysing your data from included studies, is the performance of any outcomes particularly dependent on presentations at meetings or appearance in conference abstracts? Is this performance confirmed by subsequent publication?

(Source: Chan et al., 2008)

SUMMARY

Synthesis is not the mere process of assembling the raw ingredients of the review (i.e. the individual studies) but also includes the more creative elements of seeking patterns, examining for consistency, and identifying the divergent or disconfirming case. In this way, it is prerequisite to exploring reasons for variations, discrepancies and inconsistencies. This exploration, together with a more general testing of the robustness of findings, constitutes the next phase of the review analysis.

Analysis is a high-order research skill required when undertaking any systematic approach to reviewing the literature. In contrast to synthesis, analysis is often presented as a naturally occurring sequel with little in the way of formal procedures. Nevertheless formal procedures do exist and are informed by recognised methods of quantitative analysis. These include the use of **Funnel plots** (for the investigation of publication bias), **subgroup analysis** (for exploring commonalities that exist at a level beneath that of the complete population of studies) and sensitivity analysis (for testing the robustness of results to particular assumptions). Once you have used these analytical techniques to explore the internal validity of the review, you can turn your attention to examining external validity. Your observations relating to applicability, generalisability, replicability and implementation fidelity will shape your likely recommendations for research and for practice. Once such recommendations are drafted and exist in a fluid or malleable state, attention can turn to how best to present the report, the focus for Chapter 10.

 key learning points

- Data extraction is a key step towards synthesis and it is helpful to picture what the final synthesis might look like before selecting data to be extracted.
- Numerous approaches to synthesis exist and the reviewer will find it informative to look at existing published methods and examples before selecting a methodology that is fit for purpose.
- A reviewer can select from a large range of types of data presentation, including textual, graphical, numerical and tabular approaches.
- Analysis initially involves testing the robustness of your synthesis in light of what you know about the quality of included studies.
- Particular concerns relate to the presence of dissemination- and publication-related biases.
- Having assessed the overall robustness, your attention will focus on the extent to which the findings may be applied within the specific context of your review.

frequently asked questions

FAQ 8.1 Should I perform a rapid review?

Rapid reviews are typically used when decision makers face a time-critical decision (Khangura et al., 2014). Rapid reviews are characterised by the time window within which a decision is required and by close interaction with the commissioner – the Audience & Purpose of our TREAD mnemonic (see Chapter 3). Where time is not an issue a systematic review is to be preferred – primarily because it takes elaborate precautions to avoid bias. Mays and colleagues (2005a) distinguish between reviews for decision support and those for knowledge support (see Chapter 2). Reviews for knowledge support offer a generalisable foundation for practice and/or research which is worth waiting for. Reviews for decision support provide a contingent and context-specific answer within a time-limited expiry date.

Rapid reviews are typically either abbreviated, conceding rigour to deliver on time, or accelerated, by preserving rigour but requiring more resources. A review team should initiate a frank and open discussion with those commissioning the review to clarify how the review is to be used, limitations of the method, and the impact of streamlining on the uncertainty of conclusion. In a risk averse context a robust yet delayed **systematic review** may offer a more effective policy lever than a superficial rapid review where its contribution has been devalued following close scrutiny.

FAQ 8.2 How do I decide which method of meta-analysis to use?

A meta-analysis combines the results from two or more primary studies statistically. Essentially you have a choice between a fixed-effects model or a random-effects model. A fixed-effects model considers the set of studies included in the meta-analysis and assumes that a single true value underlies all of the study results. The model assumes that if all the studies that address the same question were infinitely large and completely free of *bias*, they would yield identical estimates of the effect. Assuming that studies are free from *risk of bias*, observed estimates of effect will only differ from each other because of *random error*. In contrast a random-effects model assumes that the studies included are a random sample of a population of studies addressing the question posed in the meta-analysis. Because of inevitable differences in the patients, interventions and outcomes among studies that address the research question, each study estimates a different underlying true effect, and these effects will have a normal distribution around a mean value. The random-effects model takes into account both within-study variability and variability in results beyond what can be attributed to within-study variability. The random-effects model is less likely to demonstrate that an intervention is effective when it is not; it is more conservative. If you have concerns about the heterogeneity of your included studies then it would be best to use the random-effects model.

FAQ 8.3 What software is available for performing a meta-analysis?

As with most types of software for supporting a systematic review there is a range of options, some fee-based and others freely available. Comprehensive Meta-analysis is considered by many as an easy-to-use commercial package (as its names suggests it is purpose-designed). A general widely used statistical software package is STATA which may be available under license within your academic institution. This performs most of the required meta-analytic statistical procedures but cannot be used to manage the whole review. In contrast the Cochrane Collaboration's RevMan software has been designed for preparing and maintaining Cochrane reviews and is freely available. Bax et al. (2007) have reviewed a variety of software packages for meta-analysis.

FAQ 8.4 What if the studies in my meta-analysis are of variable quality?

If you are trying to investigate possible causes of variability in your review then you should conduct a sensitivity analysis. This is equally true in this case where it is the study quality that is variable. Essentially sensitivity analysis involves repeating an analysis under different assumptions – for example, assuming that studies of any quality are included versus assuming that only high quality studies are included. You can then identify how 'sensitive' the overall review result is to bias from the poorer quality studies.

■■■■■■ suggestions for further reading ■■■■■■

Crombie, I.K. and Davies, H.T.O. (2009) *What is Metaanalysis?* 2nd edition. London: Hayward Medical Communications.
A brief educational briefing that summarises meta-analysis in a concise easy-to-read format.

Deeks, J.J., Higgins, J.P.T. and Altman, D.G. (eds) (2011) Analysing data and undertaking meta-analyses (Part 2, Chapter 9). In J.P.T. Higgins and S. Green (eds), *Cochrane Handbook for Systematic Reviews of Interventions*, Version 5.1.0 (updated March 2011). The Cochrane Collaboration. Available at: www.cochrane-handbook.org (last accessed 9 March 2016).
Authoritative chapter from the *Cochrane Handbook* summarising current thinking on meta-analysis.

Higgins, J.P.T, Altman, D.G. and Sterne, J.A.C. (eds) (2011) Assessing risk of bias in included studies (Part 2, Chapter 8). In J.P.T. Higgins and S. Green (eds), *Cochrane Handbook for Systematic Reviews of Interventions*, Version 5.1.0 (updated March 2011). The Cochrane Collaboration. Available at: www.cochrane-handbook.org (last accessed 9 March 2016).
Companion chapter to the previous item from the *Cochrane Handbook* describing risk of bias procedures from those who have developed them.

Pope, C., Mays, N. and Popay, J. (2007) Methods for evidence synthesis. In C. Pope, N. Mays and J. Popay (eds), *Synthesizing Qualitative and Quantitative Health Evidence: A Guide to Methods*. Maidenhead: Open University Press, 45–114.
Good overview of approaches across both quantitative and qualitative methods.

Sterne, J.A.C., Egger, M. and Moher, D. (eds) (2011) Addressing reporting biases (Part 2, Chapter 10). In J.P.T. Higgins and S. Green (eds), *Cochrane Handbook for Systematic Reviews of Interventions*, Version 5.1.0 (updated March 2011). The Cochrane Collaboration. Available at: www.cochrane-handbook.org (last accessed 9 March 2016).
Further chapter from *Cochrane Handbook*, an authoritative contribution on publication biases.

REFERENCES

Alfirevic, Z., Keeney, E., Dowswell, T., Welton, N.J., Dias, S., Jones, L.V., Navaratnam, K. and Caldwell, D.M. (2015) Labour induction with prostaglandins: a systematic review and network meta-analysis. *BMJ*, **350**, h217.

Alias, M. and Suradi, Z. (2008) Concept mapping: a tool for creating a literature review. In A.J. Cañas, P. Reiska, M. Åhlberg and J.D. Novak (eds), *Concept Mapping: Connecting Educators Proceedings of the Third International Conference on Concept Mapping*. Tallinn and Helsinki: Tallinn University, 96–99.

Arai, L., Britten, N., Popay, J., Roberts, H., Petticrew, M., Rodgers, M. and Sowden, A. (2007) Testing methodological developments in the conduct of narrative synthesis: a demonstration review of research on the implementation of smoke alarm interventions. *Evidence and Policy*, **3**, 3, 361–83.

Atkins, S., Lewin, S., Smith, H., Engel, M., Fretheim, A. and Volmink, J. (2008) Conducting a meta-ethnography of qualitative literature: lessons learnt. *BMC Medical Research Methodology*, **8**, 21. DOI: 10.1186/1471-2288-8-21.

Bafeta, A., Trinquart, L., Seror, R. and Ravaud, P. (2014) Reporting of results from network meta-analyses: methodological systematic review. *BMJ*, **348**, g1741.

Barnett-Page, E. and Thomas, J. (2009) Methods for the synthesis of qualitative research: a critical review. *BMC Research Methodology*, **9**, 59. DOI: 10.1186/1471-2288-9-59.

Bax, L., Yu, L.-M., Ikeda, N. and Moons, K.G. (2007) A systematic comparison of software dedicated to meta-analysis of causal studies. *BMC Medical Research Methodology*, **7**, 40. DOI: 10.1186/1471-2288-7-40.

Baxter, S., Killoran, A., Kelly, M.P. and Goyder, E. (2010) Synthesizing diverse evidence: the use of primary qualitative data analysis methods and logic models in public health reviews. *Public Health*, **124**, 2, 99–106.

Booth, A. and Carroll, C. (2015) Systematic searching for theory to inform systematic reviews: is it feasible? Is it desirable? *Health Information & Libraries Journal*, **32**, 3, 220–35.

Booth, A., Meier, P., Shapland, J., Wong, R. and Paisley, S. (2010) *Alcohol pricing and criminal harm: a rapid evidence assessment of the published research literature*. Sheffield: School of Health and Related Research, University of Sheffield, UK.

Booth, A., Meier, P., Stockwell, T., Sutton, A., Wilkinson, A., Wong, R., Brennan, A., O'Reilly, D., Purshouse, R. and Taylor, K. (2008) *Independent Review of the Effects of Alcohol Pricing and Promotion: Part A. Systematic Reviews*. Sheffield: School of Health and Related Research, University of Sheffield, UK.

Braithwaite, J. (2010) Between-group behaviour in health care: gaps, edges, boundaries, disconnections, weak ties, spaces and holes. A systematic review. *BMC Health Services Research*, **10**, 330.

Budgen, D., Turner, M., Brereton, P. and Kitchenham, B. (2008) Using mapping studies in software engineering. Proceedings of PPIG 2008, Lancaster University, 195–204.

Caldwell, D.M. (2014) An overview of conducting systematic reviews with network meta-analysis. *Systematic Reviews*, **3**, 109.

Chan, A.W. and Altman, D.G. (2005) Identifying outcome reporting bias in randomised trials on PubMed: review of publications and survey of authors. *BMJ*, **330**, 7494, 753.

Chan, A.W., Hróbjartsson, A., Jørgensen, K.J., Gøtzsche, P.C. and Altman, D.G. (2008) Discrepancies in sample size calculations and data analyses reported in randomised trials: comparison of publications with protocols. *BMJ*, **337**, a2299.

Chua, S.L., Chen, D.-T. and Wong, A.F.L. (1999) Computer anxiety and its correlates: a meta-analysis. *Computers in Human Behavior*, **15**, 5, 609–23.

Clinkenbeard, P.R. (1991) Beyond summary: constructing a review of the literature. In N.K. Buchanan and J.F. Feldhusen (eds), *Conducting Research and Evaluation in Gifted Education: A Handbook of Methods and Applications*. New York: Teachers College Press, 33–50.

Combs, J.P., Bustamante, R.M. and Onwuegbuzie, A.J. (2010) An interactive model for facilitating development of literature reviews. *International Journal of Multiple Research Approaches*, **4**, 2, 159–82.

Cooper, H. and Dorr, N. (1995) Race comparisons on need for achievement: a meta-analytic alternative to Graham's narrative review. *Review of Educational Research*, **65**, 4, 483–8.

Cooper, H. and Hedges, L.V. (eds) (1994) *The Handbook of Research Synthesis*. New York: Sage.

Cooper, H.M. (1982) Scientific guidelines for conducting integrative research reviews. *Review of Educational Research*, **52**, 2, 291–302.

Cresswell, J.W. (2003) *Research Design: Qualitative, Quantitative, and Mixed Method Approaches*, 2nd edition. Thousand Oaks, CA: Sage.

Crombie, I.K. and Davies, H.T.O. (2009) What is meta-analysis? 2nd edition. *What is ... ?* **1**, 8: 1–8.

Crowther, M., Avenell, A., MacLennan, G. and Mowatt, G. (2011) A further use for the harvest plot: a novel method for the presentation of data synthesis. *Research Synthesis Methods*, **2**, 2, 79–83.

Davies, H.T.O. and Crombie, I.K. (1998) What is meta-analysis? *What is......?* **1**, 8, 1–8.

de Craen, A.J., van Vliet, H.A. and Helmerhorst, F.M. (2005) An analysis of systematic reviews indicated low incorporation of results from clinical trial quality assessment. *Journal of Clinical Epidemiology*, **58**, 3, 311–13.

Dekkers, O.M., von Elm, E., Algra, A., Romijn, J.A. and Vandenbroucke, J.P. (2009) How to assess the external validity of therapeutic trials: a conceptual approach. *International Journal of Epidemiology*, **39**, 1, 89–94.

Denyer, D., Tranfield, D. and Van Aken, J.E. (2008) Developing design propositions through research synthesis. *Organization Studies*, **29**, 2, 249–69.

Dinh-Zarr, T.B., Sleet, D.A., Shults, R.A., Zaza, S., Elder, R.W., Nichols, J.L., Thompson, R.S. and Sosin, D.M. (2001) Task force on community preventive services. Reviews of evidence regarding interventions to increase the use of safety belts. *American Journal of Preventive Medicine*, **21**, Suppl. 4, 48–65.

Egger, M. and Davey Smith, G. (1998) Meta-analysis: bias in location and selection of studies. *BMJ*, **316**, 61–6.

Evans, D. (2007) Integrative reviews of quantitative and qualitative research: overview of methods. In C. Webb and B. Roe (eds), *Reviewing Research Evidence for Nursing Practice*: Systematic Reviews. Oxford: Blackwell, 135–148.

Ganann, R., Ciliska, D. and Thomas, H. (2010) Expediting systematic reviews: methods and implications of rapid reviews. *Implementation Science*, **5**, 56.

Glass, G.V., McGaw, B. and Smith, M.L. (1981) *Meta-analysis in Social Research*. Beverly Hills, CA: Sage.

Graham-Matheson, L., Connolly, T., Robson, S. and Stow, W. (2006) A systematic map into approaches to making initial teacher training flexible and responsive to the needs of trainee teachers. Technical report. In: *Research Evidence in Education Library*. London: EPPI-Centre, Social Science Research Unit.

Gray, C. and Malins, J. (2004) *Visualizing Research: A Guide to the Research Process in Art and Design*. Burlington, VT: Ashgate.

Greenhalgh, T. (2014) *How to Read a Paper: The Basics of Evidence-based Medicine*, 5th edition. London: BMJ Books.

Greenhalgh, T., Kristjansson, E. and Robinson, V. (2007) Realist review to understand the efficacy of school feeding programmes. *BMJ*, **335**, 7625, 858.

Grimshaw, J.M., Thomas, R.E., MacLennan, G., Fraser, C., Ramsay, C.R., Vale, L., Whitty, P., Eccles, M.P., Matowe, L., Shirran, L., Wensing, M., Dijkstra, R. and Donaldson, C. (2004) Effectiveness and efficiency of guideline dissemination and implementation strategies. *Health Technology Assessment*, **8**, 6, 1–72.

Hammersley, M. (2001) On 'systematic' reviews of research literatures: a 'narrative' response to Evans and Benefield. *British Educational Research Journal*, **27**, 543–54.

Harker, J. and Kleijnen, J. (2012) What is a rapid review? A methodological exploration of rapid reviews in Health Technology Assessments. *International Journal of Evidence-Based Healthcare*, **10**, 4, 397–410.

Hart, C. (1998) *Doing a Literature Review: Releasing the Social Science Research Imagination*. London: Sage.

Hartling, L., Ospina, M., Liang, Y., Dryden, D.M., Hooton, N., Krebs Seida, J. and Klassen, T.P. (2009) Risk of bias versus quality assessment of randomised controlled trials: cross sectional study. *BMJ*, **339**, b4012

Kavanagh, J., Trouton, A., Oakley, A. and Harden, A. (2005) *A Scoping Review of the Evidence for Incentive Schemes to Encourage Positive Health and Other Social Behaviours in Young People*. London: EPPI-Centre, Social Science Research Unit.

Khangura, S., Polisena, J., Clifford, T. J., Farrah, K. and Kamel, C. (2014) Rapid review: an emerging approach to evidence synthesis in health technology assessment. *International Journal of Technology Assessment in Health Care*, **30**, 1, 20–7.

Kitchenham, B. (2007) *Guidelines for Performing Systematic Literature Reviews in Software Engineering* (Version 2.3). EBSE Technical Report: EBSE-2007–01. Software Engineering Group, School of Computer Science and Mathematics, Keele University, Staffordshire.

Lewis, J.A. and Ellis, S.H. (1982) A statistical appraisal of post-infarction beta-blocker trials. *Primary Cardiology*, Suppl. 1, 31–7.

Lewis, S. and Clarke, M. (2001) Forest plots: trying to see the wood and the trees. *BMJ*, **322**, 7300, 1479–80.

Lexchin, J., Bero, L.A., Djulbegovic, B. and Clark, O. (2003) Pharmaceutical industry sponsorship and research outcome and quality: systematic review. *British Medical Journal*, **326**, 7400, 1167–70.

Light, R.J. and Pillemer, D.B. (1984) *Summing Up: The Science of Reviewing Research*. Cambridge, MA: Harvard University Press.

Lipsey, M.W. and Wilson, D.B. (2001) *Practical Meta-analysis*. Applied Social Research Methods series (Vol. 49). Thousand Oaks, CA: Sage.

Lucas, P.J., Baird, J., Arai, L., Law, C. and Roberts, H.M. (2007) Worked examples of alternative methods for the synthesis of qualitative and quantitative research in systematic reviews. *BMC Medical Research Methodology*, **7**, 4.

Lundh, A. and Goetzche, P.C. (2008) Recommendations by Cochrane Review Groups for assessment of the risk of bias in studies. *BMC Medical Research Methodology*, **8**, 22.

Mays, N., Pope, C. and Popay, J. (2005a) Systematically reviewing qualitative and quantitative evidence to inform management and policy-making in the health field. *Journal of Health Services Research and Policy*, **10**, Suppl. 1, 6–20.

Mays, N., Pope, C. and Popay, J. (2005b) Details of approaches to synthesis – a methodological appendix to the paper, systematically reviewing qualitative and quantitative evidence to inform management and policy making in the health field. Report for the National Co-ordinating Centre for NHS Service Delivery and Organisation R and D (NCCSDO), London School of Hygiene and Tropical Medicine.

Mills, E., Jadad, A.R., Ross, C. and Wilson, K. (2005) Systematic review of qualitative studies exploring parental beliefs and attitudes toward childhood vaccination identifies common barriers to vaccination. *Journal of Clinical Epidemiology*, **58**, 11, 1081–8.

Mulrow, C. (1994) *Rationale for Systematic Reviews*. London: BMJ.

National Collaborating Centre for Methods and Tools (n.d.) *Methods: Synthesis 1. Rapid Reviews: Methods and Implications*. [fact sheet]. Hamilton, ON: National Collaborating Centre for Methods and Tools. Retrieved from www.nccmt.ca/pubs/Methods_Synthesis1.pdf.

Neupane, B., Richer, D., Bonner, A. J., Kibret, T. and Beyene, J. (2014) Network meta-analysis using R: a review of currently available automated packages. *PloS One*, **9**, 12, e115065.

Neyeloff, J.L., Fuchs, S.C. and Moreira, L.B. (2012) Meta-analyses and Forest plots using a Microsoft Excel spreadsheet: step-by-step guide focusing on descriptive data analysis. *BMC Research Notes*, **5**, 1, 52.

Ogilvie, D., Fayter, D., Petticrew, M., Sowden, A., Thomas, S., Whitehead, M. and Worthy, G. (2008) The harvest plot: a method for synthesising evidence about the differential effects of interventions. *BMC Medical Research Methodology*, **8**, 8.

Pawson, R. (2001) *Evidence Based Policy: II. The Promise of 'Realist Synthesis*. ESRC UK Centre for Evidence Based Policy and Practice. London: Queen Mary, University of London.

Pawson, R., Greenhalgh, T., Harvey, G. and Walshe, K. (2004) *Realist Synthesis: An Introduction*. Manchester: ESRC Research Methods Programme.

Petticrew, M. and Roberts, H. (2006) *Systematic Reviews in the Social Sciences: A Practical Guide*. Oxford: Blackwell.

Polisena, J., Garritty, C., Umscheid, C. A., Kamel, C., Samra, K., Smith, J. and Vosilla, A. (2015) Rapid Review Summit: an overview and initiation of a research agenda. *Systematic Reviews*, **4**, 1, 1–6.

Popay, J., Roberts, H., Sowden, A., Petticrew, M., Arai, L., Rodgers, M. and Britten, N. (2006) Guidance on the conduct of narrative synthesis in systematic reviews. A Product from the ESRC Methods Programme.

Randolph, J.J. (2009) A guide to writing the dissertation literature review. *Practical Assessment, Research and Evaluation*, **14**, 1–13.

Rodgers, M., Arai, L., Popay, J., Britten, N., Roberts, H., Petticrew, M. and Sowden, A. (2009) Testing methodological guidance on the conduct of narrative synthesis in systematic reviews: effectiveness of interventions to promote smoke alarm ownership and function. *Evaluation*, **15**, 49–73.

Rosenthal, R. (1991) *Meta-analytic Procedures for Social Research*, revised edition. Newbury Park, CA: Sage.

Rowley, J. and Slack, F. (2004) Conducting a literature review. *Management Research News*, **27**, 4, 31–9.

Rumrill, P.D. and Fitzgerald, S.M. (2001) Using narrative reviews to build a scientific knowledge base. *Work*, **16**, 165–70.

Ryan, R.E., Kaufman, C.A. and Hill, S.J. (2009) Building blocks for meta-synthesis: data integration tables for summarising, mapping, and synthesising evidence on interventions for communicating with health consumers. *BMC Medical Research Methodology*, **9**, 16.

Schünemann, H.J. and Moja, L. (2015) Reviews: Rapid! Rapid! Rapid!... and systematic. *Systematic Reviews*, **4**, 1, 1–3.

Sedgwick, P. (2012). How to read a forest plot. *BMJ*, **345**, e8335.

Slavin, R.E. (1986) Best-evidence synthesis: an alternative to meta-analysis and traditional reviews. *Educational Researcher*, **15**, 9, 5–11.

Smith, G.D. and Egger, M. (1997) Meta-analysis of randomised controlled trials. *Lancet*, *350*, 1182.

Song, F., Parekh, S., Hooper, L., Loke, Y.K., Ryder, J., Sutton, A.J., Hing, C., Kwok, C.S., Pang, C. and Harvey, I. (2010) Dissemination and publication of research findings: an updated review of related biases. *Health Technology Assessment*, **14**, 8, 1–193.

Sterne, J.A., Sutton, A.J., Ioannidis, J., Terrin, N., Jones, D.R., Lau, J., Carpenter, J., Rücker, G., Harbord, R., Schmid, C.H., Tetzlaff, J., Deeks, J.J., Peters, J., Macaskill, P., Schwarzer, G., Duval, S., Altman, D.G., Moher, D. and Higgins, J. (2011). Recommendations for examining and interpreting funnel plot asymmetry in meta-analyses of randomised controlled trials. *BMJ*, **343**, d4002.

Thomas, J., Harden, A., Oakley, A., Oliver, S., Sutcliffe, K., Rees, R., Brunton, G. and Kavanagh, J. (2004) Integrating qualitative research with trials in systematic reviews. *BMJ*, **328**, 7446, 1010–2.

Tugwell, P., Petticrew, M., Kristjansson, E., Welch, V., Ueffing, E., Waters, E., Bonnefoy, J., Morgan, A., Doohan, E. and Kelly, M.P. (2010) Assessing equity in systematic reviews: realising the recommendations of the Commission on Social Determinants of Health. *BMJ*, **341**, c4739.

Turley, R., Saith, R., Bhan, N., Rehfuess, E. and Carter, B. (2013) Slum upgrading strategies involving physical environment and infrastructure interventions and their effects on health and socio-economic outcomes. *The Cochrane Database of Systematic Reviews*. DOI: 10.1002/14651858.CD010067.pub2.

Turner, J., Preston, L., Booth, A., O'Keefe, C., Campbell, F., Jesurasa, A., Cooper, K. and Goyder, E. (2014) What evidence is there for a relationship between organisational features and patient outcomes in congenital heart disease services? A rapid review. Southampton (UK): NIHR Journals Library; *Health Services and Delivery Research*, **2**, 43.

Umoquit, M.J., Tso, P., Burchett, H.E. and Dobrow, M.J. (2011) A multidisciplinary systematic review of the use of diagrams as a means of collecting data from research subjects: application, benefits and recommendations. *BMC Medical Research Methodology*, **11**, 1, 11.

Vadeboncoeur, C., Townsend, N. and Foster, C. (2015) A meta-analysis of weight gain in first year university students: is freshman 15 a myth? *BMC Obesity*, **2**, 22.

Watt, A., Cameron, A., Sturm, L., Lathlean, T., Babidge, W., Blamey, S., Facey, K., Hailey, D., Norderhaug, I. and Maddern, G. (2008) Rapid versus full systematic reviews: validity in clinical practice? *Australian and New Zealand Journal of Surgery*, **78**, 11, 1037–40.

Webb, G., Shakeshaft, A., Sanson-Fisher, R. and Havard, A. (2009) A systematic review of workplace interventions for alcohol-related problems. *Addiction*, **104**, 3, 365–77.

Wheeldon, J. and Faubert, J. (2009) Framing experience: concept maps, mind maps, and data collection in qualitative research. *International Journal of Qualitative Methods*, **8**, 68–83.

Whittemore, R. and Knafl, K. (2005) The integrative review: updated methodology. *Journal of Advanced Nursing*, **52**, 5, 546–53.

Williamson, P.R. and Gamble, C. (2005) Identification and impact of outcome selection bias in meta-analysis. *Statistics in Medicine*, **24**, 1547–61.

Zief, S.G., Lauver, S. and Maynard, R.A. (2006) Impacts of after-school programs on student outcomes: a systematic review. *The Campbell Library*, **2**, 3. DOI: 10.4073/csr.2006.3.

SYNTHESISING
AND ANALYSING
QUALITATIVE STUDIES

 **in a nutshell**

How to synthesise and analyse qualitative studies

- Typically qualitative data are summarised in the form of themes or constructs.
- Qualitative data can also be summarised and synthesised in narrative, tabular and sometimes graphical form.
- Your choice of synthesis method is primarily determined by the respective balance between the need to aggregate and the need to interpret findings from the studies.
- You should also consider whether the units of analysis are the individual studies, the themes or the findings within the studies.
- Integrating quantitative and qualitative data requires either an additional integrative review, a framework for bringing the data together, translation of data into a common format, or a methodology that accommodates both types of data, either sequentially or in parallel.

INTRODUCTION

Qualitative methods allow you to gather detailed and specific information and, most importantly, go beyond statistical associations by investigating the localised and complex mechanisms of both events and process (Miles and Huberman, 1994). Whether you are conducting a quantitative or a qualitative review synthesis involves identifying patterns within your data. In contrast to a quantitative review, which seeks to summarise all the data economically within a single estimate of the overall strength and direction of effect, a qualitative review seeks to identify any commonalities emerging from your data. Importantly, you are looking to discover whether there are any exceptions to an overall pattern or 'rule' (Booth et al., 2013b). You must recognise that the value of your review does not lie in merely identifying and bringing together related studies. By *juxtaposing* findings from different sources you may potentially achieve insights not previously recognised by the authors of individual studies. Furthermore you may be able to *integrate* your data to produce an overarching, new explanation or theory which attempts to account for the range of findings (Mays et al., 2005a). Bear in mind, too, that these 'synthetic' insights may not relate only to the findings (what the individual authors found) but may also relate to how the studies have been carried out (meta-method). You may be able to use differences in the methods of the studies to explain inconsistencies in their findings or, ultimately, to make recommendations on how such studies might best be conducted in the future.

Explicit to synthesis is the principle that you are 'making a new whole out of the parts' (Pope et al., 2007). Your manufactured 'new whole' may form a new line of argument, a new theory or a new 'bottom line'. Conceptual 'building blocks' (studies or findings) can be rearranged within an existing fabrication (for example a theory or framework), integrated with new studies or used to produce an entirely new construction (Anderson et al., 2013b). Gough, Thomas and Oliver (2012b) characterise these functions around the GET mnemonic; findings from a review can help to **G**enerate, **E**xplore or **T**est theory. Indeed some iterative methods may move between more than one of these functions. For example realist synthesis moves between the **G**eneration and **T**esting of theory (Pawson et al., 2004) while framework synthesis **T**ests an existing framework before **G**enerating new theory from that data imperfectly accommodated within the original framework (Carroll et al., 2011, 2013; Booth and Carroll, 2015).

SYNTHESIS-ANALYSIS: AN ITERATIVE PROCESS

For many methods of qualitative evidence synthesis, the processes of synthesis and analysis are iterative rather than linear. A finding may be generated by the process of synthesis. The reviewer might seek to confirm the presence of this finding in the existing data using some analytical technique. Indeed many analytical techniques are common to multiple types of synthesis. The distinction between synthesis and analysis is therefore most useful in defining the tools available for each process from which the reviewer selects judiciously.

OVERVIEW OF APPROACHES TO QUALITATIVE SYNTHESIS

Synthesis relies heavily on pattern recognition. Thus Hart emphasises techniques such as *analogy* (looking for similarities between different phenomena), *metaphor* (thinking about one thing as if it were the same as another), and *homology* (looking for direct and corresponding relationships between natural and synthetic structures, e.g. between nature and human society) (Hart, 1998). These techniques translate readily to evidence synthesis (Tranfield et al., 2003; Greenhalgh and Russell, 2006). Furthermore Hart and other authors emphasise how important it is to use the basic critical and analytical components of *comparison* and *contrast* (Hart, 1998; Cresswell, 2003; Gray and Malins, 2004):

[Some] references may be organized chronologically in parts of your review where you may be evaluating developments over time; some may be arranged thematically, demonstrating similarities and allowing you to make creative connections (cross-currents) between previously unrelated research; and some arranged to demonstrate *comparison and contrast* perhaps using a common set of criteria as an 'anchor'. (Gray and Malins, 2004)

You can use comparison and contrast within a literature review to compare study by study (usually only possible with a limited number of items for inclusion) or by findings (i.e. similarities and differences across studies). Within a larger literature review, as carried out for a dissertation or thesis, you may want to combine both approaches.

Qualitative approaches to synthesis may be broadly characterised as **aggregative**, **configurative** and **integrative**. Aggregative synthesis is primarily a 'stocktaking' activity, typically embodied in mapping exercises. An aggregative synthesis answers such questions as: What are the main types of study for this particular phenomenon? What are the principal themes across multiple studies? Are there any populations that are either not represented at all or poorly represented across studies? Configurative synthesis principally involves trying to capture the whole rounded-out picture of a particular phenomenon. It addresses such questions as: How do the individual themes identified across studies relate to one another? Are all perspectives captured within any potential explanations of the phenomenon? What are the main areas of agreement or dissonance across studies and how might they be explained? Integrative approaches to synthesis seek to bring together different types of data (either bringing together data from quantitative and qualitative studies or triangulating across different types of data or different types of method). For example you might integrate qualitative thematic data with responses from surveys. Just as primary mixed method studies are variously interpreted as studies integrating quantitative and qualitative study components or studies integrating data collected through different methods, so too might mixed methods synthesis integrate similarly diverse types of data. Integrative synthesis may answer such questions as: How might the findings across different methods be reconciled, if at all? Can I explain apparent inconsistencies between findings from different methods? How does the bringing together of different data sources reveal possible gaps in the current research base? As mentioned in Chapter 8 you can use either qualitative or quantitative approaches for summarising qualitative data (as when the occurrence of themes or words is quantified by **content analysis**) (Mays et al., 2005b).

Dixon-Woods and colleagues (2004) identify no fewer than 12 *qualitative* approaches to research synthesis (Box 9.1).

 box 9.1

Twelve qualitative approaches to synthesis

1. Narrative synthesis
2. Grounded theory – constant comparison
3. Meta-ethnography

(Continued)

(Continued)

4. Meta-synthesis
5. Meta-study
6. Logical analysis
7. Data analysis techniques
8. Metaphorical analysis
9. Domain analysis
10. Hermeneutical analysis
11. Discourse analysis, and
12. Analytic induction

Three approaches in particular, **narrative synthesis** (Snilstveit et al., 2012), **meta-ethnography** (Campbell et al., 2011) and **realist synthesis**, have experienced accelerated growth across disciplines (Denyer and Tranfield, 2006; Armitage and Keeble-Allen, 2008). **Thematic synthesis** continues to represent one of the most accessible methods of qualitative synthesis. Bearman and Dawson (2013) look at the complementary strengths of **thematic analysis (synthesis)**, meta-ethnography and realist synthesis. Garside (2008) has compared meta-ethnography and **meta-study**. Recent years have witnessed an attempt to move beyond simple documentation of methods to an attempt to identify which method of synthesis is most appropriate under what circumstances (Kastner et al., 2012; Paterson, 2012). Before looking at specific techniques of synthesis we examine a key step on the path to synthesis, namely data extraction.

EXTRACTING QUALITATIVE DATA FOR YOUR REVIEW

Data extraction is key in demonstrating that you have followed a systematic approach. When extracting data you are systematically identifying information relevant to a review's research questions. You may find it tempting to cut-and-paste large quantities of text from the portable document format (PDF) of articles into your data extraction form. Alternatively you may be similarly tempted to code entire articles having imported them into a qualitative data analysis package such as NVivo. Just because you can, does not mean that you should! Return to your review question and only extract those data that are relevant, or potentially relevant, to your question.

Quantitative systematic review is often criticised for the de-contextualisation of source data. A corresponding challenge for qualitative systematic reviews is to preserve information about contextual factors from the included studies (Fu et al., 2015) to help explain differences across studies. You should seek to handle different studies, with their different designs and publishing conventions, in a consistent manner. An important consideration is deciding what data you will extract and how to do this. Data extraction requires that you pre-specify and then examine which elements of data are present in each individual study report (Munn et al., 2014). For qualitative systematic reviews some authors decide not to extract to purpose-designed forms but prefer to import the PDFs of articles direct into qualitative data analysis software such as NVivo (Toye et al., 2014). Extracting data in this way recognises that interpretive reviews possess characteristics that challenge the process of data extraction described in Chapter 8.

The raw data of a qualitative systematic review are ideas or concepts. Ideas or concepts need not be constrained within a single 'Results' section of a paper but might appear in both the 'Results' and 'Discussion' sections. When synthesising qualitative research you will often need to go back and re-read the original findings, thus allowing you to compare emerging ideas to the concepts as originally written. Uploading a PDF version of the complete study onto NVivo software allows a review team to code conceptual findings wherever they appeared within the paper, and compare individual team interpretations in one database. NVivo offers a feature, particularly useful for collaborative analysis, that allows you to record and compare team member interpretations. It also allows the researchers to write and link, through a process of 'memoing', to specific data in order to keep track of developing ideas. It also permits classification of study characteristics such as: author; journal; year of publication; number and age of participants; source and country of participants; method of data collection (e.g. interviews); methodological approach (e.g. grounded theory). Data extraction, therefore, is typically underpinned by assumptions of an 'extract once, read multiple times' way of working. It may therefore be less useful in the context of a 'read multiple times, code multiple times' model of working as necessitated by more interpretive review processes which require ongoing grounding in the primary studies.

While Pawson and colleagues are not enthusiasts of data extraction they do summarise succinctly its overall intent:

> The conventional systematic reviewer proceeds by lining up primary studies that have made it through the quality filter, fine-tuning the set of characteristics through which to compare them, combing through each source to extract precisely the same nugget of information from each, and recording these data onto a standard grid (often reproduced as an appendix to the review). (Pawson et al., 2004)

You can display extracted or coded qualitative data in the form of matrices, graphs, charts or networks (Whittemore and Knafl, 2005). Such displays help you visualise patterns and relationships within and across the constituent studies. This provides a good starting point for interpretation and subsequent analysis (Knafl and Webster, 1988; Sandelowski, 1995). Pawson and colleagues (2004) observe that qualitative reviews are increasingly subjected to a process analogous to that used in quantitative systematic review:

> Qualitative reviews increasingly conform to this expectation about completing comprehensive and uniform extraction sheets. A crucial difference on this variant, however, is that grid entries can take the form of free text and usually consist of short verbal descriptions of key features of interventions and studies.

 toolbox

Data extraction

The toolbox for this chapter contains a sample data extraction form that you can use as a template for your own review (see Table 9.1).

(Continued)

(Continued)

Table 9.1 Sample data extraction form for qualitative study

Data extracted by:	Date:	Ref ID:

Full paper screen:

Question		If Yes	If No
1	Is the study 2003 onwards?	Continue	Exclude
2	Does the intervention being evaluated include one or more of the following: Aspirin, NSAIDs, Vitamins, Minerals, Calcium, Folic acid, dietary supplements generally?	Continue	Exclude
3	Does the study report, as an outcome, people's attitudes, perceptions or beliefs concerning the taking of one of more of the agents listed above?	Continue	Exclude
	Include or exclude?		
	Note: *any population group may be included*		

Title of review			
Publication details			
	Reference number		
Author(s)	Year		
Title of article			
Title of journal			
Volume	Issue		Pages

Study details	Location / country			
	Research question / objectives			
Participants	Population			
	Age			
	Age (Mean/Range)	Mean		Range
	Gender	Male (n)	Female (n)	Not specified (n)

Ethnicity

Recruitment / sampling
(e.g. inclusion criteria, response rate, test of any differences between those who participated and those who did not)

Intervention　**Agents / nutrients**

Outcomes　**What is being evaluated?**

Data Collection　**Method**

(e.g. survey, focus group, interviews)

Validation and recording
(e.g. is survey tool validated; are interviews transcribed and is respondent validation used?)

Data Analysis　**Method**
(e.g. descriptive statistics (%) reported only; analysis of transcripts employing a stated method)

Findings *(data must be verbatim quotes or authors' statements clearly based on data)*

How are results presented?

Verbatim Quotes [Italics]	Author Statements [Normal]	**Author Statements supported by Verbatim Quotes [Bold]**

Theme 1

Theme 2

Theme 3 *(Repeat as necessary for all subsequent themes)*

(Continued)

(Continued)

Authors' conclusions		
Comments	*Limitations, reviewer comments, etc.*	
References	**Possible new includes**	
	Background papers	

The value of data extraction for qualitative research depends upon whether the overall intent is aggregative (bringing multiple studies together in a common format to facilitate assimilation and summing up) or **interpretive** (where data extraction is enhanced by creative techniques to optimise the explanatory value of the data). The units of extraction in this case are specific findings and illustrative excerpts from the text.

A GENERIC APPROACH TO QUALITATIVE EVIDENCE SYNTHESIS

While distinctions between different methodologies are conceptually useful, it is helpful to think generically in terms of the synthesis and analysis processes common across the different methods (Garside, 2008). Broadly speaking these synthesis and analysis processes fall into four main sub-processes:

1. Initial assessment of study reports.
2. Analysis and synthesis.
3. Preliminary analysis and interpretation.
4. Full analysis and interpretation.

The *initial assessment of study reports* requires a preliminary reading and re-reading of the studies for inclusion. To engage with reports at this level you may decide to use a short structured form against which you extract provisional relevant information. You are not seeking to achieve full-blown data extraction but, instead, to produce a brief aide-memoire against which to characterise individual studies. You may be able to identify 'sibling study' reports to contribute additional conceptual richness or contextual thickness (Booth et al., 2013a). By sensitising yourself to the literature you may also be able to 'surface' underlying methods or theories within the studies, either individually or collectively, perhaps as small clusters of related studies. The contribution of methods or theories may be explicit, for example in citation of a named theory, or implicit, through using the terminology or concepts of a recognisable theory. Examining studies that ostensibly share the same methodological or theoretical heritage enables you to identify where studies lack 'theory fidelity' to their claimed origins (Field et al., 2014). For example, a study citing use of 'opinion leaders', a concept drawn implicitly from Roger's Theory of Diffusion, may reveal that recruitment of such individuals was conducted opportunistically and not true to the agreed characteristics of 'opinion leaders' (Booth et al., 2013a). This particular programme is less successful than other programmes that implement the theoretical characteristics more faithfully. This initial assessment also helps you establish the utility and relevance of this initial set of studies to the review question. You may be able to identify where individual studies lie relative to one another on a utility versus rigour trade-off and help to inform purposive study selection and sampling.

Analysis and synthesis will involve further reading and re-reading of study reports. However, at this stage you will move from considering the studies as individual reports towards examining these as a body of evidence. The constant comparison method may prove useful as a mechanism for continually moving between the findings of individual studies and the synthetic findings from the studies considered so far. Your challenge is to extract findings from these studies without losing a sense of the context and relationships within each report. This more detailed reading allows you to focus on more technical aspects of the reporting and to start thinking about whether the methods used are appropriate. You are not seeking to implement some hierarchy of study design but rather to consider the suitability of each method to the particular research question under examination.

Preliminary analysis and interpretation moves you away from the detail of the individual reports to more of a meta-level of analysis. You will start to categorise the findings from the studies. Making sense of qualitative studies, and exploring the presence of patterns, may be facilitated by techniques of narrative synthesis covered in Chapter 8, e.g. mind maps, logic models, tabulation, etc. At this stage you will start to explore relationships in the data both within and between studies.

Full analysis and interpretation moves you beyond the elementary synthesis techniques used in the preliminary stages to more formal methods of synthesis such as thematic synthesis, framework synthesis or meta-ethnography. Suri and Clarke (2009) identify three components of a synthesis that are particularly useful at this stage of the process:

1. Pursuing a line of argument.
2. Examining consistencies.
3. Identifying the disconfirming case.

Engaging with the findings at this depth yields insights into meta-level study features, for example how findings have been informed by a particular research tradition or the development of concepts over time. Incompatibility between certain theoretical or ideological stances is revealed. For example, our study of community engagement revealed a schism between top-down governmental approaches and the more participatory bottom-up approaches (Harris et al., 2015). At this stage the reader is in a position to factor in the influence of study quality on the findings. While most synthesis approaches steer the reader towards identifying patterns of similarity they are now particularly active in seeking the divergent or disconfirming case. Where the data are sufficiently rich you may proceed to theory development – perhaps by constructing if-then causal chains or logic models.

Britten and colleagues (2002) describe the steps they took to facilitate the comparison and translation of papers. They created a grid in Microsoft Excel with each author's name and year of paper recorded in a separate column and concepts derived from the papers being entered into the rows. Second order constructs from each paper were then entered into the grid. Constructs generated by the review team (third order constructs) were developed after comparing the second order constructs across the papers. By ordering their third order constructs along a timeline, influenced by an index paper they were able to develop a 'line of argument' which explored the progression of patients' responses to heart failure. The review team also sought actively to identify anomalous findings.

Britten and colleagues (2002) then employed an iterative process and dialogue in order to refine third order constructs and generate a conceptual model. Their 'line of argument', derived from the model, is that patients pass through five stages as they seek a sense of safety and wellbeing when living with heart failure. As a final process of validation they returned to their original papers to establish that no theme had been missed. They also consulted on the model with their study group and their patient and public advisory team for comment.

As Whittemore and Knafl (2005) make clear many more techniques are available to populate our repertoire (see Table 9.2) during the iterative phases of synthesis and analysis.

After considering techniques for handling data, we look at how such activities may be undertaken within the context of different types of data presentation, namely textual, graphical, numerical and tabular.

Table 9.2 Elements of data analysis

Elements	Application within synthesis methods
Noting patterns and themes	Meta-ethnography, thematic synthesis
Seeing plausibility (ensuring conclusions make good sense)	Meta-ethnography
Clustering	Content analysis, framework synthesis, meta-ethnography, thematic synthesis
Making metaphors	Meta-ethnography, meta-narrative review
Counting	Cross-case analysis, meta-analysis, meta-summary
Making contrasts/comparisons	Meta-ethnography, meta-narrative review
Partitioning variables	Framework synthesis, meta-ethnography, meta-analysis
Subsuming particulars into the general	Meta-analysis, meta-ethnography
Noting relations between variables	Logic models, realist synthesis
Finding intervening variables	Logic models, realist synthesis
Building a logical chain of evidence	Logic models, realist synthesis
Making conceptual/theoretical coherence	Concept maps, logic models, meta-ethnography, meta-narrative review, realist synthesis

(Based on Miles and Huberman, 1994)

PLANNING YOUR SYNTHESIS STRATEGY

A key early stage in the process of synthesis is planning your initial **synthesis strategy** – how you will approach the literature once it has been assembled (Kitchenham, 2007).

You may in fact need to switch from your initial strategy (see Box 9.2) to a more appropriate alternative as patterns from the literature become clearer.

box 9.2

Planning your synthesis strategy

1. Decide whether to read swiftly through all papers OR to work through papers in detail one by one.
2. Decide upon the method of documentation (memos, notes, structured form).
3. Select a starting paper (e.g. an **index paper** – according to age, conceptual richness, number of citations, source discipline, etc.).
4. Decide on an approach for subsequent papers (chronological, purposive sampling, maximum variation sampling, etc.).
5. Construct cross-case comparisons (e.g. tabulation, etc.).

You may prefer to start with a holistic approach that involves reading through the body of literature, with very little hesitation or interruption, perhaps occasionally **memo-ing** or annotating with brief points to which you will return later (Finfgeld-Connett, 2009). Alternatively you might begin with an index paper against which you will compare all subsequent papers. Considerable variation exists in how this index paper is identified or defined and this reflects genuine variety in what each review is trying to achieve; it may be the earliest paper, the most cited paper, the richest in terms of either data or conceptual development, etc. Garside and colleagues (2008) justify their selection of the index paper for their review of the experience of heavy menstrual bleeding as follows:

> In the event, [Paper X] was chosen as an index paper against which the other papers were compared, as this was the only one with a strong conceptual framework. Other papers, while organising data under emergent themes, showed little attempt to provide explanatory concepts.

In this instance, the interpretive nature of their review (a meta-ethnography), with its endpoint of creating explanatory models, justified an approach targeted at conceptual richness.

Alternatively your topic may be more suited to a sampling approach. The literature may fall within individual cognate disciplines from which you wish to sample. In their review on the diffusion of innovations Greenhalgh and colleagues (2005) drew on the thinking of Kuhn (1962) and purposively attempted to capture the development of concepts within different disciplines and they sampled accordingly.

While your *initial* synthesis strategy is open to subsequent refinement and change, you will nevertheless need a reasonably clear picture of your direction of travel. Clearly if you intend to read and review an entire body of literature, albeit centred on a focused question, it is not so critical in which order you handle the papers. Each paper receives an equal opportunity to be compared with all previous papers, perhaps using the **constant comparative method**. If, however, your final intention is to sample judiciously from the literature, perhaps until a point of **informational redundancy** and/or **theoretical saturation** (Combs et al., 2010) then you need to be confident that you have constructed your sampling frame appropriately. As Atkins and colleagues (2008) observe:

Key difficulties with this approach include how to establish the population of studies from which to sample without first identifying all relevant studies. It is also unclear how data saturation is determined in a synthesis, where access to the original data is limited, and little guidance on this is available.

Cognitive research indicates that the human brain often finds it inordinately easier to identify overall patterns or similarities in data ahead of being able to spot inconsistencies or exceptions to the rule (Petticrew and Roberts, 2006). This trait holds several dangers to the objectivity of the review process. You are likely to be subconsciously influenced to impose explanatory patterns over data that is either not present or non-apparent. As Bergman and Coxon (2005) state:

> Of course, skilled authors are able to selectively make authority arguments that bolster a particular line of argument, so this strategic verification of knowledge, although effective and widespread, is the most threatening to the integrity of a study and its results.

Furthermore, we are more likely to accept data that support our underlying opinion and to reject or explain away data that are uncomfortable or do not fit easily. While 'line of argument' is dealt with first for these reasons, it is very important that equal time and attention is paid to the more nuanced findings from inconsistencies or contradictions. Indeed, a review team should consciously construct mechanisms to maximise opportunities to 'challenge' a persuasive or seductive line of argument (Booth et al., 2013b). It is important to make sure that those closest to the data, especially when junior members of the team, are given the opportunity to challenge and resist interpretations within which data are inappropriately 'shoehorned'.

GETTING STARTED IN QUALITATIVE SYNTHESIS

For qualitative data we generally advise that you start by considering the two more accessible methods of synthesis, namely thematic synthesis and framework synthesis. Both methods are based on corresponding methods used for many years for analysis of primary qualitative data, namely thematic analysis and framework analysis.

Thematic synthesis

Thematic synthesis aims to provide a consistent analysis of content across included studies (see Box 9.3). It seeks to identify the range of factors that is significant for understanding a particular phenomenon. It then seeks to organise those factors into the principal (interpretive) or most common (aggregative) themes.

 box 9.3

Thematic synthesis

What is it?

Thematic synthesis is based upon **thematic analysis**, a method often used to analyse data in primary qualitative research. Thematic synthesis uses a comparable type of analysis to bring together and integrate the findings of multiple qualitative studies within systematic reviews. It includes three principal stages, although these overlap to some degree: free line-by-line coding of the findings of primary studies; the organisation of these 'free codes' into related areas to construct 'descriptive' themes; and the development of 'analytical' themes.

What can I use it for?

This method has particularly been used in systematic reviews that address questions about people's perspectives and experiences (Harden et al., 2004, 2006; Thomas et al., 2003, 2007). These perspectives may relate to a particular programme or intervention. Alternatively, they may concern attitudes to a particular condition (e.g. poor housing) or disease (e.g. stroke). Such literature often involves identification of barriers or facilitators. If you are conducting a mixed methods review you can use thematic synthesis to generate hypotheses that you then test against the findings of quantitative studies.

How has it been used?

Morton and colleagues (2010) describe using thematic synthesis to examine the views of patients and carers in treatment decision making for chronic kidney disease. This involved line-by-line coding of the findings of the primary studies and development of descriptive and analytical themes. Their review included 18 studies, 14 focusing on preferences for dialysis, three on transplantation, and one on palliative management. They identified the centrality of four major themes: confronting mortality, lack of choice, gaining knowledge of options and weighing alternatives. They concluded that a preference to maintain the *status quo* may explain why patients often stick with their initial treatment choice.

Framework synthesis

Just as **thematic synthesis** draws its origins from **thematic analysis**, **framework synthesis** is analogous to **framework analysis**, also used in primary qualitative research. It stems from recognition that the sheer volume and richness of qualitative research poses a challenge for rigorous analysis. Framework synthesis (Box 9.4) offers 'a highly structured approach to organising and analysing data by utilising an *a priori* "framework" – informed by background material and team discussions – to extract and synthesise findings' (Barnett-Page and Thomas, 2009). You can then express the resulting synthesis in the form of a chart for each key factor or variable identified. Finally you can use tabular presentation to map the concept under study, to explore consistencies and to identify the disconfirming case.

 box 9.4

Framework synthesis

What is it?

Framework synthesis is based on framework analysis, outlined by Pope and colleagues (2000). It draws upon the work of Ritchie and Spencer (1993) and Miles and Huberman (1994).

(Continued)

(Continued)

Its rationale is that qualitative research produces large amounts of textual data in the form of transcripts, observational fieldnotes, etc. Framework synthesis offers a highly structured approach to organising and analysing data (e.g. indexing using numerical codes, rearranging data into charts, etc.). It is distinct from other methods outlined in this chapter in using an a priori 'framework' to extract and synthesise findings. Although it is largely a deductive approach new topics may be developed, added to and incorporated with those topics already present in the framework as they emerge from the data (Cooper et al., 2010). You can express the synthetic product in the form of a chart for each key dimension identified. You can then use this chart to map the nature and range of the concept under study and find associations between themes and exceptions to these (Brunton et al., 2006).

What can I use it for?

Framework synthesis is most suitable where a general conceptual model or framework already exists and is well-established and, consequently, where concepts are 'secure'. However, it does also hold the potential for new topics to be developed and incorporated as they emerge from the data, allowing use of a contingent 'best fit' model that will be enhanced and developed by the addition of new data (see Box 9.5 below).

How has it been used?

Brunton et al. (2006) applied the framework synthesis approach to a review of children's, young people's and parents' views of walking and cycling. Results of 16 studies of children's, young people's and/or parents' views were synthesised and combined with the results of 15 intervention evaluations to summarise available evidence about the effectiveness and appropriateness of interventions to promote a shift from car travel to more active forms of transport. They identified that children often saw themselves as responsible transport users, that their views might differ from those of their parents, and that themes identified from the evidence differed in importance and content depending on the children's age, sex, socioeconomic status and location.

 box 9.5

Best fit framework synthesis

What is it?

Best fit framework synthesis seeks to capitalise on the inherent advantages of both framework synthesis and thematic synthesis to derive a methodology that is particularly suited to pragmatic situations, such as the production of **health technology assessments**. It does this by starting with a 'good enough' framework, populating it with as much of the data as possible without forcing the data to fit. Following this initial deductive phase, you can handle the remaining data inductively, creating new themes until all the data are processed. While framework synthesis described above, and its primary data predecessor framework analysis, have always accommodated the subsequent inductive addition of data, the best fit framework approach is characterised by the conscious and explicit engineering of a distinct two-stage process. This ensures that there is a clear audit trail for themes derived from the original framework and those subsequently identified by the inductive process of thematic synthesis. In addition to added transparency the method also facilitates project management and version control by keeping the two stages phased and sequential, rather than iterative.

What can I use it for?

Best fit framework synthesis is most suitable where you are unable to identify a model or framework that represents a close match to the data being extracted. For example, in its original application a review team were unable to identify a conceptual model that sufficiently depicted the phenomenon of taking substances such as aspirin to prevent bowel cancer. However, they identified a model that looked at factors influencing women who were taking dietary supplements. Despite differences in age group, and between a single gender issue and a problem affecting both genders, factors influencing their behaviour, such as the effect of friends and family and the media and fears of adverse effects, were common to both health issues. As a general rule of thumb, a match of between 60% and 80% of the data to the chosen framework offers a relative advantage over thematic synthesis. Subsequent variants merge several competing frameworks for a well-theorised area (workplace smoking prevention) to create a more comprehensive meta-framework for data extraction (Carroll et al., 2013). Logic models and policy frameworks (Walt and Gilson, 2014) are also suggested as potential structures for data extraction (Booth and Carroll, 2015) where theoretical frameworks do not exist.

How has it been used?

Examples of the best fit framework synthesis approach are not yet plentiful although increasing rapidly. As Dixon-Woods (2011) comments:

> Framework-based synthesis is an important advance in conducting reviews of qualitative synthesis. The 'best fit' strategy is a variant of this approach that may be very helpful when policy makers, practitioners or other decision makers need answers quickly, and are able to tolerate some ambiguity about whether the answer is the very best that could be given.

PROGRESSING TO MORE ADVANCED FORMS OF SYNTHESIS

If thematic synthesis and framework synthesis are the most accessible methods of qualitative synthesis then meta-ethnography is one of the most prevalent, being particularly suited to interpretive purposes. **Reciprocal translation, line of argument synthesis** and **refutational synthesis** (see below) have received particular prominence as constituent procedures within meta-ethnography (Noblit and Hare, 1988). Melendez-Torres et al. (2015) point out that reciprocal translation is the foundation of most qualitative synthesis methods. More broadly the associated sub-procedures of mapping similarity, ensuring exclusivity and avoiding overlap, and creating secure and well-defined concepts are the building blocks of many interpretive processes, such as creating a taxonomy, producing a framework or meta-framework, developing a coding scheme or generating a thematic synthesis.

Meta-ethnography

Pursuing a line of argument

Thinking around the line of argument with regard to synthesis is most developed within the type of review known as meta-ethnography. Meta-ethnography is an interpretive approach that seeks to preserve the social and theoretical contexts in which findings emerge (Noblit and Hare, 1988: 5–6). Noblit and Hare state that the aim of a *line of argument* synthesis is to discover a 'whole' among a set of parts'. Meta-ethnography involves open coding to identify emergent categories and then *constant comparison* of metaphors across studies. As Pope et al. (2007) observe, this process is essentially based on inference. You use published narratives of research within a narrow predefined field to construct an explanatory theory or model. A major weakness however is that your interpretation is only one possible reading of the studies (Noblit and Hare, 1988). It is therefore feasible for another investigator to produce an entirely different reading (Noblit and Hare, 1988). Nevertheless, meta-ethnography (see Box 9.6) is the most commonly practised form of qualitative synthesis (Britten et al., 2002; Campbell et al., 2003; Dixon-Woods et al., 2007). Campbell and colleagues (2003) argue that meta-ethnography is:

> Perhaps the best developed method for synthesising qualitative data and one which clearly had its origins in the interpretivist paradigm, from which most methods of primary qualitative research evolved.

 **box 9.6**

Meta-ethnography

What is it?

A technique used to translate concepts across individual studies. It involves:

1. Reciprocal translation (establishing where studies share common overarching concepts or themes, even where expressed in different terms).
2. Line of argument synthesis (establishing where studies contribute to a shared line of thought, identified through inference).
3. Refutational synthesis (establishing the extent to which studies contradict or refute each other) (Noblit and Hare, 1988).

What can I use it for?

Typically you can use meta-ethnography to extend existing theory or develop new theory.

How has it been used?

Siau and Long (2005) synthesised five different stage models of e-government using meta-ethnography. They were able to translate the stages within different models into one another (reciprocal translation) and thus to develop a new e-government stage model. The new e-government stage model had five stages: web presence, interaction, transaction, transformation and e-democracy.

Meta-ethnography is comparable to a grounded theory approach to the extent that it uses open coding and identifies categories emerging from the data (Tranfield et al., 2003). It draws heavily on the constant comparative method (Beck, 2001). First you would identify and list key metaphors (themes, perspectives, phrases, ideas and/or concepts) from each individual study (Noblit and Hare, 1988). You would then 'put together' these metaphors by linking them across studies. In such a way, you would seek to provide a holistic account of the phenomenon (Suri, 1999). Many qualitative researchers consider the results of a study to be specific to one particular context at one point in time (Campbell et al., 2003). Noblit and Hare (1988) argue that all synthesis involves interpretation as the reviewer gives meaning to the sets of studies under consideration. Importantly, meta-ethnography enables you to translate the studies into their own social understanding. However, you should remember that you are seeing the synthesised studies through the worldview of a translator, the reviewer (Noblit and Hare, 1988). As such, advocates of the approach argue that translations are unique forms of synthesis that preserve the interpretive qualities of the original data by:

> carefully peeling away the surface layers of studies to find their hearts and souls in a way that does least damage to them. (Sandelowski et al., 1997)

Reciprocal translation

An important feature of the line of argument component of synthesis is what Noblit and Hare (1988) label 'reciprocal translation'. The importance of reciprocal translation is illustrated in Table 9.3.

In Cell D, two papers describe the same phenomenon and use the same terms or language to describe this phenomenon. In this case, one assumes a 'direct translation' between the two papers. This is the most straightforward type of translation. It is common where agreed definitions or classifications are used within a single discipline (e.g. stress and coping in the nursing literature). In contrast, in Cell A, different terms are used by two papers to refer to different phenomena. Each of the two papers adds to the conceptual richness of the line of argument. So, for example, the psychological and educational literature may yield completely different facets for an umbrella term of 'Identity'. Given that a second paper has no similarity with the first means we can be confident that theoretical saturation is not yet reached. We can also see the value of sampling articles from different disciplines. We may, however, find it consequently more difficult to establish a relationship between unconnected concepts from both papers – unless we subsequently find a third paper containing both concepts.

Table 9.3 A conceptual grid for reciprocal translation

	Terms do not match	Terms match
Ideas/concepts do not match	Neither terms nor ideas/concepts match (A)	Terms match but refer to different ideas/concepts (C)
Ideas/concepts do match	Ideas/concepts match but assigned different terms (B)	Both terms and ideas/concepts match (D)

More problematic are translation scenarios where ideas/concepts coincide but terms do not (Cell B). These are most typical where different disciplines explore a phenomenon independently and yet arrive at a similar conclusion (Curran et al., 2007). Here you need to decide which of two terms is to be preferred, or indeed whether to settle for a third term that represents a middle ground or that adequately captures the richness of both previous terminologies.

Finally, you may encounter translation scenarios where terms coincide but ideas/concepts do not. Clearly you would not want to conflate both meanings within a shared terminology when they are intended to convey different meanings. Typically, therefore, you would assign an independent term to each concept. Alternatively, you might favour one term. You would need to be explicit that this term is not to be used for its subordinate meaning, where an alternative term, derived from an alternative source, should be preferred.

You may find such a process difficult to follow at an abstract or theoretical level. We shall therefore illustrate these principles with an easy experiment that you could conduct with some of your colleagues (see Box 9.7).

 box 9.7

A simple illustration of qualitative synthesis

Ask your colleagues to each provide three phrases to describe their perfect holiday. Some may be very clear and specific, e.g. 'good waves for windsurfing'. In this example there is little possibility for confusion with another concept, although further clarification might be needed as to what precisely this requires. What, however, if two or more colleagues use such phrases as 'good weather'? – clearly this will differ between different settings (e.g. temperate versus tropical settings) and different types of holiday (beach versus skiing holiday). Further clarification is required to see if these colleagues have similar or different ideas in mind. Alternatively, colleagues may use different terminology (e.g. 'many places of interest' and 'rich cultural heritage'). In this case, you will need to establish whether these two phrases do actually 'translate' into the same concept or idea. If by 'many places of interest' a colleague means restaurants, bars and discos it is less likely that reciprocal translation between the two phrases is appropriate! Of course the difficulty of this process is compounded in the case of published studies because it is not usually possible to go back to your informants to clarify exactly what was meant.

As illustrated by the preceding examples the whole process of constructing a line of argument synthesis is iterative with each additional study used to test or challenge the robustness and validity of the evolving argument. For this reason, the constant comparative method is often used as the practical means by which such arguments are developed. An alternative would be to split studies to be included between one group, used to develop the argument or theory, and another group, used to test or validate the emerging theory. Dividing studies in this way could either be done randomly, to ensure that both groups of studies are similarly representative, or purposively according to a particular characteristic such as age group, country, ethnic group, organisation type, etc. So, in this latter example, if you were looking at models of outreach for underserved groups you might build up a theory or model based on the literature in general and then examine the extent to which such generalised findings apply to a specific subset of studies relating to refugees or traveller populations. Such an approach is particularly suited to dissertation or thesis requirements where a generalised theory is explored within the context of a specific population or context to meet the requirement to generate 'new knowledge'.

Examining consistencies

You should not simply catalogue all the themes or variables from the individual studies and then amalgamate these into a long master list. Following a pruning or paring down process, by which you identify synonyms and carry out reciprocal translation, you examine possible groupings of the patterns in your data. You are trying to sensitise yourself to major patterns in potential influencing factors such as context, intervention type, etc. In a qualitative review, these factors resemble themes or constructs that emerge from the synthesis process.

Data comparison is a key step. This involves examining data displays for primary source data in order to identify patterns, themes or relationships. If you identify patterns in the data, you can start to think about the relationship between these variables or identified themes. Perhaps a tension exists; one desirable attribute is only achieved at the expense of a competing desirable attribute. In our review of workplace-based e-learning (Carroll et al., 2009) students valued the ability to work at their own pace and yet also valued feedback. An educator experiences a tension in that they may need to schedule their availability for feedback but this is not possible if requests for feedback come at any time from students working at their own pace.

Such tensions are unsuited for display in linear form. You will find it preferable to draw a **conceptual map** including the identified variables (themes) (Brown, 1999) and relationships between them (e.g. synergistic or antagonistic). The conceptual map groups similar variables in close proximity. If there is a pathway effect, i.e. one factor precedes another time-wise, you can also display this effectively via the conceptual map. As a more complete picture emerges of the relationships between variables or themes you can start to engage with existing theories or even start to develop hypotheses with which to populate an emergent theory.

Although creativity is a very important feature of this stage of pattern seeking and interpretation, it is important that, at all times, you try to ensure that you ground any theories or hypothesis in your data. Conclusion drawing and verification is required if you are to move from the 'particulars into the general'. As new data are accommodated, you will need to continually revise any conclusions or conceptual models so that they continue to be inclusive (Miles and Huberman, 1994). You will need to verify any patterns, themes, relationships or conclusions with your primary source data to ensure that these are both accurate and confirmable (Miles and Huberman, 1994). At this stage, you will be particularly vulnerable to a *cognitive bias* such as premature analytic closure (being locked into a particular pattern) (Miles and Huberman, 1994) or the exclusion of pertinent evidence because it is inconvenient or extraneous to your theorising (Sandelowski, 1995).

To use our earlier example about a holiday, you might group individual data into overarching constructs, such as weather, location, attractions, companions, food and drink, etc. You may then wish to trace particular responses back to particular respondent characteristics: for example, are males more likely to mention food and drink? Do younger respondents have a tendency to focus on extreme sports or strenuous activities? You may therefore need to re-examine the data in light of such differences. Furthermore, there may be tensions or conflict between some of the characteristics – if, for example, large numbers of respondents desire 'peace and quiet' and equally large numbers require 'excitement'. Identification of such tensions may lead you to explore in more detail their implications or practical manifestations. In our holiday example you might ask, 'How does a couple with conflicting expectations of a perfect holiday resolve such a conflict?' You may subsequently come up with such models or constructs as 'taking turns' (strict alternation), 'separate lives' (separate holidays), 'anything for a quiet life' (grudging acquiescence), 'together and then apart' (two holidays/year) or 'your turn now but I'll cash in the goodwill chip when I need it' (delayed trade-off).

Clearly examining the data for consistencies requires more intensive engagement with the data than identification of an overarching line of argument. Typically you will move from broad questions such as 'What works?' towards more nuanced interpretations such as 'What works under what circumstances?' (Pawson, 2001).

IDENTIFYING THE DISCONFIRMING CASE

One contrast between systematic approaches to the literature and more traditional narrative reviews is a need to test the robustness of the emerging review product. As Whittemore and Knafl (2005) state:

> Analytical honesty is a priority; the data analysis process is made transparent with rival explanations and spurious relationships thoughtfully explored.

While such an approach may seem daunting, particularly to the novice researcher, it is essential if the review is to establish itself as a reliable and authoritative contribution to the evidence base.

Identification of the negative or disconfirming case is commonly regarded as the most difficult component of the synthesis process (Whittemore and Knapfl, 2005). It is particularly challenging when conflicting results are equally compelling and derive from high quality reports. Booth and colleagues (2013b) identify several strategies to encourage a genuine diversity of perspectives and interpretations. These include specific roles within the team, engineering different researcher viewpoints and triangulation across data sources. Of course, individual studies may differ from the main body of studies across a wide range of aspects, i.e. they are genuine 'outliers'. In such cases, you may wish to reconsider whether it truly makes sense to include these within an overarching analysis or whether they should be analysed separately.

Because you might potentially be led towards a wrong conclusion it is critical that you take steps to document your hunches and other intuitive steps in the process. This allows you to retrace your steps to a point of divergence and reconstruct an alternative line of argument. As well as testing the premises for your thinking with a supervisor or mentor, you may find it useful to check your assumptions with stakeholders or user representatives. However, you should not automatically assume that your line of reasoning is wrong just because your perceptions are not confirmed by other parties. After all, by synthesising the literature you are accessing privileged insights not easily discerned by an individual researcher immersed in one particular context. However, if conflicting evidence or conflicting viewpoints persist, you will probably not be able to reconcile such perspectives within your own individual review. You may then suggest that further research, using a specific design that aims to resolve this conflict, is needed to examine the issue.

METHODS OF QUALITATIVE SYNTHESIS

Notwithstanding differences in the nature of quantitative and qualitative data you have the same four tools of synthesis at your disposal, namely *textual, numerical, tabular* and *graphical*. Within qualitative synthesis textual approaches occupy the principal place. In addition to narrative synthesis, which is genuinely adaptable to both paradigms, textual approaches include basic techniques from primary qualitative analysis such as **thematic synthesis** and **framework synthesis** as well as specific interpretive methods such as meta-ethnography, **meta-narrative** and **critical interpretive synthesis**. Tables 9.4 and 9.5 illustrate some approaches to synthesis found in different types of review.

Table 9.4 Approaches to synthesis in different types of reviews

Type of review	Approaches used to synthesis	Application	Review example
Qualitative systematic review	Meta-ethnography. Conceptual model. Graphical display. Narrative description.	Extraction of key concepts, translation of these concepts, construction of conceptual model of factors influencing effective dissemination. Conceptual model portrayed graphically. Graphical display of how concepts link together in Boolean relationship. Narrative description of each theme.	Constructing a model of effective information dissemination in a crisis (Duggan and Banwell, 2004).
Meta-narrative	Preliminary mapping of meta-narratives. Iterative refinement of meta-narratives. Characterisation by colour coding of philosophical positions for each. Summary tables for each position.	Sought not simply to summate the findings of different meta-narratives but to present tensions and conflicts between them. Identified key themes, each with inherent tensions – between studies with a positivist world view and those with an interpretivist, critical or recursive world view, though with some overlap.	Tensions and paradoxes in electronic patient record research (Greenhalgh et al., 2009).
Realist synthesis	Categorisation by setting and clinical application. Listing of tools. Candidate mechanisms.	For an illustrative case study identified Context-Mechanism-Outcome (CMO) configurations for lean thinking.	Lean thinking in healthcare: a realist review of the literature (Mazzocato et al., 2010).
Mixed methods review	Mapping, thematic analysis, identify five key principles as meta-themes.	Provided brief description, contextual example and key references for each knowledge translation method.	Improving the utilisation of research knowledge in agri-food public health: a mixed-method review of knowledge translation and transfer (Rajic et al., 2013).

Tabular presentation

Tabulation is often used to describe characteristics of the population, intervention, comparator and outcome (measures). You can also use tabulation for describing study characteristics (e.g. study design). You may use tabulation to report how individual studies perform with regard to study quality, thereby allowing easy identification of higher-quality studies. Tabulation is particularly valuable within the context of cross-case comparison and for 'eyeballing' patterns across rows or down columns. However, tabulation may be criticised, particularly in a qualitative or implementation context because it is necessarily reductive. Selecting data for inclusion in tables can result in a loss of important context or detail that aids interpretation of the studies. More details of tabulation, together with examples, are given in Chapter 8.

Table 9.5 Other methods used for synthesis of textual data

Method	Description	Application
Grounded theory	Grounded theory is used for analysing primary research literature. Yin (1991) suggests that grounded theory could be used for the synthesis of 'multivocal literature'. It provides a methodology for synthesising literature, identifying categories and generating theories. It utilises such methods as theoretical sampling and the constant comparative method. It therefore has some similarities with meta-ethnography which is a method specifically developed for use in secondary analysis.	Moustaghfir (2008) used grounded theory in a review to extend existing theory regarding the 'knowledge-value chain' by integrating the additional concept of dynamic capabilities. Grounded theory was used to synthesise the information and generate assumptions. The systematic review method was specifically selected as a recognised tool for theory building.
Meta-study	Paterson et al. (2001) coined a multi-faceted approach to synthesis, meta-study. This involves three components undertaken prior to synthesis. These are meta-data-analysis (analysis of findings), meta-method (analysis of methods), and meta-theory (analysis of theory). Collectively, these three elements make up 'meta-study'. These elements can be usefully conducted individually for specific purposes, or conducted concurrently to maximise cross-study insights within a 'new interpretation'. Meta-study allows the impact of methods and theory on findings to be formally explored.	Munro and colleagues (2007) used meta-theory to explore 11 behaviour change theories applicable to long-term medication adherence. They found little research on the effectiveness of these theories but several had the potential to improve adherence to long-term treatments.

Numerical presentation

Although the emphasis of qualitative systematic reviews is on textual and narrative methods of presentation, you should bear in mind that a qualitative synthesis is both descriptive and analytical. For descriptive purposes numerical counting may be important – for example, how many studies come from each country, how many studies include perspectives from patients, carers and health professionals respectively, etc.? In addition to presenting the 'epidemiology' of included studies numerical data may be used to characterise the included population, for example to determine the average age of the population or the percentage who smoke. Such details may be used in the subsequent analysis to help to explain why certain qualitative themes or factors are present in some studies but not in others within the same review.

Graphical approaches

Graphical approaches make an important contribution to synthesis by assisting in the identification of patterns. They help you visualise the relationship of parts to the overall whole. You can use graphical approaches for cross-linking across disparate features of a review, e.g. for depicting a link between study characteristics and findings. For example, you could use colour coding to indicate whether qualitative findings from a review are associated with negative (red), neutral (yellow) or positive (green) results. As Whittemore and Knafl (2005) observe:

> Creativity and critical analysis of data and data displays are key elements in data comparison and the identification of important and accurate patterns and themes.

You thus need to develop tools such as graphs, charts, forms and figures to help you visualise, sort and compare the data across all of the primary sources (Whittemore and Knafl, 2005). Graphical methods can include techniques for exploring data as well as presenting the data. You can use **mind maps**, **concept maps** and **idea webs** to map out the main themes or variables in a creative and imaginative way (Exercise 9.1). Although graphical methods of presentation are most developed for meta-analysis of quantitative studies, they are assuming increasing importance in the presentation of qualitative data. For example, some authors use linked boxes to indicate relationships between included studies with different shading depicting those that contribute to a particular theme. While such graphics conflate methodology and findings (and therefore receive further prominence in Chapter 10) you should note that graphical presentation fulfils both a **formative** function (as a review team explores patterns within their results) and a **summative** function (in presenting the findings from a **qualitative evidence synthesis**).

 exercise 9.1

Helpful graphical display

Briefly reflect on a journal article that you have recently read, not necessarily a systematic review. How did tabular or graphical display make it easier to read? Were any tabular or graphical aspects difficult to understand and interpret? If so, why?

INTEGRATING QUANTITATIVE AND QUALITATIVE DATA

To a large degree, the integration of quantitative and qualitative data is the outstanding methodological challenge for systematic approaches to reviewing the literature. Its prominence stems from several factors. Having tackled and overcome many methodological problems from the separate spheres of quantitative and qualitative evidence synthesis, it is now opportune to look at how these two synthetic products might be brought together. Second, there is an increasing awareness of the value of mixed method approaches for policy makers, including both primary research and secondary synthesis (Pope et al., 2006). Finally, and most importantly, there is recognition that answering questions on effectiveness alone is not enough. Issues of appropriateness, acceptability and equity (Tugwell et al., 2010) are equally important in the success of an intervention.

Integration of quantitative and qualitative data within a single synthetic product is one way of including diverse forms of evidence and thereby increasing the relevance of reviews for decision makers. Where **randomised controlled trials** show a high degree of heterogeneity, the inclusion of qualitative research may help to explain that heterogeneity. By eliciting a more complete picture of the research landscape for a particular topic, you can not only identify areas neglected by both paradigms (i.e. research gaps), you can also locate where promising interventions have not been evaluated for effectiveness, or conversely where effective interventions have not been assessed for acceptability or **social validity**. Furthermore, the multiple questions addressed by a **mixed method review** correspond more closely to the concerns of decision makers (Pope et al., 2006). Such reviews are particularly appropriate for the exploratory phase of a dissertation or thesis where an investigator needs to identify what is known, together with any research gaps.

Of course by amalgamating quantitative and qualitative approaches to **evidence synthesis**, itself requiring familiarity with both quantitative and qualitative primary research, you are broadening the scale of the review endeavour and increasing its technical complexity. Typically such approaches require a widening of the skills base of the team (Exercise 9.2) and may also require the formal involvement of stakeholders. Decisions on when and how to bring the two synthetic products together, whether having conducted these in parallel or serially, add further complexity to the already challenging job of project management. On the other hand, it may well be that one of the components has already been undertaken (e.g. a **Cochrane** or **Campbell Review**) and you can focus attention on the complementary role of the other review and its ultimate integration.

 exercise 9.2

Choosing your method of synthesis

Examine the different methods of synthesis outlined in this chapter. Sort them into those of current potential for your review, those that are unlikely to prove useful at present, and those for which you need to obtain further detail. Produce a draft learning plan for further reading/research on data synthesis.

- Bayesian meta-analysis.
- Critical interpretive synthesis.
- Framework synthesis.
- Grounded theory.

- Meta-analysis.
- Meta-ethnography.
- Meta-study.
- Narrative synthesis.
- Realist synthesis.
- Thematic synthesis.

Current potential	Further detail required	Not relevant at present

To find out more on data synthesis I am going to read/research:

By __/__/201_

 toolbox

Study synthesis

With a wealth of specific methods to choose from, this toolbox section picks out one exemplar of an approach to cross-study qualitative synthesis, namely qualitative data analysis. However, we would encourage you to look at the many published qualitative examples of synthesis techniques referenced in this chapter in order to identify less common tools that may assist you in your own literature review.

Qualitative data analysis

Data extraction against themes helps in the identification of patterns. Within the limited number (three studies) of reports included in the thematic matrix (see Table 9.6) for a hypothetical review on the attitudes of village communities to peripherally located supermarkets we observe that Study 1 by Greenwood and Liffey focuses exclusively on economic considerations. Studies 2 and 3 both look at convenience with regard to road traffic. Study 3 by Swathe is overwhelmingly positive whereas Studies 1 and 2 cover positives and negatives. Studies 2 and 3 carry implications for (different) health-related services.

Such a thematic matrix is a useful vehicle for pattern recognition. The themes could be derived from the data (as with grounded theory, thematic synthesis or meta-ethnography approaches) or from a published framework or model (as for framework synthesis).

ANALYSING WHAT YOU FIND

Having performed your initial synthesis, whether using narrative, qualitative or quantitative techniques or a combination of the three, you can explore what has been found and what

Table 9.6 Hypothetical thematic matrix for review on attitudes to peripheral supermarkets

	Article content		
Theme	**Greenwood and Liffey, 2010 (Study 1)**	**Verdant, 2010 (Study 2)**	**Swathe, 2011 (Study 3)**
Convenience		Good communications via main roads Ample parking	On outskirts of village therefore reduces congestion
Household economy	Reduces price of staple products (e.g. bread, milk)	Reduced petrol prices	Cheap petrol
Focus for community		Location for charitable collections Health education stands	Venue for blood transfusion service
Threat to local commerce	Challenges bespoke traders (e.g. bakers, dairies)	24-hour competition to petrol stations	
Threat to community identity	Uniform character of hypermarkets – cheap builds	Reduced use of village centre Increased use by non-locals	

is missing. The synthesis stage aims to tell you what the literature *says*. The analysis stage focuses on telling you what the literature *means*. If synthesis is analogous to a detective assembling all the clues, then analysis corresponds to making sense of them.

Essentially analysis provides you with an opportunity to assess the strength of evidence for drawing conclusions about the results of synthesis and their generalisability in your intended context. Several techniques will help you test or confirm review findings (see Box 9.8). These 'tactics' derive from the context of conducting primary research but apply equally within synthesis.

 **box 9.8**

Tactics for testing or confirming review findings

Elements

Representativeness.

Researcher effects.

Triangulating.

Weighting the evidence.

Meaning of outliers.

Using extreme cases.

Following up surprises.

> Looking for negative evidence.
>
> Make if-then tests.
>
> Rule out spurious relations.
>
> Replicate a finding.
>
> Check out rival explanations.
>
> Feedback from informants.

(Source: based on Miles and Huberman, 1994)

Examining *representativeness* requires that you explore whether the populations included in the various study samples (the study populations) match the characteristics of the population being investigated (the target population). As a reviewer you need to examine your component studies and ask yourself, 'Are any particular groups under-represented? Are any groups over-represented? Am I confident that the characteristics of a particular group are not misrepresented or misinterpreted?'

You should cultivate a healthy scepticism when exploring the likely presence of *researcher effects*. Do the researchers favour a particular programme or intervention – for example, did they influence the selection of outcomes? Or, perhaps, have they triggered inadvertent researcher effects – for example, if a qualitative researcher is a doctor has this changed the way that participants communicate or what they choose to share with her?

Triangulating the data may involve the use of different methods to research the same issue with the same unit of analysis. This may involve checking findings within a review across different study designs, different schools of thought, or different methods of data collection. It may involve comparing findings from secondary research with those from your subsequent primary research and bringing the two together in a combined discussion section. Triangulation has also been used to describe the process of comparing interpretations across multiple reviewers (Donald et al., 2005).

Weighting the evidence asks you to ensure that your conclusions are not simply based on 'vote-counting'. Not all studies are equal – you may need to look initially at the effect of ordering studies from the highest quality to the lowest quality. You can ask yourself, 'Are positive or negative aspects clustered around particular points in this ranking?'

A valuable precaution against over-generalisation is to examine the *meaning of outliers* (i.e. any studies that show particularly extreme results – either very positive or very negative) or, in a qualitative context, those that are a unique source of a particular theme. You may wish to discuss these with colleagues and topical experts, asking them, 'Can you identify one or more possible explanations for the difference in the findings?' Such explanations may be explored in the analysis, provided such data are available, or suggested as hypotheses to be explored in future research.

Associated with the exploration of outliers is the tactic of *using extreme cases*. However, whereas the stimulus for looking at outliers relates to the presence of extreme results, extreme cases are stimulated by atypical contexts. Examining the characteristics of the population and the intervention may provide an insight into better than expected or worse than expected (but not necessarily outlying) results.

Following up surprises is an intellectually rewarding tactic for exploring your data. Having a particular explanation for a pattern of results you will find it interesting to identify where one or more studies does not fit its anticipated place within the pattern. Again, you will need to do more than simply looking for outliers. The 'surprise' may lie embedded within the 'pack' of studies but not where predicted. You should record any surprises as you encounter them because, over an extended period of time, they may lose their capacity to surprise you. Your reader typically starts at a point analogous to where you were before undertaking the synthesis and analysis. You should treat them as a 'fellow traveller'. Once you have validated these surprises you can highlight them in publications, oral presentations and, where appropriate, press releases. For example, in a review of appointment reminder systems (McLean et al., 2014), we were surprised to find that, although reminders are framed in the context of the forgetful patient, poor attendance often reflects the inflexibility of a health system and its inability to handle cancellation and rescheduling. Such an observation led us to reconceptualise appointment reminder systems around the time interval required to offer freed up slots to other patients instead of being based on a mythical optimal time for the patient memory.

Looking for negative evidence is frequently overlooked, largely because synthesis impels towards commonality rather than dissonance. Such a tactic involves actively seeking disconfirmation of what you believe to be true. Within the context of qualitative evidence synthesis you may need to sample purposively from fields or disciplines outside the original sampling frame. A recent methodological paper describes how reviewers might actively manufacture opportunities to identify discrepant or refutational findings and outlines possible methods by which a team might actively seek disconfirming cases within the overall review process (Booth et al., 2013b).

Table 9.7 Unhelpful and helpful framing of if-then statements

A. Unhelpful framing of if-then statements:	
IF	**THEN**
Funding is provided for bursaries	Clinical staff are more likely to be given protected time for planning and conducting research
Clinical staff are more likely to be given protected time for planning and conducting research	Research is more likely to be completed within its planned timescale
Clinical staff are more likely to be given protected time for planning and conducting research	Research is more likely to address current organisational priorities

B. Helpful framing of if-then statements:	
IF	**THEN**
Funding agencies fund bursaries	Hospital managers give doctors protected time for planning and conducting research
Hospital managers give doctors protected time for planning and conducting research	Doctors complete research within its planned timescale
Hospital managers give doctors protected time for planning and conducting research	Doctors conduct research that addresses current organisational priorities

Where the intention of a literature review is to contribute to **programme theory** you will find it helpful to *make if-then tests*. This would require looking at two seemingly similar programmes to see if specific elements (contextual factors or mechanisms) are either present or absent. This is the approach codified in the methodology of **realist synthesis**. One possible technique is to use a spreadsheet with one column for the *if* statement and the second column for the *then*. We also find it helpful to remove any qualifying words such as 'probably' or 'may be' to turn the statements into testable hypotheses and to phrase the statements with an identifiable actor rather than in the passive voice (see Table 9.7). Although the hypotheses lose apparent nuances while they are being tested against the quantitative and qualitative data these are actually restored when the data reveal contexts in which the hypothesis is more or less likely to be true.

Several additional observations can be made about the set of if-then statements in Table 9.7 above. First, you can see the link between the first then statement and the subsequent if. In effect you are starting to construct a causal chain of if-thens. Second, the repeated if in the second and third statements reminds us that a single action may have multiple consequences. These may be positive consequences, as in the example, but equally might represent both positive and negative or intended and unintended consequences. Finally the third then statement does not make clear how 'doctors conduct research that addresses current organisational priorities'. You may find that you need to insert an extra layer of if-thens to make it a more complete causal chain, e.g. 'Doctors mobilise resources for research projects speedily'.

A **truth table**, that is a matrix codifying the presence or absence of particular factors in individual studies, may be a useful practical tool for identifying such relationships (Dixon-Woods et al., 2004; Pope et al., 2007; Cruzes and Dybå, 2010). This is similar to the thematic matrix demonstrated earlier but with binary indicators of presence or absence (e.g. 1 versus 0 or check box versus empty cell) rather than qualitative themes (see Table 9.8).

As a follow-up to the if-then testing above you will need to *rule out spurious relations*. To do this you will need to consider whether a third factor or variable may possibly explain away

Table 9.8 Hypothetical truth table for review on attitudes to peripheral supermarkets

| Study | Explanatory variables | | | | | Dependent variable |
	A	B	C	D	E	Orchestrated community opposition
Greenwood and Liffey, 2010 (Study 1)	0	1	0	1	1	1
Verdant, 2010 (Study 2)	1	1	1	1	1	0
Swathe, 2011 (Study 3)	1	1	1	0	0	0
Total	2	3	2	2	2	1

A = Convenience; B = Household economy; C = Focus for community; D = Threat to local commerce; E = Threat to community identity.

Note: Findings from this hypothetical truth table appear to show that orchestrated community opposition is less likely to be present if a supermarket emphasises its role as a focus for community activities.

the apparent relationship identified from the data. Ideally, your frame for investigation would include studies reporting the presence of the two conditions, the absence of each and the presence and absence of the third variable. In the example of a truth table (see Table 9.8) we may assume that promoting the benefits of the supermarket for the household economy helps to avoid orchestrated community opposition. However, the contribution from the fictional Greenwood and Liffey study shows that opposition occurs even where this factor is present.

In exploring the data you may need to refer to external data sources, for example in order to *replicate a finding*. To replicate a finding you may need to extend your sampling frame to a nearby contiguous area of literature where you may find the underlying explanatory mechanism. Alternatively, if the original literature review is not based upon a comprehensive sample, you could split your population of studies and use half of these to generate the theory or hypothesis and the other half to test and validate it.

A good analyst keeps their mind open to alternative explanations and *checks out rival explanations*. It can be informative to record the theory underpinning each study as you extract the data from each. You can then revisit these theories when you complete your synthesis. Editorial or commentary material, published in the same issue of a journal as an original study, or even ensuing correspondence in subsequent issues, may explain findings or help to reconcile them with prevalent theory.

The use of informants for validation remains controversial, principally because the synthetic product need not necessarily resemble a single contributory study. However, this is not an argument against *feedback from informants* (**respondent validation**) per se but simply against attaching undue weight to such feedback compared with the synthesis. A review team can ensure a clear definition of stakeholder roles, and a clear explanation of how they plan to use feedback, to protect against the likelihood that stakeholder consultation will overturn the findings from a well-grounded synthetic product.

Consider the techniques we have itemised as a toolbox from which you select according to the robustness of your synthesis and the underlying purpose of your analysis.

Weight of evidence synthesis

As mentioned in Chapter 7 if you categorise studies into low, moderate and high likelihood of bias you can distinguish between findings which provide a strong basis for confidence (strong weighting), and those which are more speculative, supported only by weak evidence. When writing the conclusions and recommendations (see Chapter 10), you should give more weight to findings from studies with a greater strength of evidence than to findings based upon less reliable studies. Many different methods exist for weighting evidence; some examine the technical performance of studies (i.e. they only factor in rigour) while others conflate rigour and relevance. For example the Social Care Institute for Excellence (SCIE) states:

> the synthesis should give greater weight to studies that directly concern the review question (topic relevance) and those people affected by the service in question, and to those studies that give greater confidence in their findings by reporting depth and detail and relevance to wider populations and contexts. Reviewers will rely on some studies more than others because they are assessed as having higher quality, and they will find themselves constantly returning to the quality judgements during qualitative data synthesis. (Coren and Fisher, 2006)

Studies can be weighted according to the following (Coren and Fisher, 2006):

1. Centrality of the study to the review topic.
2. Strength of design (in relation to answering the review question).
3. Generalisability (with respect to context of intervention, sample sizes and population, etc.).
4. Clarity of reporting of methods.

Reviewer effects

It would be naïve to expect that literature reviews, even those that embody systematic approaches, are neutral vehicles for research findings. Naturally, a review reflects the 'perspectives, preferences and propensities' (Sandelowski, 2008) of its reviewers. These may be detected at every stage of the process from the conception of the review and the selection of the principal research question through to study identification, selection and assessment. It can be further identified in the processes of synthesis and analysis. The last of these stages, analysis, is an appropriate juncture for considering the likely effect of researcher effects both in the component studies and in the review itself.

Systematic reviews make much of the virtue of their objectivity, embodied in their methods and in their explicit reporting. However, the reality is that the most they can aspire to is what an expert commentator refers to as 'disciplined subjectivity' (Sandelowski, 2008). As an honest reviewer you will seek to conduct an analysis, explicit or otherwise, of the likely challenges posed to objectivity by your own preoccupations and prejudices. You will recognise that the outcomes of your systematic review are 'situated, partial and perspectival' (Lather, 1999) and you will seek to communicate these limitations to your reader.

Critical reflection

Critics of systematic approaches to reviewing the literature (Hammersley, 2002) imply that slavish adherence to a review method reduces it to 'essentially an unscholarly or unanalytical pursuit and that it can be conducted by anyone' (Wallace et al., 2003). If such a criticism is to be countered, then a review team, or a single reviewer operating in conjunction with a supervisor or mentor, should actively manufacture opportunities to 'ensure critical reflection on the applicability of the review questions, meaningful data extraction, interpretation and synthesis of the research studies' (Wallace et al., 2003). Indeed Dixon-Woods et al. (2006b) embody critical reflection and interpretation within a review process labelled 'critical interpretive synthesis'. This method builds upon Sandelowski's previously mentioned concerns regarding the subjectivity of the review process. It moves from the formal **critical appraisal** of individual studies specified by many review methods to a 'critique' of literatures, namely the studies as a body. Such an approach facilitates the development of mid-range theory. More importantly it challenges the assumptions that may underpin individual studies. The review team likens their analysis to that undertaken in primary qualitative research moving from individual papers to themes and then on to the critique. They explicitly state that:

> A key feature of this process that distinguishes it from some other current approaches to interpretive synthesis (and indeed of much primary qualitative research) was its aim of being

> *critical*: its questioning of the ways in which the literature had constructed [the phenomenon], the nature of the assumptions on which it drew, and what has influenced its choice of proposed solutions. (Dixon-Woods et al., 2006b)

Critical interpretive synthesis accounts for the voice of 'the author', explicitly and reflexively, while rejecting the pretence that another review team using similar methods would arrive at the same interpretation. Critical interpretive synthesis also blurs any distinction between synthesis and analysis, explicitly endorsing an iterative approach:

> Our critique of the literature was thus dynamic, recursive and reflexive, and, rather than being a stage in which individual papers are excluded or weighted, it formed a key part of the synthesis, informing the sampling and selection of material and playing a key role in theory generation. (Dixon-Woods et al., 2006b)

Such a creative approach may provide a useful mechanism for critiquing the significant bodies of literature from different disciplines and schools of thought associated with the early stages of a dissertation or thesis. At the same time it provides challenges in the lack of a formal documented method, the difficulties of establishing a formal audit trail and issues relating to how it should be reported. As Dixon-Woods and colleagues acknowledge:

> However, it is important to note that, as with any qualitative analysis, full transparency is not possible because of the creative, interpretive processes involved. Nonetheless, the large multidisciplinary team involved in the review, and the continual dialogue made necessary by this, helped to introduce 'checks and balances' that guarded against framing of the analysis according to a single perspective. (Dixon-Woods et al., 2006b)

Subgroup analysis

When examining a qualitative body of research you move iteratively between examining the whole and scrutinising the component parts. Data extraction and coding reveal different groups or 'families' of studies, perhaps sharing population, intervention, methodological or contextual characteristics. You should explore whether such a subgroup, defined by its study characteristics, shares its characteristics with the total review population or whether it might prove the exception to the rule. For example, in a review of e-learning among health professionals, where studies of doctors are in the majority, do findings from the overall interpretation transfer to the subgroup of nurses represented by a smaller proportion of studies or even to another group represented by a single study?

Qualitative sensitivity analysis

As defined in Chapter 8, sensitivity analysis is the formal 'exploration of what ifs' (Greenhalgh, 2014). Sensitivity analysis is increasingly recognised as important in systematic approaches to qualitative research. Typical indications for performing sensitivity analysis in a qualitative evidence synthesis are given in Box 9.9. What is less clear, however, is the action to be taken once such sensitivities have been identified.

box 9.9

Reasons for considering a sensitivity analysis (qualitative)

Consider conducting a sensitivity analysis where:

- you have had persistent doubts about whether a study is eligible for inclusion within a review; would exclusion of this study result in the disappearance of one or more themes from your synthesis?
- you have identified significant differences in the quality of included studies; are particular themes only present in poorer quality studies or are they distributed across both good and poor quality studies?
- you are uncertain whether included studies are heterogeneous or homogeneous; qualitatively do studies have more in common than they have dissimilarity and how important are such similarities or differences likely to be in explaining the overall phenomenon?
- you observe that one study has results very different from the rest of the studies (i.e. it is an obvious outlier); qualitatively does that study have important differences from all other studies or does it simply reflect a similar number and type of differences as are present in other studies?
- you have assumed equivalence between apparently related themes; how open is your assumption to an alternative interpretation or nuance?
- you consider the overall framework or itemisation of themes to be particularly influenced by one individual study (e.g. the most content rich, the earliest, etc.); can you still find evidence of all the themes were you to exclude this study? (Bear in mind too that later authors may have a vested interest in emphasising additional or alternative themes – do they acknowledge the conceptual legacy of the earlier paper in their citations or were such themes simply not identified?)

Several commentators, including Pawson (2006b) and Dixon-Woods et al. (2006a), point out that excluding an entire study on the basis of an appraisal of study quality may not be appropriate. Pawson, for example, argues that:

> the 'study' is not the appropriate unit of analysis for quality appraisal in research synthesis. There are often nuggets of wisdom in methodologically weak studies and systematic review disregards them at its peril. (Pawson, 2006b)

Identifying gaps

Qualitative reviewers will want to be assured that their literature sample is adequate; whether they have identified *all* studies (comprehensive sampling), whether they have enough studies (purposive sampling), or whether they have identified the right studies (theoretical sampling). Preparation of a review is an ongoing and continuous process. New studies appear continuously; chasing cited references may repeatedly extend the review task, and reading in adjacent literature may imperceptibly cause **scope creep** (see Chapter 5). You must therefore agree the mechanisms by which you are going to close the door on further studies. You must not terminate study identification too early, especially as an increasing number of journals will not accept a manuscript if the literature search has not been updated within the last 12 months.

For an interpretative review you should evaluate, with a colleague, supervisor or mentor, whether theoretical saturation is likely to have been achieved. Typically a **formative** presentation of evidence takes stock of what you have found to date:

> This evidence might include literature review maps/diagrams, matrices, or outlines that indicate main themes, subthemes, categories, subcategories, patterns and sequencing of ideas. (Combs et al., 2010)

 **toolbox**

Data analysis

The key to the robustness of the results from a review is some consideration of the presence or absence of bias. The CERQual approach is applied to individual review findings from a qualitative evidence synthesis (Lewin et al., 2015). Critical to the application of CERQual is an understanding of what a review finding is:

> *an analytic output from a qualitative evidence synthesis that, based on data from primary studies, describes a phenomenon or an aspect of a phenomenon.*

CERQual aims to transparently assess and describe how much confidence decision makers and other users can place in individual review findings from syntheses of qualitative evidence. Confidence in the evidence requires that you assess the extent to which the review finding is a reasonable representation of the phenomenon of interest against four separate components (see Table 9.9). This assessment communicates the extent to which the research finding is likely to be substantially different (that is, enough to change a policy or practice decision) from the phenomenon of interest.

Table 9.9 Components of the CERQual approach

Component	Definition
Methodological limitations	The extent to which there are problems in the design or conduct of the primary studies that contributed evidence to a review finding
Relevance	The extent to which the body of evidence from the primary studies supporting a review finding is applicable to the context (perspective or population, phenomenon of interest, setting) specified in the review question
Coherence	The extent to which the pattern that constitutes a review finding is based on data that are similar across multiple individual studies and/or incorporates convincing explanations for any variations across individual studies
Adequacy of data	An overall determination of the degree of richness and/or scope of the data as well as the quantity of data supporting a review finding

Each CERQual component (see Table 9.9) is assessed individually, often requiring iteration between components such as coherence and adequacy (Lewin et al., 2015), before a final overall assessment of confidence in the review finding is produced (see Table 9.10).

Table 9.10 The CERQual approach – definitions of levels of confidence in a review finding

Level	Definition
High confidence	It is highly likely that the review finding is a reasonable representation of the phenomenon of interest
Moderate confidence	It is likely that the review finding is a reasonable representation of the phenomenon of interest
Low confidence	It is possible that the review finding is a reasonable representation of the phenomenon of interest
Very low confidence	It is not clear whether the review finding is a reasonable representation of the phenomenon of interest

Finally a summary of qualitative findings table is produced, depicting the finding, the assessment for the finding, a brief explanation and identification of the contributing studies. See Table 9.11 for a (fictional) example.

Table 9.11 The CERQual approach – example of a summary of a (fictional) qualitative findings table

Objective: To identify, appraise and synthesise qualitative research evidence on the barriers and facilitators to use of group approaches for postpartum support (fictional example)

Perspective: Experiences and attitudes of women about group-based approaches in any country

Included programmes: Programmes delivered to support women in the postnatal period, either including group approaches for mutual support or for delivery of a group-based intervention

Review finding	CERQual assessment of confidence in the evidence	Explanation of CERQual assessment	Contributing studies
While mothers appreciated opportunities to meet with other women practical constraints, such as transport difficulties, child care and lack of co-operation of their partners, impacted negatively on their attendance	Moderate	Finding based on adequate data, from studies that generally had minor methodological limitations, displayed reasonable coherence and represented a wide geographical spread	Busse et al. (2001); Wagen et al. (2001); Descartes et al. (2002); Inomota (2011); Musoke et al. (2014); Nyakango et al. (2015)

(Continued)

(Continued)

Review finding	CERQual assessment of confidence in the evidence	Explanation of CERQual assessment	Contributing studies
Some mothers were demoralised when comparing their progress against other members of the group	Low	Finding based on studies with minor methodological limitations. These studies displayed reasonable coherence, but the finding was based on two studies only, from Hong Kong and Kenya respectively	Kasi et al. (2011); Nyakango et al. (2015)
Women, particularly first-time mothers, appreciated the sharing of practical tips (e.g. nappy changing, breast feeding) and coping strategies (e.g. infant crying) by others in the group	High	Finding based on adequate data from studies with minor methodological limitations; and with good coherence, conducted across a wide range of populations and contexts	Duipers et al. (1994); Knappe et al. (2001); Saurbaum et al. (2004); Rasch (2005); Terry et al. (2006); Tao Ling et al. (2013)

How review findings are defined and presented depends on many factors, including the review question, the synthesis methods used, the intended purpose or audience of the synthesis, and the richness of the data available (Gough et al., 2012a). The large number of approaches to qualitative synthesis range from those that aim to identify and describe major themes, to those that seek more generalisable, interpretive explanations that can be used for theory-building. Furthermore, many syntheses use both approaches or include findings that are neither descriptive or interpretive.

MATCHING THE ANALYSIS TO THE REVIEW PURPOSE

Having considered the variety of techniques that comprise the analysis section of the reviewer's toolkit, we shall revisit the sample reviews used throughout this book to see how they utilise analytical techniques to match their purpose (see Table 9.12).

Revisiting the review question(s)

You should return to your review protocol and question throughout the review project, for example when checking items against the scope or for planning your synthesis strategy. It is particularly important to do this at the analysis stage. By now you have been so intensively and extensively engaged with the literature that your review could shift from being question-driven to literature-driven. You need to check that the questions you are answering are those identified

Table 9.12 Examining methods of analysis used in reviews

Type of review	Methods of analysis used	Application of methods	Review example
Scoping review	Identifying gaps. Checking with authors of primary studies (i.e. projects in progress).	Identifies absence of systematic reviews on use of incentives in young people. Identifies existence of significant work in progress to inform future reviews. Following discussion with funders identified need for systematic review on effectiveness and implementation aspects.	A scoping review of the evidence for incentive schemes to encourage positive health and other social behaviours in young people (Kavanagh et al., 2005).
Mapping review	Identifying gaps. Subgroup analysis.	Failed to find research that explicitly considers how to make initial training responsive to individual needs of trainee teachers. Reports most common aspects of training. Concludes further research is needed in this area.	A systematic map into approaches to making initial teacher training flexible and responsive to the needs of trainee teachers (Graham-Matheson et al., 2006).
Systematic review	Use of validity assessment. Sensitivity analysis. Identifying gaps.	Identified considerable methodological problems that limit internal validity and generalisability of results. Emphasises implications for future research. Suggests possible avenue of future research.	A systematic review of work-place interventions for alcohol-related problems (Webb et al., 2009).
Qualitative systematic review	Identifying gaps.	Proposes model of dissemination. Identifies role for opinion leaders and need for training and education.	Constructing a model of effective information dissemination in a crisis (Duggan and Banwell, 2004).
Meta-narrative review	Identifying and characterising different research traditions. Construct a narrative for each tradition. Highlight similarities across traditions.	Used 'conflicting' findings to address higher-order questions about how researchers had differently conceptualised and studied the electronic patient record (EPR) and its implementation.	Tensions and paradoxes in electronic patient record research (Greenhalgh et al., 2009).
Realist synthesis	Organised data around context, outcomes of lean use and components of lean interventions in healthcare. Coded and categorised data within each topic using terms from articles or new descriptive terms.	Found common contextual aspects which interact with different components of the lean interventions and trigger four different change mechanisms.	Lean thinking in healthcare: a realist review of the literature (Mazzocato et al., 2010).
Mixed methods review	Thematic analysis conducted on a prioritised and representative subset of articles to identify key principles and characteristics.	Identified recommended and promising methods and important gaps and challenges.	Improving the utilization of research knowledge in agri-food public health: a mixed-method review of knowledge translation and transfer (Rajic et al., 2013)

in the original review protocol. You will also need to establish that you have identified literature that maps to each question and whether you need to conduct additional purposive searches to populate any gaps. For a mapping review, you can identify where any gaps exist, provided you are reasonably confident that you have looked in the right places. For a policy review, you may have to settle for lower quality study designs, drilling down to lower forms of evidence such as case series, case study or even expert opinion. Such decisions will impact on your description of methods, your discussion of uncertainties surrounding the evidence base, and your recommendations for action and for future research. If you used a **logic model** in depicting your review questions you could usefully map the literature against each node to gain a picture of which questions are well covered and which are data poor. Finally, revisiting your review question not only allows you to check the alignment of your review but also may suggest lines of inquiry that your analysis might take. For example, a reference in your objectives to 'evaluating the quantity and quality of the retrieved literature' may prompt you to use tables and mapping to reflect the quantity of the literature and sensitivity analysis to investigate its quality.

DISCUSSING THE LIMITATIONS OF THE EVIDENCE

Recognising the limitations of the evidence is important in placing your review findings in context (Ioannidis, 2007). You should clearly highlight how each article, and the review as a whole, has performed with regard to their **validity**, their closeness to the truth. You can thus help the reader to ascribe a level of certainty to a review's conclusions.

To discuss the limitations of your review well you will not simply list systematic errors and associated problems with validity. This would be like a plumber who meets any problems, regardless of severity, with a sharp intake of breath! Instead you should try to interpret the meaning of any errors and their likely influence. Your reader will gain a clear picture of how validity issues impact on the findings of the review.

Just as it is important to take steps to avoid being misled by biases in planning, conducting, analysing and interpreting individual primary studies, similar steps must be taken in planning, conducting, analysing and interpreting evidence syntheses. When you are conducting your overall evaluation of your review and its limitations you need to ask such questions as specified in Box 9.10.

 box 9.10

Questions to ask when assessing the likelihood of bias in your review

1. Have I clearly specified the question to be examined by my review, how included studies address this question, and the extent to which my conclusions resolve this question?
2. Have I defined explicit and objective eligibility criteria for studies to be included?
3. To what extent am I confident that I have identified all potentially eligible studies?
4. Have I ensured that the eligibility criteria are applied in ways that limit bias (possibly resulting from inappropriate acceptance or rejection)?

5. Have I assembled as high a proportion as possible of the relevant information from the included studies?
6. Have I used a variety of analyses to explore any uncertainties associated with my review findings?
7. Have I presented my findings and conclusions in a structured report with clear links between what is observed and what is concluded?

Publication bias

While typically perceived as a problem for quantitative studies Petticrew and colleagues (2008) examined publication rates of qualitative conference presentations, finding an overall publication rate of 44.2%, directly comparable to that for quantitative research. However, likelihood of publication for qualitative research was positively related to the quality of reporting of study methods and findings in the abstract as opposed to the direction and significance of results.

You should therefore explore likely publication bias with regard to qualitative studies or theoretical/conceptual studies. For qualitative studies you might use a matrix approach to examine whether any populations, age groups or countries where the phenomenon of interest is common are comparatively under-represented. For theoretical/conceptual studies you might brainstorm, either singly or with colleagues or a mentor, those disciplines that are likely to have studied the phenomenon of interest. Compare your list with the characteristics of your included studies. Are any disciplines comparatively under-represented? A specific concern when reviewing qualitative studies is labelled 'truncation bias' (Campbell et al., 2011). It refers to the tendency for the fullness of reporting for qualitative studies to be limited by constraints related to journal article word limits.

While methods for detecting and reporting the effects of publication bias are most developed for use with quantitative studies (see Chapter 8), similar questions may be asked with regard to likely reporting bias in qualitative studies or in theoretical/conceptual studies. If you used a framework approach for examining qualitative studies, you might check whether any themes, concerns or issues are missing or under-represented. You might also consider qualitatively whether any specific themes or concerns might not be reported because of stigma, peer pressure, the influence of the researcher, limitations of the methodology or concerns about confidentiality or possible reprisals. If you are conducting a review of barriers and facilitators you can examine whether (a) positive and negative expressions of the same barrier are equally present in the literature (e.g. time pressures and lack of time), albeit in different papers, and (b) whether barriers may be paired with corresponding facilitators. Of course, your subsequent analytical task is to examine whether any gaps are a feature of the data collection process, of incomplete reporting or of being genuinely unrecognised. At the same time you should acknowledge that the frequency of reporting of particular themes is not necessarily related to their importance for, as Dixon-Woods and colleagues (2006a) observe:

> it has to be acknowledged that sampling research papers is fundamentally not like sampling people. Unlike people, research papers have a vested interest in being different from one another, and are (in theory at least) only published if they are saying something new. Missing out some papers may therefore risk missing out potentially important insights.

For theoretical/conceptual studies you may wish to construct diagrams that examine citation patterns. If authors neglect to cite a particular author or school of thought working within the same field you may want to identify why this has happened. Are other authors ignorant of particular arguments or connections, are there possible conflicts or tensions, or is this an intentional omission? You may find it informative to look for patterns of cross-fertilisation or alternatively the existence of a 'silo mentality' between disciplines. All such observations may help to guide your analysis and subsequent presentation.

Triangulation

The technique of **triangulation**, a navigational metaphor, may include using multiple data sources (e.g. members of the public, those delivering a service or programme and other stakeholders), multiple data collection methods (e.g. use of in-depth interviews and focus groups), multiple disciplinary perspectives (e.g. education, management science and psychology), and comparison with existing theory (Cook et al., 2001).

METHODS FOR INTEGRATING QUALITATIVE AND QUANTITATIVE DATA

The outstanding challenge for evidence synthesis relates to the integration of qualitative and quantitative data. Interest in integration has increased recently with attention now focusing on complex interventions. As mentioned in Chapter 5 the challenges of evaluating complex interventions (Anderson et al., 2013a; Petticrew et al., 2013a) have implications for each stage of the review, including focusing the question (Squires et al., 2013), synthesising evidence (Petticrew et al., 2013b), analysis (Tharyan, 2013), heterogeneity (Pigott and Shepperd, 2013), and applicability of findings (Burford et al., 2013). Noyes and colleagues (2013) have subsequently identified a research and development agenda for systematic reviews of complex interventions.

Following Mays et al. (2005a) we identify four overall strategies for integrating qualitative and quantitative data:

1. Integrating at the review level.
2. Integrating using a common structure, framework or model.
3. Integrating through 'translation' of the data.
4. Using an integrative method.

The next section considers these four approaches in turn. Mays et al. (2005a) conclude that the 'choice of approach will be contingent on the aim of the review and nature of the available evidence'. Often more than one approach will be appropriate.

Integrating at the review level

Integrating at the review level is the approach most commonly used. Essentially it involves conducting three systematic reviews in one – a quantitative review, a qualitative review and then an integrative synthesis bringing the previously separate reviews together. For example, the EPPI-Centre at the University of London has developed methods that involve conducting separate reviews of effectiveness and of user views and then bringing the two reviews together to produce a final integrated synthesis (Thomas et al., 2004). At its simplest integration is achieved through an integrative narrative, describing both quantitative and qualitative studies. This might be supported by other practical mechanisms such as tables, graphs or diagrams as a common structure, described in the following sub-section.

Recently Whitaker and colleagues (2014) unpacked the complexity of using multiple review types to address multiple review questions in a review of repeat teenage pregnancy. Describing their endeavour as a 'streamed mixed methods review', they explored 'intervention effectiveness and cost-effectiveness, qualitative and realist synthesis of implementation factors and user engagement'. They mapped their six different review questions against six different review methods and sought to integrate the findings.

Integrating using a common structure, framework or model

A second approach is to bring quantitative and qualitative data into juxtaposition by using a common structure. This structure could be a matrix, a logic model, a conceptual framework or map, or something else. The structure might be used 'instrumentally', for example as a common tool for extracting both types of data during data extraction, or more conceptually, for example as an analytical lens for identifying patterns across the two types of data. For example a conceptual framework could be broken down into its individual elements to create a data extraction form. By using the same structure for both data types you can spot patterns or highlight gaps or incongruities. For example a particular outcome or intervention component may be highlighted as important to users by the qualitative research but may not have been included in experimental quantitative studies.

More recently the 'logic model' is being seen as a possible vehicle for bringing data from quantitative and qualitative studies together within a conceptual whole (Baxter et al., 2010). You can use logic models as a structure for organising logical processes relating to a particular intervention such as inputs, processes, outputs and outcomes (Allmark et al., 2013). They can also be used to map complex care pathways (Anderson et al., 2011; Baxter et al., 2014). Logic models, particularly valuable at the early scoping stage of the review (see Chapter 4), can be revisited as a 'scaffold' from which findings, constructs or themes may be hung.

Integrating through 'translation' of the data

Dixon Woods characterises some synthesis approaches as 'quantitising' qualitative data or 'qualitising' quantitative data. For example cross-case comparison can look for the presence or absence of different factors in a body of literature, reducing qualitative complexity into a binary presentation. Alternatively the data on the surrounding context of randomised controlled trials could be analysed thematically.

Quantitising is more common than we might imagine as it is often done subconsciously. For example when we look at the frequency of certain words or phrases in a keyword analysis we may be quantitising. Quantitising can be used to count and compare the frequency of themes but we must resist the dangers of vote-counting or of interpreting the frequency of mentions of themes as an indicator of their relative importance. Quantitising allows further statistical analysis of data, but information from rich contextual data is always lost when converting from qualitative to quantitative. In contrast qualitising is less common; it might be used to convert a demographic profile of a population into a caricature or narrative vignette, that is at the same time representative of most cases and yet true to none.

Using an integrative method

Several methods are designed to accommodate both quantitative and qualitative data within the same review process. Some explore the narrative or line of argument of included studies so they are particularly examining patterns of studies rather than patterns of findings. Examples are meta-narrative review which looks at how the same concept has evolved within different disciplines and critical interpretive synthesis which looks at how the discourse within a body of literature has been explored and problematised. We conducted a meta-narrative review to follow the two paths by which community engagement has emerged as a concern; the one a government-owned top-down approach and the other a community-owned bottom-up response. Such a philosophical difference may explain differences in sustainability or success. Critical interpretive synthesis exhibits characteristics of meta-method because the way that the research in a particular topic has been conceived and executed may have a bearing on how the topic is depicted in the literature. Realist synthesis handles both quantitative data and qualitative data, in its broadest not necessarily literature-based form, in a similar way to generate causal chains (known as CMO configurations) and then to attempt to test them. **Bayesian meta-analysis** uses qualitative data first to develop 'priors' or expectations for the data and then uses the quantitative literature to confirm or modify them. So, for example, qualitative data can be used to identify parents' concerns regarding vaccination and quantitative data can explore whether these factors had a bearing on uptake rates. Each method merits a separate chapter in a more expansive text so we will briefly introduce and characterise these and then point to further sources for follow-up as appropriate.

Some attempts have been made to integrate qualitative and quantitative data using Bayesian meta-analysis (Roberts et al., 2002). Bayesian meta-analysis (see Box 9.11) uses a serial, rather than parallel, approach in eliciting important factors or variables from qualitative data and then attempting to quantify their individual effects within a meta-analysis. By favouring quantitative data over qualitative data, such an approach is viewed as an unequal partnership.

 box 9.11

Bayesian meta-analysis

What is it?

Bayesian meta-analysis is a method of synthesis where a summary of qualitative data is used to develop a **probability distribution** (**prior distribution**), which can be tested later using a more conventional synthesis of quantitative data. In so doing, the qualitative and quantitative data are combined to produce a posterior distribution. Bayesian meta-analysis explicitly acknowledges the importance of subjective judgement within evidence-based decision making. It attempts to identify what it is reasonable for an observer to believe in light of the available data and therefore explicitly takes account of the perspective of the potential user of the analysis. In doing this, Bayesian meta-analysis recognises that perspectives are important in determining the implications of scientific research for decision making.

What can I use it for?

There are few examples of Bayesian meta-analysis (Roberts et al., 2002; Voils et al., 2009). However, they offer the potential to conduct a synthesis where different forms of evidence need to be brought together. For example you can use this method to explore the likelihood of something happening through one type of research evidence. Subsequently you can establish whether this actually happens via another type of research (usually qualitative followed by quantitative).

How has it been used?

Voils et al. (2009) examined whether people are less likely to keep taking their medicines if they have a complicated medication schedule as opposed to a more straightforward one. They identified 11 qualitative and six quantitative studies to address this question. They used information from the qualitative studies to arrive at a prior likelihood that the complicatedness of the medication schedule was a factor and then used the reports of quantitative studies to verify this.

Critical interpretive synthesis

The thinking behind critical interpretive synthesis resulted from a comprehensive review of existing methods for integrating qualitative and quantitative evidence (Dixon-Woods et al., 2004). The authors had identified deficiencies in existing methods and sought to develop a method that specifically addressed such shortcomings. These included the over-'proceduralisation' of the systematic review at the potential expense of theorising and creativity. The authors also resisted the widespread implication that the product of the review process is necessarily objective, particularly where interpretation is a stated objective of a specific review process. Pragmatically, critical interpretive synthesis (see Box 9.12) is an attempt to handle comparatively large bodies of literature addressing wide-ranging issues at a level that permitted holistic judgements of quality and coherence rather than deconstructing such issues into units of decontextualised studies that have been individually quality assessed.

 box 9.12

Critical interpretive synthesis

What is it?

Critical interpretive synthesis (CIS) aims to conduct a critique rather than a **critical appraisal**. It therefore treats the 'body of literature' as an object of inquiry, not focusing on isolated articles as units of analysis. It stimulates creative interpretations by questioning 'normal science' conventions and examines what influences the choice of proposed solutions. It is heavily

(Continued)

(Continued)

steeped in the context for the literary output. It embraces all types of evidence and is attentive to procedural defects in primary studies without necessarily excluding the contribution that flawed studies might make. It acknowledges the relevance of adjacent literatures as a creative feed, purposively sampling from those literatures in its quest to pursue its explicit orientation towards theory generation. The importance of reflexivity as a constructed part of the process, in recognition of the subjectivity of the review process, is discussed further in Chapter 10.

What can I use it for?

Critical interpretive synthesis has been purposely developed for those situations where a theorisation of the evidence is a specific intended outcome from the review. It can be seen to encourage a critique of literatures and thus to stimulate questioning of taken-for-granted assumptions about concepts and methods (Dixon-Woods et al., 2006b).

How has it been used?

Flemming (2010) used CIS to synthesise quantitative research, in the form of an effectiveness review and a guideline, with qualitative research, to examine the use of morphine to treat cancer-related pain. CIS had not previously been used specifically to synthesise effectiveness and qualitative litera-ture. The findings of the effectiveness research were used as a framework to guide the translation of findings from qualitative research using an integrative grid (compare framework synthesis). A secondary translation of findings from the qualitative research, not specifically mapped to the effec-tiveness literature, was guided by the framework. Nineteen qualitative papers were synthesised with the quantitative effectiveness literature, producing 14 synthetic constructs. Four synthesising arguments were subsequently developed drawing on patients', carers' and healthcare profession-als' interpretations of the meaning and context of the use of morphine to treat cancer pain.

Meta-narrative review

Another approach to pursuing 'lines of argument' involves use of the meta-narrative review (see Box 9.13) to explore large and heterogeneous literatures by identifying the unfolding 'storyline' of research (Greenhalgh et al., 2005). While the approach can help build an understanding of a field, findings should be seen as 'illuminating the problem and raising areas to consider' rather than 'providing the definitive answers' (Greenhalgh et al., 2005). The literature may possess adversarial characteristics, perhaps with arguments attributed to particular 'schools of thought' – again you will probably wish to sample initially from each of the most prominent stances.

 box 9.13

Meta-narrative review

What is it?

Meta-narrative reviews use a historical and philosophical perspective as a pragmatic way of making sense of a diverse literature. They acknowledge the existence of heterogeneity within the different paradigms. The questioning process starts from Kuhn (1962) by asking:

What research teams have researched this area?

How did they conceptualise the problem?

What theories did they use to link the problem with potential causes and impacts?

What methods did they define as 'rigorous' and 'valid'?

What instruments did they use?

What can I use it for?

To investigate a broad open-ended question in terms of the main research traditions, schools of thought, used to explore that question. This approach fits well with the open-ended exploratory phase that characterises the first year of most PhD work.

How has it been used?

Greenhalgh and colleagues (2009) used the meta-narrative method to examine 'conflicting' findings that illustrate how researchers had differently conceptualised and studied the implementation of the electronic patient record (EPR). They considered 24 previous systematic reviews and 94 further primary studies. The key tensions identified from the literature centred on seven conflicting tensions:

1. The EPR ('container' or 'itinerary').
2. The EPR user ('information-processer' or 'member of socio-technical network').
3. Organisational context ('the setting within which the EPR is implemented' or 'the EPR-in-use').
4. Clinical work ('decision making' or 'situated practice').
5. The process of change ('the logic of determinism' or 'the logic of opposition').
6. Implementation success ('objectively defined' or 'socially negotiated').
7. Complexity and scale ('the bigger the better' versus 'small is beautiful').

A key finding from their meta-narrative approach was that even though secondary work (audit, research, billing) may be made more efficient by the EPR, this might be at the expense of primary clinical work which may be made less efficient.

Standards for reporting meta-narrative reviews have been produced by the RAMESES initiative and training materials are available from the RAMESES website.

Realist synthesis

Pawson (2002) argues that the 'primary ambition of research synthesis is explanation building'. To this end, realist synthesis attempts to bring together different types of research data, quantitative or qualitative, with other data sources in order to identify an underlying mechanism of effect. Such a mechanism may explain why an intervention works in one context but not in a similar one. Drawing on earlier work on programme evaluation (Pawson and Tilley, 1997), Pawson (2006a) contends that research synthesis should be targeted at identifying, and subsequently developing an understanding of, these underlying generative mechanisms. Pawson (2002) proposes realist synthesis for analysing the effectiveness of policy programmes through the development and testing of theoretical ideas on intervention–outcome relations. This pragmatic approach has been likened to the use of research synthesis for developing design propositions in management and organisation studies (Denyer et al., 2008). The purpose is to 'articulate underlying programme theories and then interrogate existing evidence to find out whether and where these theories are pertinent and productive' (Pawson, 2006a). While programmes are context-specific and not generalisable, intervention–outcome combinations are. Consequently programme reviews aim at discovering context–mechanism–outcome combinations in order to know when, where and for whom to apply the programme, or elements of it. Realist synthesis therefore involves the progressive investigation of the following questions:

- What is the nature and content of the intervention?
- What are the circumstances or context for its use?
- What are the policy intentions or objectives?
- What are the nature and form of its outcomes or impacts?

Realist synthesis, therefore, uses included studies as 'case studies, whose purpose is to test, revise and refine the preliminary theory' (Pawson, 2006a). Realist synthesis (see Box 9.14) is able to accommodate research evidence from a range of study types.

 box 9.14

Realist synthesis

What is it?

Realist synthesis is used to articulate underlying programme theories and then interrogate existing evidence to find out whether and where these theories are pertinent and productive. It can be seen that the unit of analysis is the programme theory with primary data being inspected for what they reveal about the programme theory. The explicit purpose of the review is thus to test and refine programme theory. Realist synthesis therefore examines different types of evidence as they address specific questions or uncertainties within a programme. In some cases, therefore, these questions can relate to the effectiveness of a particular intervention, particularly as it might apply differentially in different contexts. In other cases, this may examine the acceptability of a programme or the attitudes of stakeholders towards it.

What can I use it for?

Realist synthesis produces 'mid-range theory', lying between minor working hypotheses from day-to-day research and broader systematic efforts to develop a unified theory (Pawson, 2002). You can use realist synthesis to examine possible theory underlying particular programmes or mechanisms to explain why it works in certain circumstances but not other apparently similar circumstances. You can examine policies or programmes at either a national level or at a local implementation level to identify variables affecting likely success or failure at either or both levels.

How has it been used?

Kane and colleagues (2010) sought a better understanding of the mechanisms by which community health workers (CHWs) might help to reduce the burden of childhood illnesses in low and middle income countries (LMIC). They examined evidence from randomised control trials (RCT) from a realist perspective to see if this yielded insight into how such roles worked. This review aimed to use evidence from the RCTs for a hypothesis-generating exercise. The review identified factors more likely to be associated with the success of programmes as well as negative mechanisms that might compromise CHW performance. This review was successful as a hypothesis-generating exercise but the RCTs did not yield sufficient specificity to go beyond hypotheses that were very general and not well refined. They identified a need to further test and refine these hypotheses in further studies.

Standards for reporting realist syntheses have been produced by the RAMESES initiative and training materials are available from the RAMESES website.

USING ANALYSIS TO EXAMINE AN INTEGRATED SYNTHESIS

Once you have performed your synthesis you are in a position to examine what happens when you bring the quantitative results and the qualitative findings together. Perhaps the take-home message is synergistic – the most effective option is also revealed as being the most acceptable or the easiest to implement. It is correspondingly easier to write recommendations for action. More typically the two evidence bases reflect a trade-off – an intervention is effective but not well accepted or a programme achieves its desired outcomes but has difficulty retaining people within the programme.

Tensions or contradictions may also exist with regard to the research agenda. Quantitative studies such as RCTs may have examined more easily measurable outcomes but the qualitative synthesis may reveal that outcomes important to the patients have been overlooked. The bringing together of both bodies of evidence thus informs the 'Discussion', 'Conclusion' and 'Recommendations'. Techniques at your disposal for bringing together both types of evidence include various forms of graphing, the use of matrices and tabulation, and the analytical techniques we have listed earlier. You could graph the quantitative studies by size of effect and compare this with the presence/absence of particular intervention components. For example the EPPI-Centre team compared health messages on fruit and vegetables with the effects on increased consumption by children (Thomas et al., 2004). They found it was ineffective to promote fruit and vegetables in the same way or to expect children to respond to messages regarding the long-term health benefits. Alternatively you could place quantitative outcomes from included studies in rows (for example patient satisfaction score) and qualitative versions of the same outcome (patient satisfaction) in columns and examine the matrix to see whether both types of data are favourable, unfavourable or equivocal (Candy et al., 2011). In a study of appointment reminders we arranged the before and after arms of studies separately according to increasing attendance rate, allowing comparison of the baseline attendance rates across studies and identification of improvement between the before and after within studies (McLean et al., 2014). We then brought in qualitative evidence on the nature of each appointment type, observing for example that person-specific appointments had higher baseline attendance rates than general population reminders for screening or blood donation appointments and attendance rates for children were higher than those for adults. On the basis of this pattern we carried out further theory-informed analysis on the role of personalisation and commitment in the effectiveness of appointment reminders.

SUMMARY

This chapter illustrates that synthesis includes the more creative elements of seeking patterns, examining for consistency, and identifying the divergent or disconfirming case. You as a reviewer will find it stimulating to explore the reasons for variations, discrepancies and inconsistencies. This exploration, together with a more general testing of the robustness of findings, constitutes analysis – a high-order research skill. Analysis is often presented as a naturally occurring sequel lacking formal procedures. Analysis involves identifying patterns to data and included studies, investigating conflicting or outlying cases, and exploring the relationships between particular variables.

Concerns about applicability, generalisability, replicability and implementation fidelity shape likely recommendations for research and for practice. Once such recommendations are drafted and exist in a fluid or malleable state, you can turn your attention to how best to present the report, the focus for Chapter 10.

 key learning points

- Data extraction is a key step in progress towards synthesis and it is helpful to derive a picture of what the final synthesis might look like before selecting the data to be extracted.
- Numerous approaches to synthesis exist and you should look at existing published methods and examples before selecting a methodology that is fit for purpose.
- Analysis initially involves testing the robustness of your synthesis in light of what you know about the quality of included studies.
- A reviewer has a large range of types of data presentation to select from including textual, graphical, numerical and tabular approaches.
- Integration of quantitative and qualitative data remains the outstanding methodological challenge for synthesis. Methods do exist for such integration but few published examples are available.

frequently asked questions

FAQ 9.1 How do I choose an appropriate method for qualitative synthesis?

Several publications open up the full range of choices in qualitative synthesis available to a reviewer. However, a smaller number wrestle with the more challenging issue of matching your review to the method of synthesis. Look back to Chapter 3 and attempt the scenarios given. Use the TREAD framework (also Chapter 3) to specify the task to be performed for your review. Consult sources that focus on selecting an appropriate method: for example Hannes and Lockwood (2011) and Noyes and Lewin (2011). The book by Gough et al. (2012a) also offers a good overview of the available choices and their theoretical underpinnings.

FAQ 9.2 Which methods of qualitative evidence synthesis are most suitable for a novice reviewer?

Review expertise is not the only consideration because familiarity with qualitative research is also required when reviewing the qualitative literature. However, concentrating only on the ease of the synthesis method we would recommend either meta-aggregation, thematic synthesis or framework synthesis. Meta-aggregation minimises the interpretive burden as the reviewer compiles themes already articulated by the authors of the primary studies, supporting these with verbatim extracts from the texts. Thematic synthesis is the synthesis equivalent of thematic analysis and is considered intuitive to the novice reviewer. However, if you lack confidence in your ability to generate new themes then you may want to try framework synthesis. Once you have gained some confidence from mapping the large proportion of the data to the framework you may feel more able to create new themes for the data not previously accommodated by the framework.

FAQ 9.3 Is software available to help with qualitative synthesis?

Software may be specific to the systematic review process or may include software designed for primary qualitative research that is only used during the synthesis and analysis stages. Eppi-Reviewer is intended for use across a wide variety of review types. It can be particularly useful when seeking to employ a common review approach across both quantitative and qualitative reviews. Similarly QARI from the Joanna Briggs Institute (JBI) is specialist software, particularly for the method of qualitative synthesis known as meta-aggregation, but is part of a suite of review programmes purpose-designed to support the review activities of the organisation. Finally qualitative data analysis software such as NVivo may be used to handle coding of texts from journal articles in the same way that they handle interview transcripts.

FAQ 9.4 Which methods of integrating quantitative and qualitative evidence are most suitable for a novice reviewer?

Many reviewers find that use of matrices, to explore correlations or inconsistencies in the data across qualitative and quantitative studies, is an intuitive way of handling the data. So, for example, themes from the qualitative data can be compared with outcomes measured in quantitative studies. Bear in mind, however, that another part of your analysis is to compare whether concepts measured both quantitatively and qualitatively are actually capturing the same phenomenon. Terms such as quality of life and patient satisfaction may have both a technical meaning and a lay meaning and these might be quite different. Be sure to highlight this. Beyond the **matrix method** you may find it helpful to map both quantitative and qualitative data against a common structure such as a logic model, or even against a conceptual framework using best fit framework synthesis.

FAQ 9.5 Should I publish my mixed methods review as one publication or two?

This dilemma is already familiar to those who publish mixed methods primary research. The trade-off is the added value of the integration of both types of evidence against word constraints that limit completeness of reporting. It is already difficult to do justice to the 'Methods' and 'Results' of a single review and mixed methods reviews serve to compound

(Continued)

(Continued)

this issue. Although the question centres on publishing one or two reviews, a third option is to publish *three* reviews – the quantitative review, the qualitative review and an integrative review. Assuming, however, that a student or review team is unable to be this prolific then you should consider an integrative review that focuses on the quantitative results published in a high impact journal and then a supplementary publication unpacking the detail of the qualitative review. Reasons for profiling the quantitative results in this way are strategic rather than methodological. Quantitative reviews tend to face a better chance of being accepted in high impact journals. Citing the integrative review in the qualitative review offers the added prospect that the study report will be located through citation searching.

suggestions for further reading

Hannes, K. and Lockwood, C. (2011) *Synthesizing Qualitative Research: Choosing the Right Approach*. Chichester: Wiley.
Tackles the bewildering choice offered by qualitative synthesis methods. Devotes a chapter to each of the main methods of qualitative synthesis together with a walk-through of each methodology and a worked case example.

Munn, Z., Tufanaru, C. and Aromataris, E. (2014) JBI's systematic reviews: data extraction and synthesis. *American Journal of Nursing*, **114**, 7, 49–54.
From a mini-series on systematic reviews from staff at the Joanna Briggs Institute (JBI), this article covers data extraction, often neglected in step-by-step guides.

Petticrew, M., Rehfuess, E., Noyes, J., Higgins, J.P., Mayhew, A., Pantoja, T., Shemilt, I. and Sowden, A. (2013) Synthesizing evidence on complex interventions: how meta-analytical, qualitative, and mixed-method approaches can contribute. *Journal of Clinical Epidemiology*, **66**, 11, 1230–43.
Part of an innovative series on complex interventions, all of which are relevant and readable, this article highlights the utility of different synthesis combinations.

Pope, C., Mays, N. and Popay, J. (2007) Methods for evidence synthesis. In C. Pope, N. Mays and J. Popay (eds), *Synthesizing Qualitative and Quantitative Health Evidence: A Guide to Methods*. Maidenhead: Open University Press, 45–114.
Probably the only text to date to give equal attention and value to both quantitative and qualitative evidence. An excellent compendium of review methods.

Ring, N., Ritchie, K., Mandava, L. and Jepson, R. (2010) A guide to synthesising qualitative research for researchers undertaking health technology assessments and systematic reviews. NHS Improvement, Scotland.
The first text to examine qualitative synthesis within the specific context of health technology assessment, this report provides a good cross-sectional view of the state of qualitative synthesis when it was written.

Saini, M. and Shlonsky, A. (2012) *Systematic Synthesis of Qualitative Research*. Oxford: Oxford University Press.

This book is strong on the standard procedures for systematic reviews of qualitative research, with applicability beyond its primary social work researcher audience. Despite its title its strengths are in the searching and appraisal, in addition to offering a clear overview of the review process.

REFERENCES

Allmark, P., Baxter, S., Goyder, E., Guillaume, L. and Crofton-Martin, G. (2013) Assessing the health benefits of advice services: using research evidence and logic model methods to explore complex pathways. *Health & Social Care in the Community*, **21**, 1, 59–68.

Anderson, L.M., Oliver, S.R., Michie, S., Rehfuess, E., Noyes, J. and Shemilt, I. (2013a) Investigating complexity in systematic reviews of interventions by using a spectrum of methods. *Journal of Clinical Epidemiology*, **66**, 11, 1223–9.

Anderson, L.M., Petticrew, M., Chandler, J., Grimshaw, J., Tugwell, P., O'Neill, J., Welch, V., Squires, J., Churchill, R. and Shemilt, I. (2013b) Introducing a series of methodological articles on considering complexity in systematic reviews of interventions. *Journal of Clinical Epidemiology*, **66**, 11, 1205–8.

Anderson, L.M., Petticrew, M., Rehfuess, E., Armstrong, R., Ueffing, E., Baker, P., Francis, D. and Tugwell, P. (2011) Using logic models to capture complexity in systematic reviews. *Research Synthesis Methods*, **2**, 1, 33–42.

Armitage, A. and Keeble-Allen, D. (2008) Undertaking a structured literature review or structuring a literature review: tales from the field. *Electronic Journal of Business Research Methods*, **6**, 2, 141–52.

Atkins, S., Lewin, S., Smith, H., Engel, M., Fretheim, A. and Volmink, J. (2008) Conducting a meta-ethnography of qualitative literature: lessons learnt. *BMC Medical Research Methodology*, **8**, 21.

Barnett-Page, E. and Thomas, J. (2009) Methods for the synthesis of qualitative research: a critical review. *BMC Medical Research Methodology*, **9**, 59.

Baxter, S., Killoran, A., Kelly, M.P. and Goyder, E. (2010) Synthesizing diverse evidence: the use of primary qualitative data analysis methods and logic models in public health reviews. *Public Health*, **124**, 2, 99–106.

Baxter, S.K., Blank, L., Woods, H.B., Payne, N., Rimmer, M. and Goyder, E. (2014) Using logic model methods in systematic review synthesis: describing complex pathways in referral management interventions. *BMC Medical Research Methodology*, **10**, 14, 62.

Bearman, M. and Dawson, P. (2013) Qualitative synthesis and systematic review in health professions education. *Medical Education*. **47**, 3, 252–60.

Beck, C.T. (2001) Caring with nursing education: a metasynthesis. *Journal of Nursing Education*, **40**, 3, 101–10.

Bergman, M.M. and Coxon, A.P.M. (2005) The quality in qualitative methods. *Forum Qualitative Sozialforschung/Forum: Qualitative Social Research*, **6**, 2, Art. 34.

Booth, A. and Carroll, C. (2015) How to build up the actionable knowledge base: the role of 'best fit' framework synthesis for studies of improvement in healthcare. *BMJ Quality & Safety*, Online First. DOI: 10.1136/bmjqs-2014-003642

Booth, A., Carroll, C., Ilott, I., Low, L.L. and Cooper, K. (2013a) Desperately seeking dissonance identifying the disconfirming case in qualitative evidence synthesis. *Qualitative Health Research*, **23**, 1, 126–41.

Booth, A., Harris, J., Croot, E., Springett, J., Campbell, F. and Wilkins, E. (2013b) Towards a methodology for cluster searching to provide conceptual and contextual 'richness' for systematic reviews of complex interventions: case study (CLUSTER). *BMC Medical Research Methodology*, **13**, 1, 118.

Britten, N., Campbell, R., Pope, C., Donovan, J., Morgan, M. and Pill, R. (2002) Using meta-ethnography to synthesise qualitative research: a worked example. *Journal of Health Services Research and Policy*, **7**, 4, 209–15.

Brown, S.J. (1999) *Knowledge for Health Care Practice: A Guide to Using Research Evidence*. Philadelphia: W.B. Saunders Co.

Brunton, G., Oliver, S., Oliver, K. and Lorenc, T. (2006) *A Synthesis of Research Addressing Children's, Young People's and Parents' Views of Walking and Cycling for Transport*. London: EPPI-Centre, Social Science Research Unit, Institute of Education, University of London.

Burford, B., Lewin, S., Welch, V., Rehfuess, E. and Waters, E. (2013) Assessing the applicability of findings in systematic reviews of complex interventions can enhance the utility of reviews for decision making. *Journal of Clinical Epidemiology*, **66**, 11, 1251–61.

Campbell, R., Pound, P., Morgan, M., Daker-White, G., Britten, N., Pill, R., Yardley, L., Pope, C. and Donovan, J. (2011) Evaluating meta-ethnography: systematic analysis and synthesis of qualitative research. *Health Technology Assessment*, **15**, 43, 1–164.

Campbell, R., Pound, P., Pope, C., Britten, N., Pill, R., Morgan, M. and Donovan, J. (2003) Evaluating meta-ethnography: a synthesis of qualitative research on lay experiences of diabetes and diabetes care. *Social Science and Medicine*, **56**, 4, 671–84.

Candy, B., King, M., Jones, L. and Oliver, S. (2011) Using qualitative synthesis to explore heterogeneity of complex interventions. *BMC Medical Research Methodology*, **11**, 1, 124.

Carroll, C., Booth, A. and Cooper, K. (2011) A worked example of 'best fit' framework synthesis: a systematic review of views concerning the taking of some potential chemopreventive agents. *BMC Medical Research Methodology*, **11**, 1, 1–9.

Carroll, C., Booth, A., Leaviss, J. and Rick, J. (2013) 'Best fit' framework synthesis: refining the method. *BMC Medical Research Methodology*, **13**, 1, 37.

Carroll, C., Booth, A., Papaioannou, D., Sutton, A. and Wong, R. (2009) UK health-care professionals' experience of on-line learning techniques: a systematic review of qualitative data. *Journal of Continuing Education in the Health Professions*, **29**, 4, 235–41.

Combs, J.P., Bustamante, R.M. and Onwuegbuzie, A.J. (2010) An interactive model for facilitating development of literature reviews. *International Journal of Multiple Research Approaches*, **4**, 2, 159–82.

Cook, D.J., Meade, M.O. and Perry, A.G. (2001) Qualitative studies on the patient's experience of weaning from mechanical ventilation. *Chest*, **120**, 6, Suppl, 469S–73S.

Cooper, K., Squires, H., Carroll, C., Papaioannou, D., Booth, A., Logan, R.F., Maguire, C., Hind, D. and Tappenden, P. (2010) Review of qualitative data on views and attitudes to the taking of agents that may be used for chemoprevention. In: Chemoprevention of colorectal cancer: systematic review and economic evaluation. *Health Technology Assessment*, **14**, 32, 79–96.

Coren, E. and Fisher, M. (2006) *The Conduct of Systematic Research Reviews for SCIE Knowledge Reviews*. Using Knowledge in Social Care Research Resource 1. London: Social Care Institute of Excellence.

Cresswell, J.W. (2003) *Research Design: Qualitative, Quantitative, and Mixed Method Approaches*, 2nd edition. Thousand Oaks, CA: Sage.

Cruzes, D.S. and Dybå, T. (2010) Synthesizing evidence in software engineering research. ESEM 10, Proceedings of the 2010 ACM-IEEE International Symposium on Empirical Software Engineering and Measurement, Association for Computing Machinery, New York.

Curran, C., Burchardt, T., Knapp, M., McDaid, D. and Li, B. (2007) Challenges in multidisciplinary systematic reviewing: a study on social exclusion and mental health policy. *Social Policy and Administration*, **41**, 3, 289–312.

Denyer, D. and Tranfield, D. (2006) Using qualitative research synthesis to build an actionable knowledge base. *Management Decision*, **44**, 2, 213–27.

Denyer, D., Tranfield, D. and Van Aken, J.E. (2008) Developing design propositions through research synthesis. *Organization Studies*, **29**, 2, 249–69.

Dixon-Woods, M. (2011) Using framework-based synthesis for conducting reviews of qualitative studies. *BMC Medicine*, **9**, 39.

Dixon-Woods, M., Agarwal, S., Young, B., Jones, D. and Sutton, A. (2004) *Integrative Approaches to Qualitative and Quantitative Evidence*, London: Health Development Agency.

Dixon-Woods, M., Bonas, S., Booth, A., Jones, D.R., Miller, T., Shaw, R.L., Smith, J., Sutton, A. and Young, B. (2006a) How can systematic reviews incorporate qualitative research? A critical perspective. *Qualitative Research*, **6**, 1, 27–44.

Dixon-Woods, M., Booth, A. and Sutton, A.J. (2007) Synthesising qualitative research: a review of published reports. *Qualitative Research*, **7**, 375–422.

Dixon-Woods, M., Cavers, D., Agarwal, S., Annandale, E., Arthur, A., Harvey, J., Hsu, R., Katbamna, S., Olsen, R., Smith, L., Riley, R. and Sutton, A.J. (2006b) Conducting a critical interpretive synthesis of the literature on access to healthcare by vulnerable groups. *BMC Medical Research Methodology,* **6**, 35.

Donald, M., Dower, J. and Kavanagh, D. (2005) Integrated versus non-integrated management and care for clients with co-occurring mental health and substance use disorders: a qualitative systematic review of randomised controlled trials. *Social Science & Medicine*, **60**, 6, 1371–83.

Duggan, F. and Banwell, L. (2004) Constructing a model of effective information dissemination in a crisis. *Information Research*, **9**, 3.

Field, B., Booth, A., Ilott, I. and Gerrish, K. (2014) Using the knowledge to action framework in practice: a citation analysis and systematic review. *Implementation Science*, **9**, 1, 172–86.

Finfgeld-Connett, D. (2009) Model of therapeutic and non-therapeutic responses to patient aggression. *Issues in Mental Health Nursing*, **30**, 9, 530–7.

Flemming, K. (2010) Synthesis of quantitative and qualitative research: an example using critical interpretive synthesis. *Journal of Advanced Nursing*, **66**, 1, 201–17.

Fu, Y., McNichol, E., Marczewski, K. and Closs, S.J. (2015) Patient–professional partnerships and chronic back pain self-management: a qualitative systematic review and synthesis. *Health & Social Care in the Community* [Epub ahead of print]. DOI: 10.1111/hsc.12223

Ganann, R., Ciliska, D. and Thomas, H. (2010) Expediting systematic reviews: methods and implications of rapid reviews. *Implementation Science*, **5**, 56.

Garside, R. (2008) A comparison of methods for the systematic review of qualitative research: two examples using meta-ethnography and meta-study. Doctoral dissertation, Universities of Exeter and Plymouth.

Garside, R., Britten, N. and Stein, K. (2008) The experience of heavy menstrual bleeding: a systematic review and meta-ethnography of qualitative studies. *Journal of Advanced Nursing*, **63**, 6, 550–62.

Gough, D., Oliver, S. and Thomas, J. (eds) (2012a) *An Introduction to Systematic Reviews*. London: Sage.

Gough, D., Thomas, J. and Oliver, S. (2012b) Clarifying differences between review designs and methods. *Systematic Reviews*, **1**, 1, 28.

Graham-Matheson, L., Connolly, T., Robson, S. and Stow, W. (2006) A systematic map into approaches to making initial teacher training flexible and responsive to the needs of trainee teachers. Technical report. In: *Research Evidence in Education Library*. London: EPPI-Centre, Social Science Research Unit.

Gray, C. and Malins, J. (2004) *Visualizing Research: A Guide to the Research Process in Art and Design*. Burlington, VT: Ashgate.

Greenhalgh, T. (2014) *How to Read a Paper: The Basics of Evidence-based Medicine*, 5th edition. London: BMJ Books.

Greenhalgh, T., Potts, H.W., Wong, G., Bark, P. and Swinglehurst, D. (2009) Tensions and paradoxes in electronic patient record research: a systematic literature review using the meta-narrative method. *Milbank Quarterly*, **87**, 4, 729–88.

Greenhalgh, T., Robert, G., Macfarlane, F., Bate, P., Kyriakidou, O. and Peacock, R. (2005) Storylines of research in diffusion of innovation: a meta-narrative approach to systematic review. *Social Science and Medicine*, **61**, 2, 417–30.

Greenhalgh, T. and Russell, J. (2006). Reframing evidence synthesis as rhetorical action in the policy making drama. *Healthcare Policy*, **1**, 2, 34.

Hammersley, M. (2002) Systematic or unsystematic, is that the question? Some reflections on the science, art and politics of reviewing research evidence. Talk given to the Public Health Evidence Steering Group of the Health Development Agency.

Hannes, K. and Lockwood, C. (2012) *Synthesising Qualitative Research: Choosing the Right Approach*. Chichester: Wiley-Blackwell.

Harden, A., Brunton, G., Fletcher, A. and Oakley, A. (2006) Young people, pregnancy and social exclusion: a systematic synthesis of research evidence to identify effective, appropriate and promising approaches for prevention and support. London: EPPI-Centre, Social Science Research Unit, Institute of Education, University of London.

Harden, A., Garcia, J., Oliver, S., Rees, R., Shepherd, J., Brunton, G. and Oakley, A. (2004) Applying systematic review methods to studies of people's views: an example from public health. *Journal of Epidemiology and Community Health*, **58**, 794–800.

Harris, J., Springett, J., Croot, L., Booth, A., Campbell, F., Thompson, J., Goyder, E., Van Cleemput, P., Wilkins, E. and Yang, Y. (2015) Can community-based peer support promote health literacy and reduce inequalities? A realist review. *Public Health Research*, **3**, 3. DOI: http://dx.doi.org/10.3310/phr03030

Hart, C. (1998) *Doing a Literature Review: Releasing the Social Science Research Imagination*. London: Sage.

Ioannidis, J.P.A. (2007) Limitations are not properly acknowledged in the scientific literature. *Journal of Clinical Epidemiology*, **60**, 4, 324–9.

Kane, S.S., Gerretsen, B., Scherpbier, R., Dal Poz, M. and Dieleman, M. (2010) A realist synthesis of randomised control trials involving use of community health workers for delivering child health interventions in low and middle income countries. *BMC Health Services Research*, **10**, 286.

Kastner, M., Tricco, A.C., Soobiah, C., Lillie, E., Perrier, L., Horsley, T., Welch, V., Cogo, E., Antony, J. and Straus, S.E. (2012) What is the most appropriate knowledge synthesis method to conduct a review? Protocol for a scoping review. *BMC Medical Research Methodology*, **12**, 1, 114.

Kavanagh, J., Trouton, A., Oakley, A. and Harden, A. (2005) *A Scoping Review of the Evidence for Incentive Schemes to Encourage Positive Health and Other Social Behaviours in Young People*. London: EPPI-Centre, Social Science Research Unit.

Kitchenham, B. (2007) Guidelines for performing systematic literature reviews in software engineering (Version 2.3). EBSE Technical Report: EBSE-2007–01. Software Engineering Group, School of Computer Science and Mathematics, Keele University, Staffordshire.

Knafl, K.A. and Webster, D.C. (1988) Managing and analyzing qualitative data: a description of tasks, techniques, and materials. *Western Journal of Nursing Research*, **10**, 195–210.

Kuhn, T.S. (1962) *The Structure of Scientific Revolutions*. Chicago: University of Chicago Press.

Lather, P. (1999) To be of use: the work of reviewing. *Review of Educational Research*, **69**, 2–7.

Lewin, S., Glenton, C., Munthe-Kaas, H., Carlsen, B., Colvin, C.J., Gülmezoglu, M., Noyes, J., Booth, A., Garside, R. and Rashidian, A. (2015) Using qualitative evidence in decision making for health and social interventions: an approach to assess confidence in findings from qualitative evidence syntheses (GRADE-CERQual), *PLOS Medicine*, **12**, 10, e1001895.

Mays, N., Pope, C. and Popay, J. (2005a) Systematically reviewing qualitative and quantitative evidence to inform management and policy-making in the health field. *Journal of Health Services Research and Policy*, **10**, Suppl. 1, 6–20.

Mays, N., Pope, C. and Popay, J. (2005b) Details of approaches to synthesis – a methodological appendix to the paper: systematically reviewing qualitative and quantitative evidence to inform management and policy making in the health field. Report for the National Co-ordinating Centre for NHS Service Delivery and Organisation R and D (NCCSDO), London School of Hygiene and Tropical Medicine.

Mazzocato, P., Savage, C., Brommels, M., Aronsson, H. and Thor, J. (2010) Lean thinking in healthcare: a realist review of the literature. *Quality & Safety in Health Care*, **19**, 5, 376–82.

McLean, S., Gee, M., Booth, A., Salway, S., Nancarrow, S., Cobb, M. and Bhanbhro, S. (2014) Targeting the Use of Reminders and Notifications for Uptake by Populations (TURNUP): a systematic review and evidence synthesis. *Health Services and Delivery Research*, **2**, 34.

Melendez-Torres, G.J., Grant, S. and Bonell, C. (2015) A systematic review and critical appraisal of qualitative metasynthetic practice in public health to develop a taxonomy of operations of reciprocal translation. *Research Synthesis Methods*. DOI: 10.1002/jrsm.1161.

Miles, M.B. and Huberman, A.M. (1994) *Qualitative Data Analysis: An Expanded Sourcebook*, 2nd edition. London: Sage.

Morton, R.L., Tong, A., Howard, K., Snelling, P. and Webster, A.C. (2010) The views of patients and carers in treatment decision making for chronic kidney disease: systematic review and thematic synthesis of qualitative studies. *BMJ*, **340**, c112.

Moustaghfir, K. (2008) The dynamics of knowledge assets and their link with firm performance. *Measuring Business Excellence*, **12**, 2, 10–24.

Munn, Z., Tufanaru, C., Aromataris, E. (2014) JBI's systematic reviews: data extraction and synthesis. *American Journal of Nursing*, **114**, 7, 49–54.

Munro, S., Lewin, S., Swart, T. and Volmink, J. (2007) A review of health behaviour theories: how useful are these for developing interventions to promote long-term medication adherence for TB and HIV/AIDS? *BMC Public Health*, **11**, 7, 104.

Noblit, G.W. and Hare, R.D. (1988) *Meta-ethnography: Synthesizing Qualitative Studies*. Newbury Park, CA: Sage.

Noyes, J., Gough, D., Lewin, S., Mayhew, A., Michie, S., Pantoja, T., Petticrew, M., Pottie, K., Rehfuess, E., Shemilt, I., Shepperd, S., Sowden, A., Tugwell, P. and Welch, V. (2013) A research and development agenda for systematic reviews that ask complex questions about complex interventions. *Journal of Clinical Epidemiology*, **66**, 11, 1262–70.

Noyes, J. and Lewin, S. (2011) Supplemental guidance on selecting a method of qualitative evidence synthesis, and integrating qualitative evidence with Cochrane intervention reviews. In J. Noyes, A. Booth, K. Hannes, A. Harden, J. Harris, S. Lewin and C. Lockwood (eds), *Supplementary Guidance for Inclusion of Qualitative Research in Cochrane Systematic Reviews of Interventions*. Version 1 (updated August 2011). Cochrane Collaboration Qualitative Methods Group. Available at: http://methods.cochrane.org/qi/sites/methods.cochrane.org.qi/files/uploads/Data%20synthesis%20supplemental%20guidance_2010%2012%2023B.doc.

Paterson, B.L. (2012) 'It looks great but how do I know if it fits?': an introduction to meta-synthesis research. In K. Hannes and C. Lockwood (eds), *Synthesizing Qualitative Research: Choosing the Right Approach*. Chichester: Wiley-Blackwell, 1–20.

Paterson, B., Thorne, S., Canam, C. and Jillings, C. (2001) *Meta-study of Qualitative Health Research*. Thousand Oaks, CA: Sage.

Pawson, R. (2001) *Evidence Based Policy: II. The Promise of 'Realist Synthesis.* ESRC UK Centre for Evidence Based Policy and Practice. London: Queen Mary, University of London.

Pawson, R. (2002) Evidence based policy: in search of a method. *Evaluation*, **8**, 2, 157–81.

Pawson, R. (2006a) *Evidence-based Policy: A Realist Perspective.* London: Sage.

Pawson, R. (2006b) Digging for nuggets: how 'bad' research can yield 'good' evidence. *International Journal of Social Research Methodology*, **9**, 2, 127–42.

Pawson, R., Greenhalgh, T., Harvey, G. and Walshe, K. (2004) *Realist Synthesis: An Introduction.* Manchester: ESRC Research Methods Programme.

Pawson, R. and Tilley, N. (1997) *Realistic Evaluation.* London: Sage.

Petticrew, M., Anderson, L., Elder, R., Grimshaw, J., Hopkins, D., Hahn, R., Krause, L., Kristjansson, E., Mercer, S., Sipe, T., Tugwell, P., Ueffing, E., Waters, E. and Welch V. (2013a) Complex interventions and their implications for systematic reviews: a pragmatic approach. *Journal of Clinical Epidemiology*, **66**, 11, 1209–14.

Petticrew, M., Egan, M., Thomson, H., Hamilton, V., Kunkler, R. and Roberts, H. (2008) Publication bias in qualitative research: what becomes of qualitative research presented at conferences? *Journal of Epidemiology and Community Health*, **62**, 552–4.

Petticrew, M., Rehfuess, E., Noyes, J., Higgins, J.P., Mayhew, A., Pantoja, T., Shemilt, I. and Sowden, A. (2013b) Synthesizing evidence on complex interventions: how meta-analytical, qualitative, and mixed-method approaches can contribute. *Journal of Clinical Epidemiology*, **66**, 11, 1230–43.

Petticrew, M. and Roberts, H. (2006) *Systematic Reviews in the Social Sciences: A Practical Guide.* Oxford: Blackwell.

Pigott, T. and Shepperd, S. (2013) Identifying, documenting, and examining heterogeneity in systematic reviews of complex interventions. *Journal of Clinical Epidemiology*, **66**, 11, 1244–50.

Pope, C., Mays, N. and Popay, J. (2006) How can we synthesize qualitative and quantitative evidence for healthcare policy-makers and managers? *Healthcare Management Forum*, **19**, 1, 27–31.

Pope, C., Mays, N. and Popay, J. (2007) *Synthesising Qualitative and Quantitative Health Evidence: A Guide to Methods.* Maidenhead: Open University Press.

Pope, C., Ziebland, S., and Mays, N. (2000) Qualitative research in health care: analysing qualitative data. *BMJ*, **320**, 114–16.

Rajić, A., Young, I. and McEwen, S.A. (2013) Improving the utilization of research knowledge in agri-food public health: a mixed-method review of knowledge translation and transfer. *Foodborne Pathogens and Disease*, **10**, 5, 397–412.

Ritchie, J. and Spencer, L. (1993) Qualitative data analysis for applied policy research. In A. Bryman and R. Burgess (eds), *Analysing Qualitative Data.* London: Routledge, 173–94.

Roberts, K.A., Dixon-Woods, M., Fitzpatrick, R., Abrams, K.R. and Jones, D.R. (2002) Factors affecting the uptake of childhood immunisation: a Bayesian synthesis of qualitative and quantitative evidence. *The Lancet*, **360**, 1596–9.

Sandelowski, M. (1995) Qualitative analysis: what it is and how to begin. *Research in Nursing and Health*, **18**, 371–5.

Sandelowski, M. (2008) Reading, writing and systematic review. *Journal of Advanced Nursing*, **64**, 1, 104–10.

Sandelowski, M., Docherty, S. and Emden, C. (1997) Qualitative metasynthesis: issues and techniques, *Research in Nursing and Health*, **20**, 4, 365–71.

Siau, K. and Long, Y. (2005) Synthesizing e-government stage models – a meta-synthesis based on meta-ethnography approach. *Industrial Management and Data Systems*, **105**, 4, 443–58.

Snilstveit, B., Oliver, S. and Vojtkova, M. (2012) Narrative approaches to systematic review and synthesis of evidence for international development policy and practice. *Journal of Development Effectiveness*, **4**, 3, 409–29.

Squires, J.E., Valentine, J.C. and Grimshaw, J.M. (2013) Systematic reviews of complex interventions: framing the review question. *Journal of Clinical Epidemiology*, **66**, 11, 1215–22.

Suri, H. (1999) The process of synthesising qualitative research: a case study. Annual Conference of the Association for Qualitative Research, Melbourne.

Suri, H. and Clarke, D. (2009) Advancements in research synthesis methods: from a methodologically inclusive perspective. *Review of Educational Research*, **79**, 1, 395–430.

Tharyan, P. (2013) Introducing conceptual and analytical clarity on dimensions of complexity in systematic reviews of complex interventions. *Journal of Clinical Epidemiology*, **66**, 11, 1202–4.

Thomas, J., Harden, A., Oakley, A., Oliver, S., Sutcliffe, K., Rees, R., Brunton, G. and Kavanagh, J. (2004) Integrating qualitative research with trials in systematic reviews. *BMJ*, **328**, 1010–12.

Thomas, J., Kavanagh, J., Tucker, H., Burchett, H., Tripney, J. and Oakley, A. (2007) *Accidental Injury, Risk-taking Behaviour and the Social Circumstances in which Young People Live: A Systematic Review*. London: EPPI-Centre, Social Science Research Unit, Institute of Education, University of London.

Thomas, J., Sutcliffe, K., Harden, A., Oakley, A., Oliver, S., Rees, R., Brunton, G. and Kavanagh, J. (2003) *Children and Healthy Eating: A Systematic Review of Barriers and Facilitators*. London: EPPI-Centre, Social Science Research Unit, Institute of Education, University of London.

Toye, F., Seers, K., Allcock, N., Briggs, M., Carr, E. and Barker, K. (2014) Meta-ethnography 25 years on: challenges and insights for synthesising a large number of qualitative studies. *BMC Medical Research Methodology*, **14**, 80. DOI: 10.1186/1471-2288-14-80.

Tranfield, D., Denyer, D. and Smart, P. (2003) Towards a methodology for developing evidence-informed management knowledge by means of systematic review. *British Journal of Management*, **14**, 207–22

Tugwell, P., Petticrew, M., Kristjansson, E., Welch, V., Ueffing, E., Waters, E., Bonnefoy, J., Morgan, A., Doohan, E. and Kelly, M.P. (2010) Assessing equity in systematic reviews: realising the recommendations of the Commission on Social Determinants of Health. *BMJ*, **341**, c4739.

Voils, C., Hasselblad, V., Crandell, J., Chang, Y., Lee, E. and Sandelowski, M. (2009) A Bayesian method for the synthesis of evidence from qualitative and quantitative reports: the example of antiretroviral medication adherence. *Journal of Health Services Research and Policy*, **14**, 4, 226–33.

Wallace, A., Croucher, K., Quilgars, D. and Baldwin, S. (2003) Meeting the challenge: developing systematic reviewing in social policy. Paper presented to Social Policy Association Conference, University of Teeside, 16 July.

Walt, G. and Gilson, L. (2014) Can frameworks inform knowledge about health policy processes? Reviewing health policy papers on agenda setting and testing them against a specific priority-setting framework. *Health Policy Plan*, 29, Suppl. 3, 6–22.

Webb, G., Shakeshaft, A., Sanson-Fisher, R. and Havard, A. (2009) A systematic review of workplace interventions for alcohol-related problems. *Addiction*, **104**, 3, 365–77.

Whitaker, R., Hendry, M., Booth, A., Carter, B., Charles, J., Craine, N., Edwards, R.T., Lyons, M., Noyes, J., Pasterfield, D., Rycroft-Malone, J. and Williams, N. (2014) Intervention Now To Eliminate Repeat Unintended Pregnancy in Teenagers (INTERUPT): a systematic review of intervention effectiveness and cost-effectiveness, qualitative and realist synthesis of implementation factors and user engagement. *BMJ Open*, **4**, 4, e004733.

Whittemore, R. and Knafl, K. (2005) The integrative review: updated methodology. *Journal of Advanced Nursing*, **52**, 5, 546–53.

Yin, R.K. (1991) Advancing rigorous methodologies: a review of 'towards rigor in reviews of multivocal literatures'. *Review of Educational Research*, **61**, 3, 299.

WRITING, PRESENTING AND DISSEMINATING YOUR REVIEW

 **in a nutshell**

How to write up, present and share your review findings

- Writing up and presenting data from a systematic approach to the literature requires that you consider your audience and your message.
- Increasingly reporting standards specify what you should include when reporting your review.
- Typically you should consider both recommendations for research and recommendations for practice.
- You should choose methods for data presentation that illustrate key messages from your review.

INTRODUCTION

As mentioned throughout this book, many inherent advantages of systematic approaches to reviewing the literature relate to the transparency and auditability of the review product. While a subject expert may be tempted to present minimal detail on the methods of the review, preferring to concentrate on the findings, it is the methods that contribute to the credibility and objectivity of the final review. As a review author, you must not only consider the nature of your topic and the methods of your chosen type of review. You must also give detailed consideration to your audience. As Major and Savin-Baden (2010) emphasise:

> in presenting the synthesis, it is critical for synthesists to speak directly to a specific intended audience. Further we suggest that the selection of an intended audience is likely to drive decisions about how the synthesis is presented.

IDENTIFYING RECOMMENDATIONS FOR ACTION

Having completed your review you may be able to identify methods or interventions that can be utilised in practice. Not all review results will automatically be able to be used in this way. Many factors will have a bearing on whether research may be applied within a specific context (Dekkers et al., 2009). If you are going to be able to apply the results of your review to the outside world, you will need a good picture of the context in which these are to be implemented. You may already have such a picture as a practitioner-researcher. Alternatively, you may need to engage with a steering group to advise on the implications of your findings.

You can also tailor your recommendations through consultation documents, interim presentation of results to review commissioners, stakeholder conferences and presentations at professional meetings. This iterative process, when your findings are fresh and their interpretation still fluid, is as integral to the analysis phase as to the subsequent presentation and dissemination. Other factors involved in judging how you may apply your review findings to the external world may be more technical, informed by a detailed knowledge of the eligibility criteria for your review (Dekkers et al., 2009). If you decide to focus your review for practical and logistic reasons this may limit its wider applicability to populations outside your main focus.

A further constraint on your recommendations for practice is the extent of reporting of included studies. You may not have sufficient information in the original reports for you to judge the external validity and applicability of included studies. Glasziou and colleagues (2008) examined reports of non-drug treatments that had been shown to be promising and found deficiencies in the description of interventions that made it impossible to replicate these in practice. Even where the characteristics of the intervention itself are clearly described there may be correspondingly little detail on *how* it has been implemented. Work on **implementation fidelity** identified at least six factors that may determine how well an intervention actually works in practice when compared with its evaluation in empirical studies (Carroll et al., 2007).

HIGHLIGHTING RECOMMENDATIONS FOR FUTURE RESEARCH

Any review has the potential to identify research gaps. However, the familiar semi-serious injunction for all researchers to start writing up with the statement 'Further research is needed' is rightly treated with caution. Given that one of the objectives of the review is to consolidate a body of evidence, you should seek to be as specific as possible about what is lacking in research conducted to date. Does a theoretical framework already exist for the review area? If so, does it require further exploration or validation? If not, are we any further in identifying what its essential features might be? Have any population groups that might benefit from an intervention been under-researched or completely neglected? Has the potential effectiveness of an intervention been mooted or already explored in small-scale studies? How large does a rigorous **randomised controlled trial** need to be to establish such effectiveness conclusively? Are any adjustments to an intervention, suggested by stakeholders or by qualitative synthesis, yet to be investigated for effectiveness? Are the right outcomes being measured and reported (Moher et al., 2007)?

The American Educational Research Association (2006) explains how new research can contribute to existing research (see Box 10.1). These purposes apply equally well to the main contributions of evidence synthesis (see Exercise 10.1).

 box 10.1

The contribution of evidence synthesis to existing research

Theory testing or validation: if a review is a contribution to an established line of theory and empirical research, it should make clear what the contributions are and how the study contributes to testing, elaborating or enriching that theoretical perspective.

Theory generation: if a review is intended to establish a new line of theory, it should make clear what that new theory is, how it relates to existing theories and evidence, why the new theory is needed, and the intended scope of its application.

Problem solving: if a review is motivated by practical concerns, it should make clear what those concerns are, why they are important, and how this investigation can address those concerns.

Fact finding: if a review is motivated by a lack of information about a problem or issue, the problem formation should make clear what information is lacking, why it is important, and how this investigation addresses the need for information.

 exercise 10.1

The contribution of new research

Look at the four contributions that new research can make to existing research (see Box 10.1). Which seem particularly relevant to your own review? Are any contributions that your review might make not covered by these four generic headings?

CONSIDERING YOUR AUDIENCE

Why might a particular review fail to capitalise on structured methods of review presentation? Concerns with technical detail or methodological niceties may interfere with the intended message or may even lead to them being considered boring (Greenhalgh, 2012). The measured, cautious tone of a review with its acknowledgement of nuances may mask the potential usefulness of the review findings. In particular, the comprehensive identification of similar evidence in multiple contexts and circumstances may appear to offer contradictory advice. The source reports may lack the detail required to replicate an intervention or programme, even when demonstrated to be effective. The Template for Intervention Description and Replication (TIDieR) checklist represents a recent attempt to improve reporting of intervention characteristics (Hoffman et al., 2013; Hoffman et al., 2014). The review team may have addressed a deliberately narrow question to make it easier to conduct the review. This may limit the range of options covered thereby constraining its usefulness and applicability. Particular sectors of the community may be excluded, either from the evidence base or from the review conclusions. Finally, the time taken to conduct the review may mean that the preferred option has changed or been overtaken by external events. Clearly a review team should try to anticipate many concerns early in the review process, particularly at the commissioning and scoping stages (see Chapter 5). This chapter therefore focuses on aspects that are yet to be determined prior to writing up the review.

No review product has a *single* target audience (Hammersley, 2002). However you should always be able to identify the *primary* audience for your review:

> whenever we address a particular audience we have to take account of what we can assume they already know, what they would and would not be interested in, and perhaps also what they might misinterpret. (Hammersley, 2002)

You should therefore seek to prioritise those aspects of presentation that relate to the primary audience without compromising too much on the needs of other, secondary, audiences (see Exercise 10.2). However, you will also need to add the all-too-important ingredient of political context to any technical requirements:

> We need to take account of the politics of how reviews are received and read by audiences. The reception of reviews is often driven by audiences' current preoccupations, and guided by relatively fixed preconceptions. (Hammersley, 2002)

Political concerns may appear less important if the intended output is an academic piece of work, particularly for a dissertation or doctorate. However, you will often need to adapt the tone of the accompanying narrative to the prior state of belief of the audience and where you intend them to be upon completion of the review. Do you need to exhort, reason, cajole or even berate? To a certain degree, the tone you adopt depends upon whether you are trying to encourage your audience to adopt some new method or technique (start-starting), to dispense with an ineffective practice (start-stopping), to maintain proven good practice (stop-stopping), to resist the lure of an ineffective technology (stop-starting) (Nicoll et al., 2000) or simply to open their minds to a tentative future possibility.

 **exercise 10.2**

Consumers of your review

In marketing terms, we think about a synthesis product in terms of its primary audience (the main consumers of your review) and its secondary audiences (others who may be interested in your review. For example, the primary audience of a review included in your thesis might be

(Continued)

(Continued)

the external examiner and secondary audiences might be your supervisor, other academics in your discipline and, possibly, practitioners in your chosen field.

For your own review complete the following grid.

Primary audience(s)	What do I already know about their reading preferences? How could I find out more about their reading preferences?
Secondary audience(s)	What do I already know about their reading preferences? How could I find out more about their reading preferences?

Writing for research funders

Research funders want you to reassure them that they have made a wise investment of the money entrusted to your care. They are particularly interested in incremental knowledge gains made as a result of the review. They will also be interested in the added value that a systematically conducted review offers over and above other possible research approaches, whether these involve primary research or other types of synthesis. Finally, they will want to know if you have identified any other areas for research, either follow-up questions identified in the course of your review or proximate areas that you have not covered in your own work. Your research funders will find it particularly helpful if you identify first what is already known about the topic, and second what this review adds. You will find it helpful to summarise your own review as two boxes of bulletpoints and then to use this structure to construct your own conclusions.

A further feature of interest is *recommendations for future research*. The ubiquitous conclusion 'More research is needed' is justifiably viewed with disdain (Phillips, 2001). If you have spent many person-hours immersing yourself in the literature covered by the review, you will quite rightly be expected to be able to identify specifically what has or has not been researched or where considerable uncertainty remains. It is also helpful if you give a clear idea of the specific question and the type of research required in future to provide an answer (see EPICOT+ in the tools section of this chapter). Rather than generate a seemingly endless list of areas for future research, you should think in terms of a finite amount of funds and prioritise research that is both feasible and important. You should continue to write as an honest broker and not as a potential beneficiary of future research commissioned in the area; if you subsequently happen to benefit from a gap that you have highlighted, then this is an unexpected bonus.

Writing for policy makers

Although policy makers will wish to know that the conclusions of your review are based on high-quality research studies wherever possible, they are particularly interested in the external validity (or generalisability) of your review (Ahmad et al., 2010). In other words, they want to know the extent to which the results of your review can be reasonably applied or generalised to a definable population/populations in a particular context. If studies have not been conducted within the setting of interest, they will want to know any limitations or reservations they might have in applying results across contexts. They will also want to have an idea of the limitations of the evidence in terms of any unresolved areas of uncertainty.

You should particularly bear in mind that policy makers need reviews for decision support (to provide answers or direction) rather than for knowledge support (Pope et al., 2006). Reviews that plumb lower-level study types, provided that you clearly state the consequences of doing so, add value over general non-actionable conclusions that 'robust studies are unable to provide answers'. Similarly, policy makers appreciate a more holistic picture of all issues to inform their decision (i.e. they should 'address the full range of questions asked by managers and policymakers') rather than a simple lens offering an answer to a very tightly focused question. Increasingly, models of iterative interaction involve decision makers in the entire review process, from asking the research questions to providing a context for the question under study (Lavis et al., 2006; Pope et al., 2006).

As well as a focus on pragmatic answers, policy makers are interested in how reviews are presented. In particular it is helpful if they can be:

> more easily scanned for relevance, decision-relevant information, and factors that would influence assessments for local applicability. (Lavis et al., 2006)

In some cases, this need has led to reviews being presented in the 1:3:25 format (involving corresponding numbers of pages for take-home messages (1), the executive summary (3), and the full systematic review (25) (Lavis et al., 2005, 2006).

Writing for practitioners

A well-conducted systematic review is invaluable for practitioners. Many feel overwhelmed by the volume of literature in their discipline. As a consequence they often prefer summaries of information to publications of original investigations (Williamson, 1989). Review articles can help practitioners keep up to date. High-quality systematic reviews can define the boundaries of what is known and what is not known and can help to avoid knowing less than has been proven. Single studies rarely provide definitive answers, but systematic reviews can help practitioners solve specific problems. By critically examining primary studies, systematic reviews improve understanding of why different sources of research evidence yield conflicting or inconsistent answers. By quantitatively combining the results of several small studies, **meta-analyses** can create more precise, powerful and convincing conclusions. In addition, **systematic reviews** including multiple studies may better inform decision makers about whether findings can be applied to specific subgroups of the population.

Several commentators have expressed concern at the limitations of systematic reviews where evidence is limited, for example in so-called empty reviews (Yaffe et al., 2012) or where there is only a single study (Pagliaro et al., 2010). Practitioners seem to favour having some evidence, albeit of low quality, over no evidence. It is essential to consult with current practitioners so that a rigorous technical process is not applied to studies of an intervention that no longer reflects standard practice, producing an outdated review (Pagliaro et al., 2010). Similar reservations relate to the length of reviews (typically 40 pages or more) and the unhelpfulness of their recommendations for practice (Pagliaro et al., 2010). Clearly, such concerns have implications for the writing up of reviews; many relate back to the scoping of the review (see Chapter 5).

Writing for the research community

The research community is particularly interested in well-conducted reviews because these help to identify gaps in the evidence base and provide a quantitative basis for informing new research initiatives. Typically, a researcher responding to a funding call will seek to find a systematic review or overview around which they can build their argument for a research proposal. In particular contexts, a systematic review may be of significant value in designing new studies (Cooper et al., 2005). However, it is still true to say that reviews are not as heavily used in the design of studies as we might expect. Within medicine, there has been a recent and welcome trend to require that study authors identify related studies when presenting their own primary research. This imperative seeks to reduce the numbers of 'islands without continents, i.e. primary studies that fail to make a connection with their own evidence base (Clarke and Chalmers, 1998). Increasingly funders provide vignettes as part of the tender documentation that refer to findings from relevant systematic reviews. Certainly, the inclusion of encouragement in guidelines for publication or for funding applications to consider and cite review results is a trend to be welcomed.

Writing for the media

It is frequently observed that the interests of the review author and the journalist fail to correspond. At best, the interaction between these two parties may seem a short-lived marriage of convenience. Certainly the 'discovery value' of research synthesis pales alongside the dramatic laboratory experiment or the miracle cure. Nevertheless a review author can place great store by the fact that findings from a review carry more accumulated weight than a single study.

In 1996 Smith bemoaned the absence of systematic approaches to reviewing the evidence base:

> We are, through the media, as ordinary citizens, confronted daily with controversy and debate across a whole spectrum of public policy issues. But typically, we have no access to any form of a systematic 'evidence base' – and therefore no means of participating in the debate in a mature and informed manner. (Smith, 1996)

Fortunately this situation has been undergoing gradual change over the last 20 years. Reviewers are starting to emphasise that the methodology of synthesis may result in the first occasion when one has been able to see the whole picture from otherwise conflicting research. Another selling point is the cumulative number of subjects, patients, studies or events that the review considers when compared with a single paper. Table 10.1 illustrates ways in which reviewers have attempted to communicate the features of their approach to journalists and, ultimately, to the public.

Writing for the public

A review author has two particular challenges in communicating the results of their review to the public. The first relates to the specific knowledge associated with the topic. This typically requires the simplification of concepts, definition of unfamiliar terms and the use of

Table 10.1 Lay explanations of systematic reviews from media reports

Definition	Source
'Systematic reviews are an important tool for scientists; unlike ordinary reviews, they are seen as original research and help to provide clarity in areas of uncertainty. The basic underpinning of a systematic review is that the process of conducting the review is pre-specified and that the review itself is as comprehensive as possible within these pre-specified limits. Reviews that are not systematic are much more prone to bias, especially with regards to the selection of papers included for review'.	*The Times*: Great minds: attack science at your own risk (7 January 2010)
'... the treatment they receive whether alternative or mainstream, is based not simply on single studies but on a systematic review of all the evidence available'.	*The Times*: Effective medicine (27 May 2006)
'In its thoroughness, transparency and even-handedness this review is, we believe, the only scientifically defensible assessment of the evidence worldwide'.	*Sunday Times*: Letters to the editor: let us come clean on water fluoridation (18 May 2003)
'One good-quality summary of the research (a systematic review), which included almost 900 people'.	*Guardian*: Heel pain, what treatments work? (2 March 2010)
'A systematic review is a thorough look through published research on a particular topic. Only studies that have been carried out to a high standard are included. A systematic review may or may not include a meta-analysis, which is when the results from individual studies are put together'.	*Guardian*: Heel pain, what treatments work? (2 March 2010)
'Researchers ... pooled together data from 15 studies looking at pain-killer use and Alzheimer's. More than 14,600 participants were involved. Observational studies had previously suggested ... but the results were inconclusive'.	*Daily Mail*: Pill 'cure' for Alzheimer's (18 July 2003)
' ... the result was not statistically significant. However, this may only have been because the number of studies specifically evaluating the effects of aspirin was small'.	
'The findings come from a review of 25 studies ... the University researchers said: "This systematic review contributes a rigorous and objective synthesis of the evidence for added benefits ...".'	*Daily Mail*: Jogging in the park boosts energy and improves mood more than going to the gym (10 August 2010)

more easily accessible terminology. However, the second relates to the nature of the review product, its methodology and its inherent advantages over single studies and over other types of (non-systematic) review.

You will find it helpful in this context to use a definition of the review that, rather than focusing simply on the technical superiority of the methods used, stresses the relative advantage of the methodology.

WHAT IS REQUIRED

There are many reasons why systematic approaches to the literature are considered valuable when presenting research findings. We consider just four attributes under the acronym of CART (*c*larity-*a*uditability-*r*eplicability-*t*ransparency). In highlighting the relative importance of these four criteria (while not necessarily attempting to put the CART before the horse!) we deliberately exclude criteria such as comprehensiveness (a claimed virtue for quantitative systematic reviews), present in some but not all such systematic approaches.

Clarity

While clarity has always been a desired characteristic in scientific communication, albeit seen more in the breach than the observance, systematic approaches to the literature frequently seek to take these to a further degree. Clarity should be present in the research question, in the methodology, in the presentation of findings, in discussing the limitations of method and/or evidence and in relating the conclusions back to the original question. Furthermore the structured nature of the reporting for many such approaches imposes a further clarity on the review product as a whole making it easier to navigate and interpret.

Auditability

Creating an audit trail has always been a requirement of good quality research and it should come as no surprise that it similarly figures in the context of evidence synthesis. The reviewer seeks to carefully document all of the steps that are taken in conducting the review. This audit trail serves as documentation to make clear the evidence that supports each finding, where that evidence can be found, and how that evidence was interpreted (Randolph, 2009). It may be used subsequently to defend a finding or interpretation, although typically systematic approaches to the literature seek to anticipate and forestall such potential criticism.

Replicability

The quest for reproducibility has long been a major driver in the development of systematic approaches to reviewing the literature. Research indicates that the conclusions of one narrative review can differ completely from another review written by a different author, even when exactly the same articles are reviewed (Light and Pillemer, 1984). In preference to reproducibility, which suggests the repeatability of laboratory experiments, many commentators favour the term **replicability**. This recognises that the intention may well be to create a finished product that closely resembles its predecessor. In a sense we recognise that 'the mould was broken' when a systematically conducted review was completed, but by giving careful attention to detail and use of many of the same techniques, we can minimise inconsistencies and produce a product that is essentially similar. Such inconsistencies are still present in more systematic approaches, but at least their influence is more readily identified, more completely understood, and appropriate remedial actions attempted. For example Popay and colleagues (2006) demonstrated, in an interpretive context, that *even the same reviewer* may develop a different line of argument on successive days. Furthermore, there is increasing recognition that, even for the **gold standard** systematic review, differences in search methods or the differential application of inclusion criteria can result in different review products. As multiple reviews start to appear on identical or at least closely related topics, it becomes clearer that the focus should be more on identifying and explaining such differences rather than eliminating them completely.

In qualitative evidence synthesis, reviewers may decide to reveal their own pre-existing biases and discuss how those biases might have affected the review. This approach, known as **reflexivity**, mirrors that encouraged for primary qualitative research where the investigator reflects on the effect of their own position as researcher. Indeed, one approach to qualitative synthesis, that known as **critical interpretive synthesis**, harnesses personalised interpretation which acts against **replicability**. Such approaches belong within a research tradition of recognising that there are multiple truths and that by constructing a narrative, in the form of a review, the reviewer is privileging one of many possible interpretations.

In contrast, in quantitative evidence synthesis the reviewer is encouraged to take a neutral perspective, acting as an honest broker with the data and presenting the review findings as fact. Such reviews belong within a tradition where the reviewer seeks to communicate a single truth but many factors (biases), whether conscious or subconscious, may deflect them from their intention. Mechanisms for handling the dangers of personal interpretation in quantitative reviews are crude by comparison; typically a **conflict of interest statement** identifies areas that relate almost exclusively to financial interest. To equate bias primarily with financial interest is to overlook the fact that researchers will include professionals delivering a service, parents of children receiving an educational intervention, carers of relatives receiving a healthcare or social care provision, taxpayers financing policy interventions, etc. The quest to minimise the effect of bias, or at least to make it easier to identify it where it may likely exist, will no doubt lead ultimately to a declaration or statement of prior beliefs. In this way the reader would be able to identify, for example, where an educator stands with regard to a teaching intervention or a clinician in connection with a new drug or surgical treatment.

Transparency

It is common to see claims of transparency for systematic reviews (The PLoS Medicine Editors, 2007), such as the following statement from the international **Campbell Collaboration** (n.d.):

> A systematic review uses transparent procedures to find, evaluate and synthesize the results of relevant research. Procedures are explicitly defined in advance, in order to ensure that the exercise is transparent and can be replicated.

While the quality of transparency is linked to replicability, it is typically attributed to the availability of supporting documentation such as procedure manuals. To date, little attention has been paid to the fidelity with which such procedures have been followed – the implication, albeit a suspect premise, is that the manual acts as a guarantor for all review products associated with that documentation. This is, perhaps, one step too close to the 'eminence based' practice of the past which judged published outputs according to their author or the journal in which they were published. The emphasis should be on the ability of the reader to make their own judgements on review quality. The redeeming feature of transparency is that it makes such judgements more practicable.

A SAMPLE REVIEW STRUCTURE

Once you have completed the data extraction, quality assessment, synthesis and analysis of the literature, you will need to consider how your review will be structured and written. The key to a good academic paper is the ability to present the findings in such a way that it demonstrates your mastery of the review topic. To some extent, the structure of your review will depend upon its purpose. For example, systematic reviews have a clear structure that must be followed and that will dictate for the most part how the writing should be undertaken. However, many readers will be conducting their review as part of a coursework assignment, research proposal or research dissertation. As such you will need an overall direction of travel and a few major signposts but you will be able to maintain some freedom in how your writing is structured. The structure of your review report should be immediately apparent to its reader. It is therefore important to be logical, and you will find that some key elements will need to be included in *all* literature reviews (Aveyard, 2014) (see Box 10.2).

 **box 10.2**

Key elements in reporting a literature review

1. Title.
2. Abstract.
3. Introduction.
4. Methods.
5. Results.
6. Discussion.
7. Conclusion.

This structure is familiar in that it uses the IMRAD (*i*ntroduction-*m*ethods-*r*esults-*a*nd-*d*iscussion) format required when presenting any primary scientific report (Burns and Grove, 2007). This is also the structure largely employed when following the PRISMA statement used to report 'full-blown' systematic reviews in peer-reviewed journals (see the section on reporting standards later in this chapter). The only areas of difference are that the conclusion becomes subsumed under the heading of 'Discussion' and the seventh element becomes 'funding'. The PRISMA statement aims

> to help authors report a wide array of systematic reviews to assess the benefits and harms of a health care intervention. PRISMA focuses on ways in which authors can ensure the transparent and complete reporting of systematic reviews and meta-analyses. (Moher et al., 2009)

However, as already demonstrated, the similarities between PRISMA and generic approaches to study reporting make it a useful template for reviews using systematic approaches in any discipline. We shall expand on each of these seven areas. However, the reader is referred to the most up-to-date version of the PRISMA statement.

Title: increasingly, scientific reports not only include a meaningful title indicating the subject but also, following a colon, a subtitle indicating the study type such as, 'The impact of learning on unemployed, low-qualified adults: a systematic review'. Alternatively a **meta-analysis** may have a title such as: 'A systematic review and meta-analysis of set-shifting ability in eating disorders'. The important point is that, by having the study type in the title, you increase the chance of a reader identifying and retrieving the study report from internet or database searches and of an indexer coding it correctly when adding terms to a database record. The importance of indicating the study type in the title is true for other systematic approaches such as 'a rapid evidence assessment', 'a meta-ethnography', etc.

Abstract: structured abstracts improve the chance that your work will be identified. They also prompt the author to provide essential details concerning the review. Typical headings that can be used for a review abstract include background; objectives; data sources; study eligibility criteria, participants and interventions; study appraisal and synthesis methods; results; limitations; conclusions and implications of key findings; systematic review registration number. In essence, the abstract is a review in miniature and a reader should be able to identify immediately how well you searched, how many studies you reviewed and what your main conclusions are. Typically, the abstract should not exceed 250–300 words although you should check individual journals for their specific requirements. The abstract should be sufficiently informative to provide the reader with a brief picture of the overall findings; it should therefore reveal and not tantalise (e.g. avoid statements such as 'The review goes on to describe findings of critical importance to all practitioners', but state briefly instead what these findings are). Generally, commentators recommend that the abstract is undertaken last so that it reflects the final emphasis of the review that it summarises (Hendry and Farley, 1998).

Introduction: this will provide essential details concerning the starting point for the review. These will include a rationale for the review in the context of what is already known and a structured statement of the review question using either **PICOS** (Participants, Interventions, Comparisons, Outcomes and Study design) or some equivalent such as **SPICE** (Setting, Perspective, phenomenon of Interest, Comparison, Evaluation) or **PICOC** (Population, Intervention, Comparison, Outcomes, Context). Typically we encourage review authors to provide a convincing argument for the importance of the review in terms of how common the problem is, how serious its consequences, how costly it is, and its impact both on services and on society more widely. If genuine controversy exists, perhaps seen in significant variations in practice, this should be acknowledged and both sides of the argument characterised as even-handedly as possible.

Methods: the length of literature reviews varies considerably and word limits must be considered when assigning the proportion of the available coverage between the methods and the results, discussion and conclusion. While the extent of the description of methods depends on the type of review you are undertaking and the degree of rigour it requires, it is probably best to start from a complete list of possible items for inclusion and then to pare this down according to your specific requirements. If the review is a formal production for a government agency or an international collaboration, you may wish to indicate where a review protocol exists and how it may be accessed. Some journals will allow you to submit your review protocol as supplementary online material. You might then proceed through such data elements as the eligibility criteria, the information sources accessed, the search strategies, and the process for study selection. Guidelines have been suggested for reporting search strategies (Booth, 2006; Higgins and Green,

2011; Sampson et al., 2008; Sampson et al., 2009) (see Table 10.2) although evidence suggests that these have been imperfectly implemented (Yoshii et al., 2009).

You would continue with details of the data collection process and the list of data items or variables of interest. Formal review processes, as used by the Cochrane Collaboration, then require details of the risk of **bias** within individual studies (i.e. a description of methods used for quality assessment) and the risk of bias across studies (see sections in Chapter 8 on **publication bias** and **selective reporting**). You will also give details of the data being summarised whether by quantitative summary measures (e.g. risk ratio, difference in means), or by qualitative concepts or themes. Finally, having described your methods of synthesis you will proceed to your methods of analysis (see Chapters 8 and 9). Again, these may be either quantitative (**sensitivity** or **subgroup analyses**, meta-regression) or more qualitative assessments of the robustness of the results and possible explanations for findings.

At this point we have reviewed just over half of the items expanded in more detail in the 27-item PRISMA checklist. Only now have we reached the results. This emphasises that, while you as a reviewer may be most interested in the review question and its findings, the reader first needs convincing that your review product is up to the task.

Results: this section starts with a quantitative summary of the number of items identified and then moves on to the detail of the individual studies. A subsection on study selection will give numbers of studies screened, assessed for eligibility, and included in the review, with reasons for exclusions at each stage. Increasingly there is a requirement, as with the PRISMA statement, to produce a flow diagram. Our experience is that this is a useful aid for the reader for any type of review utilising systematic approaches. Tabulation is important in describing the study characteristics (e.g. study size, PICOS, follow-up period) and in providing an easy look-up reference point to the individual citations in the reference list. Again you will present results for your assessments of the risk of bias within studies and the risk of bias across studies. These assessments will typically

Table 10.2 Guidelines for reporting search strategies

Cochrane (effectiveness) Reviews (Higgins and Green, 2011).	Qualitative systematic reviews (Booth, 2006) (STARLITE)	
Databases searched	S:	Sampling strategy (e.g. purposive, theoretical, comprehensive)
Name of host	T:	Type of studies
Date search was run	A:	Approaches (other than electronic subject searches covered in the electronic sources section), e.g. hand searching; citation snowballing, etc.)
Years covered by search	R:	Range of years (start date to end date)
Complete search strategy	L:	Limits
One or two sentence summary of the search strategy	I:	Inclusion and exclusions
Language restrictions	T:	Terms used
	E:	Electronic sources (reports databases used and, optimally, search platforms, and vendors to assist in replication)

precede the very important sections reporting the results of individual studies and the synthesis of results respectively. Such sections utilise presentation features including tables and **Forest plots** for each meta-analysis and thematic summaries, diagrams and displays for qualitative data. If using a thematic approach, the account should flow logically from one section or theme to the next, to maintain continuity and consistency (Beyea and Nicholl, 1998). This can be achieved by summarising each theme or section and outlining how it is related to the theme that follows.

Discussion: up to this point you have provided the reader with the 'crude' evidence, so you now need to proceed to the *discussion* which corresponds to the 'refined' by-products that allow the findings to be utilised and interpreted by its 'consumer'. You should start with a summary of evidence giving particular attention to the strength of evidence associated with each finding. Having previously identified the main audiences for your review, you should seek to provide each of these with the information they need to answer their particular issues or questions. As Cronin and colleagues (2008) identify, you will also need to spend a significant amount of time discussing the limitations of your review both in terms of the characteristics of the included studies, any inconsistencies and contradictions, and what you have or have not been able to do in relation to the review as a whole. They highlight that your role here is to summarise and evaluate evidence about your topic, pointing out similarities and differences and offering possible explanations for any inconsistencies uncovered (Polit and Beck, 2006). If your literature review has been conceived and designed to inform the objectives, design or conduct of a follow-up primary study, any gaps in knowledge that have been identified should feed into the purpose of the proposed study. In some cases, it may also be possible to use developed themes to construct a conceptual framework or **logic model** to inform the study (Baxter et al., 2010). Finally, you will return to what was previously known, as described in your 'Introduction', to provide a general interpretation of the results in the context of other evidence, and implications for future practice and/or research (*conclusions*). All reviews will be able to provide some recommendations or implications for practice and for research, with the emphasis between each being determined by the extent to which the review question could be answered. If you are following the PRISMA statement you will conclude with *funding*, describing sources of funding for the systematic review and other support (e.g. supply of data) as well as the role of funders for the systematic review. As previously mentioned, this may be an appropriate juncture to identify other types of *conflict of interest*. It should also act as a prompt to you in providing *acknowledgements* to those who provided substantive support to the review but do not qualify for authorship.

Exercise 10.3 now asks you to apply what you have just learnt about report structure to your own review.

 **exercise 10.3**

Producing a draft report structure

Produce a draft report structure for your review using the sections described above. Try to allocate an appropriate word limit to each section based on the size and scope of your review and its intended focus.

STANDARDS FOR THE REPORTING OF REVIEWS

Increasing recognition of the importance of transparency in scientific research, particularly given that much is financed from the public purse, has led in recent years to a veritable industry of publication guidelines and templates for presentation. While few can argue against the benefits of effective communication, opinion is more divided when it comes to such publication conventions. Some would argue that attempts to homogenise the presentation of research make published reports more bland and less informative. In addition, it can introduce a tendency to conceal rather than reveal; for example, encouragement of stock phrases such as 'References were followed up and contact was made with authors' may mask individual differences that are in themselves revealing. Finally, the contents of checklists may focus on the instrumentality of a review, not its overall quality. For example, it is generally agreed that it is good practice to include an appendix with a complete search strategy on a primary bibliographic database (or on all databases according to *Cochrane Handbook* requirements: see Lefebvre et al., 2011). The same methods section that reports a detailed search process on bibliographic databases may, however, include a statement such as 'Internet searches were conducted using Bing'. Focusing on one easily measured aspect at the expense of a less easily measured but equally important alternative is like bolting a gate with a yawning gap in the fence.

As a reviewer of other people's studies, as opposed to being a review author, you can benefit from standardised reporting of individual primary studies. Standardised reporting makes the task of creating data extraction forms, using standard quality assessment checklists and tabulating data, more straightforward. However, as we have implied, this may be at the expense of informative detail of context or revealing slips in the reporting of methods.

Systematic reviews were, after randomised controlled trials, one of the first recipients of reporting standards. The quality of reporting of meta-analyses (QUOROM) statement (Moher et al., 2009) has existed for over a decade and has more recently been replaced by the PRISMA statement. Furthermore, separate conventions have been published for systematic reviews of observational studies (MOOSE) and for systematic reviews of diagnostic tests (STARD). Recent years have seen a tentative statement produced for reporting qualitative systematic reviews (ENTREQ) (Tong et al., 2012). However, this is still to be subjected to consensus processes. These statements typically contain standard headings under which specific detail is reported. They may also include a checklist of individual elements to be reported. Finally, a flow diagram of the progress of studies throughout the review process is frequently required, analogous to the flow diagram for patients through a trial required by the CONSORT statement (Schulz et al. and CONSORT Group, 2010). A book compiling publication reporting standards for both primary and secondary studies has recently been published (Moher et al., 2014) (see Exercise 10.4).

Notwithstanding the progressive emergence of such standards there is considerable variation in how mechanisms such as the flow diagram are used. Some authors use a strictly *chronological* approach, others superimpose a *logical* structure that may disguise inconsistencies or multiple iterations, yet others re-interpret the diagram as a means of describing *methodological* decision points (Hind and Booth, 2007). While each approach may be useful in different contexts such inconsistencies are potentially confusing.

Table 10.3 Most common standards for reporting studies

CONSORT Statement: Consolidated Standards Of Reporting Trials	The CONSORT Statement is intended to improve the reporting of a randomised controlled trial (RCT), enabling readers to understand a trial's design, conduct, analysis and interpretation, and to assess the validity of its results. It emphasises that this can only be achieved through complete transparency from authors.
PRISMA Statement (formerly QUOROM): Preferred Reporting Items for Systematic Reviews and Meta-Analyses	Statement aims to help authors report a wide array of systematic reviews to assess the benefits and harms of a healthcare intervention. PRISMA focuses on ways in which authors can ensure the transparent and complete reporting of systematic reviews and meta-analyses.
PRISMA-P: Preferred Reporting Items for Systematic review and Meta-Analysis Protocols	Contains 17 items considered to be essential and minimum components of a systematic review or meta-analysis protocol.
eMERGe Project: Developing guidelines for meta-ethnography reporting	New project (2016) in response to identified deficiencies in reporting of meta-ethnography (France et al., 2014).
ENTREQ Statement: Enhancing transparency in reporting the synthesis of qualitative research (Tong et al., 2012)	Statement seeks to help researchers report the stages most commonly associated with the synthesis of qualitative health research: searching and selecting qualitative research, quality appraisal and methods for synthesising qualitative findings.
MOOSE Statement: proposal for reporting meta-analysis of observational studies in epidemiology (Stroup et al., 2000)	Proposed checklist contains specifications for reporting, including background, search strategy, methods, results, discussion and conclusion. Use of checklist should improve usefulness of meta-analyses for authors, reviewers, editors, readers and decision makers.
RAMESES (Realist And Meta-narrative Evidence Syntheses: Evolving Standards): Meta-narrative reviews (Wong et al., 2013a)	Project aimed to produce preliminary publication standards for realist systematic reviews.
RAMESES (Realist And Meta-narrative Evidence Syntheses: Evolving Standards): Realist synthesis (Wong et al., 2013b)	Project aimed to produce preliminary publication standards for meta-narrative reviews.
STARD Statement: Standards for Reporting Studies of Diagnostic Accuracy	The objective of the STARD initiative is to improve the accuracy and completeness of reporting of studies of diagnostic accuracy.
STARLITE Statement: Standards for Reporting Literature Searches (Booth, 2006)	The mnemonic STARLITE (sampling strategy, type of study, approaches, range of years, limits, inclusion and exclusions, terms used, electronic sources) is used to convey the essential elements for reporting literature searches.
STROBE Statement (and STREGA): STrengthening the Reporting of OBservational studies in Epidemiology, guidelines for the reporting of genetic association studies (STREGA)	STROBE is an international collaboration of epidemiologists, methodologists, statisticians, researchers and journal editors involved in the conduct and dissemination of observational studies. A subsequent workshop developed guidelines for the reporting of genetic association studies (STREGA).

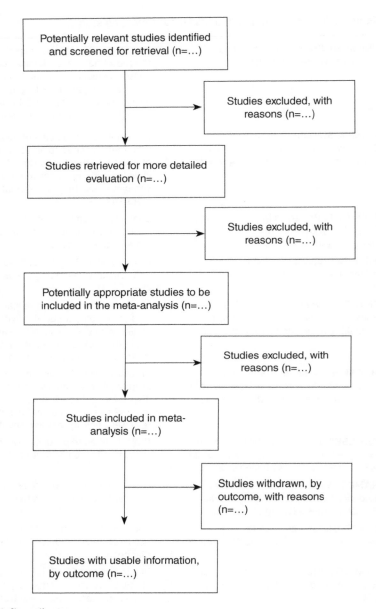

Figure 10.1 PRISMA flow diagram

exercise 10.4

Identifying and using reporting guidelines

Many guidelines for reporting, generic and specific, are contained at the useful EQUATOR Network Website. The main standards relating to reviews are given in Table 10.3.

Look at the EQUATOR Network Website. Which guidelines are most informative for your review? Identify the guideline and its source reference in the boxes provided. Once you find a reporting guideline appropriate to your review, revisit your draft review structure and revise it in view of the requirements.

- Reporting Guideline   Reference Citation

Flow of included studies

One of the most valuable, and self-evidently useful, features of the PRISMA statement is the flowchart for included studies. Indeed, such a flowchart is of potential value to other less-structured types of review, both in accounting for studies during conduct of the review and in subsequently reporting the review method. The PRISMA flow diagram (see Figure 10.1) depicts the flow of information through the different phases of a systematic review. It maps out the number of records identified, included and excluded, and the reasons for exclusions. At each stage, the vertical 'plughole' continuation box and the horizontal 'overflow' box should combine to total the number of studies in the preceding box, ensuring that studies are accounted for at each point of the process. The main caution in using such a diagram relates to the difference between references and papers (many duplicate references may have been identified from multiple databases) and the subsequent difference between papers and studies (one study may be represented by reports in multiple papers) (Hind and Booth, 2007). Indeed it may be helpful to signal transparently the transition from references to papers and from papers to studies.

USE OF TABLES AND FIGURES

Tables and figures can summarise vast quantities of data (as an alternative to an extensive description in the form of narrative text) or as a vehicle for illustrating and supporting what is already present in the narrative. Typically these will be used for a combination of both purposes. In this connection, it will be helpful to draw a distinction between 'summary tables' which are typically to be found within the text and tables of extracted data which are more likely to be included as appendices.

Useful subjects for summary tables will include a summary of:

1. study characteristics (e.g. number of participants, setting, study design, etc.);
2. methodological quality (e.g. whether comparative, which outcome measures have been used, response rates or completeness of follow-up, etc.);
3. results (an effect size (or list of themes) for each study; any confidence limits, etc.).

Such summary tables may typically be included within the main body of the text unless the number of included studies exceeds about 20. This is because they are less likely to provide the same disruption to the flow of the text as the more fully reported data extraction tables which may be placed in an appendix to increase the auditability of the review product.

If you have combined studies within a meta-analysis, then your report may include one or more Forest plots. While many meta-analysis software packages allow the export of such Forest plots, you must be aware that this technical facility may not completely meet the needs of publication (Schriger et al., 2010). If you need to relabel or even redraw such a display, you must pay careful attention to such details as the orientation of the diagram (is more of an outcome better or worse?), the captioning (what exactly is the outcome of interest?) and the point of no effect (does the Forest plot present a ratio? – in which case the point of no effect is represented by one – or does it present a difference? – in which case the point of no effect is signified by zero).

USE OF APPENDICES AND OTHER SUPPORTING FEATURES

While there is little formal guidance on what should and should not be included within appendices for a report of a structured literature review, an informal consensus is emerging as evidenced within published reports. Of course a major consideration will be whether the review is being published within a word-limited paper journal or within a larger technical report. The emergence of increasing numbers of online journals as a vehicle for systematic reviews has led to increasing flexibility with regard to published appendices. Typically, the following will be found in appendices:

1. At least one search strategy (and possibly all available search strategies) used for the review.
2. A sample data extraction form.
3. A list of excluded studies (only for those studies appearing to meet the Inclusion criteria but not included) with a brief reason for their exclusion.
4. Data extraction tables for included studies.
5. The checklist used (unless commonly available).
6. Results of quality assessments.

As awareness of the requirements for rigorous conduct and reporting increases, this list is likely to become even further expanded.

ACCURATE REFERENCING

The importance of a structured approach to the recording of bibliographic information on included studies has already been emphasised (Chapter 7). Every type of literature review should conclude with a full bibliographical list of all the books, journal articles, reports and other media referred to in the work. Every citation in the text must appear in the bibliography (reference list) and vice versa. Formally structured approaches to the literature such as systematic reviews frequently make a distinction between supporting materials from the background which go into a general reference list and a list of included studies. Analysis of supporting references for **Cochrane Reviews** yields one of the Collaboration's more memorable titles: 'Three bibles, three dictionaries, and nearly 25,000 other things' (Clarke and Clarke, 2000). You will find that it will save you much time at the critical stage towards the end of your review if you compile your list of references as you identify each new item. Although the internet has made reference checking much easier, it remains a time-consuming procedure and you cannot guarantee that other authors have correctly recorded their own references. Many academic supervisors use the reviews of their supervisees for regular updates in their main topics of interest. You therefore have an added incentive to ensure that your reference list is accurate.

 toolbox

Presenting your findings

A key challenge, once the literature review process has been completed, is to decide upon an appropriate method for presenting your findings to your chosen audience. This 'Tools' section looks firstly at the highly structured 1:3:25 report format increasingly favoured by policy makers. It then turns its attention specifically to the reporting of meaningful recommendations for future research using the EPICOT+ structure proposed by representatives of the Cochrane Collaboration and the Centre for Reviews and Dissemination.

1:3:25 report format

The 1:3:25 report format, used by such organisations such as the UK Home Office, Health and Safety Executive, and the Canadian Health Services Research Foundation, stems from recognition that writing a research summary for decision makers is not the same as writing an academic journal article. Because the reviewer has a different objective they are required to take a different approach.

Every 1:3:25 report follows the same guidelines: it begins with one page of main messages; followed up by a three-page executive summary; and concluded with findings presented in no more than 25 pages of writing, in language that is easy for a lay person to understand. Details of these three sections are as follows.

Main messages (the '1'): one page of main message bullets reporting the lessons decision makers can take from your review. These go beyond a summary of findings because they have to tell the audience what your findings mean for them. Writing main messages is a challenge for researchers who are typically trained to provide an objective and detached view of the evidence. You will have to strike a balance between having something of interest and practical importance to report without going beyond what is actually present within your review.

Executive summary (the '3'): these are your findings condensed for consumption by a busy decision maker. Such an executive summary is problem-focused and therefore uses the journalistic technique of presenting the more meaningful content at the top, followed by the background and context, and less important information further down. In this context, you should resist the temptation to labour the meticulous detail of the review methodology – this can be used as a subsequent guarantor of rigour once the findings have been assimilated, understood and interpreted.

(Continued)

(Continued)

The report (the '25'): the 25-page report of your review allows more detail, but nevertheless requires a greater succinctness than typically observed in a final report. Take time to show it to your decision-maker partners. Seven categories of information are recommended for inclusion in the report:

- *Context:* the policy issue or managerial problem with a clear statement of the PICOS review question.
- *Implications:* state what your review findings mean for decision makers, targeting the implications at your main stakeholders but trying to anticipate other audiences who may be interested in your work.
- *Approach:* outline your review methods, including the type of review undertaken, the database sources and search strategies used, the numbers of studies found and the overall methods of synthesis and presentation. Brief details of limitations of the methods should be given, with a fuller explanation provided in a technical appendix.
- *Results:* summarised in a concise and informative way using a full array of graphical and tabular means to highlight key themes and messages. Subsidiary results will be placed in an appendix.
- *Additional resources:* supportive materials (e.g. publications and websites) to help decision makers follow up issues raised by your review.
- *Further research:* resisting the blanket 'further research is needed', this should frame specific questions that remain to be answered together with suggested research designs to address them.
- *References and bibliography:* typically using the Vancouver numbered reference style, with references at the end of the report.

It is typically a challenge to condense the content of a systematic review, or even a rapid evidence assessment, within the 25-page strictures of this format. Nevertheless, creative use of appendices and judicious but rigorous reporting can achieve this aim.

The EPICOT+ format for reporting research recommendations

In 2005, representatives of organisations commissioning and summarising research met to develop guidelines for improving the presentation of recommendations for further research (Brown et al., 2006). They proposed the EPICOT format as the basis for a statement on formulating research recommendations. Subsequently, they identified several optional components of varying levels of relevance and their ensuing discussion resulted in the proposed EPICOT+ format (see Box 10.3).

 box 10.3

Suggested format for research recommendations on the effects of treatments (EPICOT+)

Core elements

E Evidence (What is the current state of the evidence?)

P Population (What is the population of interest?)

I Intervention (What are the interventions of interest?)

C Comparison (What are the comparisons of interest?)

O Outcome (What are the outcomes of interest?)

T Time stamp (Date of recommendation)

Optional elements

d Disease burden or relevance

t Time aspect of core elements of EPICOT

s Appropriate study type according to local need

OTHER TYPES OF REVIEW

The more structured the review, the more likely the existence of guidelines for reporting that particular type of review. Some sources seek to apply a structured description of methodology and of presentation of findings to those types of review that lie towards the middle of the structured–unstructured continuum. For example the *Journal of Advanced Nursing* has unilaterally produced guidelines for *concept analysis* reviews. These require 'concept analysis' to appear in the title and the aims to be stated as: '*This paper is a report of an analysis of the concept of X'*. The structured abstract will include fields commonly associated with a systematic review such as data sources and review methods. Typically, such an analysis includes a justification of the importance of the concept, details of the concept analysis method used (including quality assessment if present), and results presented according to the accepted terminology of the method (e.g. attributes, definition, antecedents, consequences). The discussion includes an assessment of whether the definition constitutes a middle-range descriptive theory or middle-range explanatory theory.

Arksey and O'Malley (2005) suggest several approaches suitable for presenting a narrative account of findings, specifically from a *scoping review*. It is important to point out that your choice of approaches will depend upon the data you have previously 'charted' from the component studies. The first approach is what we describe as the 'epidemiology' of the literature. Basically, just as a population can be described in terms of its basic characteristics such as the number of males/females, age distribution, ethnic constitution, fertility rate, etc., so too can a 'population of studies' be similarly characterised. This involves a 'basic numerical analysis of the extent, nature, and distribution of the studies included in the review'. To achieve this, authors would produce

tables and charts mapping: the distribution of studies geographically and for the different [population] groups; the range of interventions included in the review; the research methods adopted and the measures of effectiveness used. (Arksey and O'Malley, 2005)

Such an analysis helps to inform the commissioners of the review in that 'it sheds light on the dominant areas of research in terms of intervention type, research methods and geographical location' (Arksey and O'Malley, 2005). It also enables the researchers to 'quickly get a flavour of the main areas of interest, and consequently where the significant gaps were', invaluable when presenting their subsequent recommendations.

An alternative and possibly complementary approach is to organise the literature thematically, perhaps by a shared characteristic such as intervention type. Arksey and O'Malley (2005) identified 11 such different intervention types. Ideally, categories should be mutually exclusive to minimise duplication and the consequent risk of double-counting but this will not always be possible. As has been previously mentioned, the reviewer will also be constrained by the degree of completeness of reporting of the component studies. Here you will face the choice as to whether to have a minimum dataset of that data that are complete for each study or a more extensive matrix with many empty cells. To a certain extent, this will be determined by whether your focus is on the mapping of the existing evidence base, or the identification of gaps. Furthermore, for a **scoping review** or **mapping review**, where it is not always possible to provide a detailed assessment of component studies, you will be heavily dependent upon the classifications and terminology suggested by the authors themselves rather than constructing your own, more specific taxonomy.

These two primary choices were determined by the authors' own priorities for their scoping review and should not be construed as implying the superiority of these two approaches. Indeed, the authors acknowledge that they could have equally organised studies by the 'theoretical or conceptual positions adopted by authors'. This illustrates that the reviewer must preserve some clarity in their reporting of data so that readers can determine any potential bias in reporting or recommendations. In order to achieve a consistent approach to reporting the authors developed a 'template' for each of the 11 component groups. This required a template that

> began with a small table summarising basic characteristics of all the studies included in that particular intervention group, and was followed by commentary written under the following nine headings: interventions; sample sizes; participants; research methods; outcomes; evidence relating to effectiveness; economic aspects; UK studies; gaps in the research. (Arksey and O'Malley, 2005)

The value of such a structured approach was apparent in that it allowed reviewers, and indeed readers,

> to make comparisons across intervention types; identify contradictory evidence regarding specific interventions; identify gaps in the evidence gaps about individual interventions and across interventions as well as consider possible 'new frontiers' (such as the Internet). (Arksey and O'Malley, 2005)

Other structured approaches to presenting review findings might include a chronological approach, a dialectic approach between competing schools of thought, or a meta-narrative approach as described in Chapter 9 (Greenhalgh et al., 2005) which will characterise the literature according to source discipline.

SUMMARY

Clearly, the intense and prolonged effort that goes into producing your literature review that harnesses systematic approaches will only be fully exploited if you give careful consideration to the intended audience for your review. Your intended audience will determine the language and the format of your final review. We have seen that you may need secondary products, such as plain language summaries (Santesso et al., 2006; Glenton et al., 2010; Rosenbaum et al., 2011), 1:3:25 reports (see Toolbox section) and briefings (Carroll et al., 2006) to target the information preferences of your intended audience. In addition, all reviews have multiple audiences so you must give attention to using multiple channels.

 key learning points

- It is critical when writing a systematic review to base what you write and how you present it on a detailed knowledge of the intended audience.
- In addition to your primary audience your review will have other audiences and you should try, therefore, to factor in their interests.
- Systematic approaches to presenting your methodology and findings will demonstrate clarity-auditability-replicability-transparency (CART).
- Published reporting standards may help in the clear and transparent presentation of your methodology and findings.
- In addition to a structured academic report you may need to consider other methods of presentation for your review including plain language summaries and briefings.

frequently asked questions

FAQ 10.1 How do I identify reporting standards that relate to my systematic review?

It is very challenging to keep up to date with the appearance of reporting standards. Fortunately the EQUATOR (**Enhancing the QUAlity and Transparency Of health Research**) Network Website seeks to compile an index of standards in searchable form. Entries are grouped together into categories together with a brief description and links to external resources. Once you have located the name of an appropriate standard you will find that a high proportion of reportings standards are available via open access. Several websites, such as PRISMA, also make available helpful checklists or reporting templates.

FAQ 10.2 Is it compulsory to use reporting standards where available?

As this book has emphasised, part of the value of systematic approaches to reviewing the literature is transparency in reporting methods. Reporting standards are often the

(Continued)

(Continued)

result of extensive consultation and even a formal Delphi process. Some might consider it arrogant or foolish to ignore all that collective and free advice on how to report your review more clearly. Many journals are adding reporting statements to the requirements of their 'Instructions to Authors' and some even require a completed checklist to demonstrate compliance with a particular standard. However, even if this is not the case you will find that most peer reviewers will have a similar set of reporting characteristics in mind when they review your work. Take the opportunity to anticipate the information that they will want to see by following an appropriate reporting guideline. Remember too that these standards are only a guide. If you identify a particular need for reporting your review then do try to innovate within the overall framework. For example you may want to adapt the PRISMA flowchart of studies through the review to illustrate some methodological point.

FAQ 10.3 How can I create greater impact for my systematic review?

If your organisation, the commissioning organisation or a journal publisher produces press releases, you may want to work closely with the press office to produce an accurate yet public-friendly version of your review. Increasingly social media are used to flag up the appearance of new systematic reviews. Produce a tweet version of your review on Twitter with an abbreviated URL link. Better still, create a sequence of four or five related tweets, each focusing on a different 'take home message', and release them over a period of seven to ten days. Have you thought about creating a YouTube video for your review? Often a graphic depiction of your review results will stick in your mind longer than a printed message.

━━━ suggestions for further reading ━━━

Aveyard, H. (2014) How do I present my literature review? And other key questions. In H. Aveyard (ed.), *Doing a Literature Review in Health and Social Care: A Practical Guide*, 3rd edition. Maidenhead: Open University Press, 147–58.
A useful guide on the entire review process, this chapter focuses on the presentation and write-up.

Major, C.H. and Savin-Baden, M. (2010) 6 - Presenting the synthesis. In C.H. Major and M. Savin-Baden (eds), *An Introduction to Qualitative Research Synthesis: Managing the Information Explosion in Social Science Research*. Abingdon: Routledge, 89–104.
Authoritative text on qualitative synthesis in education, includes examples of reviews and tabulation.

Moher, D., Altman, D., Schulz, K., Simera, I. and Wager, E. (2014). *Guidelines for Reporting Health Research: A User's Manual*. Chichester: Wiley.
Multi-author compilation of current reporting standards for health research.

Pope, C., Mays, N. and Popay, J. (2007) Organising and presenting evidence synthesis. In C. Pope, N. Mays and J. Popay (eds), *Synthesizing Qualitative and Quantitative Health Evidence: A Guide to Methods*. Maidenhead: McGraw-Hill, 117–52.
Versatile guide on all aspects of systematic reviews concludes with a chapter on presentation.

Robertson-Malt, S. (2014) Presenting and interpreting findings. *American Journal of Nursing*, **114**, 8, 49–54.
Part of a series presenting a step-by-step guide to systematic review, this article focuses on the end of the process, namely presenting and interpreting findings. This article particularly details what should be included when presenting the findings of a systematic review to ensure these can be translated into clinical practice.

REFERENCES

Ahmad, N., Boutron, I., Dechartres, A., Durieux, P. and Ravaud, P. (2010) Applicability and generalisability of the results of systematic reviews to public health practice and policy: a systematic review. *Trials*, **11**, 20.

American Education Research Association (2006) Standards for reporting on empirical social science research in AERA publications. *Educational Researcher*, **35**, 6, 33–40.

Arksey, H. and O'Malley, L. (2005) Scoping studies: towards a methodological framework. *International Journal of Social Research Methodology*, **8**, 1, 19–32.

Aveyard, H. (2014) How do I present my literature review? And other key questions. In H. Aveyard (ed.), *Doing a Literature Review in Health and Social Care: A Practical Guide*, 3rd edition. Maidenhead: Open University Press, 147–58.

Baxter, S., Killoran, A., Kelly, M.P. and Goyder, E. (2010) Synthesizing diverse evidence: the use of primary qualitative data analysis methods and logic models in public health reviews. *Public Health*, **124**, 2, 99–106.

Beyea, S. and Nicholl, L. (1998) Writing an integrative review. *AORN Journal*, **67**, 4, 877–80.

Booth, A. (2006) 'Brimful of STARLITE': toward standards for reporting literature searches. *Journal of the Medical Library Association*, **94**, 4, 421–9.

Brown, P., Brunnhuber, K., Chalkidou, K., Chalmers, I., Clarke, M., Fenton, M., Forbes, C., Glanville, J., Hicks, N.J., Moody, J., Twaddle, S., Timimi, H. and Young, P. (2006) How to formulate research recommendations. *BMJ*, **333**, 7572, 804–6.

Burns, N. and Grove, S.K. (2007) *Understanding Nursing Research – Building an Evidence Based Practice*, 4th edition. St. Louis, IL: Saunders Elsevier.

The Campbell Collaboration (n.d.) What is a systematic review? The Campbell Collaboration. Available at www.campbellcollaboration.org/what_is_a_systematic_review/ (last accessed 17 October 2015).

Carroll, C., Cooke, J., Booth, A. and Beverley, C. (2006) Bridging the gap: the development of knowledge briefings at the health and social care interface. *Health and Social Care in the Community*, **14**, 6, 491–8.

Carroll, C., Patterson, M., Wood, S., Booth, A., Rick, J. and Balain, S. (2007) A conceptual framework for implementation fidelity. *Implementation Science*, **2**, 40. DOI: 10.1186/1748-5908-2-40.

Clarke, M. and Chalmers, I. (1998) Discussion sections in reports of controlled trials published in general medical journals. Islands in search of continents? *JAMA*, **280**, 280–2.

Clarke, M. and Clarke, T. (2000) A study of the references used in Cochrane protocols and reviews: three bibles, three dictionaries, and nearly 25,000 other things. *International Journal of Technology Assessment in Health Care*, **16**, 3, 907–9.

Cooper, N.J., Jones, D.R. and Sutton, A.J. (2005) The use of systematic reviews when designing studies. *Clinical Trials*, **2**, 3, 260–4.

Cronin, P., Ryan, F. and Coughlan, M. (2008) Undertaking a literature review: a step-by-step approach. *British Journal of Nursing*, **17**, 1, 38–43.

Dekkers, O.M., von Elm, E., Algra, A., Romijn, J.A. and Vandenbroucke, J.P. (2009) How to assess the external validity of therapeutic trials: a conceptual approach. *International Journal of Epidemiology*, **39**, 1, 89–94.

France, E.F., Ring, N., Thomas, R., Noyes, J., Maxwell, M. and Jepson, R. (2014) A methodological systematic review of what's wrong with meta-ethnography reporting. *BMC Medical Research Methodology*, **19**, 14, 119.

Glasziou, P., Meats, E., Heneghan, C. and Shepperd, S. (2008) What is missing from descriptions of treatment in trials and reviews? *BMJ*, **336**, 7659, 1472.

Glenton, C., Santesso, N., Rosenbaum, S., Nilsen, E.S., Rader, T., Ciapponi, A. and Dilkes, H. (2010) Presenting the results of Cochrane Systematic Reviews to a consumer audience: a qualitative study. *Medical Decision Making*, **30**, 5, 566–77.

Greenhalgh, T. (2012) Outside the box: why are Cochrane reviews so boring? *British Journal of General Practice*, **62**, 37.

Greenhalgh, T., Robert, G., Macfarlane, F., Bate, P., Kyriakidou, O. and Peacock, R. (2005) Storylines of research in diffusion of innovation: a meta-narrative approach to systematic review. *Social Science and Medicine*, **61**, 2, 417–30.

Hammersley, M. (2002) Systematic or unsystematic, is that the question? Some reflections on the science, art, and politics of reviewing research evidence. Text of a talk given to the Public Health Evidence Steering Group of the Health Development Agency, October.

Hendry, C. and Farley, A. (1998) Reviewing the literature: a guide for students. *Nursing Standard*, **12**, 44, 46–8.

Higgins, J.P.T. and Green, S. (eds) (2011) *Cochrane Handbook for Systematic Reviews of Interventions*, Version 5.1.0 (updated March 2011). The Cochrane Collaboration. Available from: www.cochrane-handbook.org (last accessed 9 March 2016).

Hind, D. and Booth, A. (2007) Do health technology assessments comply with QUOROM diagram guidance? An empirical study. *BMC Medical Research Methodology*, **7**, 49.

Hoffmann, T.C., Erueti, C. and Glasziou, P.P. (2013) Poor description of non-pharmacological interventions: analysis of consecutive sample of randomised trials. *BMJ*, **347**, f3755.

Hoffmann, T.C., Glasziou, P.P., Boutron, I., Milne, R., Perera, R., Moher, D., Altman, D.G., Barbour, V., Macdonald, H., Johnston, M., Lamb, S.E., Dixon-Woods, M., McCulloch, P., Wyatt, J.C., Chan, A. and Michie, S. (2014) Better reporting of interventions: template for intervention description and replication (TIDieR) checklist and guide. *BMJ: British Medical Journal*, **348**, g1687.

Lavis, J., Davies, H., Gruen, R., Walshe, K. and Farquhar, C. (2006) Working within and beyond the Cochrane Collaboration to make systematic reviews more useful to healthcare managers and policy makers. *Healthcare Policy*, **1**, 2, 21–33.

Lavis, J., Davies, H., Oxman, A., Denis, J.L., Golden-Biddle, K. and Ferlie, E. (2005) Towards systematic reviews that inform health care management and policy-making. *Journal of Health Services Research and Policy*, **10**, Suppl. 1, 35–48.

Lefebvre, C., Manheimer, E. and Glanville, J. (2011) Searching for studies (Part 2, Chapter 6). In J.P.T. Higgins and S. Green (eds), *Cochrane Handbook for Systematic Reviews of Interventions*, Version 5.1.0 (updated March 2011). The Cochrane Collaboration. Available from: www.cochrane-handbook.org (last accessed 9 March 2016).

Light, R. and Pillemer, D. (1984) *Summing Up: The Science of Reviewing Research*. Cambridge, MA: Harvard University Press.

Major, C.H. and Savin-Baden, M. (2010) 6 – Presenting the synthesis. In C.H. Major and M. Savin-Baden (eds), *An Introduction to Qualitative Research Synthesis: Managing the Information Explosion in Social Science Research*. Abingdon: Routledge, 89–104.

Moher, D., Altman, D., Schulz, K., Simera, I. and Wager, E. (2014) *Guidelines for Reporting Health Research: A User's Manual*. Abingdon: Wiley.

Moher, D., Liberati, A., Tetzlaff, J., Altman, D.G. and The PRISMA Group (2009) Preferred reporting items for systematic reviews and meta-analyses: The PRISMA statement. *PLoS Medicine*,
6, 7, e1000097.

Moher, D., Tetzlaff, J., Tricco, A.C., Sampson, M. and Altman, D.G. (2007) Epidemiology and
reporting characteristics of systematic reviews. *PLOS Medicine*, **4**, 3. DOI: http://dx.doi.
org/10.1371/journal.pmed.0040078.

Nicoll, A., Lynn, R., Rahi, J., Verity, C. and Haines, L. (2000) Public health outputs from the
British Paediatric Surveillance Unit and similar clinician-based systems. *Journal of the Royal
Society of Medicine*, **93**, 11, 580.

Pagliaro, L., Bruzzi, P. and Bobbio, M. (2010) Why are Cochrane hepato-biliary reviews under-
valued by physicians as an aid for clinical decision-making? *Digestive and Liver Diseases*, **42**,
1, 1–5.

Phillips, C.V. (2001) The economics of 'more research is needed'. *International Journal of
Epidemiology*, **30**, 4, 771–6.

The PLoS Medicine Editors (2007) Many reviews are systematic but some are more transparent
and completely reported than others. *PLoS Medicine*, **4**, 3, e147.

Polit, D. and Beck, C. (2006) *Essentials of Nursing Research: Methods, Appraisal and Utilization*, 6th
edition. Philadelphia: Lippincott Williams and Wilkins.

Popay, J., Roberts, H., Sowden, A., Petticrew, M., Arai, L., Rodgers, M. and Britten N., with Roen,
K. and Duffy, S. (2006) *Guidance on the Conduct of Narrative Synthesis in Systematic Reviews:
A Product from the ESRC Methods Programme*. Version 1. Manchester: Economic and Social
Research Council.

Pope, C., Mays, N. and Popay, J. (2006) Informing policy making and management in healthcare: the place for synthesis. *Healthcare Policy*, **1**, 2, 43–8.

Randolph, J.J. (2009) A guide to writing the dissertation literature review. *Practical Assessment,
Research and Evaluation*, **14**, 1–13.

Rosenbaum, S.E., Glenton, C., Wiysonge, C.S., Abalos, E., Mignini, L., Young, T., Althabe, F.,
Ciapponi, A., Marti, S.C., Meng, Q., Wang, J., De la Hoz Bradford, A.M., Kiwanuka, S.N.,
Rutebemberwa, E., Pariyo, G.W., Flottorp, S. and Oxman, A.D. (2011) Evidence summaries
tailored to health policy-makers in low- and middle-income countries. *Bulletin of the World
Health Organisation*, **89**, 54–61.

Sampson, M., McGowan, J., Cogo, E., Grimshaw, J., Moher, D. and Lefebvre, C. (2009) An evidence-based practice guideline for the peer review of electronic search strategies. *Journal of
Clinical Epidemiology*, **62**, 9, 944–52.

Sampson, M., McGowan, J., Tetzlaff, J., Cogo, E. and Moher, D. (2008) No consensus exists
on search reporting methods for systematic reviews. *Journal of Clinical Epidemiology*, **61**, 8,
748–54.

Santesso, N., Maxwell, L., Tugwell, P.S., Wells, G.A., O'Connor, A.M., Judd, M. and Buchbinder,
R. (2006) Knowledge transfer to clinicians and consumers by the Cochrane Musculoskeletal
Group. *Journal of Rheumatology*, **33**, 11, 2312–8.

Schriger, D.L., Altman, D.G., Vetter, J.A., Heafner, T. and Moher, D. (2010) Forest plots in reports
of systematic reviews: a cross-sectional study reviewing current practice. *International Journal
of Epidemiology*, **39**, 2, 421–9.

Schulz, K.F., Altman, D.G., Moher, D. and the CONSORT Group (2010) CONSORT 2010
Statement: Updated Guidelines for Reporting Parallel Group Randomised Trials. *PLoS
Medicine*, **7**, 3, e1000251.

Smith, A.F.M. (1996) Mad cows and ecstasy: chance and choice in an evidence-based society.
Journal of the Royal Statistical Society, **159**, 3, 367–83.

Stroup, D.F., Berlin, J.A., Morton, S.C., Olkin, I., Williamson, G.D., Rennie, D., Moher, D.,
Becker, B.J., Sipe, T.A. and Thacker, S.B. (2000) Meta-analysis of observational studies in

epidemiology: a proposal for reporting. Meta-analysis Of Observational Studies in Epidemiology (MOOSE) group. *JAMA*, **283**, 15, 2008–12.

Tong, A., Flemming, K., McInnes, E., Oliver, S. and Craig, J. (2012) Enhancing transparency in reporting the synthesis of qualitative research: ENTREQ. *BMC Medical Research Methodology*, **12**, 1, 181.

Williamson, J.W., German, P.S., Weiss, R., Skinner, E.A. and Bowes, F. III (1989) Health science information management and continuing education of physicians: a survey of U.S. primary care practitioners and their opinion leaders. *Annals of Internal Medicine*, **110**, 151–60.

Wong, G., Greenhalgh, T., Westhorp, G., Buckingham, J. and Pawson, R. (2013a) RAMESES publication standards: meta-narrative reviews. *BMC Medicine*, **11**, 20.

Wong, G., Greenhalgh, T., Westhorp, G., Buckingham, J. and Pawson, R. (2013b) RAMESES publication standards: realist syntheses. *BMC Medicine,* **11**, 21.

Yaffe, J., Montgomery, P., Hopewell, S. and Shepard, L.D. (2012) Empty reviews: a description and consideration of Cochrane systematic reviews with no included studies. *PLoS One*, **7**, 5, e36626.

Yoshii, A., Plaut, D.A., McGraw, K.A., Anderson, M.J. and Wellik, K.E. (2009) Analysis of the reporting of search strategies in Cochrane systematic reviews. *Journal of the Medical Library Association*, **97**, 1, 21–9.

GLOSSARY

adjacency – a term relating to the searching of electronic databases. When using adjacency in a search, you are specifying that words should be searched together in a phrase (e.g. 'heart attack', 'housing market') to yield a smaller and more precise set of results.

aggregative – adjective relating to a type of review that is concerned with assembling and pooling data (either quantitative as with meta-analysis or qualitative as with thematic synthesis). To achieve such aggregation requires that there is basic comparability between phenomena.

analytic/analytical – the facility to use analysis to discern patterns, trends or themes to data or the properties of tools that assist in such analysis.

AND – a Boolean operator (q.v.), that is syntax entered into a search engine or database, that specifically requires two or more concepts to be present in an item (e.g. an abstract) for it to be retrieved (e.g. eat AND drink).

applicability – the application of the results from individual studies or from a review of studies of a study population to individual people, cases or settings in a target population.

attrition – the loss of participants during the conduct of a study.

attrition bias – a type of selection bias caused by attrition (loss of participants).

author searching – a term relating to the searching of electronic databases or internet sources for one or more authors known to be working in a review topic area.

Bayesian meta-analysis (Bayesian synthesis) – a specific type of meta-analysis whereby statisticians express their belief about the size of an effect by specifying some prior (up front) probability distribution before seeing the data. On completing the meta-analysis, they update that belief by deriving a posterior (after the fact) probability distribution, taking the data into account. Some commentators suggest that qualitative research may be used to inform the prior belief, e.g. parents' attitudes to vaccination.

best evidence synthesis – a method of synthesis that, like realist synthesis, draws on a wide range of evidence (including single case studies) and explores the impact of context, often employing an iterative, participatory approach.

bias – systematic error in individual studies or in a review that can lead to erroneous conclusions about an intervention, programme or policy.

bibliographic databases – a database of bibliographic records typically containing references to the published journal literature (although its scope may also include newspaper articles, conference proceedings and papers, reports, government and legal publications, patents, books, etc.).

black box effect – a term typically used within the study of complex interventions to describe when the intervention is not sufficiently defined to distinguish which configuration of components has produced a measured change in outcome.

blind – when a study design is referred to as blind, this means the treatment a person has received or, in some cases, the outcome of their treatment is not known by individuals involved in the study. This is to avoid them being influenced by this knowledge. The person who is blinded could be either the person being treated, their caregiver or the researcher assessing the effect of the treatment (single blind), two of these people (double blind) or all three of these people (triple blind).

Boolean logic – a system of logical operators (most commonly AND, OR and NOT) used for specifying information to be retrieved from a computer (bibliographic) database.

Boolean operator – a term (most commonly AND, OR and NOT) used to specify the preferred relationship between two or more concepts to be retrieved from a computer (bibliographic) database. For example (eat AND drink; train OR bus; adult NOT child).

Campbell Collaboration – a non-profit organisation that applies a rigorous, systematic process to review the effects of interventions in the social, behavioural and educational arenas, in order to provide evidence-based information in the shape of systematic reviews.

case-control study/ies – observational (i.e. non-experimental) study/ies that compare patients who have a disease or outcome of interest (cases) with patients who do not have the disease or outcome (controls). The research team looks back (retrospectively) to compare how frequently the exposure to a risk factor (e.g. smoking) is present in each group to determine the relationship between the risk factor and the disease (e.g. lung cancer).

changes clause – a term originally applied to the documentation of changes to provisions in government contracts but, in this context, used to refer to documented changes to a review plan or protocol.

checklist(s) – systematised list(s) of criteria used to assess the quality of a published research study in order to ensure that a standardised approach can be used in an attempt to minimise bias.

citation searching – a term relating to the searching of electronic databases or internet sources for items that have cited, or been cited by, an article or study known to be relevant to a review topic. This specialised function is only available on a limited number of databases such as Web of Knowledge, CINAHL and Google Scholar.

cite-while-you-write – the facility to use a reference management package alongside a word processing package so that a reviewer can place markers (numerical document identifiers) as they write their article and then automatically generate a bibliography upon its completion.

Cochrane Collaboration – an international organisation of over 10,000 volunteers in more than 90 countries that aims to help people make well-informed decisions about health by preparing, maintaining and ensuring the accessibility of systematic reviews of the benefits and risks of healthcare interventions.

Cochrane Library – a collection of databases in medicine and other healthcare specialities, including full-text systematic reviews provided by the Cochrane Collaboration and annotated bibliographic records supplied by other organisations.

Cochrane Review – a systematic summary of evidence of the effects of healthcare interventions intended to help people make practical decisions on focused health issues.

cohort study/ies – an observational study, commonly used in medicine and social science, in which a defined group of people (the cohort) is followed over time. The outcomes of people in subsets of this cohort are compared, to examine those who were exposed or not exposed (or exposed at different levels) to a particular intervention or other factor of interest.

complex intervention – interventions that contain several interacting components.

concept analysis – a type of analysis required to identify and determine the scope of a concept designated by a given term as it is used in the literature of a particular subject field.

concept map(s) – a diagram showing the relationships among concepts. Concept maps are useful graphical tools for organising and representing the knowledge covered by a review.

concept mapping – the process of using a diagram or related graphical tool to represent the knowledge covered by a review.

conceptual map – see **concept map**.

confidence value – a range of values considered to represent the likely range of values (i.e. the lowest and highest values) for a given population of effect sizes within a given margin of error (e.g. 95%).

configurative – an adjective relating to a review approach that addresses open questions, typically answered with qualitative data and more iterative methods that interpret specific examples of things, by examining experiences and meaning to generate and explore theory.

conflict of interest statement – a written declaration, typically accompanying a systematic review or a primary research study, that documents where individuals involved with the conduct, reporting, oversight or review of research also have financial or other interests, from which they can benefit, depending on the results of the research/review.

confounding – the presence of one or more variables, in addition to the variable of interest, that makes it impossible to separate their unique effects leading to incomplete or incorrect conclusions.

confounding variable(s) – an unforeseen and unaccounted-for variable that poses a threat to the reliability and validity of an experiment's outcome.

constant comparative method/constant comparison – a research methodology that, when applied to reviews, requires the comparison of findings from an additional study with findings from previously reviewed studies in the quest for additional insights.

content analysis – the process of organising written, audio or visual information into categories and themes related to the central questions of a study or review.

controlled vocabulary – a carefully selected set of terms used in a bibliographic database, such that each concept is described using only one term in the set and each term in the set describes only one concept.

conversion ratio – a term originally from the domain of business which, in this context, relates to the number of references that need to be examined in order to identify one study for inclusion in a review.

critical appraisal – the use of explicit, transparent methods to assess the data in published research, by systematically considering such factors as validity, adherence to reporting standards, methods, conclusions and generalisability.

critical interpretive synthesis – an approach to the synthesis of qualitative and quantitative data used in situations where theorisation of the evidence is required. Critical interpretive synthesis encourages a critique of literatures and the questioning of taken-for-granted assumptions about concepts and methods.

critical path – the path through a series of activities relating to a review, taking into account interdependencies, in which late completion of activities will impact on the review end date or delay a key milestone.

cross-sectional survey(s) – a specific research design that involves observation of some subset of a population at the same point in time, looking simply at occurrence without being able to establish causation.

database bias – a specific form of location bias (q.v.) that relates to the likelihood of a particular journal being indexed in a database and therefore to the likelihood of its constituent articles being identified through systematic literature searches. This may relate to language of publication or location of publisher, or other characteristics related to the database or the publishing industry.

data dredging – is the inappropriate (sometimes deliberate) use of processes such as data mining to uncover misleading relationships in data. These relationships may be valid within the test set but are not statistically significant within the wider population.

data extraction – the process of retrieving and coding relevant variables from primary studies in order to facilitate comparison and the observation of patterns, themes or trends.

data mining – data processing using sophisticated search capabilities and statistical algorithms in large pre-existing databases as a way to facilitate the discovery of patterns, themes or trends.

data synthesis – the process of summarising the contents of original studies using textual, graphical or tabular means.

descriptive – summarising data according to their patterns or characteristics as opposed to analytical which examines the relationships between data.

descriptive data synthesis – summarising studies descriptively (i.e. what the literature looks like) rather than analytically (what the literature tells us).

descriptive mapping – describing the scope of a topic according to the characteristics of its constituent literature.

descriptors – used to index a reference in a bibliographic database such as MEDLINE. Thesaurus terms, subject headings and keywords are all descriptors.

disconfirming case – a case or example that that does not fit emergent patterns and allows the researcher to identify and evaluate alternative explanations.

duplicate citations – the result of literature searching across multiple databases whenever there is significant overlap in journal coverage.

electronic database(s) – databases, most typically bibliographic databases, that can be used to speed up the process of study identification.

empty reviews – systematic reviews around clearly focused questions that have been unable to identify any studies that fulfil the requirements for both relevance and rigour and therefore contain no included studies.

equipoise – literally, a situation of genuine uncertainty within the expert medical community over whether a treatment will be beneficial. Within the context of systematic reviews it can also be used to indicate genuine uncertainty within the pattern of results from included studies on whether a treatment is beneficial.

evidence base – information gathered by a reviewer that characterises what is known about a topic, typically from higher quality studies.

evidence-based policy – the application of principles from evidence-based practice to the making of decisions at a population level regarding effective programmes and policies.

evidence-based practice – the integration of individual professional expertise with the best available external evidence from systematic research.

evidence summary – a brief, often rapidly produced, evidence product designed to inform decision makers; it typically includes such features as a structured question, a bottom-line result, bulletpoints and tabulation of evidence.

evidence synthesis – the process of summarising the contents of original research, typically of higher quality studies.

exclusion criteria – the standards or criteria used to specify the circumstances in which a person is disqualified from being included in a trial and, by extension, the standards used to determine whether an individual paper is disqualified from inclusion in a systematic review.

exhaustivity – the extent to which all possible sources are covered in the quest to identify relevant studies for a review.

explanatory variables – variables that may be used to explain the cause of a particular result or finding.

external validity – the extent to which the effect of an intervention, programme or policy being investigated in a study or review might be expected to occur in other participants or settings.

fixed effects analysis – an analysis using a statistical model that treats all measurements as if those quantities were non-random. A fixed effects analysis is therefore more likely to underestimate the effect of variation and, correspondingly, to overestimate the effect of an intervention, programme or policy.

footnote chasing – checking a particular item's (for example a journal article) footnotes, endnotes and reference list for relevant items.

Forest plot (or blobbogram) – a graphical display designed to illustrate the relative strength of effects in multiple studies addressing, and quantifying the effects for, the same question.

formative – an adjective describing those aspects of a review that appear throughout its conduct and may thus inform its ultimate form and content.

framework analysis – the process of analysing primary data using an existing framework or model as an organising structure to facilitate the analysis.

framework synthesis – a process of synthesis that is analogous to the use of framework analysis but in this case is used to analyse data from multiple studies within a review.

free-text – a retrieval term referring to when a search engine examines all of the words in every stored document in an attempt to match search words supplied by the user, not just terms pre-specified as entry terms by an indexer.

Funnel plot – a graphical device for exploring the likelihood of publication bias by plotting a measure of study size against a measure of effect size, and thereby seeking to identify any likelihood of missing populations of studies.

Gantt chart – a project management tool that seeks to convey project tasks, timescales, deliverables and dependencies.

generalisability – the extent to which findings from research conducted in one time and place can be applied to populations in another time and/or place.

gold standard – a metaphorical term used to describe the extent to which a particular study or characteristic may be used as a basis for comparison with other studies or characteristics.

grey literature – information produced by government, academics, business and industry in electronic and print formats not controlled by commercial publishing, (i.e. where publishing is not the primary activity of the producing body).

grounded theory – procedures developed within primary data analysis, and subsequently applied to secondary research, that seek to provide a method for generating theory grounded in the data in the absence of an *a priori* theory or hypothesis.

hand searching – a complementary method of searching that requires systematic scanning of the contents of key journals in order to offset perceived deficiencies in database coverage or indexing.

health technology assessment – a type of review commonly conducted for health policy makers that seeks to inform decisions about the effectiveness and cost-effectiveness of a particular procedure, programme, policy or intervention, typically within a tightly constrained timeframe.

heterogeneity – the extent to which studies demonstrate variation across a range of key variables.

heterogeneous – this refers to the extent to which studies included in a systematic review display variability. Such variability may relate to differences in the included participants, interventions and outcomes, or to diversity in study design and the consequent risk of bias. These differences may in turn contribute to variability in the intervention effects being evaluated in the different studies (statistical heterogeneity).

hierarchical vocabulary – vocabularies used to index citations, such as MeSH on the MEDLINE database, which are often organised in a hierarchical structure, with broader terms (for example 'Anatomy') at the top of the list, and narrower terms below (for example 'Digestive System').

hierarchy/ies of evidence – an approach to defining the quality of research studies based on their study design, favouring studies that are comparative, prospective and protected against systematic error or bias.

homogeneity – the extent to which studies exhibit shared characteristics across a range of key variables.

idea web(s)/idea webbing – a form of concept mapping regarded as particularly valuable in making sense of a complex phenomenon or programme.

implementation fidelity – the degree to which an intervention, programme or policy can be seen to have been put into practice as originally intended.

incident knowledge – newly appearing knowledge that makes a contribution to an improved understanding of a particular topic area.

inclusion criteria – the standards or criteria that have to be fulfilled in order for a person to be eligible to be included in a trial and, by extension, the standards used to determine whether an individual study is eligible for inclusion in a systematic review.

index paper – a paper that is regarded as being rich in content and is therefore considered an appropriate starting point for a subsequent investigation of a series of papers.

information explosion – a social phenomenon that describes the state at which information is being produced at a rate quicker than it can be identified, organised, managed or retrieved.

information literate – the facility of an individual to be able to undertake basic information-processing tasks.

information overload – the point at which an individual has too much information and is therefore unable to process it effectively.

information retrieval – a set of techniques and procedures used to specify and identify relevant items from a data source such as an electronic database.

informational redundancy – a point at which further information fails to add additional value to knowledge or understanding already established from previously identified studies.

integrative review – originally a type of review that sought to integrate findings from a number of research papers; nowadays more commonly used to describe a review that integrates both quantitative and qualitative data together in the same review product.

internal validity – the extent to which the design and conduct of a study are likely to have prevented bias and therefore the results may be considered reliable.

interpretive – a type of review that seeks to use the process of synthesis as a means of explaining a particular phenomenon.

language bias – a form of bias relating to the original language of a publication. It is characterised by a tendency for reviews to be more likely to include studies published in the language of that review.

language of publication bias – a systematic bias caused by the increased/decreased likelihood of a research paper containing positive or negative results as a function of the language in which it is being published.

law of diminishing returns – the phenomenon that as one extends searching across more and more databases the yield becomes correspondingly less productive.

limit function – a facility on bibliographic databases that allows the searcher to restrict search results by date, language or publication type in order to make the retrieval results more manageable.

line of argument (synthesis) – a component method of meta-ethnography that seeks to organise findings from multiple studies into a single explanatory line of argument.

literature search(ing) – the product from/process of identifying published or non-published items for inclusion within a review output using either database subject-based techniques or supplementary techniques such as hand searching, follow up of references and citation searches.

location bias – an umbrella term referring to any form of bias relating to the location(s) in which a study is originally conducted. Most commonly, but not necessarily, associated with language bias, it may result in a review being less likely to include studies that originate from a particular region of the world (e.g. the systematic exclusion of studies from low and middle income countries).

logic model(s) – a visual representation showing the sequence of related events connecting the need for a planned programme with the programme's desired results or short-term and long-term outcomes. A logic model may be used at the beginning of a review to plan a review strategy or towards the end as a framework for interpreting and presenting the findings.

longitudinal – study design in which the same subjects are observed repeatedly over a period of time.

lumping – the action of deciding to undertake a broad review in preference to several related, but individual, reviews on the basis of commonalities shared by the population, interventions and/or outcomes (compare with **splitting**).

mapping review – a rapid search of the literature aiming to give a broad overview of the characteristics of a topic area. Mapping of existing research, identification of gaps and a summary assessment of the quantity and quality of the available evidence help to decide future areas for research or for systematic review.

matrix method – a method for integrating two types of variables or two types of data within a table or matrix where one type is assigned to the rows and the other to the columns. The method is long-established but has enjoyed renewed interest as a potential method for integrating quantitative and qualitative data.

meaningfulness – the value that an individual or population ascribes to a particular intervention, programme or policy as established from the personal opinions, experiences, values, thoughts, beliefs or interpretations of the individuals themselves, their families or significant others.

memo-ing – the process of documenting observations on a research process conducted by a researcher or reviewer as their work progresses.

MeSH (Medical Subject Headings) – a controlled vocabulary (thesaurus) for the purpose of indexing journal articles in databases such as MEDLINE.

meta-analysis – the process of combining statistically quantitative studies that have measured the same effect using similar methods and a common outcome measure.

meta-ethnography – the most common method of synthesis of qualitative research, originally used to synthesise ethnographies but now used to refer to the synthesis of other study types, typically with the objective of theory generation.

meta-method – a type of synthesis that seeks to derive insights from studying the characteristics of different methods used to investigate a shared phenomenon.

meta-narrative – a type of synthesis that seeks to explore large and heterogeneous literatures from different research traditions or disciplines by following the unfolding storyline or narrative from each.

meta-study – the process or technique of synthesising research reports by using various methods to retrieve, select and combine results from previous separate but related studies. Meta-study is a generic term that includes meta-analysis and meta-synthesis. Meta-study also relates to a specific technique that variously examines the methods (meta-method), theory (meta-theory), data (meta-data-analysis) and genertated constructs (meta-synthesis) from a body of studies.

meta-summary – a type of quantitatively oriented synthesis developed to accommodate the distinctive features of topical and thematic survey findings typically produced from qualitative descriptive studies.

meta-synthesis – a generic term describing the science of bringing studies together and examining them for shared characteristics and patterns. Typically the term is used in connection with synthesis of qualitative studies but, strictly speaking, it may also be applied to quantitative meta-analysis.

meta-theory – a type of synthesis that seeks to synthesise multiple theories from research papers examining a shared phenomenon.

methodological filter(s) – standardised search strategies designed to retrieve studies of a particular methodology type.

mind map(s) – a diagram used to represent words, ideas, tasks or other concepts linked to, and arranged around, a central key word or idea.

mixed method(s) review – a literature review that seeks to bring together data from quantitative and qualitative studies integrating them in a way that facilitates subsequent analysis.

narrative review – the term used to describe a conventional overview of the literature, particularly when contrasted with a systematic review.

narrative synthesis – a systematic process of describing the shared properties of a group of studies included in a review primarily through text but augmented by tabular and graphical displays of data.

NOT – a Boolean operator (see above), that is syntax entered into a search engine or database, that explicitly requires that one concept is present in an item (e.g. an abstract) and the other is absent for it to be retrieved (e.g. Female NOT Male).

number needed to read (NNR) – a measure of how many items (for example journal abstracts) need to be read to find one of relevance.

observational study/studies – a study that investigates the effects of an intervention or programme where the assignment of subjects is outside the control of the investigator.

open label – a type of clinical trial in which both the researchers and participants know which treatment is being administered.

open source software – a method for the distribution of software without charge which allows the source code to be modified or developed in the public domain subject to the fulfilment of prespecified terms and conditions.

OR – a Boolean operator (see above), that is syntax entered into a search engine or database, that allows for the presence in a single item (e.g. an abstract) of either one concept or an alternative concept or both in order for it to be retrieved (e.g. fruit OR vegetables).

pearl-growing – the process of identifying a known highly relevant article (the pearl) as a means to isolate terms on which a search can subsequently be based.

PICOC – an acronym, coined by Petticrew and Roberts (2006), to capture a precise review question by specifying the five elements of Population, Intervention, Comparison, Outcome, Context.

PICOS – an acronym describing an approach to formulating or specifying a review question according to the elements of Population, Intervention, Comparison, Outcome and Study design.

point estimate – a single point or value considered to represent the most likely approximation for a given population of effect sizes (e.g. a mean value).

practically significant – a difference observed in a study or review that is considered by professionals to be important enough to be worth achieving.

prevalent knowledge – the knowledge that exists on a topic at a particular point in time.

primary study/ies – original research studies; compare secondary studies which are reviews or syntheses.

prior distribution – the specification, in advance of a test or experiment, of the distribution of an uncertain quantity.

PRISMA (Preferred Reporting Items for Systematic reviews and Meta-Analyses) – a standard for the reporting of systematic reviews and meta-analyses in the published journal literature (formerly QUOROM).

probability distribution – a statistical function that identifies either the probability of each value of a random variable (when the variable is discrete), or the probability of the value falling within a particular interval (when the variable is continuous).

process evaluation – a type of study used in complex interventions research that aims to provide more detailed understanding of interventions to inform policy and practice. Examines aspects such as implementation, mechanisms of impact (how participants interact with the intervention) and context (how external factors influence the delivery and functions of the intervention).

programme theory – an idealised model that shows how programme features interact to influence performance indicators, and produce desired outcomes. It comprises three components: (i) a problem definition; (ii) programme components linked together to create a programme logic; and (iii) a link between the programme logic and programme activities through the use of performance indicators.

prospective – a prospective study asks a specific study question (usually about how a particular exposure affects an outcome), recruits appropriate participants, and looks at the exposures and outcomes of interest in these people over the following months or years.

proximity – the specification of two search terms to be close to each other, e.g. in a phrase or within the same sentence, in order for a document to be retrieved from a database.

publication bias – the tendency for researchers, editors and pharmaceutical companies to handle the reporting of experimental results that are positive (i.e. they show a significant finding) differently from results that are negative (i.e. supporting the null hypothesis) or inconclusive. Typically this is evidenced in an increased likelihood of publication.

qualitative – adjective relating to the facility by which a phenomenon may be effectively expressed in terms of its (non-numerical) characteristics.

qualitative evidence synthesis – an umbrella term increasingly used to describe a group of review types that attempt to synthesise and analyse findings from primary qualitative research studies.

qualitative study/ies – an approach to research that is concerned with eliciting the subjective experiences of participants. Qualitative research may entail a choice of methodologies such as ethnography, grounded theory and phenomenology, and may use a variety of methods of which questionnaire, interview and participant observation are the most common.

quality assessment – the systematic process of examining the internal and external validity of studies for potential inclusion in a review so as to evaluate their individual contributions to the overall 'bottom line' of that review.

quality of conduct – the attribute of a review that relates to how well its processes and procedures have been carried out.

quality of reporting – that attribute of a review that relates to how well its processes and procedures have been documented.

quantitative – adjective relating to the facility by which a phenomenon may be effectively expressed in numerical values.

random effects analysis – an analysis using a statistical model that allows for random variation among populations. A random effects analysis therefore provides a more conservative estimate of an effect size and is less likely to overestimate the effect of an intervention.

randomised controlled trial(s) (RCT) – a study design considered to be the most rigorous method of determining whether a cause–effect relationship exists between an intervention and an outcome. As such systematic reviews of randomised controlled trials provide the best available evidence of effectiveness. The strength of the RCT lies in the process of randomisation that should allow both intervention and comparison to be compared on an equal basis when considering the effect of an intervention.

rapid evidence assessment – a tool for obtaining a rapid overview of the available research evidence on a policy issue, as comprehensively as possible, within the constraints of a given timetable. It uses elements of scoping review and mapping review methodologies.

rapid review – a systematic approach to the literature characterised by its limited window of opportunity and by substantive interaction between the commissioner and the review team.

Rapid reviews may either use accelerated systematic review methods to deliver a similar quality product within a shorter timescale or, alternatively, may use abbreviated methods with acknowledged implications for the quality of the output.

realist synthesis – a method for studying complex interventions in response to the perceived limitations of conventional systematic review methodology. It involves the identification of contexts, mechanisms and outcomes for individual programmes in order to explain the differences, intended or unintended, between them.

reciprocal translation – a component technique of meta-ethnography which involves exploring the extent to which an idea or concept used by one author accurately represents use of a related idea or concepts by other authors.

reference management – the management of bibliographic references, and sometimes full-text papers, typically through electronic means so that they may be identified, stored, retrieved and used effectively.

reflexivity – the capacity of a researcher to consider the effect that their relationship to the subject or participants of a study may have on the conduct and interpretation of that study.

refutational synthesis – a stage of meta-ethnography (q.v.) where the reviewer is involved in a purposive search for phrases, metaphors and themes that refute any emerging patterns that have emerged from included data.

reliability – the extent to which a particular result measured at a particular point in time accurately captures the likely result of a similar measurement made at another point in time.

replicability – the extent to which a result or measurement achieved by one researcher or reviewer could be achieved by another researcher or reviewer working independently.

replicative – the property of causing replication.

reproducibility – the property of any scientific study by which results obtained from one experiment can be reproduced, either by the same or another investigator, by repeating the method as described. In the context of systematic reviews it refers to the extent to which review methods, if followed as described, would, at least in theory, produce the same results.

research question (Chapter 5) – a precisely stated question that specifically conveys what the researcher will attempt to answer.

research synthesis – a form of synthesis that seeks to synthesise only data obtained through the medium of research.

respondent validation – (also known as member checking) a technique used by researchers to help improve the accuracy, credibility, validity and transferability of a study. Typically the interpretation and report (or a portion of it) are given to members of the sample (respondents/informants) in order to check the authenticity of the work. Feedback from the members of the sample serves as a check for whether the interpretation is viable.

retrospective – a retrospective study looks backwards and examines exposures to suspected risk in relation to the outcome(s) being investigated.

review protocol – a document compiled at the beginning of a systematic review project that outlines the review topic and the methods to be used in conducting the review.

risk of bias tool – an instrument developed by the Cochrane Collaboration to assist in the identification and presentation of data on the likelihood of particular types of bias both in an individual study and in a group of studies.

scope creep – the tendency for any review to expand the work required without due consideration of costs and the implications for timely production.

scope note – a function of some bibliographic databases (such as MEDLINE) that defines thesaurus terms and gives information on use and synonyms.

scoping – the process of identifying the characteristics of a topic and its associate literature in order to determine a feasible strategy for a subsequent review.

scoping review – a type of review that has as its primary objective the identification of the size and quality of research in a topic area in order to inform subsequent review.

scoping search – a type of literature search that seeks to determine rapidly and efficiently the scale of a predefined topic to inform the subsequent conduct of a review.

screening (also known as sifting or study selection) – using pre-defined inclusion and exclusion criteria to examine the relevance of studies retrieved in the literature search, to identify those appropriate for inclusion in your systematic review.

search filters – a generic term for any collection of search terms designed to optimise retrieval from a bibliographic database. Such terms may be topical (i.e. related to the subject content of items to be retrieved) or methodological (pertaining to the methodology of retrieved items).

search strategy – the plan for retrieval of information on a chosen topic and, more specifically, the combination of search terms used to retrieve relevant items.

selection bias – a systematic error in choosing subjects for a particular study that results in an uneven comparison whether such subjects represent people (for a primary research study) or papers (for a literature review).

selective reporting bias – the selection, on the basis of the results, of a subset of analyses to be reported.

sensitivity – a diagnostic term, appropriated by information retrieval, to refer to the capacity of a search strategy to identify all relevant items (i.e. not missing any relevant items) on a particular topic.

sensitivity analysis – in this context, an analysis used to determine how sensitive the results of a systematic review are to changes in how it was done. Sensitivity analyses assess how robust the results are to assumptions made about the data and the methods that were used.

sibling studies – a term devised within the Cochrane Qualitative and Implementation Methods Group to describe additional studies associated with a particular index study (e.g. a feasibility study, qualitative study and process evaluation associated with a randomised controlled trial).

snowballing – literature-searching technique that involves locating a relevant source paper and then using this paper as a starting point for either working back from its references or for conducting additional citation searches.

snowball sampling – an epidemiological term used to describe the sampling procedure whereby sampling of a small group of subjects (or papers) helps to define an appropriate strategy and sample for further sampling.

social validity – in this context, the selection of interventions, programmes or policies on the basis that they are socially acceptable.

specificity – a diagnostic term, appropriated by information retrieval, to refer to the capacity of a search strategy to identify *only* relevant items (i.e. not retrieving any irrelevant items) on a particular topic.

SPICE – an acronym describing an approach to formulating or specifying a review question according to the elements of Setting, Perspective, phenomenon of Interest, Comparison and Evaluation.

splitting – the action of deciding to undertake a number of narrowly focused reviews on adjacent topics in preference to a single broad review on the basis of meaningful differences between elements of the population, interventions and/or outcomes (cf. **lumping**).

statistically significant – a measurable statistical result that is unlikely to have been achieved by chance.

study selection – the process of applying inclusion and exclusion criteria to an initial set of documents in order to arrive at a manageable set of includable studies.

subgroup analysis – a set of procedures that follows up analysis of an entire study population (people or papers) by looking for patterns in one or more subsets of that population.

subject index(es) – listings, either printed or electronic, that seek to provide retrieval of items in a predefined topic area or discipline.

summative – an adjective describing those aspects of a review that can only be assessed or evaluated as it approaches its completion.

synonyms – in literature searching, different words likely to be used by authors or other researchers with a similar meaning to a word that you have selected to describe your own topic e.g. 'car', 'motor vehicle' and 'automobile'.

synthesis strategy – an approach to planning the subsequent synthesis and analysis of a review by attempting to pre-specify review procedures. Typically a synthesis strategy is based on a preliminary assessment of the likely nature of the data and a knowledge of the purpose for which the review is to be used.

systematic review – a review of a clearly formulated question that uses systematic and explicit methods to identify, select and critically appraise relevant research and to collect and analyse data from the studies that are included in the review.

systematic search – a literature search that aims for comprehensiveness by applying a 'system' to finding the evidence.

test for heterogeneity – a formal statistical test used, prior to meta-analysis, to examine quantitatively the extent of variability or differences between studies in the estimates of effects.

text mining – the analysis of 'natural language' text, for example the words contained in the title or abstract of a journal article. In the context of systematic reviews, text mining can assist many of the processes, such as scoping the literature, identifying search terms, study selection.

textwords – exact words found in the title and/or abstract of an article that can be used to retrieve its details from a bibliographic database. Often called keywords.

thematic analysis – a method often used to analyse data and identify themes in primary qualitative research.

thematic synthesis – the use of methods, analogous to thematic analysis in primary qualitative research, in systematic reviews to bring together and integrate the findings of multiple qualitative studies.

theoretical saturation – the point within an interpretive review at which all data can be coded into an existing category; new categories are not emerging, and the existing category structure appears stable or secure.

thesaurus – a list of words showing similarities, differences, dependencies and other relationships to each other and mapping words used by database users to the actual words utilised by the constructors of that database.

transferability – the ability to apply results of research in the context of one or more study populations to the context of a target population. Also, the extent to which a review invites its readers to make meaningful connections between elements of the review and their own experiences.

transparency – the use of a set of policies, practices and procedures to help to make the contents and process of a review accessible, usable, informative and auditable to its readers.

triangulation – a term from primary qualitative research that refers to the use of two or more methods or sources to collect data on a particular phenomenon. Findings established from multiple sources are more likely to be valid and discrepancies or inconsistencies across sources will merit further investigation. In the specific context of literature reviews triangulation may refer to the use of findings from different study types or methods, from quantitative and qualitative research, or from different disciplines or schools of thought.

truncation – a truncation symbol is a character (determined by the database, such as an asterisk or dollar sign) which can be substituted, when searching databases or search engines, for various endings of the stem of a word (e.g. organi* for organisation, organization, organised, organized).

truth table – a matrix using binary notation to show all possible truth-values for a particular factor, derived from the truth-values of its component studies. It is particularly useful for examining the possible relationships between factors or variables.

validity – the degree to which a result (of a study or a review) is likely to be true and free of bias (systematic errors).

vote-counting – a (typically derogatory) term for the process by which the likelihood of a review finding being correct is determined simply by the numbers of studies reporting a favourable or unfavourable result.

wildcard – a wildcard character is a character (typically a question mark) that may be substituted, when searching databases or search engines, for any of a defined subset of all possible characters (e.g. wom?n for woman or women).

INDEX

Tables and Figures are indicated by page numbers in **bold**.